ADLERIAN COUNSELING AND PSYCHOTHERAPY

Second Edition

Don C. Dinkmeyer

Don C. Dinkmeyer, Jr.

Len Sperry

Merrill Publishing Company
A Bell & Howell Information Company
Columbus Toronto London Melbourne

*To Rudolf and Tee Dreikurs, our teachers and friends, who have
fostered and stimulated the growth of Adlerian psychology
throughout the world; and to our wives and mothers.*

Published by Merrill Publishing Company
A Bell & Howell Information Company
Columbus, Ohio 43216

Photo credits: pp. x & 8, Alfred Adler Institute of Chicago; pp. 22 & 156,
David Strickler/Strix Pix; pp. 42, 84, 186, & 252, Merrill Publishing/
Mary Hagler; pp. 62, 218, & 292, Tom Hubbard; p. 134, Merrill
Publishing/Lloyd Lemmerman; p. 170, Christopher Reddick; pp. 236 &
316, Jo Hall.

This book was set in Serifa.

Administrative Editor: Vicki Knight
Production Coordinator: Molly Kyle
Cover Designer: Cathy Watterson

First edition © 1979 by Wadsworth Publishing Company, Inc.
Library of Congress Catalog Card Number: 86-62373
International Standard Book Number: 0-675-20614-6
Printed in the United States of America
1 2 3 4 5 6 7 8 9—92 91 90 89 88 87

Foreword

Alfred Adler proposed that his psychology should be a "psychology of use." The second edition of *Adlerian Counseling and Psychotherapy* is based on this premise.

After contact with professors, editors, and graduate students across the country, the authors have expanded the text of the earlier edition in a number of ways. The chapter on Psychopathology has been reconceptualized to relate the DSM-III to Adlerian constructs. New chapters on Health Care Counseling and Counseling and Psychotherapy with the Elderly, written by a new author, a psychiatrist whose expertise is in the areas of health psychology and the elderly, expand the scope of the textbook and reflect the increasingly diverse applications of Adlerian psychology. Research studies are included to support principles.

The authors have actively solicited information from others whose expertise could clarify important principles, such as the lifestyle and priorities and how family systems theories parallel Adlerian approaches to family therapy. The authors have also adhered to the recommendations and comments of reviewers, editors, and formalized evaluations of graduate students.

The authors have thus enriched the text with extensive revisions of a number of chapters and have added three new chapters to keep step with the variety of ways practitioners apply principles of Adlerian psychology. I believe the second edition of *Adlerian Counseling and Psychotherapy* is a major contribution to the field of Counseling Psychology.

Roy M. Kern
Professor, Georgia State University

Preface

An increasing number of disciplines embrace the tenets of Individual Psychology. Adlerian ideas continue to dramatically influence the fields of psychology, psychotherapy, social work, and counseling. The North American Society of Adlerian Psychology steadily grows in membership. Although it is now fifty years since the death of Alfred Adler and more than a decade since the death of his most influential disciple, Rudolf Dreikurs, there is a resurgence of interest in Adlerian psychology. One sees evidence of this interest in the proliferation of books and educational materials and in higher attendance at conventions.

The second edition of *Adlerian Counseling and Psychotherapy* will satisfy the growing interest in this practical psychology. It is designed for use in counselor education programs and in the training of psychologists, social workers, and psychiatrists who are interested in the basics of Adlerian counseling and psychotherapy.

We begin with a brief review of the history and current status of Adlerian counseling and psychotherapy. In Chapter 3, we discuss the development of personality and the life style—a unique Adlerian concept that finds practical application in the therapeutic process. Chapter 4 presents an Adlerian understanding of psychopathology and its relationship to the DSM-III. Chapters 5 and 6 acquaint the reader with the actual process and techniques of Adlerian counseling and psychotherapy. Ensuing chapters review the application of Adlerian counseling to children and adolescents, the elderly, health care settings, to group procedures, to family and marriage counseling, and to teacher and parent education.

This book is a substantial revision of our work with W.L. Pew, published in 1979. We have added chapters on the elderly, health care counseling, and a new integration of psychopathology with standard assessment tools by Len Sperry, Ph.D., M.D.

This text was conceived while the senior author worked with Rudolf Dreikurs and was begun with his encouragement and support. Sharing Dreikurs's wisdom and techniques with the readers is personally rewarding. Don Dinkmeyer, Jr., an associate editor of the *Individual Psychology* journal and vice-president of the North American Society of Adlerian Psychology, and Len Sperry collaborated in this effort to bring the ideas of Adler and Dreikurs to the attention of the counseling profession. The book also incorporates the thinking of contemporary Adlerians such as Bernard Shulman, Harold Mosak, Kurt Adler, Heinz and Rowena Ansbacher, and Walter O'Connell. The content also reflects Don Dinkmeyer, Sr.'s intensive training at the Alfred Adler Institute of Chicago with Rudolf Dreikurs, Bernard Shulman, Harold Mosak, Bernice Grunwald, Bina Rosenberg, and Raymond Corsini.

It is virtually impossible to list all the inspiring colleagues and teachers who have contributed to this book with their constructive criticism and encouragement and to express our appreciation to all of them. We are particularly indebted to Dr. Michael Nystul, New Mexico State University; Dr. Roy Kern, Georgia State University; and Bernard Shulman, Stone Medical Center, Chicago.

Special thanks to Nancy Richards and E. Jane Dinkmeyer for their excellent word processing and office management skills.

Contents

CONTENTS

1 Introduction to Adlerian Counseling and Psychotherapy

A lfred Adler's Individual Psychology is one of the oldest, and still most relevant, schools of psychological thought. It emerged during Adler's nine-year association with Freud as an alternative to Freud's approach. Adler's system, with its practical applications to psychotherapy and counseling, has continued to experience steady growth after a period of neglect that followed Adler's death in 1937. Today, Individual Psychology is acknowledged as the precursor of many current systems of thought and approaches to psychotherapy. Its impact can be detected in countless areas—among them, child rearing, marriage and family therapy, and school counseling.

A BRIEF BIOGRAPHY

Alfred Adler was born on February 7, 1870, in Penzing, a suburb of Vienna. He was the second of six children. His father was a middle-class Jewish merchant, and his mother was a housewife. In his early childhood, Adler suffered from poor health and was run over by a vehicle. As he grew older, his health steadily improved. His interest in medicine, which arose when he was very young, led to a medical degree at the prestigious University of Vienna in 1895.

Adler became a practicing physician in Vienna. In the fall of 1902, Freud invited him to join his discussion groups, which later grew into the Vienna Psychoanalytic Society, of which Adler became president in 1910. Adler resigned from the society one year later, partly because of Freud's pressures for uniformity and strict allegiance to his theory. Contrary to popular notion, Adler was not a "disciple" of Freud (he was never psychoanalyzed by him); he was a colleague, and his ideas were often in conflict with Freud's.

After he severed his ties with psychoanalysis, Adler devoted himself to developing his own system of thought. In 1912, the Society for Individual Psychology was born and counted among its members a large number of those who had belonged to Freud's Psychoanalytic Society and who had left when Adler did. After participating in World War I as a medical officer, Adler created numerous child-guidance clinics in the Vienna public schools to serve as training vehicles for teachers, social workers, physicians, and other professionals. Adler demonstrated his techniques in front of groups of professionals—an instructional idea that had never been used before. Despite their revolutionary nature, the guidance clinics grew rapidly in Vienna and throughout Europe, and, at one point, there were nearly 50 of them. But soon political and other obstacles began to interfere with the growth of Adler's psychology in Europe.

In 1926, Adler made his first lecture tour in the United States. After that, his visits became more and more frequent, and eventually, in 1935, he fled Europe and settled in the United States, where he taught and lectured extensively. He died in 1937 in Aberdeen, Scotland, while on a lecture tour, leaving his disciples, many of whom had fled the political unrest of Europe, to carry on his work.

ADLER'S LEGACY

Adler published more than 300 books and articles.[1] Countless lectures and public demonstrations attest to his commitment to a theory that would be useful not only to professionals but to the public at large. Those who inherited Adler's legacy have continued to honor his commitment by being acutely aware of the needs of the community and by keeping alive Adler's practice of public demonstration, parent- and family-education centers, and the dissemination of useful, practical information.

After Adler's death, there was a decline of interest in his work. The Nazi regime and World War II were partly responsible, causing his disciples to scatter across the European continent and beyond. Many of them came to the United States. Here they found extreme resistance to Adler's work, which was seen as the antithesis of Freudian psychology. This erroneous perception of Adler's ideas here, the destruction of Adler's accomplishments in Europe, and the preeminence of the Freudian Approach were the main causes of the temporary decline in the recognition of Adler's contributions and in the number of practitioners of Individual Psychology.

Rudolf Dreikurs

Rudolf Dreikurs, a prolific writer and founder of the Alfred Adler Institute in Chicago, nurtured the growth of Adlerian psychology in the United States during the period of heavy psychoanalytic dominance.

Dreikurs emigrated to America in 1937 to escape Nazi persecution. His dream was to establish Adlerian child-guidance centers throughout the world. Among the numerous contributions he made to Individual Psychology before his death in 1972, especially important are his understanding of children and his unique insights into the counseling process.

Inspired by the basic Adlerian principle that all behavior has a purpose, Dreikurs formulated the four goals of misbehavior in children. He

---

[1] Of special interest to counselors and psychotherapists are *The Practice and Theory of Individual Psychology* (Totowa, N.J.: Littlefield, Adams, 1958); *What Life Should Mean to You* (New York: Capricorn, 1958); *Understanding Human Nature* (Greenwich, Conn.: Fawcett, 1969); and *The Neurotic Constitution* (New York: Arno, 1972).

saw in those goals—attention, power, revenge seeking, and display of inadequacy—the explanation for all of a child's disruptive behavior. By categorizing misbehaviors in terms of their goals, Dreikurs offered parents and teachers an invaluable tool for dealing more effectively with children's mistaken efforts.

Dreikurs also made some interesting contributions to the area of counseling. He stressed that the interview with a client is a valuable opportunity for the counselor to show that he or she is not perfect and to offer insights not as indisputable truths but as tentative hypotheses. In Dreikurs's opinion, the counselor should look at each interview as if it might be the last. Anytime the client leaves the interview without having learned something, the counselor has failed. Dreikurs would begin each session by asking the client "What do you remember from last time?" stressing the client's responsibility for his or her own change and the continuity from session to session. It was Dreikurs who first introduced the multiple-therapist procedure to psychotherapy as a teaching method for both therapist and client.

Rudolf Dreikurs was a colorful and courageous theorist and practitioner. His insights continue to reach thousands through his writings and the continuing work of those he encouraged during his lifetime. A highly readable biography, *The Courage to be Imperfect* (Terner and Pew, 1978), gives insight into a fascinating man who battled massive odds with tremendous strength.

ADLER, A MAN AHEAD OF HIS TIME

Adler left a wealth of ideas and techniques that still serve the counseling profession well. His son, Kurt, a practitioner in New York City, has gathered what he considers the most significant examples of his father's pioneering contributions to psychotherapy and counseling (Adler, n.d.).

Alfred Adler was the first to work publicly with clients by practicing group and family therapy in front of large audiences of doctors, teachers, parents, and others. He used these demonstration settings so that other professionals could learn by observing the counseling interaction at work. No other practitioner had ever risked or shared as much as Adler did through these public demonstrations.

Adler explained neurotic symptoms as "safeguards" against threats to one's self-image and against the challenges of the outside world. Freud, instead, saw neurotic symptoms as defense mechanisms against the repression of internal, instinctual drives. Freud's interpretation of neurotic symptoms was later amended by his daughter, Anna, who recognized the existence of defenses against external, and not only internal, demands.

The existence of such defenses was first recognized in children and later extended to include the whole gamut of safeguarding devices that are employed by humans of all ages.

Adler suggested that a child's bedwetting problem has a psychological, as well as a physiological, component. Contemporary research suggests that many instances of bedwetting are in fact physiologically based but that the physiological element alone is not sufficient to explain the problem. To thousands of pediatricians who rarely find a physiological cause for bedwetting, Adler's understanding of the interaction between psychic and physiological factors is still valid today, just as it was more than 75 years ago.

In the 1920s, Adler predicted that two more generations would pass before women would achieve true equality. Women's successful struggle for equality in the past decade attests to the accuracy of this prediction. Adler didn't see much difference between domination by males and domination by tyrannical regimes like those that oppressed Europe before and during his lifetime. Instead of indulging in the popular contemporary misconception of women's inferiority, Adler stressed that inequality makes loving relationships and mutual cooperation impossible. His commitment to the equality of all people is reflected in Tyra Boldsen's plans for a monument commemorating the enfranchisement of women. Boldsen, a Danish sculptor and an early "liberationist," planned a sculpture that would have many women but only one man—Adler.

FROM AUTOCRACY TO DEMOCRACY

Adler's model fits a democratic era. The revitalization of counseling through Adler's ideas has paralleled the democratic revolution that has profoundly affected not only our institutions but our strategies for changing behavior, beliefs, and feelings. A therapist-dominated approach, like Freud's, was appropriate in an autocratic era. When powerful leaders dominated the masses, parents and schools controlled children, and minorities were ignored, it was fitting that the therapist would authoritatively prescribe and the client would passively accept the therapist's wisdom. The client's passive position on the therapist's couch alluded to the nature of the relationship and to the power of the helper. In an age of democracy, when people demand to be treated as equals, Adler's basic approach offers a model that is consistent with the times, since it views the client as a full and equal participant in the counseling process.

The shift from autocratic to democratic procedures has brought about a revolution in counseling and psychotherapy. In the past, the training of psychiatrists, psychologists, and social workers was often heavily influenced by the psychoanalytic school of thought. Emphasis was on cause and effect, on human drives, and on a mechanistic view and explanation of behavior. While the psychoanalytic theory still has a large following, there is an increasing acceptance of other approaches—for example, rational-emotive therapy, behavior modification, reality therapy, transactional analysis, and client-centered therapy (Corsini, 1979). All these approaches share the belief that people are decision-making beings responsible for their own behavior and capable of changing it.

Walter O'Connell (1976), a past president of the North American Society of Adlerian Psychology, referred to the attitude of many contemporary practitioners and theorists as a "yes, but" acceptance of Adlerian principles. He pointed out that none of them (he specifically mentioned Viktor Frankl, Colin Wilson, Ernest Becker, Ira Progoff, and Rollo May) call themselves Adlerians, yet their belief in human development parallels Adler's. All of these "friends" acknowledge many of Adler's ideas in their own contributions to psychology, yet they qualify their similarities.

CURRENT STATUS

The North American Society of Adlerian Psychology (NASAP) is Individual Psychology's central organization in the United States and Canada. The society was founded in 1952, largely through Dreikurs's efforts. Dreikurs edited the *Journal of Individual Psychology* after Adler's death and disseminated Adlerian concepts across the North American continent, as well as abroad. Through his efforts and those of his colleagues, numerous local societies and organizations have emerged.

There are Adlerian training institutes in several cities, including Chicago, New York, and Minneapolis. When NASAP recently celebrated its 30th anniversary, it had more than 1,000 members. Although not yet impressive in numbers, the Adlerian movement is experiencing steady growth, and so is the number of practitioners who operate according to its guidelines.

The quarterly journal *Individual Psychology* now alternates issues devoted to theory and research and practice and application. NASAP has established six Interest Sections: Clinicians, Adlerian Counseling and Therapy, Family Education, Theory and Research, Education, and Business and Organizations.

NASAP's annual convention is held each Memorial Day weekend; an annual Conference in Orlando, Florida, each February exposes many new people to Adlerian concepts. Dozens of regional and local meetings and workshops are conducted each year across the United States and Canada. NASAP is a member of the International Association of Individual Psychology (IAIP). Once every three years, IAIP meets at a new site to bring together people who are interested in Individual Psychology; the last meeting drew attendance from more than 12 countries from Europe to Japan.

Successful practical applications of Adlerian tenets across the North American continent are so numerous that they exceed the scope of a brief review. In Chapters 15 and 16 we will discuss applications for parents and teachers, who have derived many practical educational concepts.

REFERENCES

Adler, K. (n.d.). *Alfred Adler, a man ahead of his time.* Unpublished paper.

Corsini, R.J. (Ed.). (1979). *Current psychotherapies* (2nd ed.). Itasca, IL: Peacock.

Dinkmeyer, D., & Dreikurs, R. (1963). *Encouraging children to learn: The encouragement process.* Englewood Cliffs, NJ: Prentice-Hall.

O'Connell, W. E. The "friends of Adler" phenomenon. *Journal of Individual Psychology,* 32 (1), 5–17.

Terner, J., & Pew, W. L. (1978). *The courage to be imperfect: The life and work of Rudolf Dreikurs.* New York: Hawthorn.

2 Theoretical Foundations of Adlerian Counseling

T he Adlerian counseling process applies general theories of behavior to specific individual concerns and challenges. The principles set forth in this chapter are drawn from the writings of Alfred Adler and Rudolf Dreikurs, as well as from those of their colleagues and students.

Eva Dreikurs Ferguson summarizes Adler's development of the theory:

> In the early nineteen hundreds, when he was a physician helping patients with sick bodies, Adler developed a psychological theory that was based on organ inferiority. A broader theory, developed between approximately 1910 and 1920, focused on personality and child development and on ways the individual can strive to overcome feelings of inferiority. In the late 1920s and until 1937 he focused on the fundamental need of every person to belong to the human community and to feel he or she has a place. He postulated that *individual* striving was to contribute, whereas *society* strives from a minus to a plus and towards an ideal of perfection. (Ferguson, 1984, p. 2)

Adler's early work established a foundation that has stimulated furthur theories. His contribution is acknowledged by proponents of many current theories of human behavior. Adlerian concepts have stimulated a number of practical approaches to counseling with individuals, groups, and families and have seen application in schools, universities, and various agencies, as well as in private practice.

The purpose of a counseling theory is to set the foundations of the relationship between counselor and counselee, thereby helping counselors improve their effectiveness. Theory also provides guidelines for making observations about what occurs in the counseling process. It is the position of the authors that counselors must have an explicit theory of human behavior.

The assumption underlying Adlerian counseling theory is that people are indivisible, social, decision-making beings whose actions and psychological movement have purpose. Each person is seen as an individual, within a social setting, with the capacity to decide and to choose.

ALL BEHAVIOR HAS SOCIAL MEANING

One of the basic premises of the Adlerian approach is that we are primarily social beings and that our behavior can be understood only in terms of a social context. Interaction with others is a continuous, lifelong process that begins in infancy, when we are entirely dependent on others for our very survival. Later, we need to cooperate with others to realize our goals and function fully.

Each human being is born with the capacity to develop what Adler called *Gemeinschaftsgefühl*. Narrowly translated as "social interest," it is the willingness to cooperate with others for the common good and the awareness of the universal interrelatedness of all human beings. As members of the human community, throughout life all of us must meet three major *life tasks*, which Adler defined as society, work, and sex. Adler believed that the extent to which a person successfully shares with others, contributes through work, and forms a satisfying relationship with a member of the other sex is a revealing indicator of the individual's overall personality and level of maturity.

Awareness of the social significance of all behavior allows counselors to better understand their clients. The school counselor looks at the social microcosms of peer groupings and teacher/student relationships for an understanding of adolescent behavior. Although similar microcosms exist in business and organizational structures, an adult's world is more diverse than that of an adolescent, and the adult's social situation is more the result of personal choice. This makes the task of understanding the social significance of adult behavior more difficult.

Regardless of the counselee's age, an understanding of her social behavior is essential. For example, an adult may characterize herself as "shy." Instead of merely focusing on causation, such as an unhappy childhood or cold family relationships, what is the present social significance of the shyness? What does this person gain from being shy?

A great deal of importance is placed on making the counseling relationship an immediate and warm interaction between equals. Assuming that the counselor has adequate social skills, the counseling relationship demonstrates the client's current social-interaction skills. Is the client concerned with power or revenge? Is the client trying to prove inadequacy?

The Goal of Belonging

Throughout life, the goal of belonging is a fundamental expression of human nature. We decide which groups are important to us and strive to gain their acceptance. The countless formal and informal groupings that exist in any society attest to our goal of belonging and to having a certain place that we value. Many of our problems and anxieties stem from the fear that we will not belong or be accepted by groups we seek to join. When we perceive that we cannot do the job or make the grade, we fear we will not be accepted by others. Our sense of belonging remains unfulfilled, and we become anxious and unhappy.

In the schools, teachers can use the natural social environment of the classroom to provide situations that utilize the need to belong. Effectively organized group discussions and activities enhance both the development of the individual and that of the group. The adult's world is not as easily structured as that of the child, but the same principles operate. Our goal of belonging creates loyalties to family, individuals, professional and social groups, fraternal orders, and athletic teams—to name just a few.

Shulman indicates that Adler saw social interest, the goal of belonging, as both inherent and potential factors in our lives:

> The tendency of human beings to form attachments (social feelings) was considered by Adler to be a fact of life. The striving of the human is always in some way connected with human bonding. Social interest is the expression of this tendency in a way that promotes human welfare. Some aspects of social interest are innate as in the infant's tendency to bond to its mother. However, social interest is a potential that must be developed through training in cooperation with productive endeavor. (Shulman, 1985, p. 248)

We relate to one another with varying degrees of success. A measure of psychic health is the extent and effectiveness of one's current interaction with others. Creative negative interpretation of self can be reversed by encouraging the client to increase and improve interaction with others, so he or she can experience self-worth and, at the same time, be given the opportunity to share his or her abilities with others. Thus, the focus shifts from self to others.

THE HUMAN PERSONALITY HAS UNITY AND DEFINITE PATTERNS

Another basic premise of the Adlerian approach is the irreducible wholeness of the individual. The person is seen as a dynamic, unified organism moving through life in definite patterns toward a goal. Fragmenting the personality by causal or analytical explanations denies this wholeness. Through synthesis, an understanding of the individual is based in the unity and purpose of the individual's behavior. An example illustrates this point.

> Linda is a 9-year-old child with a high IQ, as measured by individual psychological tests, and with considerable creativity and spontaneity. Yet, she is failing in all of her school subjects. Many might say that this behavior doesn't make sense. However, if one focuses on Linda's patterns of move-

ment instead of focusing on specific elements (such as high IQ and low grades), one sees the meaning and goal of Linda's behavior. By failing to function, Linda becomes special. Mother and Father now give her a great deal of attention by tutoring her every evening and showing great concern. Linda has become a special case that must be dealt with in a special manner both at school and at home. If one is able to conceptualize Linda's behavior at its holistic level, one can clearly see that it does have a goal and also social meaning.

The importance of understanding the patterns of behavior is illustrated in typical case studies. No matter how much information an institution gathers about an individual's intelligence, interests, and achievements, these data cannot speak for themselves. Until one is able to see the relationship between behavior and data and observe the pattern and purpose of the behavior, it is difficult to develop remedial or corrective actions. Counseling techniques that gather much data and concentrate heavily on a counselee's past history often fail to take into account this tremendously important relationship. For the counselor to be effective, the meaning of behavior must be clear with regard to its unity and central function. As Dreikurs (1953) indicated, "The doctrine of the unity of the personality gave Individual Psychology its name. This name, which is so often misunderstood, is derived from the latin word 'individuum,' which literally means 'undivided,' 'indivisible' (in-dividere)" (p. 56).

This view requires that we take a holistic, rather than reductionistic, approach. It suggests that we look at all actions in the light of the individual's chosen style of life. The way people organize themselves as whole persons influences their perception of life and their transactions with others. For example, if Susan is primarily concerned with being noticed, in some instances she will try to be recognized by being the best in anything she can do well—such as tennis, cards, or other activities. In other instances, however, she will not even try, because she will receive equal recognition for her failure to function. Since it is more important for Susan to be noticed than to be successful, she may be a "noticeable failure" in some aspects of her life. Thus, both failure and success can make sense in terms of a person's particular style of life.

BEHAVIOR HAS A PURPOSE

According to Adler, all human behavior has a purpose. Behaviors that may seem inexplicable become understandable once we know their goal or purpose.

The contrast here is obviously with those who believe that behavior is governed by causality alone and that it can be explained in mechanical terms. From an Adlerian point of view, all our actions are seen in relation to their goal-directed nature, and the goal can have an urgent, imperative quality. The goal, then, gives direction to our striving, and it becomes the final cause—the final explanation. Thus, instead of always looking back to a possible cause, we look to the future goal as the "cause."

This is how Adler stated the importance of goals:

> If we know the goal of a person, we can undertake to explain and to understand what the psychological phenomena want to tell us, why they were created, what a person has made of his innate material, why he has made it just so and not differently, how his character traits, his feelings and emotions, his logic, his morals, and his aesthetics must be constituted in order that he may arrive at his goal. (Ansbacher & Ansbacher, 1956, p. 196)

Adler's view is echoed by Allport, Rogers, and Faust. In his book *The Nature of Personality* (1950), Allport concludes that goal striving is the essence of personality and that knowing the goal provides an understanding of how the person is moving psychologically.

Rogers (1951) observes that "behavior is basically the goal-directed attempt of the organism to satisfy its needs as experienced, in the field as perceived" (p. 491). He also notes that from this concept of motivation "all the effective elements [of motivation] exist in the present. Behavior is not 'caused' by something which occurred in the past. Present tensions and present needs are the only ones which the organism endeavors to reduce or satisfy" (p. 492).

Faust (1966) describes essentially the same principle:

> In the modification of behavior it is not so much whether a particular stimulus does, in fact, assure the organism of survival that counts, as it is a matter of how the organism perceives the stimulus or the meaning which the stimulus possesses for the organism's survival. . . . While frequently individuals appear to engage in behavior which according to adults and even peers is destructive, the premise is that from the individual's point of view or interpretation this behavior has certain kinds of meaning to him in terms of his personal significance, self-esteem and method of finding a place and thus he behaves in the way in which he must.

This teleological approach implies that the goals of behavior are always created by the individual and are not the result of preceding events, as the causal approach maintains. Our uniqueness ultimately rests in this "creative power." Behavior is thus understood not only as a response to a stimulus but also in terms of the intervening variable of the person who makes a creative decision about that stimulus.

This emphasis on the purposive nature of behavior is a recognition of humans' freedom of choice; it acknowledges that people evaluate and interpret life according to the goals they choose for themselves. In pursuing the goal, the individual employs his unique cognitive and emotional abilities. *Private logic* refers to the individual's cognitive constructs that serve in pursuit of a goal and represent a set of "personal truths" that guide the individual. Private logic is not necessarily in line with common sense; for example, "I haven't gotten any mail today; therefore, no one cares about me" is a statement that may make sense in terms of a person's private logic but not in terms of what we might call "common logic."

Besides cognitive constructs, the pursuit of a goal also involves emotions. A common misconception is that human emotions are uncontrollable, passive reactions to environmental input—like the tears produced by the tear ducts in response to an onion. Emotions can be used purposefully to control others and to achieve goals. The cliché "Control your emotions!" may actually mean (often more accurately) "Don't use your emotions to control me!" The child who screams until he gets his way already understands emotions as a useful goal-achieving tool.

All forms of behavior, including misbehavior, are the results of the creative choices we make in selecting and pursuing our goals. When we are confronted with a bright adolescent who doesn't perform in school and has become a "juvenile delinquent," we may say "It doesn't make sense," simply because we don't recognize his purpose. Behavior always makes sense to the person, if not to others. The goal may not always be fully known to the individual; nonetheless, the person operates in the direction of the goal and according to the interpretation he gives to the goal.

Awareness of the goal, therefore, provides the counselor with some clues for corrective action. A study of causes, on the other hand, may provide only a list of factors that are likely to seem beyond the counselor's and counselee's control.

The Goals in Children's Actions

The goal-directed nature of behavior can perhaps be best understood in terms of the goals of child misbehavior. Dreikurs (1957) refers to these goals as:

Attention getting

Struggle for power or superiority

Desire to retaliate or get even

Display of inadequacy or assumed disability

Children who use attention-getting techniques (for example, annoying behavior) desire attention so much that, rather than being ignored, they will seek attention negatively. Some children receive attention by being successful, some by demonstrating their charm, and others by being a nuisance.

Children whose goal is power are out to show you that they can do as they please and will not do what you want them to do. Even when you defeat them, they are all the more convinced of the value of their goal, and next time will only employ a more effective method to achieve their goal, to be the boss.

Children whose goal is revenge seek their place by being extremely unlikable. Their feelings have been hurt, and they want to hurt in return. It is their pride to develop a mutual antagonism. These children do not mind being called vicious; after all, their goal is to retaliate. For them, to be as horrible as possible is a form of success.

Children whose goal is to display inadequacy are so discouraged that they cannot believe they can be significant. They use or develop inadequacy as a protection, so that nothing is required or expected. By not participating or contributing, they hope to avoid what they see as an even more devastating experience—to try and to fail.

We counselors can become more aware of these goals by observing the child's behaviors, by checking our own spontaneous reactions to such behavior, and by noting the child's responses to correction. As we observe our spontaneous reactions, we keep in mind that what we feel most inclined to do often points to the child's intentions. If we feel annoyed and want to admonish and correct, the child is probably just trying to keep us busy with him. When we feel personally challenged and want to show the child that he can't do that to us, we are engaged in a power contest. Feeling hurt and outraged points to the child's desire to get even with us or society. Most certain of all these clues is the despair we feel with a nonproducing but able child. School and parents don't know what to do, and we are impressed with the child's total inability. By leaving him alone, we do what the deeply discouraged child expects.

Another indicator of the child's goal is his response to correction. If he desires only attention, he will stop when corrected, although not for long. If he wants power, an adult's efforts to stop him will worsen his behavior. The vengeful child will become more violent, while the child who displays inadequacy will continue to endure, possibly without any sincere attempt at action.

Ambivalence or indecisiveness can also be seen as purposive activity, in that it permits the child to gain time and postpone a decision so as to keep things as they are. All psychological behaviors and transactions are purposeful, whether active, passive, or supposedly ambivalent. There is no behavior without a goal, and close observation of child as well as adult behavior reveals such goals. In the adult, the goals are more complex, but still govern the individual's actions.

What we said earlier about counseling in general also applies to child counseling. If satisfactory change is to occur, counselors must understand the purpose of children's behavior as well as their feelings. A school counselor, for example, may see Linda's inexplicably poor grades as the "problem," when they are only symptoms that lead to the purpose of her behavior. Viewing the problem instead as the result of Linda's belief and goal—"I can get more attention by being the worst"—gives the counselor direction for the counseling process.

STRIVING FOR SIGNIFICANCE EXPLAINS OUR MOTIVATION

The striving for significance takes its direction from the individual's subjectively conceived goal of success (self-ideal). In our highly competitive society, we are urged, expected, and even demanded to excel, to be *more than* others. From birth, one experiences the subjective feeling of being less than others. Adlerian psychology recognizes the family as the first group in which each individual strives to find a significant place. The search for significance occurs when one experiences the subjective feeling of being less than others (inferiority feelings) and then engages in attempts to compensate.

Our inferiority feelings are generally the result of faulty self-evaluation. We arrive at faulty self-evaluations by answering "incorrectly" such questions as "Who and what am I?" and "How do I master the environment?" There is abundant proof of our capacity to give the "wrong" answers to these and similar questions and to mistakenly conclude that we are worthless. Even the extreme act of suicide is often the result of subjective inferiority feelings rather than the outcome of an objective assessment of one's true worth.

The striving for significance is in essence a movement toward fulfillment of the goal to achieve unique identity and to belong. This movement toward a unique identity is the motivating force behind all human activity—the master motive. Adlerians see this process, too, from a teleological rather than causal perspective—as a pull by the goal rather than a push by the drive. (Most organismic approaches share the Adlerian recognition of one master motive. Positive attainment of the goal has been variously called self-actualization, self-expansion, or competence.)

The power of the striving for significance is most apparent in the adolescent struggle for uniqueness, a struggle that often sets the young in conflict with adults. Defiance of traditional norms, sometimes expressed in unusual style of clothes, unique language, and unconventional behavior, is one way adolescents affirm the difference between themselves and their parents and other adults, thus satisfying in some way their increasing need for personal autonomy. Similar techniques are used by other groups that need to proclaim their uniqueness to achieve the goal of being different and yet relate to others in the group through common beliefs and behavior.

Each of us seeks identity in different ways. As previously noted, this search often takes the form of "bad" behavior, from children's misbehavior to adult resistance or even illegal actions. Sometimes we observe an individual who is putting all her energy into her work, essentially giving up in other areas. This behavior, too, is a manifestation of the striving for significance. If we ask "How does this behavior help the person to be significant, as she perceives significance?" we discover that the individual perceives that she can be significant only in her area of work. Thus, she gives all of herself to something in which she can succeed and be special and withdraws from other areas in which she cannot. In other cases, when an individual recognizes that he cannot succeed at being the best, he will try to succeed at being the worst. Failure to function can sometimes, as we have seen, bring as much attention and power as brilliant performance.

Because motivation must be seen in the light of a person's striving for significance, as he perceives significance, it is imperative that counselors recognize a person's particular behavior, set of attitudes, and series of relationships as a revelation of how that person believes he fits into his social context. A question counselors always ask themselves is "How is the person seeking to be known?" Most ways of behaving that are eventually accepted by the person reflect the current concept of self. When individuals see themselves as inadequate in social skills, inept in social relationships with the opposite sex, or unable to cope with other tasks, they tend to behave on the basis of their beliefs, not on the basis of facts (Fullmer & Bernard, 1964). This "unrealistic" view of self and environment, however, can also be used positively. Many explorers and adventurers throughout history would have never made it if their convictions had not contradicted "facts."

BEHAVIOR IS A FUNCTION OF SUBJECTIVE PERCEPTION

We *learn* to perceive life; that is, early in life, we acquire a perception of ourselves and the world around us—a subjective point of view. As pointed out earlier, to understand people's behavior, one must come to recognize the significance of the inner, subjective experience and its influence on all our decisions.

A discouraged individual is actually in a different internal environment than an individual who feels adequate and has self-esteem. Discouragement anticipates lack of success, and the behavior of a discouraged person actually provokes responses from others that, by validating this anticipation, reinforce the discouraged interpretation of the life situation. Each person plays a dynamic role in the development of her subjective view of self and life. People are not reactors; they are actors.

For the Adlerian, it is crucial that the individual be understood in terms of the meaning a given event has for that person. This position is similar to Arthur Combs's view that all behavior is a function of the individual's field of perception at the instant of behaving (Combs, 1954). We tend to behave according to how things appear to us, and, when our perception changes, our behavior changes accordingly. Perception thus determines behavior perhaps more than "reality" does. Combs also indicates that when perceptions are vague and indistinct, behavior will be similarly ambivalent. Conversely, when perceptions are clear and accurate, behavior will be precise and efficient. In essence, behavior is a function of perception.

The Adlerian counselor is engaged in a continuous attempt to see with the client's eyes and hear with the client's ears—to get into the client's world for the purpose of making it available to the client and to the significant others in the client's environment. This is how Rogers (1951) cogently states the reason for this constant attempt: "The best vantage point for understanding behavior is from the internal frame of reference of the individual himself" (p. 492). It is for this reason that Rogerians place great emphasis on the helping relationship and on the need to develop empathy so the counselor can more accurately perceive the client's point of view. It is apparent that, the more accurately we communicate, the more adequately we will comprehend the client's vantage point.

This position has far-reaching implications for the counselor. For example, it implies that the counselor must avoid as much as possible any personal bias. If a counselor feels that a client's chosen life style needs to be changed, the counselor must ask herself whether this feeling reflects what appears to be a real concern of the client or the counselor's own bias.

The counselor must have the capacity to comprehend what counselees really say and to help them clarify why they feel that way. Once clients examine and become aware of their own points of view, the counselor can help them consider alternate views and different behaviors.

Idiographic versus Nomothetic Laws

Adlerians are more concerned with concrete laws that apply characteristically to a specific individual in relation to his style of life (idiographic laws) than with abstract laws that apply generally but include many exceptions (nomothetic laws). This point of view is shared by Combs and Snygg (1959), who indicate that the real challenge to psychology is the phenomenological, or subjective, approach. This means the counselor must seek to understand the behavior of the counselee from the counselee's point of view. The focus is on understanding people as they perceive themselves rather than as they appear to others.

The idiographic approach assumes that psychology has meaning only insofar as it postulates a theory that helps us help a specific human being to live in a way that is personally satisfying and socially acceptable. It should be clear, therefore, that this approach goes beyond the general normative descriptions that arose in child-development theory and in Freud's psychoanalytic psychiatry regarding certain predetermined characteristics and stages.

The idiographic view implies that the counselor must comprehend how a person acquired a particular value system and how that system operates in the decisions the client makes with regard to life and life tasks. The counselor will then be able to understand the basis of the individual's decisions, the goals he is trying to achieve, and the things he values. Also, the counseling process becomes a channel through which the individual is better able to develop value systems that, by being consistent with his particular society and community, permit him to live more effectively. In some instances, the counselor helps the individual explore a new set of values through a value-conflict situation.

For example, after complaining about four successive unhappy romances, a young woman concludes "They were all so unsatisfactory. Men are such disappointments!" If the counselor is able to see an idiographic rule in this woman's life style—"My man must be perfect, or I must move on"—he may also be able to help the client become aware of her self-defeating approach and do something about it.

ADLERIAN PSYCHOLOGY IS A PSYCHOLOGY OF USE, NOT OF POSSESSION

Adlerians believe that, at any given moment, one will do that which is most useful or which best accomplishes one's purpose and striving; one will not do that which interferes with one's goal. This principle can be seen at work in the varying ways individuals make use of their heredity and environment. If someone appears to have considerable physical or intellectual capacity but chooses not to utilize it, we see someone who has determined that he is not adequate and cannot function in terms of those specific capacities. The concern should therefore be "What does the person *do* with his ability?" rather than "What does the person possess?"

Whether in school, agency, institutional, or private setting, the counselor is often given much data about a client's intelligence, achievement, and personality. Sometimes this mass of information may be counterproductive, since it may hide the patterns and meaning of behavior. The Adlerian counselor is more interested in what *use* the person makes of her heredity, environment, and experiences. By focusing on the client's motivation, decisions, and conclusions, a more practical and effective counseling relationship is achieved. A simple review of test scores and reports is seldom useful in counseling, unless it points to patterns.

REFERENCES

Allport, G. W. (1950). *The nature of personality.* Reading, MA: Addison-Wesley.

Ansbacher, H. L., & Ansbacher, R. R. (Eds.). (1956). *The individual psychology of Alfred Adler.* New York: Harper & Row.

Combs, A. W. (1954). Counseling as a learning process. *Journal of Counseling Psychology,* 1 (1), 31–36.

Combs, A. W., & Snygg, D. (1959). *Individual behavior: A perceptual approach to behavior* (rev. ed.). New York: Harper & Row.

Dreikurs, R. (1953). *Fundamentals of Adlerian psychology.* Chicago: Alfred Adler Institute.

Dreikurs, R. (1957). *Psychology in the classroom.* New York: Harper & Row.

Faust, V. (1966, July). Role of the elementary school counselor: Freeing children to learn. Address to U.S. Office of Education, Washington, DC.

Ferguson, E. D. (1984). *Adlerian theory: An introduction.* Vancouver, BC: Adlerian Psychology Association of British Columbia.

Fullmer, D. W., & Bernard, H. W. (1964). *Counseling: Content and process.* Chicago: Science Research Associates.

Rogers, C. R. (1951). *Client-centered therapy.* Boston: Houghton-Mifflin.

Shulman, B. H. (1985). Cognitive therapy and the individual psychology of Alfred Adler. In M. J. Mahoney and A. Freeman (Eds.), *Cognition and psychotherapy* (pp. 243–258). New York: Plenum.

White, R. Motivation reconsidered: The concept of competence. *Psychological Review,* 66, 297–333.

3 The Development of Personality and the Life Style

W hat makes a human being unique? Why do even identical twins display distinctly different personalities? When are personality differences first visible in human development?

Human infants enter the world with certain genetic endowments and find themselves in particular human environments. They continue after birth to react to external stimuli and also to play an active role that influences their environment. This is particularly true of their social environment—the small group of humans that each child relates to on a fairly constant basis. Through what appears at first to be almost a trial-and-error process, children "learn" what works and what doesn't work. Whatever seems to work, they persist in; whatever fails to influence the significant persons about them (their social field), they discard. So each new situation is met with an ever-increasing backlog of "experience." But the experience is not reality; it is the infant's subjective interpretation of reality and the conclusions she draws from experience.

Some critics will say this view imposes our adult biases on an incomplete human who is only a bundle of disorganized drives and instincts. But that criticism fails to take into consideration the tremendous creative power of infants and small children and perpetuates an unrecognized prejudice against children. Actually, even at birth a human being has the capacity to make important contributions to another human being. By nursing at the mother's breast, the baby facilitates the third stage of labor, reduces maternal hemorrhage, and relieves breast congestion. Yet, this unique ability is often overlooked and denied, and a subtle dehumanization process begins as the infant is whisked off to a sterile nursery.

We can learn a great deal about the infant's ability to perceive and make choices when we see a normal baby with deaf-mute parents. The infant soon "learns" that sound is ineffective, so he screws up his face, gets red, flails his arms and legs, and "cries" without sound. Later he may learn to have a temper tantrum by stamping on the floor so that his parents can feel the vibrations.

Children actively create their personalities, but, although children may be good observers, they are often poor interpreters. They come to conclusions about themselves and life that are based on faulty judgments. As they create their guidelines and establish their blueprints for the future, children tend to operate with an "only if" absurdity. For example, a child may conclude "Only if I am pleasing (or in control, or comfortable, or good, or competent, or right), can I really belong." This kind of thinking is based on the faulty assumption "I don't really belong." Actually a newborn child is already a full-fledged member of the human community and can never become more human, or belong more than he or she already does (Chess,

Thomas, & Birch, 1965). Yet most of us spend a great deal of time and energy looking for a place we already have, not realizing that we have our place merely by virtue of our existence.

The "only if" premise is based on what we fear most. If we are bent on pleasing, our most awesome fear is of rejection. If control is our priority, humiliation is what we hope to avoid. If comfort has precedence, the worst thing is stress. And if moral superiority is what we value most, the feeling of meaninglessness is what we must avoid at all costs. The Adlerian view is that infants establish a number-one priority very early, perhaps within the first year, and that it is along this guiding line that they begin to construct their personalities, which will include a complex of prejudices, biased perceptions, conclusions, and convictions.

Since this process goes on preverbally, as older children or adults we are only dimly aware of our own style of living—that is, the personality we have constructed for ourselves. Developing a life style is, however, not only economical for the child (he doesn't have to start from scratch with each new experience), but absolutely essential for survival.

INFLUENCES ON THE DEVELOPING PERSONALITY

Genetic Factors

We have as yet no evidence to support genetic effects on the development of personality. In fact, in identical (one-egg) twins, who have exactly the same genetic makeup, we often see strikingly different personalities. One explanation for this difference appears frequently when we interview adult identical twins. After relating precisely the same early recollection, the twins usually reach quite opposite conclusions about the incident—which is another way of saying that it doesn't matter so much what we are born with or what we are born into but how we perceive it and what we do about it.

Constitutional Factors

We are unable to measure the effects of the various body systems, such as the endocrine system or the central nervous system, on personality development, except in cases of obvious physical or mental defect. But we know that intelligence, although not static, is still something of a factor in influencing life style, since intelligence is a necessary tool for coping behavior.

A healthy, handsome boy or girl will experience certain environmental reactions and find certain opportunities that are different from those that some of their friends will meet. Similarly, intelligent children see alternatives that duller children miss. But it is not the constitutional trait itself that is causative; what is important is how the youngster perceives the trait.

> Sally was always a gifted child and grew into a talented art student. As she approached young adulthood, her work drew increasing attention and praise from her teachers. But Sally's number-one priority was pleasing, which is a way of saying that she never really believed that she was gifted, and her talent, which eventually propelled her into a highly successful career in the graphic arts, was always much more appreciated by others than by Sally.

If a child is born with a physical defect, she may be discouraged and operate as if she had a deficiency, or she may overcompensate and, perhaps, become an outstanding athlete despite her deficiency. All children make their own decisions as to how they perceive their genetic endowment and the environmental situation they find themselves in.

Critical Periods

Montessori and others have quite clearly demonstrated that there are *critical periods* for developing certain traits or abilities. Some human skills require practice from a very early age. If they are learned later, they are acquired only with great difficulty, if at all. According to Montessori, a critical period is a short span of time during which a particular learning— for example, reading—takes place with relative ease. If the child does not develop some reading skills during this critical period, it is often difficult later to teach the child to read. "Children pass through definite periods in which they reveal psychic aptitudes and possibilities which afterwards disappear" (Montessori, in Standing, 1962, pp. 119-120).

Examples of skills that are developed during certain critical periods include the newborn's ability to swim with fishlike movements when immersed in water—an ability that is subsequently lost and never recovered in the same form. For many children and adults, learning to swim the second time may be quite difficult. Newborn infants, if held upright over a flat surface, will also "walk" with well-coordinated alternating steps. This ability, too, is lost, only to be retrieved—often with considerable effort—in the latter part of the first year or in the first part of the second year of life.

Cultural Factors

Culture provides a child with a particular way of looking at the world, thus emphasizing some tendencies in the development of the life style. For example, in Greece and in some of the Latin American countries, the culture is still quite autocratic and male dominated. It is not surprising that, in these countries, both boys and girls tend to grow up with exaggerated ideas about the importance of males. In North America the culture can be characterized as competitive. Competition seeps into all our relationships, including family relationships, providing a cultural influence that leads most children to be very competitive.

Prenatal and Perinatal Factors

Although methods of studying the developing fetus are becoming more and more sophisticated, we know very little about the prenatal period. Nevertheless, it seems logical to assume that the fetus processes stimuli and decides in some primitive sense what to make of the stimuli. Legend has George Gershwin developing his gift for syncopated rhythm as a result of the paroxysmal tachycardia that his mother had during pregnancy; that is, he was subjected for nine months to irregularity of heartbeat, which perhaps predisposed him toward syncopated rhythm.

Perinatal describes the critical period just before, during, and immediately following birth. Although only recently have scientists paid much attention to this period, studies already show that this is a critical time of life. For example, if a mother holds her unclothed newborn baby immediately after delivery, she is significantly more likely to talk with the child as a 2-year-old than the mother who has been denied that experience.

Family Influences

Each child is born into a certain social milieu, and his interpretation of his role in that cast of characters is crucial.

Birth order

Many studies have been published concerning birth order, but most are relatively meaningless, since they don't consider the child's attitude and movement, the formation of alliances and opposing groups within the family, and the unique ways children approach the social situation in their search for a place for themselves. In other words, these studies don't take into consideration children's perception of their birth order. For example, if a firstborn child is severely retarded, the second child may take over and function as the firstborn. Another child, preceded by a stillborn, might be treated as a more special "firstborn" than usual.

Birth order, then, must be explained dynamically by taking into consideration how much the child influences the other members of the family and how they influence the child. It is important to remember that all of a child's strivings are directed toward satisfying a feeling of belonging. Pepper (1971) emphasizes that no two children are ever born into the same family situation. With the birth of each child, the situation and, therefore, the environment changes because (1) the parents are older and more experienced or more discouraged; (2) the parents may be more prosperous; (3) the parents may have moved to another neighborhood; and (4) because of divorce or death, there may be a stepparent.

The *only child* has a potentially difficult start in life, since he spends his early childhood among adults. But this is not necessarily a disadvantage. It is true that the only child may be pampered and, as a consequence, may expect to be the center of interest. But it is also true that he has the opportunity to be the only beneficiary of the adults' roles as models and educators and, therefore, may become a more competent and cooperative participant in the life of the family.

The *firstborn's* position often puts the oldest child in a favored spot, but this may be only temporary, since all first children undergo the experience of being dethroned. First children, then, have the choice of trying to maintain the number-one position, or holding their competitor back in the number-two position, or becoming discouraged and letting themselves be overrun by the second child. Naturally, there are innumerable variations in between these alternatives.

The *second child* may feel that he is in a constant race and often develops a personality that is the opposite of the first child's personality, particularly if the two children are close in age and of the same sex. If a third child arrives, the second child also becomes a "squeezed" child. As such, he has one of two general tendencies—to let himself be pushed down by his older and younger siblings or to elevate himself at their expense.

The *youngest child* has the tendency to either try to overtake all the others or to remain a baby, expecting help, service, and consideration. In large families, the children usually divide into subgroups. A family of seven, for example, may be seen by the youngest as made up of three older kids, two middle kids, and two little kids. This means that, when we look for subgrouping in a family, we must do so from the point of view of the person whose life style we are trying to understand and keep in mind that this point of view is not the same for all the children in the family.

Shulman (1973) emphasizes that the ordinal positions are "psychological" more than chronological, citing the instance in which a firstborn may be dethroned and play the role of the middle child and the second born, by virtue of overrunning the first, actually plays the role of the first born.

Family constellation

"Family constellation" describes the sociopsychological configuration of a family group (Shulman, in Nikelly, 1971). The personality characteristics of each family member, emotional bonds between family members, birth order, the dominance or submission of the various members, their age differences, sex of the siblings, and size of the family are all factors in the family constellation. A child's position in the family constellation exerts a strong influence on the development of the child's personality. Therefore, as we shall see later, it is essential that the therapist or counselor take position into consideration to understand the client's dynamics.

The developing child is trying to find her place in a particular group's order, and it makes a difference how close or distant the family members are, who was born when, how the siblings perceived their position in the birth order, and who is the boss, or at least who is seen as boss (if there is one). The family constellation does not directly describe a particular child. Rather, it offers a dynamic way of understanding, for example, the fact that first and second children are often quite different in personality, particularly if they are close in age and of the same sex. An only boy among girls, or an only girl among boys, may experience the family constellation in a special way, particularly if that family favors either boys or girls. The much larger family presents, of course, many more possibilities. There may be, for example, subgroupings within the sibling group, so that a child who is the "eldest" of the younger group may share some of the characteristics of the firstborn child. In some larger families, there is a need for more cooperation, and the culturally provided competition may not have as deleterious an effect as in smaller families.

Family atmosphere

Dewey (in Nikelly, 1971) describes a number of typical family atmospheres to which the growing child reacts. These reactions can develop in the direction of accepting the attitudes and values shared by the family, in the direction of rejecting them, or in a direction somewhere between these two.

The attributes the children in a particular family share—such as love of reading, musical aptitude, or athletic ability—are a reflection of the family atmosphere. They express shared family values. In a family that values athletics, it is quite likely that all children will, to some degree, be athletically inclined. The attributes that are not shared by the children are, to some extent, a product of the atmosphere of competition within the family, which grows out of the competition between the parents. For example, if one parent is neat and the other is messy, some of the children are likely to be neat and some messy. If the mother constantly passes judgment on her husband, we can expect that the children, following in their mother's footsteps, will constantly pass judgment on their spouses.

As another example of how children respond to the family atmosphere, all five children in a family may exhibit an unusual interest in music (a shared family value, since both parents are musical). However, each child chooses a different instrument, and one child finds a unique place for herself by being "tone deaf" and making her musical contribution through percussion. The musical talent, then, represents the family atmosphere of shared family values. The difference in the way the talent is manifested is the result of the competition among the siblings. In this family, if one parent had been musical and the other had not, we might have expected two or three children to be musical and the others to be relatively uninterested in music.

Here are some of the family atmospheres described by Dewey and their characteristics.

The *rejective* atmosphere is exemplified by parents who fail to separate the deed from the doer and who constantly criticize and reject their children.

The *authoritarian* atmosphere is rigid, stresses obedience, and is likely to produce either extremely conforming or extremely rebellious children.

In an atmosphere of *martyrdom*, suffering nobly is greatly valued. The spouse of an alcoholic, who by his or her "heroic" behavior ends up by encouraging the partner's drinking, is a classic example of this situation.

In the *inconsistent* atmosphere, the children don't know what to expect of others or what is expected of them. However, Dreikurs often observed that most of the time in such atmosphere it is the adults, rather than the children, who are confused and that it is usually the parents who need to learn to become a match for their children.

The *suppressive* atmosphere limits the freedom to express thoughts and feelings and sometimes stimulates excessive daydreaming or produces children who are very good at "putting up a front." Examples of this kind of family is a family made up of humorless people or a group of very narrowly religious people, who talk little among themselves and are not demonstrative.

The *hopeless* atmosphere can be described with the term used by Satir—"funereal." She says: "Everyone suffers from severe discouragement, which is highly contagious, and boundless pessimism'' (Satir, 1972, p. 9). Children who grow up in a funereal family are often like dreary little adults—humorless, friendless, nonspontaneous. It is as if they never learned to play.

The *overprotective* atmosphere denies children the opportunity to learn to be responsible for their own behavior.

The *pitying* atmosphere often stimulates the development of ''victims,'' who become so creative and flexible in their capacity to suffer that they can suffer about anything.

The *high-standards* atmosphere leads the children to feel that they are never good enough.

The *materialistic* atmosphere underplays the significance of human relationships and often produces life failures both among those who want to be ''the best'' and among those who, despairing at being the best, may work at being ''the worst.''

The *disparaging* atmosphere is characterized by frequent criticism. The parents operate as if anybody who is not a member of the family is an outsider, thus teaching their children the basic skills of prejudice.

In the *inharmonious* atmosphere, the children grow up feeling that they are in an enemy camp.

In deeply troubled families, one of two opposite atmospheres may prevail—a very *disorderly* atmosphere or a very *orderly* atmosphere. An example of a disorderly family is a family in which bickering and fighting go on almost constantly, from the time the first family member gets up in the morning to the time the last one goes to bed at night. An example of an overorderly atmosphere is a family in which the new stepmother—long single and highly efficient as a nurse—tries to operate the family like a hospital ward and fails to establish any kind of rapport with her stepchildren, who refuse to accept her disciplinary attitude and avoid her company as much as they can.

Early Experiences

Early experiences, no matter how dramatic or potentially traumatic, are not specifically causative of personality traits, because each child will determine for herself the significance of the experience. The power of the subjective interpretation of reality is apparent, for example, if one interviews adult identical twins about some shared incident that occurred quite early in their lives. It is clear from their recollections that the twins do remember the same incident; but, as we indicated earlier, when they are asked to pinpoint the most vivid moment in the incident and how they felt at that moment, their answers are likely to indicate that they experienced the incident totally differently.

Impasses

We call *impasse* what the child decides he must avoid at all costs. If we are correct in assuming that the number-one priority is chosen very early, we can speculate that the impasse has something to do with the family situation and the methods of training. People with a number-one priority of control probably have perceived themselves in their childhood as being overpowered and overcontrolled. People with a number-one priority of superiority have often grown up in a family where good and bad, right and wrong, success and failure were emphasized and shaming was a common method of child training. People with a number-one priority of superiority seem to have felt very doubtful about their belonging as very young children and have probably concluded that meaninglessness or nothingness is the most difficult thing to imagine. People with a number-one priority of comfort have probably experienced much stress or pain and decided to organize their life so as to avoid repetition of that discomfort. People with a number-one priority of pleasing often have been literally rejected in some way and have experienced one or more kinds of behavior on the part of their parents that betrayed significant lack of respect for the dignity of the child.

THE LIFE STYLE

In Adlerian psychology, the term *life style* refers to a person's basic orientation toward life. As the Ansbachers (1956) observe, the term denotes a dynamic state rather than a rigid and static entity. From this point of view, it is more or less equivalent to terms such as *personality, psyche, character,* and *ego.*

Since a person's life style is based on one's private logic, develops out of one's life plan, and is powered by the fictional goal one establishes for himself, we can begin our discussion of life style by analyzing these three basic concepts. A comprehensive review of all the recent research on Adlerian psychology and the life style can be found in Mosak and Mosak's *A Bibliography for Adlerian Psychology*, 1985.

The Private Logic

The general knowledge of what is right and what is wrong, of what one should do and what one should not do, can be looked at as a kind of common sense (Dreikurs, 1969). When people don't do what a situation calls for, they are often operating on the basis of their private logic, which may differ widely from the logic of the human community. Behind every action are plans, goals, expectations, and decisions that cause the behavior but of which we are only vaguely aware. Most of our actions are the consequences of thinking processes that we don't recognize and often prefer not to know but that, nevertheless, have a definite influence on our actions. All of these thinking processes, which never reach the threshold of consciousness, can be considered part of the private logic.

> Whenever we act contrary to our conscience then we are acting with the sense of our "private" logic. This does not occur only when we want to evade the requirements of the situation. In daily life we do not deal with actual realities but operate with a subjective impression of the world, which is not always in accordance with reality. We call this subjective evaluation of events the "phenomenological field" within which each human being is moving, and which is valid only for him alone. We never can conceive of "facts" as such. We only have a more or less accurate impression in our imagination of the "facts," but these impressions are used in determining our actions, our attitudes and our goals. (Dreikurs, 1969, pp. 70–71; quotation translated by Pew)

The mental precursors—that is, the cognitive processes that take place below the threshold of consciousness and, yet, determine our actions—involve a hierarchy of goals that have one characteristic in common: the fact that we are unaware of them. First, there are the far-reaching basic goals of the life style. These are the fictions according to which we act and of which we are not conscious. Different factors contribute to this remarkable situation. First, these attitudes form when we are so young that we are hardly able to understand consciously what is happening within or around us. But more significantly, the reason we are unable to know these fictitious goals lies in the very necessity of subjectivity. Each of us has to act "as if" our judgment were the only possible and absolutely correct one.

Although long-term goals provide the substance of the life style, we have the power to take different attitudes toward current events. In other words, our own self-created limitations within the life style still do not limit our individual creative power—that is, the ability to make decisions about immediate situations. Since we are never rigidly forced to assume an attitude, make a decision, or establish a goal, we must also recognize the short-range goals that we set for ourselves in the immediate experiences of our lives.

In addition to long-range and short-range goals, private logic also includes a form of thinking that Dreikurs called *hidden reason*. Most of us not only don't recognize the reason we do something, but are also unaware of the process that goes on in our minds and that results in that reason. The "hidden reason" therefore appears to be an unconscious justification and force behind movement toward the goals in a given situation.

To be aware of that process, we would have to imagine that we could examine our own minds whenever we said or did something. Nevertheless, when a counselor (or someone else) accurately guesses the hidden reason, the feeling of being understood is often so overpowering that even a psychotic or a juvenile delinquent is unable to hold himself back from admitting the reason for his behavior.

The Life Plan

Small children are not prepared to deal with the demands of life. To cope, they must learn the rules of the game of the human community—a community experienced almost exclusively through the family, which seems to represent "life" and the "human condition." All difficulties children encounter are experienced personally and interpreted as difficulties that everyone encounters, just as all successes are incorporated and interpreted as examples of successful living.

To escape what appears as destiny and to find clarity and predictability in the disorientation of life, children develop safeguarding mechanisms and fictional solutions to problems, without which it would be impossible for humans to orient themselves. A fiction creates an illusion of secure values. We operate under the assumption that we can feel safe only under some circumstances and that we can be worthwhile only if we act in certain ways. The child constantly creates and operates in terms of dichotomies—good or bad, on top or at the bottom, masculine or feminine, and so on. All that makes up the character of a human is none other than the manifestation of a certain plan the person has laid down as a child in preparation for living. The life plan grows out of the constant repetition of attempts to cope with real or imagined difficulties. Out of this plan develops the life style, which, like a characteristic musical theme, accompanies the individual throughout life.

The Fictional Goal

Each person develops in early childhood a fictional image of what she needs to be like to be safe, to be superior, to feel belonging, and so forth. The actualization of this fictional image becomes the central goal of the life style and, as a consequence, limits to some extent the range of the individual's actions.

The life plan and its fictional goal are the outcomes of the child's assessment of his experiences. This assessment is often inaccurate because, although children are excellent observers and have extraordinarily sharp perception, they lack the experience and maturity necessary to evaluate their observations adequately. Children's perceptiveness is perhaps due in part to their lacking a set style of life. Without a set style, one is open to all possible perceptions instead of limited by a style of life that almost completely prevents the experience of "pure" perception. Guided by the fictional goal, children do the best they can to find for themselves a style of life that gives them an immediate feeling of belonging and promises a greater sense of belonging for the future. The style of life they seek is also one that gives them a sense of superiority as they define it for themselves. Once set, the style of life tends to become self-perpetuating.

Because the life style and the guiding fictional goal are so intimately related, the guiding fiction tends to approximate the life style. One's guiding fiction is a certain image of the world and of oneself; therefore, a person's life style is likely to be such that the observer can rather accurately infer the individual's guiding fiction.

The concept of life style also—and especially—refers to our manner of handling ourselves with respect to our self-chosen guiding fictional goal. This means that, since our creativity is practically limitless (especially when it comes to the manner of staging our own lives), there is nothing in any given guiding fiction that forcibly entails a set style of life. Thus, even after having formulated our guiding fictional goal and, to that extent, limited the range of our actions, we still have a tremendous amount of freedom in the choices we constantly make with regard to our style of living.

Development of the Life Style

The style of living is created in the course of an ongoing drama that takes place in the theater of the family, with parents and siblings all playing a part—a drama in which the child functions as his own director and whose last act he has already sketched out in broad outlines. The nuclear family *is* society to the small child, and the child's efforts to find a place in this society influence how he creates his life style. In elucidating an individual's life style, the counselor tries to get some idea of what it was like to be in that childhood drama, what roles were played by the different actors, and how the "director" interpreted the drama—that is, what role he played and what conclusions he drew about himself and life.

The drama analogy helps us see the role of another element in the construction of the life style. This element is the order of appearance of each actor on the stage—the birth order. We must keep in mind, however, that the importance assigned to this element is always the doing of the "director"; it is a value judgment on the part of the individual whose personality we are trying to understand. We can make some general guesses about someone's personality if we know her ordinal position. These guesses, however, will be based on *nomothetic laws*, such as "Oldest children are...," "Middle children tend to be...," and so on. But the actual case can be quite different, depending on how the individual sees the situation and what she does about it—*idiographic laws*. Nomothetic laws concerning the family constellation help reveal the individual's idiographic laws—that is, the individual's life style.

Understanding the role the family constellation plays in the creation of one's life style always involves trying to reconstruct the drama from her point of view. Drawing a diagram of the family constellation helps the counselor perceive patterns. This family-constellation diagram is from Mary's point of view.

Helen	George	
33	35	
Mary	Susan	Bobby
13	– 2 years	– 5 years

The diagram often reveals the existence of more than two "parents." Aunts, uncles, grandparents, and much older siblings can all be "parents" from the viewpoint of the child if they were an intimate part of the family drama during the years (up to age 6 or 7) in which the child was creating his style of living. For the diagram to be complete, it should also include brothers and sisters who have died.

Earlier in the chapter, we discussed the various factors that influence personality development. One's style of living is the result of the individual's subjective interpretation of these factors. The weight of each is creatively determined by the individual. We have mentioned, for example, genetic endowment and environmental influences; both are important, but the individual determines the degree of importance. Children create their life style from raw materials, which also include the method of training by the parents, the cultural influences in the immediate and larger community, as well as illnesses, injuries, and hospitalizations—all grist for the mill. During those first few years, children will have created their own idiosyncratic answers to: Who am I? What is life? What must I do? What is good? What is bad? Children create their own unique private logic, which, to some extent, will make each of them different from any other human being.

Dreikurs points out that we don't know how many typical life plans exist, but probably no two human beings share the same ideas and goals. Still, we find considerable similarities in styles of living. Perhaps it is the poverty of our language that forces us to use the same words for different observations and experiences. McLuhan says "All reading is guessing." Communication in any form, then, will always be an approximation both as it is sent and as it is received. It is also conceivable that each culture has a dominant perceptual mode and that its members share similar ideals and values.

Some styles of living are relatively broad, providing a basis for the solution of almost all life problems, while others have such a narrow base that they run the risk of failing. Despite the inherent cognitive defects in life style, any individual can get along quite reasonably until such time as the life style is challenged by the realities of life. Remember: the style of living is self-created and is also self-consistent. After the first years of life, each new experience merely confirms convictions. An individual will report the same early recollections with the same basic themes year after year, with little influence from outside reality. In other words, the individual has created her own convictions (or fictions) about what she must become and what she can expect of life, of the outside, and of other people.

Mosak divides these convictions into four groups: (1) the self-concept—the convictions I have about who I am; (2) the self-ideal (Adler's term)—the convictions concerning what I should be or am obliged to be in order to have a place in the world; (3) the Weltbild (picture of the world)—the convictions about the nonself (world, people, nature, and so on) and what the world demands of me; and (4) ethical convictions—the personal "right/wrong" code (Mosak & Dreikurs, 1973).

Life Style and Counseling

The concept of life style is extremely useful in counseling as both a tool and an attitude. Adlerian counselors believe that life style is self-created; therefore, they are likely to approach their clients with a positive attitude—the attitude that, as long as there is life, people can grow and change. If we instead view personality as the result of inevitable internal or external forces, one has reason to be less optimistic, for genetic influences are relatively unchanging, and the childhood environment cannot be relived.

Children tend to move in line with the expectations of the adults around them. Even in such dramatic cases as those of children suffering from Down's syndrome (mongolism), parents' expectations can make a great difference. Actually, some of the intellectual deficit in Down's syndrome may not be related to lack of genetic endowment but, rather, to a defect in the facial musculature that makes it difficult for the child to respond nonverbally to the parents. If parents don't provide the retarded child with the variety of stimulation they would offer to a more responsive child, the intellectual deficit may relate to sensory deprivation and to distorted interaction with other people. Even institutionalized "retardates" have been shown to be "rootless and rejected, rather than defective, children" (Braginsky & Braginsky, 1971). These children can be quite skillful in the art of manipulating the staff, can appear "dumber" or "brighter" at will, and demonstrate a wide range of adaptive behaviors.

Even merely gathering the data necessary to elucidate a style of living, without any interpretation on the part of the counselor, is useful. Hearing clients describe their childhood family atmosphere and constellation and some of their interpretations about their position in the family often provides the counselor with extremely useful information toward the goal of understanding her clients. In fact, in some cases, standard history taking and administration of test batteries may add little more.

When clients tell about their childhood family constellation and atmosphere, in a sense they are reliving the situation and the vivid moments and emotional experiences connected with it. By sharing the clients' emotional experiences, the counselor achieves deeper understanding and is in a better position to help clients discover more alternatives in their lives. With the help of the counselor, clients come to see themselves and all of their biases, guidelines, and convictions more vividly. It is as if a mirror were being held up in front of them, and they can then decide which basic convictions they want to keep and which basic mistakes they choose to alter.

A change in the life style is not necessarily the goal in counseling, because within a given style of living rests a wide range of behavioral alternatives. For example, one man's life style may include the conviction "I must fight to belong." If this conviction is challenged, the person might react with "What do you expect me to be—a doormat?" There are many other alternatives between being a fighter and being a doormat.

Some warnings are in order. Elucidating life style is *not* for the purpose of predicting behavior, but rather for the purpose of understanding and helping another human being. Also, people often use their style of living as an excuse: "What can you expect of me? It's my life style." Finally, we need to distinguish between life style, as we use the term here, and an individual's modus operandi, such as a suburban life style versus an inner-city life style. The style of living is what makes an individual unique, what distinguishes him from every other human being.

Functions and Mistaken Attitudes of the Life Style

Shulman (1973) describes several functions of the life style. He refers to the life style as the cognitive blueprint, the "rule of rules," and the "unique law of movement" for each individual. He sees life style as the "formal cause" of behavior and as governor as well as feedback. Shulman also believes that we can quite accurately define the functions of life style as we see them in operation.

Shulman points out that oversimplification, exaggeration, and mistaking the part for the whole are three common mistakes in logic that are also common in style of living. It is useful to list as part of the formulation of life style (see Chapter 6) the basic mistakes that usually lie beneath the threshold of consciousness. Sometimes these mistakes begin as appropriate attitudes; that is, they were appropriate in the childhood situation but are no longer appropriate for the adult. Shulman (1973) categorizes these basic mistakes into six groups.

1. Distorted attitudes about self—for example, "I am less capable than the others."
2. Distorted attitudes about the world and people—for example, "Life is unpredictable" or "People are no damn good."
3. Distorted goals—for example, "I must be perfect" or "I must never submit."
4. Distorted methods of operation—for example, excessive competitiveness, excessive pride, or ignoring what one doesn't wish to confront.
5. Distorted ideals—for example, "A real man is always heroic" or "The only thing worth being is a star."
6. Distorted conclusions: (a) pessimism—for example, "I am doomed to failure" or "Life is nothing but a trap"; (b) X (love, reason, money, or whatever) conquers all; (c) cynicism—for example, "Everyone is out only for himself" or "There is always an ulterior motive"; (d) fanaticism—for example, "This is the best of all possible systems" or "I'm the only one who has the 'real' truth."

Types of Life Styles

This brings us to the issue of the advantages and disadvantages of typologies. Labeling the client may be a comfort to the counselor but a disservice to the client. As soon as we place someone in a particular category, our tendency is to overlook the person's complexities and subtleties—those special nuances that make a person unique. It is far too easy to move from the position of seeing people in terms of labels to a position of disrespect, however subtle. Most people are quick to pick up on our failure to treat them with dignity and respect. Also, although personality typing may help us organize our thinking, we should take care that our clients don't use typology as an excuse: "Well, that's me. I'm a pleaser, you know!" Personality typing can also reduce our expectations as counselors, thus resulting in lack of respect for our clients.

With these warnings in mind, we can draw some generalizations about types of life styles (Mosak, 1971).

"Getters" try to expend as little effort as possible, while hoping for extravagant returns. Only if the world will give them special due are they willing to contribute. Generally, they look for the payoff and tend to renege on their side of the deal.

"Drivers" want to succeed and achieve, often beyond anyone's wildest dreams. They behave as if total success or "nothingness" were the only alternatives.

"Controllers" like order, their order. They fear chaos and try to keep the unexpected to a bare minimum. Unfortunately for them, other people keep behaving spontaneously, thus disrupting their system.

"Victims" and "martyrs" are similar in their "noble" suffering. However, a martyr will suffer for a cause, while a victim will suffer for anything. Victims, then, are more flexible and creative—perhaps.

"Good ones" satisfy their sense of superiority by being more competent, more useful, more right, or holier than others. They narrow their life styles by obeying the rule that only by excelling in whatever area of moral perfection they have chosen can they truly belong. Needless to say, very few others measure up to these people's high standards.

None of these types is inherently bad. It depends always on what the individual does with his convictions, as we discussed in Chapter 2. Thus, each type may make great contributions, but often for the wrong reasons and at times almost accidentally. Actually, in practice we seldom see pure types. More often we see blends, because individuals' styles of living are infinitely varied. The more we learn about a person, the more unique and creative that person becomes in our eyes.

It is essential that the therapist or counselor clearly understand the process through which individuals create their personality, their life style. As we said earlier, the prototype of the life style is already apparent in the first few years of life, by the time the child is 2 or 3. Probably, by the time the child is 4 or 5, the basic structure of the life style is well organized and will remain essentially the same throughout life unless challenged by major experiences or through therapy.

This basic structure is like a foundation that remains relatively unchanged but on which can be developed a broad variety of superstructures. The foundation includes the individual's self-created final fictional goal—one's idea of how security, belonging, superiority, perfection, or completion can be achieved. All aspects of the personality can be seen as movement in the direction of the final goal. All behavior, then, makes sense if we understand people's private logic, where they think they must go and how they think they must get there. All external influences, important as they may be, have been and will be filtered through the "intermediary psychological metabolism." Each individual will have a different reality, because each individual is totally dependent on his subjectivity. All of us always function "as if"—as if perfection or completion were precisely as we have defined it and as if the only way to move in the direction of perfection or completion were along the guidelines we have set up for ourselves in early childhood.

These concepts of reality, however, are open to change. If the individual has created them in the first place, she can create new ones to take their place—new ones that are more in the direction of courage and social interest. Change comes about as the therapist or counselor consistently challenges each basic mistake, thus helping the client see how counterproductive—at times even ridiculous—these concepts of reality are.

REFERENCES

Ansbacher, H.L., & Ansbacher R.R. (Eds.). (1956). *The individual psychology of Alfred Adler.* New York: Harper & Row.

Braginsky, D.D., & Braginsky, B.M. (1971). *Hansels and Gretels: Studies of children in institutions for the mentally retarded.* New York: Holt, Rinehart & Winston.

Chess, S., Thomas, A., & Birch, H. (1965). *Your child is a person: A psychological approach to parenthood without guilt.* New York: Viking.

Dreikurs, R. (1969). *Grundbegriffe der Individualpsychologie.* Stuttgart: Ernst Klett Verlag.

Hooker, D. (1954). Early human fetal behavior, with a preliminary note of double simultaneous fetal stimulation. *Proceedings of the*

Association for Research in Nervous and Mental Disease.
Baltimore: William & Wilkins.

Moore, O.K. (1964). Autotelic responsive environments and exceptional children. In J. Hellmuth (Ed.), *The special child in century 21.* Seattle: Special Child Publications of the Sequin School.

Mosak, B., & Mosak, H. (1985). *A bibliography for Adlerian psychology* (Vol. 2). New York: McGraw-Hill.

Mosak, H.H. (1971). Lifestyle. In A. G. Nikelly (Ed.), *Techniques for behavior change.* Springfield, IL: Charles C Thomas.

Mosak, H.H., & Dreikurs, R. (1973). Adlerian psychotherapy. In R.J. Corsini (Ed.), *Current psychotherapies.* Itasca, IL: Peacock.

Nikelly, A.G. (Ed.). (1971). *Techniques for behavior change.* Springfield, IL: Charles C Thomas.

Pepper, F.C. (1971). Birth order. In A. G. Nikelly (Ed.), *Techniques for behavior change.* Springfield, IL: Charles C Thomas.

Satir, V. (1972). *Peoplemaking.* Palo Alto, CA: Science and Behavior Books.

Shulman, B.H. (1973). *Contributions to Individual Psychology.* Chicago: Alfred Adler Institute.

Standing, E.M. (1962). *Maria Montessori: Her life and work.* New York: New American Library.

4 Psychopathology

T his chapter has three purposes: to describe Adler's basic view of normality and psychopathology and extend and clarify it; to compare the Adlerian view with the nosological or classification system of the Diagnostic and Statistical Manual, Third Edition (DSM-III); and to describe the more common patterns of psychopathology in terms of early life experiences, mistaken convictions, and symptom formation.

ADLERIAN VIEWS OF PSYCHOPATHOLOGY

The Basic Theory

According to Adlerian theory, healthy, nonpathological people typically move through life meeting various tasks with courage and common sense. This is the meaning of *social interest*, but it does not suggest that the individual is perfect. Occasionally, a healthy person uses private logic, experiences some discouragement, and feels a sense of inferiority for which he compensates in ways that are outside the reaches of social interest. Most people believe that imperfections and failures are part of the human condition. On the other hand, pathological persons believe they must be perfect and justify their thinking and actions as the only way to achieve perfection. To Adler, all personality dysfunction was the outcome of erroneous conceptions of how to achieve personal superiority. For the most part, he believed that these faulty conceptions were formed early in life (Adler, 1956).

A *neurotic disposition*, Adler's term for the predisposing conditions that can result in psychopathology, stems from childhood experiences characterized either by overprotection or neglect, or by a confusing admixture of both. From these experiences, the young child develops a set of psychological convictions (about self, the world, and life goal, which become the life style) of his inability to develop mastery or cope with the tasks of life. This conviction is confounded and reinforced by the child's perception of a frankly hostile, punishing, or depriving environment at home or school, or one that is subtly demanding or frustrating. Rather than providing encouragement to seek mastery and achievement, these experiences leave the youngster feeling discouraged and fearful. Rather than experiencing trusting and loving relationships, the young child becomes distrustful and manipulative. To compensate for these exaggerated feelings of insecurity and anxiety, the child becomes self-centered and uncooperative.

The dysfunctional life style is an inflexible life style. Problem solving is based upon a self-protective "private sense" rather than a more task-oriented and socially useful common sense. Once this set of faulty psychological convictions has coalesced and self-protective patterns of coping have been established, it becomes difficult for the individual to see or respond to life in any other way. The result is that the dysfunctional individual cannot productively cope with the tasks of life nor really enjoy the rewards of his labors, much less his relationships with others. In contrast, a set of psychological convictions and coping patterns that are shaped positively by the child's healthy experiences of mastery, creativity, and loving and pleasurable relationships result in a flexible life style.

Adler presented a unitary theory of psychopathology wherein the individual uniquely "arranges" his symptoms as excuses for not meeting the tasks of life or to safeguard his self-esteem, either by aggression or distancing himself from others. Adler discriminated dysfunctional behavior along the dimensions of social interest and degree of activity. For instance, the neurotic has more social interest than the psychotic. The neurotic responds to life tasks with "Yes, but . . . ." With "yes" he acknowledges his social responsibilities; with "but" he presents his symptoms to excuse his responsibility. Mosak (1984) describes two types of "yes, but" responses: "Yes, but I'm sick," which is the classic response of the psychoneurotic; and "Yes, but I defy it," the acting-out response of the character neurosis or personality disorder. The psychotic's response to life tasks is "no," and he cuts himself off from the common world. As to activity level, Adler noted a low degree in neurotic conditions such as depression and obsessive-compulsion, with a higher degree in anxiety neurosis, schizophrenia, and alcoholism. The highest levels were in manics and criminals, particularly murderers (Adler, 1964a).

Developments in the Theory

Adler believed that three main components were common to all psychopathology: discouragement, faulty perceptions, and life style beliefs. Furthermore, he posited that an undeveloped social interest and personality dysfunction were basically the outcome of an erroneous way of living. This represents Adler's views on normality versus abnormality at the time of his death; at the outset of his career, Adler felt that psychopathology stemmed from various organ inferiorities. This was a rather biological and reductionistic position. Later, his view changed to a more intrapsychic one in which dysfunctional behavior was seen as a conflict between inferiority and superiority feelings. He described the "neurotic disposition" as the predisposing factor in the development of neurosis. The term *pampered life style* eventually replaced this term. Still later, Adler developed a more sociopsychological view in which psychopathology represented movement toward self-importance at the expense of the common good. In many respects, the last version of Adler's theory represented one of the first attempts at developing a holistic view of psychopathology (Adler, 1964b). Although it encompassed features from the biological (organ inferiority and organ dialect) and the social realms, it was primarily a theory of emotional development and dysfunction that integrated all processes through the prism of the life style:

> This is notably the case with the lungs, the heart, the stomach, the organs of excretion and the sexual organs. The disturbance of these functions expresses the direction which an individual is taking to attain his goal. I have called these disturbances the organ dialect, or organ jargon, since the organs are revealing in their own most expressive language the intention of the individual totality. (Adler, 1964)

The eminent Adlerian clinician Irvin Neufield (1954) distinguished the psychosomatic approaches from the biopsychosocial or holistic approaches like Individual Psychology. Most psychosomatic theories failed to fully appreciate the multifaceted dynamics and interdependence of *all* of the biological, psychological, and social dimensions of human existence. Failure to appreciate all of these multifaceted dimensions leads to the same narrow reductionism Neufield criticized in many psychosomatic theories.

There has been a tendency among those who espouse a holistic theory to downplay some of these multifaceted dynamics, especially the biochemical and neuropharmacological ones. This is particularly true in the treatment of depressive disorders. There is a growing awareness that depression is not a single entity but rather a *spectrum disorder*. Many people currently view depression as a group of discrete illnesses that span a biopsychosocial continuum in which symptom patterns appear to be influenced more strongly by biochemical factors at one end of the continuum and more strongly by psychological factors at the other end.

To illustrate the holistic or biopsychosocial perspective, it will be helpful to speculate about how a depressive disorder develops. We can only speculate, since there is presently no empirically validated theory or model of depression. Based on recent research findings, we can hypothesize that a person who experiences a major depressive episode is in some way genetically susceptible to depression; brain pathways and circuits that deal with emotions like pleasure are fragile and poorly buffered from external influences. Add to this some early life trauma, such as the loss or separation from a significant other, perhaps a parent, that undermines self-confidence and esteem and for which the individual responds with safeguarding patterns. Subjection to a severe psychological stressor later in life in some way echoes the early experience of loss or separation. When existing social support systems and personal coping strategies or safeguarding methods are not sufficient to neutralize this stressor, the already compromised brain biochemistry is overtaxed, resulting in the familiar biological symptoms of depression—sleep and appetite disturbance, psychomotor retardation, reduced energy, inability to experience pleasure, and somatic symptoms such as constipation and headache. This reduced physiological functioning further reinforces the individual's life style beliefs about self, the world and the future. (Pancner [1985] suggests a similar hypothesis.)

On the other hand, a dysthymic disorder (formerly called a *neurotic depression*) which probably has more psychosocial loading and less genetic and biological loading, usually presents with fewer biological symptoms and more dysfunctional life style beliefs and coping skills. Thus, it is not surprising that dysthymic disorders respond well to primarily psychological-oriented therapies, while major depressive disorders usually respond to biochemical therapies such as antidepressant medications, often in conjunction with psychotherapy. Psychotherapy will be a necessary adjunctive treatment assuming that a pampered life style or neurotic disposition interferes with functioning in the life tasks. But when there is little or no life task dysfunction, as is sometimes the situation, psychotherapy is probably not warranted. In his address, "Biochemical Theory and Adlerian Psychology," Pancner proposed the same idea. Responding to the reluctance of some psychotherapists to minimize or deny the biological aspects in their theory and practice, Pancner added:

> We need to be open to the multiplicity of factors involved in mental illness; none of us have all the answers. . . . But to become dogmatic and say "this is the only way" or "that is the only way," I think is closed. To really understand a person we have to look at them holistically, and keep all these things in mind. (Pancner, 1985)

CLASSIFICATION SYSTEMS: ADLERIAN AND DSM-III

Quite unlike other psychological systems that are based on a disease model, Adlerian theory is based on a growth model. It tends to view the dysfunctional individual as discouraged rather than as mentally ill (Mosak, 1984).

The two major types of classificatory systems of psychopathology are descriptive and psychodynamic. The *descriptive approaches* emphasize observable or reportable symptomatology. A diagnosis is made by comparing the individual's symptoms to specified criteria that represent specific diagnoses. The more formal systems suggest inclusion as well as exclusion criteria for each diagnosis to insure both reliability and validity. Thus, the descriptive approaches lend themselves to statistical data collection and analyses, and the comparison of the incidence and prevalence of diagnoses across groups and cultures. The *psychodynamic approaches* emphasize the psychological reasons or mechanisms that are considered the bases for explaining disordered behavior and symptoms. Rudolf Dreikurs was especially critical of the shortcomings of the psychoanalytic formulations of psychopathology (Dreikurs, 1967) and wrote many articles promoting the Adlerian approach to assessing psychopathology. *Psychodynamics, Psychotherapy and Counseling* (1967) is a collection of Dreikurs's most important papers on this topic.

In the Adlerian approach, observations about an individual's movement and descriptions of uniqueness are considered more valuable than diagnostic categories and classification. For didactic purposes, however, Adler did characterize four personality types: the ruling, getting, avoiding, and the healthy, socially useful. The first three types are low in social interest, so would be considered dysfunctional. Mosak (1959, 1971, 1973, 1985) briefly describes several other personality types and provides in-depth analyses of the getting and controlling types.

Adler considered the obsessive-compulsive neurosis to be the prototype of all neuroses; for Freud, the hysterical neurosis was the prototype. Indecisiveness and doubt, depreciation of others, godlike strivings, and focus on minutiae were the safeguarding methods Adler routinely noted among his compulsive neurotic patients in their seeking the goal of personal superiority. He noted that various neurotic and psychotic individuals might use different safeguarding methods, but their movement was nevertheless the same: avoidance or rejection of the life tasks.

The standard diagnostic classification adopted by many clinicians and insurance carriers in the United States is the third edition of the *Diagnostic and Statistical Manual of Mental Disorders* (1980), usually referred to as DSM-III. Unlike the Adlerian approach, with its unitary theory of psychopathology, DSM-III describes 18 distinct major classifications and diagnostic criteria for more than 200 mental disorders. Each disorder has a unique set of descriptive—rather than dynamic—diagnostic criteria. A DSM-III diagnosis can be made when the facts from an individual's history and clinical presentation match the diagnostic criteria for a particular mental disorder. In short, the DSM system is based on the medical model and a psychology of possession, while the Adlerian approach is based on a growth model and a psychology of use. Consequently, the Adlerian therapist might not be as concerned about making a DSM-III–type of descriptive diagnosis as he would be in understanding the individual's dynamics, or movement and life style themes.

Similar to the Adlerian emphasis on life task functioning, DSM-III views pathology as clinically significant behavioral or psychological syndromes or patterns associated with maladaptive functioning in one or more of three areas: social relations, occupation, and leisure. As the Adlerian approach strives toward a holistic-biopsychosocial understanding of the individual, DSM-III allows for a multiaxial classification so that interrelated biopsychosocial or systems facets of a person's life may be considered. Five axes are used:

Axis I: Clinical Syndrome(s) (e.g., Schizophrenia)

Axis II: Personality Disorder or Specific Developmental Disorders (e.g., Borderline Personality Disorder)

Axis III: Physical Disorders or Conditions (e.g., Angina)

Axis IV: Severity of Psychosocial Stressors (e.g., death of spouse; change of job)

Axis V: Highest Level of Adaptive Functioning in the Past Year (e.g., poor)

Many holistically-oriented therapists, including Adlerians, would argue for the inclusion of a sixth axis: a holistic-biopsychosocial formulation. Merely listing biopsychosocial information in the various axes does not in itself constitute a holistic formulation.

Practically speaking, can DSM categories be integrated with Adlerian theory? Mosak (1968), in what many consider a classic in the psychopathology literature, has helped a generation of clinicians to interrelate central themes or basic life style convictions with previous DSM diagnostic categories. These central themes are determined from clinical observation, psychological testing, and especially through early recollections. Mosak lists the eleven most common themes: getters; controllers; drivers; to be good, perfect, right; martyrs, victims; "aginners"; feeling avoiders; and excitement seekers; and interrelated combinations of these themes with nineteen diagnostic categories. For example, one who would traditionally be diagnosed as a depressive neurotic would likely exhibit a composite life style, in varying degrees of the getter, the controller, and the person needing to be right (Mosak, 1979). For the antisocial personality, the themes would likely be those of the getter, the aginner, and excitement seeking.

(Consult Mosak's 1968 and 1979 articles for a fuller description of this unique integration of diagnostic categories and life style themes.)

COMMON MANIFESTATIONS OF PSYCHOPATHOLOGY

The results of the monumental NIMH Epidemilogical Catchment Area (ECA) Study (1984) lists the most prevalent psychiatric disorders that, to varying degrees, incapacitate 19 percent of the U.S. population. We will discuss six of these ECA disorders: bipolar disorders; schizophrenia; depressive disorders; antisocial personality disorder; anxiety disorders; and addictive disorders. We will also discuss the borderline personality disorder and, briefly, the Adlerian interpretation of suicide. Each discussion includes a descriptive definition of the disorder and an Adlerian interpretation that focuses on childhood experiences, inferiority feelings, compensation, approach to life tasks, and resulting symptom formation.

Anxiety Disorders

Anxiety disorders were classified in DSM-I and II as neuroses or neurotic disorders. The subclasses of anxiety disorders are phobic, obsessive compulsive, panic, generalized anxiety, posttraumatic stress, and atypical anxiety. In this group of disorders, overwhelming anxiety is either the predominant disturbance, as manifested in panic and generalized anxiety disorders, or the anxiety is experienced when one attempts to master the symptoms, as in confronting the dreaded object or situation in a phobic disorder. If the anxiety is manifested when resisting an obsession or compulsion, the diagnosis is obsessive compulsive disorder. The basic feature of phobic disorders is persistent avoidance behavior related to irrational fears of a specific object, activity, or situation. Agoraphobia is one type of phobic disorder. The essential feature of panic disorder is recurrent anxiety attacks and nervousness. These attacks are characterized by a sudden onset of intense apprehension or terror, and are often associated with feelings of impending death. Basic to a diagnosis of generalized anxiety disorder is at least six months of generalized and persistent anxiety without the specific symptoms of phobic, panic, or obsessive compulsive disorders. Recurrent and persistent ideas, impulses, or images that are not voluntarily produced, or recurrent and compelling stereotyped actions that are attempts to relieve obsessions or fears are the essential features of obsessive compulsive disorders. This case illustrates an increasingly common anxiety disorder:

Mrs. G. is a 47-year-old wife of the mayor of a suburban community who sought psychotherapy because she had a fear of being in church. As the story unfolded, it became clear that she really feared leaving home. Before she developed fear of going to church, she had become uneasy while shopping and driving her children to school. The onset of this agoraphobic behavior was related to her husband's heart attack eighteen months earlier. Since he was 62 years old, she was fearful that he might have another heart attack that would prove fatal and leave her as the sole support of her children. The thought of this was unbearable, and although she was quite dependent on her husband, she could not understand her developing fear of leaving the home.

Adler taught that anxiety is used to create distance between the individual and the life tasks so as to safeguard self-esteem when one fears defeat. The neurotic is considered an ambitious person who has lost his courage, and so lives in constant dread of having his weaknesses discovered. Adler would say that the neurotic has a "hesitating attitude" or a "yes, but" response to life. This individual postpones decisions and tries to keep a safe distance from others and difficult tasks.

Agoraphobia, anxiety neurosis, and all the forms of phobias may originate at this point (the individual's unwillingness to admit his fear of defeat), but, whichever it may be, it fulfills its purpose of blocking the way to further activity. Thus, what was desired is attained—namely, the ordeal is evaded without disclosing, even to its owner, the hated feeling of inferiority. All the other symptoms, such as compulsion ideas, fits, fatigue, sleeplessness, functional disturbances such as neurotic heart, headaches, migraines and so on, develop out of the severe tension of this very difficult concealment. (Adler, 1964b, p. 11)

These neurotic patterns are laid down in early childhood. Because the pampered child is ill-prepared to perform the tasks of life, he finds his courage taxed when another child is born, school life begins, or a major change in his environment occurs, such as a move to another neighborhood or the death of a parent. The first nervous symptoms often take the form of organ dysfunction, such as abdominal pains, respiratory symptoms, enuresis, or temper tantrums. Their purpose is to compel the parents to give in to the child and relieve him of certain responsibilities. These symptoms are among the first weapons the child uses to get his own way (Dreikurs, 1950).

Bipolar Disorder (Manic-Depression)

The core feature of this syndrome is a disordered mood with both manic and depressive phases. In the beginning of its course, mania may resemble normal euphoria, but gradually becomes uncontrolled and psychotic; 20 percent of manics experience delusions and hallucinations. The depressive phase is usually profound. Attacks are usually separated by months or even years, but the person may occasionally cycle from one to the other over days or may even present contrasting symptoms simultaneously. The first episode is often manic and begins before age 30, resolving in a few months. If untreated, most go on to the depressive phase. This is a classic example of a bipolar disorder:

> Mr. C. is a 32-year-old attorney who was admitted to the psychiatric unit of the community hospital in an acute manic episode. He was extremely hyperactive, distractible, irritable, and demanding. He exhibited pressured speech, flight of ideas, and marked hostility to his wife for what he described as infidelity. Five years earlier he was treated for a depressive episode following his wife's hysterectomy surgery. Since that time he had developed manic symptoms in the early spring and depressive symptoms in the late fall. Prior to the onset of his depression he was described as perfectionistic and outgoing, and a firstborn. Between episodes, he was rather successful as a trial attorney and showed no evidence of personality deterioration.

According to Peven and Shulman (1983), Adler had relatively little to say about the dynamics of bipolar disorders. They summarize Adler's statements on this condition as: (1) an underlying cyclothymic personality disorder is present; (2) the moods alternate between feelings of exaltation and grandiosity to those of powerlessness; (3) these individuals lack faith in their own competence; and (4) mania is viewed as a maneuver to deceive self and others. In their review of the literature, Peven and Shulman found that no dynamic theory adequately accounted for this disorder, including Adler's formulation which underplays the disturbance of mood. They suggest that the neurovegetative signs of mania and depression are probably best understood as physiological rather than as primarily psychological in etiology.

In their own research evaluating extensive psychological profiles of 17 patients who met DSM-III criteria for the bipolar disorder, Peven and Shulman found eight common factors:

1. Bipolars had unrealistically high goals regarding the achievement of prominence and prestige.
2. They typically try to impress others with sideshows if they cannot achieve their goals directly.
3. Their self-image does not assure them that their goals are within reach, but they blame this on their own ineptness rather than on the unachievability of their goals.

4. They carry within themselves an inner protest against the burdens of these goals, yet they are not free to discard these goals because of their cognitive style.
5. Their cognitive style is characterized as impulsive, internally controlled, and antithetical. In other words, they are either/or people who think in the concrete extremes of right/wrong, black/white.
6. Their perceptual style is affect-based, that is, they tend to be feelers rather than thinkers. They are excitement-seekers.
7. They are extremist in what they think, feel and do.
8. They tend to be firstborns.

To Peven and Shulman, the manic phase of the illness is a heightened attempt to achieve impressive feats, while the depressive phase represents an exhausted refusal and intensified protest to participate in life when it denies achievement but nevertheless demands the burden of achieving. Based on their research, these authors do not agree with Adler's notion that bipolars have a premorbid cyclothymic personality or that mania is "a frantic attempt to force a success in the service of his goal of superiority" (K. Adler, 1961). Given the biological predisposition and the characteristic ways manic-depressives behave, the authors conclude that "mania can result from being aroused by a success or by pleasant excitement and not knowing when to stop or how to moderate the arousal. Bipolars, in fact, court the arousal since that is the way they feel most comfortable" (p. 14).

Schizophrenia

Schizophrenia represents a large group of psychotic disorders that show characteristic disturbances of language and communication, thought, perception, affect, and behavior lasting at least six months. The characteristic disturbance of thought is marked by alterations in concept formation that can lead to misinterpretation of reality, misperceptions, hallucinations, and delusions. There are genetic, biochemical, sociocultural, and several psychological theories of this group of disorders. This is an example of schizophrenia of the paranoid type:

Mrs. H. was admitted to a psychiatric hospital the day after her thirty-third birthday. For the past nine months her family had noted strange behavior characterized by withdrawal, inappropriate mood, preoccupation with religious ideas, and the delusion that her husband and other elders in her church were "trying to do away with her like they did with Christ." She was convinced that she "would be put to death" on her thirty-third birthday and accordingly had barricaded herself in her bedroom for the three days before, claiming that only if she fasted for 40 days and nights would she be able to foil the plot. In the hospital she was markedly suspicious of the entire staff, accusing them of trying to poison her food, to "crucify" her in group therapy sessions, and so on. Much of the time she was withdrawn, claiming God could not communicate directly to her if she was in the company of "heathens." Her affect was flattened and sometimes she talked readily but inappropriately.

According to Adler, the schizophrenic has very low self-esteem, which is compensated by an overly idealized and inflated goal of superiority. Because of extreme deprivation, ambivalent mothering, organic factors, prolonged illness, or separation from parents, or any combination of these reasons, the child develops a magnified sense of inferiority. This experience leads to the view that he is utterly special and great and that others are enemies who frustrate his desires. Thus, the child not only withdraws and is uncooperative, but also exploits others. He uses people around him as personifications of his difficulties and accuses them of keeping him from achieving his grandiose designs. Paranoid projection and other delusions, as well as hallucinations, are safeguards that protect him while freeing him from responsibility for the consensually validated tasks of life (K. Adler, 1958; 1979).

No one seriously doubts that this type of psychosis probably has a somatic as well as a psychological etiology. Shulman (1968, 1980) believes that a teleological factor, a mistaken life style conviction, must call forth the psychosis amid the biochemical, genetic, and environmental factors. Schizophrenia involves an element of choice.

> One becomes schizophrenic over a period of time in response to cumulative life stresses and feelings of failure. The "choice" is neither conscious nor planned ahead of time. It is a series of small steps in which one step makes it easier to take the next step so that in the end one somehow arrives at one's own hell without ever recalling the path by which one came. (Shulman, 1983, p. xv)

The schizophrenic passes through several phases during the course of his illness. Shulman describes four phases according to the psychotic symptoms that are evident to an observer. The first phase includes seclusiveness, lack of interest in normal events, deconcentration, and practicing autistic thinking. These symptoms facilitate the person's withdrawal from social integration. Symptoms of the second phase are inappropriate affect, loose associations, disgusting behavior, and even assaultiveness, which help to overcome a desire to return to the demands of social living. Symptoms in the third phase are hallucinations, delusions, impulsiveness, and other features of the "crazy game" which have the purpose of reinforcing the person's private logic and insuring the correctness of his position. Finally, as the acute phase of the illness has passed, one notes symptoms that permit reestablishment of conditional social relationships but still mark the individual as "different." These include "reserve" symptoms, obsessive compulsive, and hypochondriacal symptoms.

Depressive Disorders

Depression is a spectrum disorder ranging from symptoms of sadness, grief reactions, nonpsychotic depression or dysthymic disorders, and, finally, major or psychotic depression. The essential feature of the dysthymic disorder is a chronic disturbance of mood involving either depressed mood or loss of interest or pleasure in all or almost all usual daily activities, and associated symptoms. These symptoms must be present for at least two years, but are not sufficiently severe to qualify as a major depression. A major depression can be so profound that the individual loses contact with reality, develops delusions, and is frequently a serious suicide risk. A diurnal variation is common, with the most severe symptoms noted early in the day. The individual has early-morning awakening, disturbed appetite, somatic symptoms, and self-depracatory thoughts and guilt feelings. Whereas psychotherapy is the treatment of choice for the dysthymic disorders, medication and sometimes electroconvulsive therapy (ECT) are necessary adjuncts to psychotherapy for the major depressions. Here is an example of a major depressive disorder:

> Mrs. J. is a 41-year-old housewife who was evaluated at a community mental health center after complaining of nausea, spontaneous crying, and depressed mood. Her symptoms had begun four months earlier, following her discovery that her husband was having an affair with another woman. She noted disturbances of appetite and concentration, early-morning awakening, and somatic symptoms such as nausea, menstrual pain, and headaches, in addition to guilty feelings and dysphoric mood. No obvious psychomotor retardation was noted. She had no previous history of mood swings, but admitted that her mother had been taking antidepressant medication for the past ten years.

Much of the Adlerian theory of depression was directed toward depressive neurosis, although it has some bearing on the major depressions as well. Adler believed that depressed individuals inflate the hazards of everyday life as they strive for unreachable fictional goals, and then blame others or life circumstances for the failure to achieve those goals. The depressive displays both his anger at not getting his own way and his contempt for others. He has learned to exploit his weaknesses and complains in order to force others to give him his way and thus avoid life's responsibilities. He is willing to go to any cost to prove to others how sick and disabled he is, and in the process can escape social responsibilities. As a discouraged child, the depressive child may have used tears to tyrannize others, and was probably excessively dependent on others. He may have had difficulty in recovering from illnesses and other stresses and perhaps found it easier to extort sympathy and active help from others rather than to attempt to develop some self-sufficiency.

Kurt Adler (1961) points out the depressive's obvious disdain for others during the healthy interludes. During these times the depressive's excessive ambition takes over and he reveals his ruthlessness and unwillingness to exert efforts to achieve results. When he fails, the depressive regularly blames others, his upbringing, ill fortune, or even his very depression.

Suicide is often considered a feature of depression. In 1910, Adler proposed that suicide has a social intention. He considered adolescent suicide an act of revenge, "in which one's death is desired, partly to cause sorrow to one's relatives, partly to force them to appreciate what they have lost in the one whom they have always slighted . . . ." (Ansbacher, 1969). In later life, a beloved person, an institution, or even the world at large is chosen as the object of this revenge. Adler also believed that the potential suicide reflects low social interest and a pampered life style, and that the threat of suicide is a means of controlling others. Kurt Adler proposes that the suicidal person holds three myths about suicide: that it is a heroic act, that it will hurt others, and that it requires courage to go through with it (K. Adler, 1961).

Antisocial Personality Disorder

Previously called psychopathic or sociopathic disorders, the essential features of antisocial personality disorder are a history of continuous and chronic behavior which violate the rights of others. The onset of this disorder must begin before age fifteen, and antisocial behavior must persist into adult life. Poor occupational performance, shown by frequent job changes, absenteeism, or unemployment, a history of arrests, marital problems, impulsivity, hedonism, promiscuity, unreliability, and drug and alcohol abuse are common features. This is an example of an antisocial personality disorder:

> B.H., the 18-year-old son of well-to-do parents, was ordered to undergo psychiatric evaluation by the court. Some three weeks before the evalua-

tion, B.H. and two younger juveniles had trespassed into a cemetery after closing time and had tipped over several gravestones and attempted to break into an above-ground mausoleum. Damages were estimated at four thousand dollars. All three were found to have blood-alcohol levels that showed them to be legally intoxicated. B.H.'s parents noted problems in school as early as age nine. At age 12 he was arrested for shoplifting a small portable radio. From the age of 13 through 17 he was frequently involved in minor delinquencies but usually managed to escape punishment because of his family's position in the community, and because his father was willing and able to make restitution. B. H. was ten years older than his twin sisters, and he reported that he was never really close to anyone, including his parents. He felt no remorse for his antisocial behavior and indicated that though his parents verbally disapproved of this behavior, they encouraged it in subtle ways. At the age of 8 he began taking anticonvulsant medication after he experienced seizures following a bicycle accident. He refused to continue the medication after three weeks, even though he was told he remained at risk for repeat seizure activity.

Perhaps more than any other great pioneer in psychiatry, Adler not only had personal experience consulting with criminals but wrote extensively on the life style and treatment of the criminal. At the roots of criminality, as in the neurotic, Adler found a lack of social interest. But unlike the neurotic, the criminal does not content himself with receiving help and being a burden to others; rather, he acts as if the whole world were against him. Adler contended that as a child, the criminal develops a "cheap superiority complex" and is recognized because he can get his own way by hurting others. He distinguished three types of criminals: (1) those who had been pampered children, trained to receive and never give, who kept this pattern as adults; (2) those who were neglected as children and directly experienced the hostile world; and (3) a smaller group of so-called ugly children who rebelled because of their perceived defect. But whatever their original situation, all three types showed the same intense striving for superiority, even though they were essentially cowards. Adler found that the criminal never fought fairly; he committed offenses only when in a position of advantage. Because he often committed several crimes before he was arrested, the criminal's feeling of superiority was strengthened. He could cooperate, but only with his own kind, and Adler found him to be totally irresponsible, "always looking for reasons that 'force' him to be a criminal" (Adler, 1956).

Addictive Disorder: Alcohol, Drug and Sexual

A common understanding of the alcoholic or drug dependent individual is someone who has a pathological relationship with a mood-altering substance. For example, the alcoholic's or drug addict's relationship with the substance becomes more important than work, friends, and even family. As this relationship progresses, the addicted person needs the substance to feel normal. Ironically, feeling "normal" for the addict also means feeling isolated and lonely, since the primary relationship upon which he depends is with a substance rather than a person. There is growing awareness among professionals about common factors among the various addictive behaviors; thus, obesity, smoking, workaholism, and uncontrollable sexual behavior are coming to be considered addictions—the pathological relationship usually involves a substance, but can be a situation, such as excessive work or uncontrolled sexual behavior. In each case, the addict's relationship with his mood-altering "experience" becomes central to his life (Carnes, 1983). This case describes alcoholism or alcohol dependence with withdrawal in DSM-III terms:

> Mr. D. is a 42-year-old unmarried newspaper columnist who admits to a 20-year history of heavy alcohol use. After finishing his column one Thursday night, he started drinking with friends and continued to drink until the bar closed at 4 A.M. He returned to his apartment and slept for a few hours. Upon awakening he had no appetite for food, but proceeded to down several scotch-and-waters. Later he went to a lounge that newspeople frequent and drank wine until late that night. This pattern of all-day drinking persisted for four days. On Monday morning he went to his office and began to shake so violently while attempting to drink a cup of coffee that he spilled the hot liquid over his shirt and trousers. A few sips of brandy calmed his nerves enough to begin work on his column. When his editor asked about his whereabouts on Friday, Mr. D. could not recall and fabricated a story about being ill. Later that morning he left his office and went to see his family doctor because of "internal" tremulousness and marked tremors of the hands. When his physician questioned him about his drinking, D. reported that he had experienced about five other weekend binges over the past eight months, in which he had missed a total of ten days and for which he had used up all his sick days. He had been told by friends that he had a drinking problem but believed that he could "handle" his liquor and had refused to attend an AA meeting at the invitation of a friend. He also noted that his fiancée threatened to leave him if he didn't get some help for his drinking.

Adler observed that the beginning of an addiction is based on an acute feeling of inferiority marked by shyness, a desire for isolation, oversensitivity, irritability, and impatience, as well as by such neurotic symptoms as anxiety, depression, and sexual insufficiency. Sometimes, the craving for the mood-altering experience begins with a superiority complex in the form of boastfulness or a longing for power. He further noted that

"In all cases of addiction we are dealing with people who are seeking alleviation in a certain situation" (Adler, 1956, p. 423).

Lombardi (1973) studied the life styles of drug addicts in comparison with matched control subjects. Themes in their early recollections revealed that the addicts saw themselves as leaning-dependent persons who lacked direction in life. They had undeveloped social interest and saw the world as hostile and dangerous. Thus, the addict would not attempt to compete or excel, but responded to life with childishness, impulsivity, isolation, over-sensitivity, irritability, and impatience, and neurotic symptoms such as anxiety, depression, and sexual difficulties. The addict could only feel competent when he was "high" on drugs, which gave him a feeling of omnipotence. This individual's early life training showed signs of either overprotection or neglect and rejection. He was not prepared by role models or by his own experiences to live life as a socially responsible adult. The addicts willingly admitted to socially undesirable traits in themselves and to difficulties in forming warm and lasting interpersonal relationships.

Although he focuses primarily on sexual addictions, Carnes (1983) believes core beliefs of the sexual addict are the bases for all addictive behaviors. The faulty core beliefs are:

> *Self view* "I am basically a bad, unworthy person, and no one would love me as I am."
>
> *World view* "My needs are never going to be met if I have to depend on others."
>
> *Fictional goal* "The addictive, mood-altering experience is the most important thing in my life."

The addict does not trust people and uses strategies and safeguards such as rage, secretiveness, and manipulativeness to achieve his goal.

Borderline Personality Disorder

The borderline personality disorder is characterized by a complex presentation including diverse combinations of anger, anxiety, intense and labile affect, brief disturbances in consciousness including dissociation and depersonalization, identity confusion, volatile interpersonal relations, and impulsive behavior including self-injury. Stress can precipitate transient psychosis. This case is an example of a borderline personality disorder:

> G. W. is a 24-year-old unemployed male who was referred to the hospital emergency room by his therapist at a community mental health center after two days of sustained suicidal ideation. Mr. W. had cut his wrists on

previous occasions and had been hospitalized twice because of this suicidal gesture. He appeared to function adequately until his senior year in high school, when he became preoccupied with transcendental meditation. He had considerable difficulty concentrating during his first semester of college and seemed to focus most of his energies on finding a spiritual guru. At times massive anxiety and a feeling of emptiness swept over him, which he found would suddenly vanish if he lightly cut his wrist enough to draw blood. He had been in treatment with his current therapist for 18 months and became increasingly hostile and demanding as a patient, whereas earlier he had been quite captivated with his therapist's empathy and intuitive sense. Lately, G. W.'s life seemed to center on his twice-weekly therapy sessions. The most recent suicidal thoughts followed the therapist's disclosure that he was moving to another clinic on the West Coast.

From an Adlerian perspective, the borderline personality would originate in a family situation where the child felt unfavored and incompetent to face the demands of life. Feelings of self-pity, helplessness, and disadvantage lead the borderline to claim special privilege in coping with the world. The borderline's cognitive style is inflexible, characterized by rigid abstractions that easily lead to grandiose, idealized perceptions of people not as real people but as personifications of all good or all bad individuals. The borderline reasons by analogy from past experience and does not easily learn from new relationships. Because of his external locus of control, he usually blames others when things go wrong. If he blamed his own incompetence, he would feel even more powerless to change the situation. Accordingly, his emotions fluctuate between hope and despair because of external circumstances beyond his control. Not surprisingly, his interpersonal relationships are stormy and characterized by dependency, rebellion, and manipulativeness, because he has never learned to respond to constancy in a relationship. His self-esteem is very fragile since it fluctuates constantly with emotions. For him there is no commitment, no feeling of belonging, and little sense of obligation (Shulman, 1982).

REFERENCES

Adler, A. (1956). *The Individual Psychology of Alfred Adler.* In H.H. Ansbacher and R.R. Ansbacher (Eds.). New York: Harper & Row.

Adler, A. (1964a). *Superiority and social interest.* In H.H. Ansbacher and R.R. Ansbacher (Eds.). Evanston, IL: Northwestern University Press.

Adler, A. (1964b). *Problems of Neurosis.* In P. Mairet (Ed.). New York: Harper and Row.

Adler, K. (1958). Life style in schizophrenia. *Journal of Individual Psychology, 14* (1), 68–72.

Adler, K. (1961). Depression in the light of Individual Psychology. *Journal of Individual Psychology, 17* (1), 56–67.

Adler, K. (1979). An Adlerian view of the development and treatment of schizophrenia. *Journal of Individual Psychology, 35* (23), 147–161.

Ansbacher, H. (1969). Suicide as communication: Adler's concept and current applications. *Journal of Individual Psychology, 25,* 174–180.

Carnes, P. (1983). *The sexual addiction.* Minneapolis: CompCare Publications.

Diagnostic and Statistical Manual of Mental Disorders (3rd ed.). (1980). Washington, DC: American Psychiatric Association Press.

Dreikurs, R. (1950). *Fundamentals of Adlerian psychology.* New York: Greenburg Publishers.

Dreikurs, R. (1967). Psychodynamic diagnosis in psychiatry. In *Psychodynamics, psychotherapy, and counseling: Collected papers of Rudolf Dreikurs.* Chicago: Alfred Adler Institute.

Mosak, H. (1959). The getting type: A parsimonious social interpretation of the oral character. *Journal of Individual Psychology, 15* (2), 193–198.

Mosak, H. (1968). The interrelatedness of the neuroses through central themes. *Journal of Individual Psychology, 24* (1), 67–70.

Mosak, H. (1971). Lifestyle. In A. Nikelly (Ed.), *Techniques for behavior changes: Applications of Adlerian theory.* Springfield, IL: Charles C. Thomas.

Mosak, H. (1973). The controller: A social interpretation of the anal character. In H.H. Mosak (Ed.), *Alfred Adler: His influence on psychology today.* Park Ridge, NJ: Noyes Press.

Mosak, H. (1979). Mosak's typology: An update. *Journal of Individual Psychology, 35* (2), 92–95.

Mosak, H. (1984). Adlerian psychology. In R. Corsini and B. Ozaki (Eds.), *Encyclopedia of Psychology.* New York: Wiley–Interscience.

Mosak, H. (1985, May). Mosak's typology: Behaviors, psychopathology, and psychotherapy. Paper presented at *North American Society of Adlerian Psychology,* Atlanta, GA.

Lombardi, D. (1973). The psychology of addiction. In H.H. Mosak (Ed.), *Alfred Adler: His influence on psychology today.* Park Ridge, NJ: Noyes Press.

Neufield, I. (1954). Holistic medicine versus psychosomatic medicine. *American Journal of Individual Psychology, 10,* (3,4), 140–168.

Pancner, R. (1985, July). Biochemical theory and Adlerian psychotherapy. Audiotape, *International Association of Individual Psychology,* Montreal.

Pancner, R. (1985). Impact of current depression research on Adlerian theory and practice. *Individual Psychology: The Adlerian Journal of Individual Psychology, 41* (3), 289–301.

Peven, D. & Shulman, B. (1983). The psychodynamics of bipolar affective disorders: Some empirical findings and their implication for cognitive therapy. *Journal of Individual Psychology, 39* (1), 2–16.

Shulman, B. (1968). *Essays in schizophrenia.* Baltimore: Williams and Wilkins.

Shulman, B. (1980). *Essays in schizophrenia* (2nd ed.). Chicago: Alfred Adler Institute.

Shulman, B. (1982). An Adlerian interpretation of the borderline personality. *Modern Psychoanalysis, 7* (2), 137–153.

5 Counseling Theory

T he theory of Individual Psychology is socioteleological; it understands people as social, creative, active, decision-making beings moving toward unique goals and influenced by unique beliefs and perceptions.

Adler admonished "trust only movement." What a person does is what he truly means. This statement gives considerable direction to the counseling process. Let us first clarify, however, that our discussion focuses on counseling and therapy. There are differences between the two situations as well as similarities. Counseling is concerned chiefly with enabling someone to modify self-defeating behaviors, make effective decisions, and solve problems efficiently. Psychotherapy is more concerned with influencing the life style; changing faulty, mistaken, and self-defeating perceptions; and actually influencing the individual's beliefs and goals. Nonetheless, the same "model of man" and techniques apply to both counseling and therapy.

PRINCIPLES OF ADLERIAN COUNSELING

Socioteleological Orientation

Seeing the purposive nature of all behavior

Adlerian psychology is unique in its focus on purpose. This teleological orientation, in contrast to a historical-causal approach, has real significance for the transactions between counselor and counselee. The emphasis is not only on removal of symptoms and changing behavioral patterns, but on the counselees' understanding that they are not powerless victims of circumstances and that they act of their own accord (Dreikurs, 1953).

All of the counselee's discouragements are understood in terms of their purpose. Lack of success on the job or at school and failure to get along with people are seen not as static problems but as valuable indicators of the pattern of psychological movement. What happens as a result of this ineptness? By displaying ineptness, children may get their parents to do their homework or house chores for them. By revealing that they cannot handle certain situations themselves, adults may get someone else to handle the situations on their behalf. In the same way, the inability to face any other challenges of living may enable a person to be treated as special, may afford him control over a relationship, or may make it possible for him to exert power in some other area. The counselor's goal is to help clients see these motives and, consequently, accept the notion that all of their behavior makes sense in terms of their premises about life and that they act in a certain way because it serves some purpose for them.

For example, if a counselee complains that he is unable to find satisfaction in his relationships with women, the counselor tries to understand the purpose of this behavior—that is, how ineffectiveness with women pays off. Perhaps that ineffectiveness enables the client to feel excused from functioning in that arena and to put all his efforts into his work—an area of life in which he feels secure. Or, maybe, the man's ineptness worries his friends, and they double their efforts to "find him the right girl." Actually, he may have a large number of people concerned and involved in establishing contacts for him. Once the counselor sees the payoff of the client's behavior—the often unconscious motives of the behavior—she can help the client become aware of these motives and how they affect his life style.

Stimulating social interest

As you may recall, Adlerian psychology sees people as social beings who cooperate with others to realize their goals and function fully. Thus, Adlerians believe that mental health can be measured in terms of one's social interest, the willingness to participate in the give and take of life and to cooperate with others and be concerned about their welfare. A typical Adlerian suggestion for people who are discouraged is to become involved in helping others and to look outward instead of inward. Social interest and concern for others are contrasted with self-interest and concern only for one's own good.

People Are Creative, Decision-Making Beings

The view that people don't merely react to the stimuli around them implies that they have an active influence on the course of their lives. A simple counseling lead that helps counselees see this and assume responsibility for the events in their lives is the question "How do *you* keep *yourself* from _____ or from being involved with _____?" If a client says "I can't cooperate more with my (husband, teacher, boss)," the counselor asks her to rephrase the statements as "I will not cooperate . . . ," thereby taking full responsibility for the relationship. The counselor makes it clear that the counselee can always decide to change, but that, for some reason, it apparently suits her purpose not to change. The counselee then examines her payoff, which, as we said, may involve being treated as special, getting service, being in control of a relationship, getting even, or whatever else is rewarding.

THE GOALS OF ADLERIAN COUNSELING

Adlerian counseling has four main objectives, which correspond to four stages in the counseling process:

Establishing an empathic relationship between counselor and counselee, in which the counselee feels understood and accepted by the counselor.

Helping the counselee understand the beliefs and feelings, as well as the motives and goals, that determine his life style.

Helping the counselee develop insight into his mistaken goals and self-defeating behaviors.

Helping the counselee consider available alternatives to the problem behavior or situation and make a commitment to change.

Establishing an Empathic Relationship

The relationship Adlerian counselors seek to establish is one between equals, a collaborative effort in which counselor and counselee are active partners working toward mutually agreed-upon goals.

The counselor is responsible for providing the necessary conditions for an effective helping relationship and for utilizing skills that enable the counselee to initiate and sustain action. The counselee is not a passive recipient "being counseled" but an active party in a relationship between equals. This relationship is sometimes spelled out in a contract. The contract specifies the goals of the counseling process and the responsibilities that each equal partner in the process must undertake. This emphasis on equality and responsibility is counter to the popular notion that one goes to counseling to be "cured." In Adlerian counseling, clients recognize that they are responsible for their behavior.

The goals of the relationship are made explicit so both counselor and counselee can evaluate progress. Mutual goal alignment expresses respect for the client's capacity to direct her life and move in directions that are personally satisfying. It also ensures the counselor's willingness and commitment to help the counselee move in those directions.

Throughout the counseling process, the counselor helps the counselee become aware of, accept, and utilize her assets. Instead of engaging in continual analysis of deficits and liabilities, the counselor, recognizing the power of encouragement, offers sustained support. Only if counselees are aware of their strengths and personal power to change can they begin to change beliefs, feelings, goals, and behavior.

This positive approach that stresses assets rather than liabilities permits counselees to perceive in less threatening terms the barriers and obstacles they must face and overcome. A poor relationship at work or in the home, a mistake, or a failure is understood as an opportunity to learn and grow, not as a frightening display of inadequacy.

Confidentiality and privacy are essential elements for establishing and maintaining an effective counseling relationship. The relationship is more effective when the counselee is voluntarily engaged in the process. Individuals who are assigned to counselor custody or probation may agree to cooperate only to avoid more onerous consequences. Until the client chooses to cooperate, "counseling" will not progress.

Understanding Beliefs and Feelings, Motives and Goals

Adlerians see the life style as a personal construct, a structure built on beliefs, perceptions, and feelings about oneself and others. Therefore, to gain true understanding of the client's life style and communicate that understanding to the client, the counselor listens closely, trying to identify the person's beliefs, perceptions, and feelings. It is a special way of listening—an active attempt to understand all the verbal and nonverbal components of communication. The counselor also observes movement to identify beliefs and goals. A holistic synthesis takes place in Adlerian counseling: all material is understood in terms of how it fits the life style and how it can be used to increase understanding of one's dynamics so as to become more effective in life (Dreikurs, 1967).

The counselor is not interested in fragmentary analysis of elements; IQ, interest scores, and past history are only elements that must be understood in relation to the pattern. Instead, the counselor looks at the meaning of the total psychological movement. The focus is on the counselee's purpose as revealed through the counseling communication, which affects the whole counseling process.

Each statement is understood in relation to the preceding and ensuing statements—that is, in terms of its relationship to the counselee's pattern. When a client says "I do my best, but others are often not satisfied; yet I keep trying to make them happy," the counselor deals not only with the feeling of discouragement and despair but with the belief about the importance and purpose of pleasing. Is the client attempting to be a victim, even a martyr, through pleasing? By "doing it only for you," perhaps the goal is to make others feel indebted. Again, it is appropriate to ask "Is it that you can't or that you won't please?"

Once the counselor, by actively listening and applying the principles of holistic synthesis, has reached a thorough understanding of the client's life style, she is in a position to help the client reach the same understanding by seeing how his basic beliefs and perceptions influence his life style. The very act of communicating to the counselee that his life style makes sense and showing him explicitly how this is so has a therapeutic effect and a profound influence on the counseling relationship. Instead of a rapport of simple empathy, the relationship becomes a rapport of understanding and acceptance. True understanding of someone's life style is the highest form of empathy. When clients feel understood and accepted, they can confront their problematic behaviors and faulty premises and attempt to change them.

What beliefs are revealed in the counseling process? Here are a few: "Life is unfair," "People are no good," "I must be right," "I must please," "I'm something only if I'm first," and "Winning is everything." Even such a short list of beliefs clearly reveals people's different approaches to the challenges of living.

> *Michele:* I do everything I can to please the boss, but he's never satisfied. I can't figure him out.
>
> *Counselor:* Perhaps what you're feeling is that, if you can't please, there's no sense in trying.

Beliefs result in feelings. By empathizing with the counselee—listening closely and reflecting back feelings of anger, compassion, joy, discouragement, and excitement—the counselor helps the counselee identify feelings, the beliefs behind them, and the purpose the feelings are supposed to achieve.

> *Michele:* I do everything I can to please the boss, but he's never satisfied. I can't figure him out.
>
> *Counselor:* You're confused.

This response by the counselor leads the conversation into a discussion of feelings and enables counselor and counselee to explore the feelings more intensively. But until Michele becomes aware that her basic belief is "I must please or I won't be successful," just exploring the feelings will not enable her to become aware that her belief is influencing her feelings. Remember: it is the Adlerian position that beliefs influence feelings; your belief about being shy creates your panicky feelings and not the other way around.

Hence, while the Adlerian counselor explores feelings to understand motives, develop empathy, and improve the relationship, he always goes beyond the feelings to discuss the beliefs behind them. It is through confronting the faulty belief and seeing it as faulty that the counselee becomes aware that she is not at the mercy of her feelings but in control of them and able to change them.

> *Michele:* I do everything I can to please the boss, but he's never satisfied. I can't figure him out.
>
> *Counselor:* Is it possible that you believe that, if you can't please, there is no point in trying? Your boss's failure to recognize your efforts justifies your becoming less cooperative or even quitting.

The counselor would make this type of response only after having clearly heard the client's feelings and getting in touch with her beliefs. It is a response designed to go beyond empathy and understanding and to stimulate action. Note that the communication is tentative—"Is it possible . . . ?"—so Michele can decide for herself. At the same time, the counselor's response moves the transaction toward a consideration of purpose. It is our position that, until the counselee is in touch with her goals and intentions, she is not going to be motivated to make significant moves toward change. Awareness of purpose is accompanied by the awareness that one has chosen her purpose and has the power to change it.

This example illustrates the need for the counselor to go beyond empathy and deal with the purpose of the client's feelings, instead of merely reflecting them:

> Jim, a first-year teacher, is explaining how things go for him with his students. He says "I spend hours preparing for class. I attend special workshops and even use my personal funds to purchase materials. Despite my best efforts, the students don't appreciate my concern. They are disorderly in class, don't get involved with the material of the class, and seldom do the assignments. I give up. Why try? It's useless!"

It is apparent that Jim is deeply discouraged about his progress as a teacher. The purpose of his complaints is to give himself the justification to stop working so hard. He believes that, if he shares his despair, the counselor will be sympathetic and excuse him from the responsibility of constructively facing his students' challenge. If the counselor focuses *only* on understanding and empathizing with feelings, without trying to get at the purpose of these feelings, the dialogue between Jim and the counselor might go like this:

> *Jim:* Wow! I've tried everything with these students, but nothing works.

Counselor:	It seems pretty hopeless.
Jim:	Nobody could do anything with students like these.
Counselor:	Sounds like there's no way you can be successful. You're feeling discouraged.
Jim:	That's not all. At home. . . .

The example illustrates that mere empathy tends to stimulate more feelings of inadequacy in the counselee. A more appropriate approach is to hear and share the feelings first and then move beyond the feelings into cognition, beliefs, attitudes, and purposes, so that Jim can become more aware and motivated to change:

Jim:	Wow! I've tried everything with these students, but nothing works.
Counselor:	I get the idea that you have the belief "I can't be successful."
Jim:	I sure don't feel successful.
Counselor:	I have a hunch that the students sense that and deal with you on the basis of your belief.
Jim:	Well, I'm discouraged; nothing works!
Counselor:	Could it be that your belief that the students are impossible justifies your lack of success? By openly declaring your inadequacy, you become the victim.
Jim:	Perhaps. But what can I do?

By acquainting Jim with his beliefs and the purpose of his feelings, the counselor makes it possible for Jim to consider other alternatives.

Developing Insight into Mistaken Goals and Self-Defeating Behaviors

Perception is primary in organizing motives and the ensuing movement. We act on the basis of how we see things.

> Individual psychology holds that behavior is always a movement toward something; that behavioral movement always has a direction which is toward a goal. The goals are motivators; they act as a final cause for behavior; they are the end point of intentions. The goals themselves are often unconscious or at best dimly envisaged. (Shulman, 1985)

Most people come to counseling aware that they are doing something wrong, that they are not effective in their approach to the tasks of life. The primary function of the counselor is to help individuals recognize their mistaken ideas and understand why they act the way they do. In other words, the goal is to have clients understand the purpose of their behavior and how that behavior helps them achieve their goals, which are often unconscious.

While the counselor is empathic and accepting, he or she is also confronting. Insight about hidden purposes and goals occurs through confrontation and encouragement, as well as through interpretation and other techniques designed to facilitate self-awareness and awareness of how we interact with others. (These techniques will be discussed in detail in later chapters.) This insight into what keeps one from functioning more effectively helps clients resolve apparent contradictions and makes it possible for them to see that they must give up their mistaken goals to achieve functional behavior.

Seeing Alternatives and Making New Choices

In the final stage of the counseling process, we move toward reorientation. This is the action-oriented phase of counseling—putting insight into action—in which a variety of active techniques are used to promote movement. The beliefs are understood, the goals and purposes perceived, and the feelings accepted, clarified, and explained in the light of the accompanying beliefs and goals. Now attention is directed toward seeing alternatives and making new choices.

> Michele: I do everything I can to please the boss, but he's never satisfied. I can't figure him out.
>
> Counselor: You're discouraged and believe that, unless you please, you're a failure. This is an idea *you* have decided to accept for yourself. You could believe, instead, "I will do my best, and, if he's not pleased, that's his problem." What do you think about that?

The counselor hears the feelings, clarifies the belief and purpose, but does not reinforce it. This is often the point at which the neophyte counselor gets bogged down—for example, by echoing the counselee's ideas. The experienced counselor instead offers alternative ideas or beliefs for consideration.

Certain elements contribute to the success of the reorientation phase. Encouragement is the prime factor in stimulating change in the counselee. Encouragement generates the self-confidence and self-esteem that enable a person to act upon his concerns. As we have indicated, discouragement is one of the basic factors in failure to function. Encouragement increases confidence and courage and thus promotes change. When courage is stimulated, there is a tendency to move in more positive directions and to be open to encouragement and support from others. In turn, when counselees learn to encourage others, they experience encouragement themselves. This becomes a reinforcing cycle in which behaving courageously stimulates greater self-confidence.

Another element that promotes consideration of viable alternatives and commitment to change is the explicitness of the purposes of the counseling process. Clearly stating specific goals and purposes fosters the counselee's involvement and commitment to change.

A study of what produces change in the client revealed that insight is the factor most frequently mentioned as instrumental to therapeutic change and that change occurs through interpretation of goals and purposes (Kal, 1972). However, the clinicians surveyed in the study also stressed the importance of action outside therapy; that is, putting insights into practice by experimenting with alternative ways of behaving. Thus, insight should be considered a powerful adjunct to behavioral change but not a prerequisite, since people can make abrupt and profound behavioral changes without developing much insight.

GETTING STARTED

It is important that the counselee understand the nature of the counseling relationship from the beginning. Most individuals who come to a counselor have had no previous exposure to this type of relationship. Because of lack of experience and inaccurate impressions derived from popular magazines, movies, and television, the counselee is likely to have a number of faulty expectations about what will happen. She may anticipate that the counselor will simply listen, or perhaps supply answers to questions. She may even hope the counselor has the magical power to solve problems quickly and single-handedly.

It is therefore essential that, at the very first session, the counselor spell out his role as a helper who works with the client to gain greater insight into the client's behavior to help her move toward the change she desires. The counselor must also clarify that he can help the client consider alternatives, but that the decisions are up to the individual.

The relationship is collaborative, with no superiors or inferiors. No movement can occur until the goals for counseling are spelled out and mutually agreed upon. It is our belief that from the first session clients should begin to formulate a plan or contract concerning what they want, how they plan to get there, what is keeping them from successful pursuit of their goals, how they can modify their nonproductive behavior, and how they can use their assets and strengths to achieve their purposes.

Beth:	I understand that you can help people like me.
Counselor:	Tell me something about yourself and why you are here.
Beth:	I've been told I have good ability, but I get poor grades in school. I can't seem to get interested. My reading is weak. Do you tutor in reading?
Counselor:	I'm not a reading tutor, but I can help you find one. You seem to feel you're not living up to your expectations.
Beth:	It's not just *my* expectations. My parents are very disappointed. I'm afraid I may be flunking.
Counselor:	There is pressure from home also.
Beth:	Yeah. Dad is really mad. He says I'll never grow up and be responsible. I'm so confused I don't know what to do.
Counselor:	There's a lot of pressure from home, and you also sound discouraged about yourself. What would you like to get from our counseling sessions?
Beth:	I'd like to understand why I'm not motivated, and I'd like to learn how to get my parents off my back.
Counselor:	What should we talk about first?
Beth:	Why I'm not motivated.
Counselor:	Our purpose, then, will be to understand your motives as they relate to school and to determine what keeps you from succeeding.

During the initial stage, the counselor listens closely and moves consistently toward helping the counselee establish why she is there and what she hopes to accomplish. The interview is not open-ended, but focuses on clarifying what is being sought. Beth may later change her goals, but focus and purpose for the original contract have been established.

It is essential that counselees understand what the counselor offers and how they are expected to participate in the relationship. This necessitates that the counselor have a clear conceptualization of the process and be able to articulate it to the person seeking help. It may also be helpful to invite a new counselee to ask questions about the counselor—education, credentials, and how the counseling will be conducted.

THE EFFECTIVE HELPING RELATIONSHIP

Motives and Expectations

As mentioned, people often have faulty expectations about counseling. Since some of the counselor's expertise is in the area of motivation, she is well equipped to discern an individual's motives for seeking help. Mosak and Gushurst (1971) clarify some ways to determine the purpose and meaning of a client's statements about his motives. For example, a person may say "I'm confused and immobilized. I feel as if I'm pulled in two directions, and I can't decide." As soon as the counselor attempts to help the person attack the dilemma, the counselee responds with "Yes, but . . . ," indicating that the counselor has a good point but must certainly weigh the considerations on the other side of the issue. If a person goes through life with a "yes, but" approach, although he will surely save face, he will not go far. Neurosis is face saving, and the stance of the neurotic is a "yes, but" stance. As Mosak and Gushurst (1971) observe:

> His statement, in other words, contains the hidden intention "I'm not going to go anywhere" and the "conflict" is his method of immobilizing himself. The reasons for such immobilization vary from patient to patient, but they tend to fall into one or the other of two major categories: protection from a loss or retention of a gain. (p. 428)

By not taking a stand or choosing a direction, a person doesn't run the risk of losing something and can reap the subtle benefits while protecting his good intentions. In other words, by being undecided, a person can maintain more than one position. For example, a student complains "If I quit my job and put full effort into my studies, I can't afford school; but if I keep my job, I don't have the time to do well in my studies." As a result, this student can continue to put less than full effort into academic work. The counselor helps the counselee see that he is describing only two extremes and that there are many other alternatives in between.

Another statement heard frequently is "I guess you'd say I'm a dependent person." As Mosak and Gushurst (1971) indicate:

> From an Adlerian perspective, however, dependency is a life movement in which the individual places others in his service. Convinced of his own inadequacy and consequent exemption from responsibility, the dependent person concentrates on evoking and maintaining the assistance of others whom he sees as stronger and therefore obligated to help him. Another way of declaring impotence is contained in the statement "I can't seem to let go of myself"—and here the patient is generally referring to his feelings and his inability to live spontaneously. In reality, the manner of stating the problem conceals the patient's investment in keeping himself "held in"— keeping himself safe, in control, free of blunders and exposure. This kind of statement is frequent among controllers* and perfectionists, people who want to keep their best profile forward. (p. 429)

---

*For a discussion of the life style of the "controller," see Mosak (1973).

It is important that counselees be aware from the start that the counselor understands their motives, even motives that may be hidden from their consciousness. When the counselor responds not only to the feeling or belief but also to the purpose, the counselee's awareness expands and the possibilities for change increase. Furthermore, recognition by the counselor that one's statement makes sense—the counselor accepts the person's private logic—is a way to establish instant rapport. The ensuing task for the counselor is to move the client from his faulty private logic to acceptance of the common logic.

Real and hidden meanings

As the counselee speaks, it is important that the counselor catch the meaning of his words and their purpose. Let's consider two ways of leading.

Christopher:	I can't seem to let go of myself.
Counselor:	It's very discouraging, and you feel defeated.
Christopher:	Yes. I'd like to relax like other people, but it doesn't seem right.
Counselor:	You're really tied up.

In this dialogue, the counselor focuses on feelings and alludes to beliefs. The following dialogue moves on to possible purpose:

Christopher:	I can't seem to let go of myself.
Counselor:	You're afraid to relax.
Christopher:	Yes. If I relaxed, I could make a mistake and look like a fool.
Counselor:	It is dangerous to make mistakes. Is it possible that you feel comfortable only if you are in control and can predict what will happen?

In this dialogue, the counselor is empathic, but quickly begins to talk about beliefs and the purpose of Christopher's movement. This more active role on the part of the counselor influences the client to become more actively involved in looking at his life and the choices he makes.

Often the stated problem is not the real problem. The concerns the client expresses in the first sessions may be a way of testing whether the counselor is really listening and how perceptive she is. If it appears that the counselor is naive or overly accepting, the counselee may not have the necessary confidence to share his true concerns. Involvement with real and hidden meanings at an early stage increases the counselee's faith in the counselor's ability and enhances the possibility of early entry into the change process.

Particularly with children and spouses, there may be indications on the counselees' part that they are there because someone referred them or "made me come here." In these instances, it is important to openly discuss how the counselee feels about being sent by someone else. There may be anger and feelings of inadequacy or unfairness, which should be discussed. It is also important to clarify the counseling relationship and to build a bridge toward goal alignment by helping the client choose what he would like to work on. For example, a parent may send a child to the counselor to help her become more motivated about school, whereas the child's major problem may be with a sibling or a peer. It is more productive to begin with the child's goals than to attempt to force her to discuss what she was sent to discuss. As the relationship unfolds and as the counselor proves an effective resource in dealing with the concern expressed by the child, she will be more willing to become involved in working at the problem for which she was referred.

If one goes to counseling to appease a spouse, the counselor helps the individual determine his concerns, which may be different from those of the spouse. The client is encouraged to discuss his feelings about being sent for counseling, and it is made clear that the counselor will work with the client's perceptions of the marital relationship and not attempt to make him over to the spouse's specifications.

Negative and unrealistic expectations

People come to counseling for a variety of reasons and with different expectations. Some who are pessimistic may believe "I can't change," "Nobody can help me," "Life is unfair," or "People are no good." They expect little to happen, and their negative expectations often become self-fulfilling prophecies; their discouraged outlook and faulty self-defeating beliefs about life actually interfere with their involvement in counseling. It is important to get a clear contract with those who have negative expectations, otherwise they may decide to stay in counseling just to prove that nothing can be accomplished. The purpose of negative expectations (to keep from moving) or the purpose of resisting counseling (to prove that nothing can happen) should be confronted. Only if counselees see how their mistaken perceptions influence their experiences can they possibly be helped to change.

Other clients may have ridiculously high expectations of the counseling process. They may also be very dependent and attempt to transfer responsibility for their progress to the counselor. They may believe "Life owes me everything," "Others must protect me," "I can do no wrong," "Others are at fault," or "My problems are simple. If you are competent, you should be able to help me in a short time." This last type of client, if he doesn't see rapid changes and many encouraging signs of progress, is quick to blame the lack of progress on the counselor or the situation.

In the first session, the counselor should clarify what she can offer— careful listening, empathy, understanding, clarification of counselee beliefs, and insight into counselee purposes and behavior to help stimulate action and change. Counselees are expected to be honest, open, congruent, involved, and committed to considering alternatives and making choices. The counselor can help, but for movement to occur, counselees must put their understanding to work and be committed to specific change.

As counselees recognize that counseling is work and that the counselor anticipates their full involvement and cooperation, they understand the process as a collaborative one, in which the counselee must not only talk, but decide and act as well.

Ingredients

Education and training of counselors and psychotherapists were once less systematic than they are today. It was believed that counseling skills could be developed just by reading the theories of established leaders in the field, almost by osmosis. Professionals had some supervision during training, but the training was not systematic, and specific programs focusing on skill development were not available.

The research of Rogers, Gendlin, Kiesler, and Truax (1967) and that of Truax and Carkhuff (1967) presented the first evidence that professional counseling and psychotherapy may be "for better or for worse." The evidence was based on research showing that the results of professional counseling are difficult to predict and that all counselors are not equally effective and therapeutic, even if they have had the same training.

These findings led to studies of the ingredients of effective helping. It became apparent that the counselor's ability to function in specific emotional and interpersonal dimensions has a significant influence on the counselor's "for better or worse" effectiveness.

The interpersonal dimensions determined to be essential ingredients of the helping relationship were identified by Rogers and his colleagues (1967) as empathy, unconditional regard, and congruence; and by Truax and Carkhuff (1967) as accurate empathy, nonpossessive warmth, and genuineness.

Carkhuff (1972) reported:

Perhaps the most important extension within helping has been to expand the helper dimensions from responsive to initiative dimensions. Thus, the original formulations emphasizing helper empathy, unconditional regard and congruence were complemented by the more action-oriented dimensions of helper concreteness (Truax & Carkhuff, 1967), confrontation and interpretations of immediacy. (Carkhuff, 1969 [p. 7])

The Helper's Perceptual Organization

It has become increasingly apparent that counselors need more than theory. They need a clear understanding of the dynamics of behavior change and the specific skills necessary to implement this change. But to be effective, counselors also need a perceptual organization (that is, a system of beliefs and perceptions) conducive to a helping relationship with their clients.

Combs and his colleagues at the University of Florida (Combs, Soper, Gooding, Benton, Dickman, & Usher, 1969) researched the perceptual organization of workers in the helping professions—for example, counselors and parole officers—and found a high degree of similarity of perceptual organization among effective workers in the numerous helping professions. More specifically, these researchers identified the beliefs that effective helpers share. Here are some of them.

Beliefs about what people are like

Effective helpers perceive others as having the capacity to deal with and find solutions to their problems. They don't doubt people's capacity to handle themselves and their lives. They see others as friendly and essentially well intentioned. They recognize and respect the worth and dignity of others.

Effective helpers see others as essentially developing and unfolding from within, not as the products of external events, easily molded and directed. They regard people's behavior as dependable, because they believe that behavior is predictable and understandable. They see others as potentially fulfilling and enhancing, rather than impeding or threatening, to the self.

Beliefs about what they themselves are like

Effective helpers feel fundamentally adequate. Thus, they can attend to the needs of others and identify with them. Effective helpers see themselves as essentially dependable and as having what it takes to cope with events. They see themselves as wanted and basically likable.

Beliefs about what their purpose is

Effective helpers perceive their purpose as one of freeing, rather than controlling, people—assisting, releasing, and facilitating, rather than controlling, manipulating, and coercing.

Effective helpers tend to be more concerned with large than with small issues. They are more likely to be self-revealing than self-concealing. They are more concerned with furthering processes than with achieving goals. Their purposes are altruistic rather than narcissistic.

Beliefs about the approach to the counseling task

The basic approach of the effective helper is a concern with people rather than with things—whether objects, events, rules, or regulations. Effective helpers are likely to approach others subjectively, or phenomenologically, since they are more concerned with people's perceptual experience than with objective facts.

Combs and his colleagues' contribution to the understanding of the counseling process cannot be stressed enough. Not only have they directed attention to the importance of the helper's perceptual organization; they have also provided the counseling field with valuable guidelines as to what beliefs make a helper effective. If a counselor's beliefs are not congruent with those described by Combs, the client is less likely to benefit from the counseling relationship.

It should be clear from examining the beliefs of effective counselors that the opposing beliefs can truly interfere with a successful counseling process. It is therefore important that all counselors in training be exposed to intensive experiences in interpersonal communication, which will help them get in touch with their own beliefs and with the ways these beliefs can help or hinder the counseling process. It is also important that experienced counselors continue to participate in group experiences to keep receiving feedback about their beliefs and their effect on their practice.

THE ADLERIAN COUNSELOR

Characteristics

The counselor's portrait that emerges from the studies we have discussed is remarkably similar to the portrait of the good Adlerian counselor.

Throughout this chapter, we have stressed the elements that constitute the essence of the Adlerian counselor's role. In light of the preceding discussion, some of these elements are worth mentioning again here.

Counselors frequently choose a theory of counseling that fits their personality as well as their values. We Adlerians are no exception; we, too, have models that influence the way we approach the counseling process. First of all, we are active participants; we collaborate with the counselee, and, at the same time, we recognize and accept responsibility for the process. We bring this active dimension to the counseling process through concern with the purpose of behavior and the unique laws of psychological movement. As we listen, we are more than merely empathic and reflective; we also attend to how the client's message reveals beliefs and goals and how we might intervene most productively to help the client see how his beliefs and goals influence his feelings and approach to life tasks.

Through chosen responses, we direct the discussion toward consideration of all these elements, since we are constantly aware that moving from empathic reflection to tentative confrontation accelerates the process. We do not wait for some magic moment in which the client, having processed all of this information, develops a sudden awareness of why she is functioning in a certain manner and how she might change. Our commitment is to active procedures, such as confrontation, interpretation, and disclosure. These procedures not only challenge the client's beliefs and goals, but influence her to translate insight into specific actions and behaviors that reflect the change that has occurred in her beliefs, self-concept, and goals.

It is increasingly apparent that our personalities are principal tools in the helping process (Combs et al., 1969). While it is important to have a theory of personality and to be acquainted with a variety of counseling techniques, this knowledge must be integrated into the personality of the helper. The counseling process necessitates creative and spontaneous response to the changing interpersonal demands of the helping relationship. Regardless of our theoretical orientation, we are behavior models for our counselees. They are influenced by our views, values, goals, and feelings, and we must keep this in mind all the time.

Here are some of the most important characteristics of the good Adlerian counselor.

Awareness of one's beliefs

The counselor must be able to answer clearly the questions "Who am I?" "What do I believe?" and, most important, "How do my beliefs affect my counseling?" Good counselors are aware that they too (not just the counselees) can have mistaken beliefs about counseling and the counselor's role. Thus, they explore their reasons for being in a helping profession and know the motives, goals, attitudes, and feelings that can create "blind spots."

Awareness of one's feelings

Counselors are trained to listen to others' feelings and to pick up nonverbal indicators of feelings. But they must also be aware of their own feelings, particularly as they affect the counseling process. Involvement with their counselees can inspire enthusiasm about progress or discouragement about setbacks or lack of movement. When this occurs, counselors need to ask themselves why they are so personally tied to the fluctuations in their counselees' lives.

If the counselee grows, that growth is a result not only of the counselor's good work but also of the counselee's understanding and initiative. In the same fashion, failure to make progress is often a result of the client's unwillingness to apply what she has learned. Although failure to progress may result from faulty diagnosis or the counselor's inability to help the individual move from insight to outsight, counselors should not assume that there is an automatic relationship between their behavior and progress. A skilled consultant can be most helpful to a counselor who is experiencing difficulties in a counseling relationship. The consultant can help clarify whether lack of progress is due to faulty diagnosis, ineffective communication by the counselor, or lack of motivation on the part of the counselee. But the essential point the counselor must keep in mind is that no progress can occur without the counselee's cooperation.

Awareness of the counselor's modeling role

Whether or not they intend to, counselors serve as models to their counselees. The counselee is sensitive to the counseling relationship and expects the counselor to be able to handle his own personal relationships effectively, so they don't interfere with his professional life. A counselor with a confused and stormy personal life is less believable as a professional resource. If a counselor's own children, marriage, or friendships are not satisfying, that counselor's ability to help others may be questionable. This does not suggest that counselors must be free of problems, but that they must be aware of the powerful impact their own life styles have on their counselees.

To effectively influence the counseling process, counselors must understand how their clients perceive them and what type of model they communicate. Our counselees often learn more from what we do and how we approach our own challenges in living than from what we say.

Schmidt and Strong (1970) studied the factors that distinguish "experts" from "inexperts" from the standpoint of counselees. Helpers perceived as expert treated counselees with friendly, attentive behavior. They spoke courageously and with confidence and were able to move quickly to the heart of the problem. Those perceived as "inexpert" were tense, fearful, rambling, and uncertain, and they communicated their disinterest.

High ethical standards

Counselors must be trustworthy and concerned about their counselees' welfare. They must not reveal confidential information. Although ultimate allegiance is to society, the counselor's primary responsibility is to the counselee. Whatever is discussed in the private session can be shared with others only with the counselee's consent and only when there is clear danger to the counselee or others. Counselors must be dependable and responsible; that is, they must have a strong commitment to a set of ethical behaviors. Counselors who work in school districts will need to clarify their ethics to students, teachers, and administrators.

Awareness of the conditions that are essential to the counselee's development

If counselors are to help counselees lead a more satisfying life and achieve the purpose for which they come to counseling, certain conditions are essential. Good Adlerian counselors are aware of the following conditions and willing to meet them.

Empathy   Seeing the world the way the counselee perceives it. This comes by accurately perceiving the individual's feelings and being able to communicate this perception to the counselee. It involves understanding the individual's private logic and beliefs as well as emotions.

Caring and concern   These are demonstrated by verbal and nonverbal attending and by showing deep and genuine concern about the welfare of the counselee.

Genuineness and openness   Both are greatly facilitated by the counselor's self-disclosure. Self-revelation can become the basis of a constructive relationship, since the counselor's words are congruent with his actions.

Positive regard and respect The counselor shows these attitudes for the counselee's individuality and worth as a person.

Understanding and clarification of the meaning and purpose of the individual's behavior Through the counselor's tentative hypotheses and disclosure, counselees develop insight into the motivations that direct their lives.

Action-oriented techniques The use of these techniques, such as confrontation and encouragement, enables the counselee to change.

REFERENCES

Carkhuff, R. R. (1969). *Helping and human relations: A primer for lay and professional helpers* (2 vols.). New York: Holt, Rinehart & Winston.

Carkhuff, R. R. (1972a, b). New directions in training for the helping professions. Part 1: The development of systematic human resource development models. *The Counseling Psychologist, 3*(3), 4–11. Part 2: Toward a technology for human and community resource development. *The Counseling Psychologist, 3*(3),12–30.

Combs, A. W., Soper, D. W., Gooding, C. T., Benton, J. A., Jr., Dickman, J. F., & Usher, R. H. (1969). *Florida studies in the helping professions* (University of Florida Monographs, Social Sciences No. 37). Gainesville: University of Florida Press.

Dreikurs, R. (1953). *Fundamentals of Adlerian psychology.* Chicago: Alfred Adler Institute.

Dreikurs, R. (1967). *Psychodynamics, psychotherapy, and counseling.* Chicago: Alfred Adler Institute.

Kal, E. (1972). Survey of contemporary Adlerian clinical practice. *Journal of Individual Psychology, 28*(2), 261–266.

Mosak, H.H. (1973). The controller: A social interpretation of the anal character. In H. Mosak (Ed.), *Alfred Adler: His influence on psychology today.* Park Ridge, NJ: Noyes Press.

Mosak, H. H., & Gushurst, R. S. (1971). What patients say and what they mean. *American Journal of Psychotherapy, 25*(3), 428–436.

Rogers, C., Gendlin, E. T., Kiesler, D. J., & Truax, C. B. (1967). *The therapeutic relationship and its impact.* Madison: University of Wisconsin Press.

Schmidt, L. D., & Strong, S. R. (1970). "Expert" and "inexpert" counselors. *Journal of Counseling Psychology, 17*, 115–118.

Shulman, B. (1985). Cognitive therapy and the individual psychology of Alfred Adler. In M. J. Mahoney and A. Freeman (Eds.)., *Cognition and psychotherapy.* New York: Plenum.

Truax, C. B., & Carkhuff, R. R. (1967). *Toward effective counseling and psychotherapy: Training and practice.* Chicago: Aldine.

6

Phases and Techniques of the Counseling Process

T he Adlerian counseling process consists of four phases: establishment of the relationship, analysis and assessment, insight, and reorientation. All leading theorists, from Freud through Rogers and Carkhuff, have stressed the importance of the counseling relationship, and its necessary conditions have been set forth in a variety of ways. This chapter elaborates the phases and techniques of the counseling process and amplifies the Adlerian view of the relationship between counselor and counselee.

THE RELATIONSHIP

Dreikurs (1967) states the nature of the relationship:

> The proper therapeutic relationship, as we understand it, does not require transference but a relationship of mutual trust and respect. This is more than mere establishment of contact and rapport. Therapeutic cooperation requires an alignment of goals. When the goals and interests of the patient and therapist clash, no satisfactory relationship can be established. Winning the patient's cooperation for the common task is a prerequisite for any therapy; maintaining it requires constant vigilance. What appears as "resistance" constitutes a discrepancy between the goals of the therapist and those of the patient. (p. 65)

Mutual Trust and Respect

Mutual trust and respect are essential elements of the Adlerian helping relationship—an equalitarian relationship in which there are no superiors and inferiors. By working in the context of a collaborative effort directed at creating psychological movement, counselees feel responsible for their own lives.

To facilitate change, Adlerian counselors use a variety of procedures. Although the techniques may be used in any facet of the interview, we will discuss them in the phase of the counseling process in which they are most likely to occur. To help you identify with the procedures, we will address you, the reader, as if you were the counselor.

Attending Behavior and Attentive Listening

The effective therapeutic relationship begins with your focusing on the concerns as presented by the counselee. That focus is facilitated if you initiate and maintain good eye contact with the client. This visual contact is not a fixed stare. Your posture is relaxed, but conveys interest and involvement through a slightly forward body position, indicating that contact is being maintained and that you are completely available. Your comments follow directly from what the person says and reinforce his free expression, without adding new data. This helps the counselee express himself spontaneously.

Establishing an effective counseling relationship requires you to be responsive to the client's communication and to clearly communicate your attentiveness. In most everyday situations, we rarely encounter people who really listen and who hear not just the words but the content, the feelings, and the intentions. Thus, coming in contact with someone who does listen is a powerful encouragement to keep talking.

> *Alan:* I feel bad about not being able to work up to my parents' expectations. I don't think I'll ever be able to meet their standards.
>
> *Counselor:* You feel it's pretty futile to try.
>
> *Alan:* I've tried, but no matter what I do, it's not enough. This feeling I have all the time that I'm not making it really makes me very angry. For example, . . .

You hear the message, follow the content and the feelings, and seek verification about what you believe you heard. Especially during the first few minutes, it is useful to just indicate what you have heard and observed. This encourages the counselee to spontaneously tell more about how he feels. It is important never to let anything pass that you have not fully understood.

Appropriate attending and listening behaviors are essential to developing mutual trust and respect in the counseling relationship. This atmosphere increases the potential for the counselor's underlying assumption about change and movement to be clearly understood and accepted by the counselee.

Counselees are made aware of the counselor's belief that they have the power to change. This belief is demonstrated by helping the individual see how "can't" often really means "won't." When a client says "I can't stop from supervising my son's homework," he may be asked to reword his statement so it is more accurate and say, instead, "I *won't* stop supervising my son's homework."

This simple technique often leads clients to recognize that they are choosing to behave in a way that keeps them in trouble. At some point, they may feel uncomfortable even when they say "I won't," because these words clearly imply that they are acting by choice. Thus, full responsibility is placed on counselees for their behavior. The counselor conveys this sense of responsibility in a respectful way that indicates the belief that, once the person is aware of the decisions he is making, he will decide for his own good.

Goal Alignment

Counseling is conversation with a purpose. Adlerians emphasize the alignment of the counselee's and the counselor's goals. The session does not consist merely of friendly conversation, acceptance, and support. It is a working session in which conversation has the purpose of developing awareness, generating insight, and stimulating movement. Cooperation and focus on a common therapeutic task are essential for change to occur. Thus, small talk is kept at a minimum, and attention is devoted to the beliefs and mistaken perceptions that interfere with one's progress in meeting the challenges of life.

An important aspect of the helping relationship is to establish a contract that clearly states why the counselee is seeking help and what she expects from counseling. Dreikurs's statement provides clear guidelines for recognizing when lack of movement or resistance arise from a discrepancy between the goals of the counselor and those of the counselee. For example, the counselor may have decided that it is important for Toni to recognize that her poor schoolwork is a symptom of a power struggle with her parents. The counselor sees Toni's behavior as an attempt to prove that no one can make her study and an indication that she enjoys the power of defeating her parents' efforts. Toni, on the other hand, seems more concerned with getting her parents off her back and with developing her own social skills. The counseling process can be effective only if it deals with what the counselee recognizes as important and wants to discuss and change. Eventually, by working with her concerns as she perceives them, Toni may also become motivated to develop a new approach to schoolwork.

In a counseling interview, you will occasionally become aware that the counselee is not working on the problem, is avoiding a topic, or is not following up on a comment you have made. It is your role to reestablish the focus by commenting on what is happening in the here-and-now conversation. Refocusing on the task enables counselees to better understand how they avoid certain issues. It also helps to reestablish the purpose of the contact and the implicit contract—to work on the concerns that keep the client from effectively meeting the challenges of life.

To align goals, you may ask "Is this the person you want to be? Can you think of a different way to act? What do you suspect will happen if you persist in this pattern?"

Claudia:	I'm very mad about the way Paul treats me, and I don't intend to stand for it.
Counselor:	You are angry and feel that you have to do something.
Claudia:	I get mad, but I get over it. Did you see that game on T.V. where the Bears lost? I was really upset.
Counselor:	I notice that, when we get to the point of discussing your anger and what to do, you usually talk about something else, as you are now. I'm wondering whether you have noticed that, too. How do you feel we can deal most effectively with this problem?

You refuse to be sidetracked and talk about how this ploy of the counselee hinders the process.

Reflection of Feelings and Empathic Understanding

There is considerable evidence that the effects of counseling are related to the counselor's level of functioning on emotional and interpersonal dimensions, such as empathic understanding (*The Counseling Psychologist,* 1972). For our purposes, empathy has been best defined by Carkhuff (1972): "Empathy involves experiencing another person's world as if you were he." Empathy is the communication of understanding. The counselor attempts to get into the counselee's world so that both counselor and counselee can understand the counselee's feelings, beliefs, and intentions.

Empathic understanding involves capturing the essence of someone's feelings and communicating the understanding to him. Carkhuff says we can be certain we have responded to a person's feelings when we have made a response that is interchangeable with the feelings expressed by the individual.

Empathy also involves concentrating on the total message. Therefore, it involves both the feelings expressed by the message and the feelings elicited in the counselor by the transaction that is taking place. Reflection of feelings helps counselees become aware of and express the feelings they are experiencing. Responding to cognitive content deals basically with the literal meaning of a person's communication; it is somewhat like listening to the words of a song without the music. Empathic understanding and reflection of feeling involve the whole message and permit both counselor and counselee to understand the feelings and motives that influence the counselee's behavior. The process is crucial to the counseling relationship because it not only increases the counselee's awareness and self-understanding but makes it possible for the counselor to develop a situation for facilitating change.

Robin: I'm tired of being controlled by the group and forced to compromise. I can't function this way.

Counselor: You are angry about the group's control and want to be free to make your own decisions.

Robin: I know I can be happier without them, because then I'll be able to decide for myself.

Productive Use of Silence

It is not always easy to appreciate the meaning and value of silence. Too often the counselor feels impelled to say something to break the silence. Unfortunately, in some instances she does so with a "closed question"—a question that requires only a yes or no on the part of the client—which only compounds the problem.

Silence can and should be used productively. Letting the counselee assume responsibility for the choice of topics is one way of doing so. By accepting silence without becoming anxious, the counselee begins to recognize his responsibility for initiating topics and sharing his concerns. After accepting the silence for a time, you might ask "What do you think is going on right now?" Another approach is to explore with the client the hidden reason for the silence—for example, "Could it be . . . ?"—and allude to a possible purpose. Is this a way for the counselee to control, get special service, retaliate, or perhaps show that nothing can be done about his situation?

Silence can indicate that the counselor and the client have not developed mutually acceptable goals. Goal alignment may not have been achieved, or there may be some false assumptions on the part of the client—for example, that it is the counselor's role to dispense advice and take full responsibility for the interview. In this situation, a reformulation of goals is necessary.

Counselee-initiated silence might mean that the individual is considering an idea, examining himself, attempting to fully understand a new insight or awareness, or evaluating new directions. These are all good reasons for silence, and you need not intervene.

However, silence may also mean avoidance. Observation may produce a clue as to the purpose of the silence. For example, if the counselee's eyes appear to be fixed upon something but not focused, it is highly probable that the person is engaged in a productive silence. If, instead, he is tense and nervous and avoids eye contact, it is possible that he is avoiding the topic. By being in touch with your own feelings during the silence, you may also be able to understand the client's purpose. Anger may indicate that the client has a desire to control; confusion, instead, may indicate that the client feels there is nothing you can do about the situation or him.

Silence can also be used to slow the pace of the interview and permit the counselee to absorb understanding of his feelings and purposes. Letting the client know that you are willing to wait without demanding that your needs be satisfied can be a very positive and reassuring way to communicate understanding and acceptance.

Nonverbal Communication

While most communication in counseling is verbal, its nonverbal components—facial expressions, body position, muscle tonus, voice tone, and breathing tempo—are also very important. Every time a person talks, all of the person talks. If you fail to comprehend this, you may miss the real message. For example, when the voice says one thing and the body says something else, a double-level message is being sent (Satir, 1972).

Nonverbal communication can be examined in terms of its global interpersonal effect. Does an individual appear to be forceful and vibrant or subdued and restricted? Does he come through as feeling inadequate, fearful, cautious, and uninvolved or does he seem to want only to intellectualize?

Satir (1972) characterizes four types of dysfunctional nonverbal responses as *placating, blaming, computing,* and *distracting.* "Placaters" agree so the other person doesn't get mad. "Blamers" are aggressive and disagree to create an impression of strength. "Computers" talk as if they had no feelings and establish their self-worth by using big words. "Distractors" behave as though problem and people were not there. Your goal is to help the person's feelings and nonverbal behavior match the verbal message—that is, help the body message and the word message be congruent.

You should also be aware of voice tone and eye contact. Posture, muscle tonus, facial expressions, and gestures all emit continuous nonverbal signals. Various possibilities to note include relaxed or stiff posture with hands clenched or relaxed. A client may sit in a posture that conveys defiance, distance, and self-control, or her facial expression may reveal anger, confusion, or recognition. The recognition reflex is that characteristic grin that communicates instantly that your client understands, regardless of what she says.

If you observe a pattern in the counselee's nonverbal communication, it is often productive to interpret the message in the form of a tentative hypothesis. You might say "It seems this is very difficult for you to talk about. . . . Could it be that the thought of it makes you angry? . . . Is it possible you feel no one could understand?" It is not necessary to inform the counselee of the source of your interpretation, unless your intent is to help the person become aware that he communicates as a whole person and you believe he is ready for such awareness. This may improve the relationship, create insight, and facilitate change.

Obviously, you must also be aware of your own nonverbal behavior and how such behavior encourages or discourages a line of exploration and conveys approval or disapproval.

Counseling means total involvement, and total involvement is often accompanied by tears. It is handy to keep a box of tissues within reach. When the counselee shows signs that he is about to cry, nonchalantly give him the tissues or actually say "It's okay to cry." If your client is fighting back tears, you can discuss what this means or inquire if he believes that crying is a sign of weakness.

Tentative Hypotheses and Encouragement

In Adlerian counseling, a great deal of effort is put into providing tentative hypotheses about the purpose of the counselee's behavior—hypotheses that are offered and discussed even in the early stages of counseling. It is important that the counselor help the client understand the purpose of his behavior. The counselor's recognition that one's behavior makes sense from one's own point of view demonstrates that the counselor's empathy goes beyond simple understanding of the feelings expressed and extends to recognition of the meaning behind the behavior. For example:

> *Tina:* I've been trying to listen to my husband's opinions; but I find they don't make sense, so I follow my own ideas.
>
> *Counselor:* You're disappointed you can't count on him.

Here the counselor only empathizes with the counselee, and this could lead to a lengthy exploration of feelings. An alternative course would be to formulate a tentative hypothesis about the relationship between husband and wife.

> *Tina:* I've been trying to listen to my husband's opinions; but I find they don't make sense, so I follow my own ideas.
>
> *Counselor:* Is it possible that you have to be in control? You seem to believe that you must be right, and this justifies negating your husband's views.

Here the counselor focuses on beliefs and meanings and conveys the message that the behavior makes sense from Tina's point of view. At the same time, by dealing with the movement instead of simply identifying the feelings, the counselor makes it more likely that the goals and beliefs influencing the feelings and the behavior will be modified.

The counseling relationship is actually enhanced by discussing tentative hypotheses. By sharing a view about the hidden motives and goals of behavior and dealing with them through interpretation, the Adlerian counselor conveys a form of empathy that makes the relationship more effective.

Encouragement is also part of the relationship from the very beginning. The whole process of attending closely to verbal and nonverbal messages, focusing on the counselee's concerns, and being sensitive to both verbalized and implied feelings is encouraging because the person feels valued. For some people, it may be the first caring and close human relationship they have ever experienced.

Disturbances That May Interfere with the Relationship

Certain psychological disturbances may interfere with the counselee's cooperation. For some, the counseling relationship is an implicit threat to self-esteem and to the habitual mode of dealing with people and meeting the challenges of living (Shulman, 1973). In his article, Shulman identifies some of the disturbances that interfere with the counseling relationship.

Fear of being defective

Coming for counseling is an admission of weakness, since one should be able to handle one's problems alone.

> Abe, a self-made man who has fought his way to the top in his profession, has nothing against his wife's and adolescent daughter's going for counseling. However, he feels very strongly that, if he should have some problems of his own, he should be able to work them out by himself.

Fear of being exposed

Sharing one's thoughts and feelings will destroy the image one wants to project.

> Betty, a 38-year-old single woman, is very interested in sex and greatly enjoys it. A successful teacher, she has learned to project the image of a well-organized, self-controlled person who is not flustered by anything. She fears that even talking of her true feelings about sex will make her attitude apparent to perceptive people around her and that it will make it even more difficult for her to control her sexual impulses.

Fear of disapproval

Revealing oneself will produce disapproval even on the part of the counselor.

> Carla, like so many women, has been trained to believe that she can belong only when she is pleasing, particularly to men. Therefore, she finds it very dangerous to reveal the anger, even rage, that underlies her incapacitating depressions.

Counselees may also use certain defenses to save their self-esteem or to defeat the counselor. Shulman (1964) categorizes those defenses:

1. *Externalization* ("The fault lies outside of me"). Externalization is employed to preserve self-esteem and shun responsibility for one's own behavior. By externalizing, the person blames others and considers himself the victim of circumstances. The varieties of externalization include:

   Cynicism ("Life is at fault"). These individuals escape responsibility for their own behavior by blaming those in charge, the "system," and so forth. They see people as getters, concerned only with meeting their own needs.

   > Dean, 30, has won and lost a fortune. He is understandably distressed but blames others for what happened. He concentrates on their behavior rather than on his own and overlooks his own greed and poor judgment, which led him to financial disaster.

   Inadequacy ("I'm just an innocent victim"). The person demonstrates incapacity and inability to function.

   > At age 32, Lynn has a long history of running away from responsibility. She never completes a program or task she sets for herself and spends months at a time incapacitated. A victim of incest as a child, she still detects injustice everywhere she turns, and, whenever demands become too pressing, she "takes a vacation."

   Rebellion ("I can't afford to submit to life"). These individuals challenge all the ordinary rules of life. They battle with life not just to win but to defeat the commonly accepted rules of society.

   > Hugh, a 25-year-old man, has pushed his crusade against the current "rules of life" and his attempt to create his own rules so far that he is hardly able to eat a meal for fear that the food has some noxious additive

or lacks the appropriate nutrients. He is a very sad Don Quixote who sees windmills wherever he turns.

Projection ("It's all their fault"). The person suspiciously blames others and shuns all responsibility for what has happened.

In a large business corporation, several of the department managers are doing poorly. The president blames them for the company's slow progress, instead of recognizing his share of responsibility for not supplying them with the information and resources they need to do a good job.

2. *Blind spots* (If I don't look at it, it will go away"). By refusing to face a problem, the person pretends the problem is not there.

Despite the fact that three of her five children have had serious psychiatric disturbance, Mary consistently avoids counseling for herself, vigorously insisting that hers is a completely normal, healthy family.

3. *Excessive self-control* ("I won't let anything upset me"). Self-control is so powerful that all emotions, pleasant or unpleasant, are strongly suppressed and the person is protected from both joy and sorrow.

Although John's 16-year-old daughter is failing in school, has no friends, and is obese, John is always smiling when he tells others that everything he tries as a father fails.

4. *Arbitrary rightness* ("My mind is made up; don't confuse me with the facts"). The person makes arbitrary decisions and allows no doubts.

Claire is a highly successful attorney. Her steel-trap mind is an advantage in her profession, but her arbitrary rightness is intolerable to her husband and children.

5. *Elusiveness and confusion* ("Don't pin me down"). These individuals attempt to conceal themselves from others by lying, pretending ignorance, or changing the subject.

Kay is a scatterbrain. She is always confused, and this gives her a convenient excuse to avoid responsibility or decision making.

6. *Contrition and self-disparagement* ("I'm always wrong"). These individuals express feelings of guilt that permit them to continue the behavior while affirming good purposes that they have no intention of carrying out.

Fred is an intelligent, verbal adolescent who tyrannizes the household with temper tantrums and then wallows in guilt feelings. When the counselor suggested that, although no living person had ever been made a saint, Fred—with his contrition and noble suffering—might be a candidate, he almost took it seriously.

7. *Suffering as manipulation* ("I suffer to control others"). These persons get what they want by protesting how much they will suffer if they don't get it. They may even put on the martyr act to glorify themselves in the eyes of others.

Things are always going wrong for Jill, and she is quick to let her family know how much she suffers. Through family counseling, the members of Jill's family are finally beginning to understand why she is always so successful at getting things her own way.

ANALYSIS AND ASSESSMENT

The phase of analysis and assessment has two purposes: understanding the life style and seeing how the life style affects the individual's functioning in the life tasks (Mosak & Dreikurs, 1973). The counselor begins by exploring the current situation and how the client approaches social relationships, work responsibilities, and the sexual role, as well as his feelings about himself. Although this investigation may be carried out in an open-ended manner that allows data to surface, information regarding the life style is generally gathered systematically by inquiring how the counselee copes with life tasks. Here are some of the questions the counselor is likely to ask.

Social relationships: How are things going in your social life? Do you have a few close friends, do you have many acquaintances, or do you feel isolated? Are you satisfied with the number of friends you have? Do you find satisfaction in your relationships with other people? Do you feel belonging and acceptance?

Work: How do things go for you in your work? Do you enjoy what you are doing? Are you successful? Are you a workaholic—overinvolved with and overcommitted to your work? What do your fellow workers (or students) think of you? How do you respond to authority? Is work a rewarding and fulfilling task, a chore, or an all-encompassing part of your life?

Sexuality: Are you glad you are a man (or a woman)? Do you wish you were of the opposite sex? Are you very masculine (or feminine)? How do things go for you in your relationships with women (or men)? Do you feel any special concerns in relating to women (or men)?

Feelings about self: How self-satisfied and self-accepting are you? What do you do for fun? How do you enjoy yourself? Do you pressure yourself? Do you feel good about yourself? Do you like yourself?

Sometimes the interviewer may also ask: What are your goals? What are the meaning and purpose of your life as you understand them?

The investigation may also involve asking counselees to rate their current feelings about success in the areas of social relationships, work, sexuality, self, spiritual life, leisure, and parenting (1 is excellent, and 5 is extremely unsuccessful and discouraging).

Paraphrasing

Paraphrasing is the process of checking with the client to be certain you understand his ideas as he intended them. Paraphrasing requires paying selective attention to content and feeding back the essence of what the client said. The process involves your mirroring the client's thoughts to see whether you are hearing accurately, as well as communicating your understanding. Thus, the task is twofold—listening intensively and accurately and expressing what you have heard so the counselee knows that he is understood.

Paraphrasing is not word swapping or parroting; it is communication of understanding. This may be achieved either by generalizing the counselee's message or by making it more specific. Because paraphrasing conveys the listener's interest, it also enhances the relationship.

> *Claudia:*   I don't know about him. At times he's very nice, but then, again, he can be very nasty.
>
> *Counselor:*   You are not sure how he's going to act. He's hard to predict.

Paraphrasing may also allude to the goal or purpose implied in the client's communication; for example, "It seems you want to get even" or "I get the impression you want to show they can't control you."

The relationship flounders if the counselor misses or misunderstands the counselee's content. While paraphrasing helps to establish the relationship, it also serves as a checkpoint in the counselor's analysis and assessment of the counselee's perceptions.

Priorities and Life-Style Scale Themes

The counselee's priorities in making decisions are also investigated. Adlerians believe that determining a person's number-one priority is a useful clinical method for quickly ascertaining one facet of the life style. For teaching purposes, Adler presented four types of number-one priorities:

ruling, getting, avoiding, and the socially useful. Adler indicated that each type of priority, unless challenged, continues to characterize the individual, thereby determining the person's unity or life style.

One point should be made clear: the concept of priorities is not used to categorize people, since every individual is too complex to be classified on the basis of type. Priorities are used to understand short- and long-range goals and to get at core convictions.

The number-one priority is determined on the basis of the person's answers to the questions "What is most important in my quest for belonging?" and "What must I avoid at all costs?" Kefir (1972) originally defined four number-one priorities: comfort, pleasing, control, and superiority. Sally might list the priorities in this order:

Important to my belonging:	To be avoided at all costs:
Comfort	Stress
Pleasing	Rejection
Control	Humiliation
Superiority	Meaninglessness

Thus, if Sally's number-one priority is comfort, she will give precedence to comfort over pleasing, control, or superiority. Her priority is based on the mistaken conviction "Only when I'm comfortable do I truly belong." The avoidance stance would be "The worst thing for me is to be under stress. I must avoid it at all costs." These avoidance priorities have a crippling effect on our lives, since they severely limit our courage and social interest.

A second approach the counselor can employ during the analysis and investigation phase is a priorities interview.

Kefir and Corsini (1974) propose that a quick assessment of a particular facet of a client's life style and core convictions could be accomplished by a clinical intervention presently referred to as investigation of the client's number-one priority. Extrapolating from the life style typology information and from Adler's original work on types, Kefir developed an interview technique to assess four basic priorities—superiority, control, comfort, and pleasing.

Superiority

Possibly the most common number-one priority is superiority in its various forms: being competent, being right, being useful, being a victim, and being a martyr. People whose number-one priority is superiority will attempt always to move toward it regardless of circumstances or others' behavior. They will also consistently evoke certain feelings in those who encounter them, usually various degrees of inferiority or guilt.

The price for superiority is overinvolvement, overresponsibility, fatigue, stress, and uncertainty about one's relationships with others.

Control

Another common number-one priority is control, which is usually one of two types: in one type, the emphasis is on control of others; in the other type, the emphasis is on control of self. People whose number-one priority is control of others consistently achieve, or at least move toward, their goal, but they also evoke feelings of challenge and resistance in those around them. Methods of control vary widely, but the number-one priority is the same. The price for this priority is distance from others.

We all know people whose number-one priority is self-control; we often call them "uptight." These people evoke feelings of frustration in others, which often lead to disinterest. Self-controllers pay an additional price of diminished spontaneity and creativity.

Comfort

Those whose number-one priority is comfort or self-indulgence will not wait for gratification; they want their pleasure their way and immediately. They get what they are after, but annoy others in the process. The price they pay is diminished productivity, since they will not risk frustration and do not want responsibility.

Pleasing

Pleasers neither respect themselves nor expect respect from others. An immediate reaction to the pleaser is "Here's a nice guy," but further acquaintanceship often evokes negative responses such as rejection, disgust, intense frustration, despair, and exasperation. The price the pleaser pays is stunted growth, alienation, often institutionalization, and retribution.

We can expand these descriptors by viewing them on an active/ passive continuum, as suggested by recent research by Wheeler, Kern, and Curlette (1985) and Langenfeld and Main (1983). An active person with a priority of superiority, for example, may lean toward martyrdom or righteousness, while a passive person may lean toward saintliness and victimization. Controllers of others may accomplish their priority actively by being tyrants, or passively by being artful dodgers. Self-controllers are likely to be more passive. Comfort seekers may pursue their goal actively by behaving at times like spoiled brats, or by sitting passively, expecting to be served.

Pleasers may be quite passive, always subordinating their desires to others', or they may be exceedingly active, continuously looking for someone to please. They evoke pity and, at first, elicit in others a desire to help them. That desire, however, may soon be replaced by frustration and despair. Active pleasers are continuously looking for what they need to do to be rewarded or stroked by others. At first we react to these individuals with pleasure, but our feelings soon turn to frustration and disgust when we see that they lack opinions and decision-making skills of their own.

Pinpointing the Priority

A counselee's number-one priority can be pinpointed by asking her to describe the minute details of a typical day—what she does and how she feels when she does things. A second technique for determining the priority is to ask the counselee directly to indicate which of the four priorities is most important. The counselor can briefly describe each priority and then ask, "Which of these four statements best describes you? 'It's most important for me to be in control . . . ,' 'It's most important for me to please others . . . ,' " and so forth through the four priorities. As an alternative the counselor may wish to create a scenario that addresses two questions as to why a client adopts a certain priority in dealing with life situations. The two basic questions are "How do I use my number-one priority to belong?" and "What must I avoid at all cost when using that chosen priority?" Kefir claims that comfort seekers avoid stress, pleasers avoid rejection, controllers avoid being humiliated by situations or others, and superiority seekers avoid meaninglessness in life.

Thus, if a client's number-one priority is comfort, he will find ways to create comfortable situations in his environment. The client's priority of comfort might be based on the mistaken conviction that "only when I am comfortable do I truly belong or am accepted by others." The converse, or the avoidance stance operating within this particular client's conviction, might be "the worst thing for me is stress, so I must avoid it at all cost." Since stress is a normal condition, one can see how a client's priority of "only if I am comfortable in life" could inhibit the courage to grow and demonstrate social interest toward others.

A third possible assessment technique is designed to measure more directly life style themes. This is a 35-item self-report instrument that the counselee may complete during the session or at home. The Kern Lifestyle Scale (1982) categorizes life style into five factors: control, perfectionist, need to please, victim, and martyr. Though descriptions of the priorities are somewhat similar, the Lifestyle Scale attempts to obtain a more expansive description of a client's life style rather than a specific aspect of the private logic. Other advantages of the instrument are that it is quick to administer, yields a quantitative profile of life style themes, and provides immediate data that may help the counselor understand the client. A further advantage is the scale's use as a research tool to further understand the life style concept. (More information on the scales, interpretation, and use are presented in Chapter 13.)

Dealing Effectively with Priorities and Life Style Themes

After a number-one priority or theme has been pinpointed and understood by counselor and counselee, alternative behaviors and attitudes can be considered. The counselor does not usually work toward changing the priority or theme; it is likely that if one is discarded, another will replace it and be just as troublesome. The counseling goal is to help clients understand the feelings they evoke in others and to determine how much they are willing to pay to maintain the priority. The goal is to lead the client away from the absurd position of "only if" ("Only if I please, can I belong" or "Only if I am in power, can I find my place") into recognizing that he can belong and find his place without going to extremes and that they do have alternatives.

> Luke was a 56-year-old stockbroker who apparently could not handle his recent demotion from office supervisor to account executive. When the therapist offered tentatively, "Could it be it's important for you to supervise others?" Luke denied this by saying, "No, I really helped more people when I managed all 15 account executives." Paraphrasing Luke's statement as "So you had more control when you were office manager," counselor and counselee agreed that the number-one priority was in fact control.

As stressed previously, however, Luke and the counselor could not have come to that insight if their relationship had not been one of cooperation in which the client felt safe and "understood." The understanding component of the relationship might well be expedited by the counselor's ability to pinpoint the number-one priority or life style theme generated from the Lifestyle Scale. When the counselor can make this connection, he can help the discouraged client understand and believe that there are alternatives to a particular problem.

Confrontation

Confrontation is a procedure by which the counselor, sensitively and perceptively, enables counselees to be aware of discrepancies between their behaviors and their intentions, their feelings and their messages, their insights and their actions, and so forth.

Shulman (1973) indicates that confrontation is the combination of a challenge and a question designed to evoke the feeling that an immediate response is required. Thus, it stimulates therapeutic movement by mirroring a counselee's mistaken goals. Shulman suggests a number of techniques, depending on the intent of the confrontation.

Confronting with subjective views

Dreikurs refers to this confrontation technique as "revealing the hidden reason." That is, the counselor confronts the client with the private justification that the client gives to himself to make his behavior acceptable in his own eyes. For example: "I'm acting this way just because I'm drunk," or "I had so little sleep that, even if I went to work, I couldn't get anything done," or "I'm too nervous" (Shulman, 1973).

Dreikurs suggests that the counselor pursue the confrontation by asking "What were you thinking of at the moment?" or "What did you say to yourself then?" He also suggests that, if the counselor wants to be understood and to make the confrontation effective, she must put the hidden reason into the counselee's words. Paraphrasing during confrontation allows clients to hear their own words from a respected individual.

Confronting with mistaken beliefs and attitudes

The beliefs and attitudes to which this type of confrontation refers are the client's basic convictions about his own nature, the world, and the meaning and requirements of life. Shulman (1973) says "These basic convictions fill in the following blanks: I am _____; life is _____; therefore _____" (p. 201). For example, the person who complains that others pick on her might be confronted with "You look, talk, and behave like a pushover; so you invite people to pick on you. Don't blame anyone but yourself, since you invite them."

Confronting with private goals

This confrontation may be used when the counselee attempts to deny a feeling you suspect is there. The confrontation is brought about by offering a tentative hypothesis such as "Could it be that you wanted to get them upset?" or "Is it possible you thought this would be an excuse?" These statements may produce a recognition reflex or an acknowledgment of acceptance of the confrontation.

Confronting with destructive behavior

This confrontation deals with the here-and-now; for example, "You just changed the subject. Were we getting too close to something?" or "I notice you are arguing about one word and ignoring the concept. How come?"

As Shulman (1973) states, "Confrontation techniques are intended to challenge the client to give an immediate response, make an immediate change or an immediate examination of some issue" (p. 205). Adlerian confrontation is intended to help counselees become immediately aware of their goals, private logic, and behavior, as well as their ability to change.

Interpretation

Interpretation deals with the reasons a person behaves a certain way—that is, with the purpose of the behavior, belief, or feeling. By shifting away from the counselee's internal frame of reference, interpretation provides a new perspective for understanding. In other words, the counselor uses this technique to help the client consider and develop a new point of view, thus gaining access to a wider range of alternatives.

Interpretation is effective only if the counselee is receptive and can understand it and use it. To minimize resistance, interpretation is usually presented in a tentative format, such as "Could it be . . . ?" or "Is it possible . . . ?" and at a time when the counselor believes the counselee is ready to hear and seriously consider the interpretation.

> *Alan:* I'm confused about how well I can do my work. I can do some of it. But, if I do well, they expect more of me, and I can't live up to their other expectations.
>
> *Counselor:* You are not sure of your ability. Could it be that you don't do too well so they excuse you?

You hear the feelings and allude tentatively to the purpose of displaying inadequacy.

"The Question"

This counseling technique, first developed by Adler, is used to determine whether a problem has an organic or a functional basis. If the person complains of a physical symptom, such as headache, difficulty in breathing, or heart tremors, you ask "What would be different if you were well?" If the basis of the condition is functional and, therefore, has a purpose, the person might say "I could meet girls," or "I could go back to work," or "I could study harder." This tells you what he is avoiding by having the physical symptom. If he does not indicate any such purpose, however, it is highly probable that there is a physical cause and that the condition is organic. While there may be a physical ailment without psychological etiology, the counselee may still use the ailment for a special purpose.

Perceiving and Responding with Concreteness

This is the procedure through which you encourage a high degree of specificity and concreteness on the part of counselees. You do so by responding with clear, concise statements that clarify the counselee's problem. Since the aim of counseling is to develop a concrete plan for action, a technique that promotes concreteness is quite useful. This approach also achieves the goal of assuring clients that you are ready to discuss concerns in detail. Finally, your concrete responses encourage clients to be concrete not only in the counseling interaction but in all of their interactions as well.

You begin by encouraging specific self-exploration and problem exploration. Once the concern has been clarified, it is appropriate to encourage the counselee to consider and explore at a lower level of concreteness the purpose of his behavior. By offering tentative hypotheses and mirroring the individual's self-defeating goal and mistaken ideas, you help the client see, in very concrete form, why he behaves as he does.

Concreteness is also your guiding principle when you help the counselee choose specific alternatives and implement action.

> *Sandy:* Well, I know I should expect trouble with children. But I come from a big family and have read a lot. Still, it doesn't relieve the pressure of guiding my children.
>
> *Counselor:* You recognize that fights between children are normal, and you'd like to find ways to reduce the pressure.

Concreteness is especially important when the counselee tends to be vague and abstract, talks in generalities, or tends to intellectualize.

> *Julie:* You don't know how some husbands might react.
>
> *Counselor A:* Some are certainly unpredictable.

Counselor A's response is not concrete and blocks progress.

> *Julie:* You don't know how some husbands might react.
>
> *Counselor B:* Tom was very quiet when you came home.

By using the indefinite *you* instead of *I*, Julie was attempting to be vague and not assume responsibility for her own statement. She referred to husbands in general, not to her husband, Tom. By being concrete and mentioning the name of her husband, Counselor B helps Julie assume responsibility for her actions and feelings.

FORMULATION OF THE LIFE STYLE

The life style denotes the basic premises and assumptions on which psychological movement through life is based. Life style can be expressed in terms of the syllogism "I am _____; the world is _____; therefore, _____" (Allen, 1971b). We believe, feel, intend, and act upon these premises, and we move psychologically to justify our point of view. Our life style is formulated from our pattern of beliefs, convictions, and attitudes.

Investigation of the life style begins with the first psychological transaction between counselor and client. Body language, tone of voice, and expressed attitudes reveal a person's style of life. Therefore, one needs to learn to understand the scripts and what the scripts really mean (Mosak & Gushurst, 1977). It is essential that, when the self-defeating or maladaptive patterns are discussed, the counselee not be made to feel accused. As Mosak and Dreikurs (1973) indicate, "the therapist will have to assist him in distinguishing between being assessed, i.e., understood, and being blamed, a distinction not easy to make or accept" (p. 55).

Analysis of the Family Constellation

The life style is formulated by assessing the individual's family atmosphere as it emerges from answers to a family-constellation questionnaire and early recollections. The family atmosphere is understood by asking questions that seek to determine the relationship between the counselee and his parents, as well as the family's values, attitudes, and disciplinary procedures. In asking these questions, the counselor is guided by a life-style form. (Appendix A shows examples of these forms.)

Adlerians believe that siblings often influence one another as much as parents influence the children and that, in many families, children influence parents as much as parents influence children. Parents, however, do set the tone for the family atmosphere, particularly in the early years.

The family-constellation questionnaire

The questionnaire provides insight into the individual's perception of self, the relationships among siblings, influential forces to which one reacted, and the experiences that affect the decisions one makes about life.

The questionnaire investigates factors that Adlerians believe to be influential, such as birth order, sibling characteristics and ratings, and transactions and interactions among siblings and between children and parents. Emphasis is not on birth order per se, but rather on the child's psychological position in the family—how the child perceived her position and what she did with it. (Refer to the topic of birth order in Chapter 3.)

Guided by the questionnaire, the counselor begins by asking the client why he is seeking counseling and how satisfied he is with the way things are going in the basic life tasks. Next, the counselor asks for a description of the counselee's parents, their names and ages, occupations, and a brief list of their outstanding personality traits. After this initial information, the counselor asks "Who was your father's favorite? And your mother's? Did your parents have ambitions for their children? What was your father's relationship with the children? And your mother's? Who was the sibling most like your father? In what ways? Most like your mother? In what ways?" Then the counselor inquires about the client's relationship with his parents and, finally, about other parental figures in the family and the effect they may have had on the client's outlook on life (Eckstein, Baruth, & Mahrer, 1975).

After posing questions about the parents and their relationships with their children, the questionnaire asks for a description of the client's siblings. The client lists each sibling, beginning with the oldest and including himself, giving name, age, and a description of character and personality traits. If siblings are deceased, they are noted in their respective positions and identified in some way—for example, with a broken circle around the name (Eckstein et al., 1975). The family-constellation questionnaire then asks "Who among your siblings was most different from you? In what respect?" If the client is an only child, he is asked "Who in your peer group was most different from you? In what ways?" The next question is "Who was most like you? In what respect?" This gives the counselor an understanding of how the client views himself, the traits with which he identifies most, and those with which he identifies least. Other questions that can be asked about the client's siblings are "Which siblings fought and argued? Which played together? Who took care of whom?"

Now the focus shifts to the client himself. The counselor asks "What kind of child were you? Did you have any unusual talents, achievements, or ambitions? What was your physical development like? Were there any physical or psychological handicaps?" The client is then asked to describe sexual development in terms of first relationships with the opposite sex, including the first sexual experiences. If the client is a woman, she may be asked to describe her experience with her first menstrual period.

The next item in investigating the family constellation is rating the client in relation to the siblings in terms of a list of attributes. To do this, the counselor takes one of the 24 attributes listed in the questionnaire—for example, intelligence—and lists, in one column, the sibling who was most intelligent and, in another column, the sibling who was least intelligent. If the client is at neither extreme, the counselor indicates the client's position in relation to the siblings.

Attribute	Most	Least
Intelligence	Mary (Sam)	George

Hence, Sam, the client, is closer to Mary in his intelligence rating.

Family dynamics

An infinite number of personalities can result from the family atmosphere, ordinal position, psychological position (the way the individual perceives and interprets his position in the family), and methods of training. The oldest child may adopt the patterns of the parent believed to have more power. For example, if father is gruff and demanding and gets his way, the child tends to copy these traits. On the other hand, if mother controls by passive-destructive methods, such as withdrawing and using silence, the child may adopt these tactics. The first child may attempt to emulate the parent's traits she considers most important or may give up because she cannot live up to those standards.

The second child is usually very perceptive of what is expected and needed to become important in the family. By noting the behavior of the first child and the behaviors valued by the parents, the second child may choose to adopt parental traits the older child has overlooked. The second child also closely identifies areas in which the first child has not succeeded and, if this provides acceptance and belonging inside the family unit, quickly moves into those territories. As Shulman (1973) states, "divergence in behavior between siblings is partly due to competition between them for a place in the sun; the second avoids the territory of the first and goes elsewhere to seek his fortune" (p. 49).

According to Dreikurs, personality traits are the children's responses to the power politics within the family group. "Similarities and differences . . . indicate alliance and competition" (Dreikurs, 1957). The siblings who are most alike are the allies (Dreikurs, 1952–53). Conversely, the siblings most different from each other are the main competitors, even though there may have been no open rivalry. Dreikurs distinguishes between rivalry and competition, describing the first as an open contest, the second as having "a much deeper impact on each child, leading to the development of opposite character traits . . . as each child seeks success where the other one fails" (Dreikurs, 1957). Competition develops mainly with the proximal sibling, the one who always had to be taken into account during the formative years. (Shulman, 1973, p. 49)

It is clear that siblings have a significant influence on the emergence of one another's personality traits. The psychological position in the family may be as important as the parents' method of training.

Thus, in summary, the analysis of a family constellation requires four things: first, a solid and comprehensive familiarity with the factors that Adlerian theory considers most influential in personality development, the implications that Adlerians find in certain types of phenomena, and the common life styles identified by Adlerians; second, the ability to recognize, discover and characterize patterns; third, the ability to compare patterns for the presence of similarities and differences; and, fourth, the ability to make accurate inferences, either by extrapolation within an already identified coherence, or through an intuitive, empathic grasp of a particular phenomenal world. (Gushurst, 1971b, p. 32)

Interpretation of Early Recollections

Early recollections are another crucial type of information the Adlerian counselor collects in the course of formulating the life style. Early recollections are specific incidents recalled from early childhood, incidents the client can remember in clear detail, almost as if he could see them, and include the feelings and thoughts at the time of their occurrence. They are not merely reports about a person's early life; they reveal beliefs, basic mistaken attitudes, self-defeating perceptions, and unique laws of psychological movement. Early recollections are valuable because, according to the Adlerian theory of personality, they are indices of present attitudes, beliefs, and motives (Mosak, 1958; Gushurst, 1971a) and because Adlerians believe that *people remember only those events from early childhood that are consistent with their present views of themselves and the world* (Adler, 1958). As Gushurst (1971b) indicates, early recollections "provide a brief picture of how an individual views himself, other people, and life in general, what he strives for in life, and what he anticipates as likely to occur in life" (p. 33).

Gushurst (1970, 1971a) has attempted to describe in an objective format what the diagnostician does when interpreting an early recollection. Gushurst has also moved toward a strategy for objectifying in a reliable and replicable way the interpretation of early recollections. Here are other writers' comments about the interpretation of early recollections.

> [Early recollections] are first interpreted thematically and second with respect to specific details. . . . The characters incorporated in the recollection are not treated in interpretation as specific individuals but as prototypes. They represent people or women in general or authority figures rather than the specific individuals mentioned. While the content of the recollection is given primary consideration, a sequential analysis provides a more rounded picture of the individual. The characteristic outlook rather than the characteristic behavior is portrayed. (Mosak, 1958, pp. 107–108)

> The main theme or pattern is to be interpreted in a manner similar with the TAT theme or the figure drawings, and are not to be broken into separate fragments. Starting with hunches, individual themes are brought together and their unity and pattern spell out a message—the client's feelings and emotions provide the main interpretative clue. (Nikelly & Verger, 1971, pp. 57–58)

The individual selects only certain events from the vast number of experiences that occurred earlier in life; she emphasizes certain aspects of each memory and downplays or completely omits others. Memory is a product of selective and evaluative processes; hence, it can provide projective data from which we infer the basic elements of the current life style (beliefs and goals). These elements influence and shape the recollection as it is articulated to the counselor.

Kopp and Dinkmeyer (1975) present a standardized procedure for use in the interview.

> Think back as far as you can to the first thing you can remember . . . something that happened when you were very young (it should be before you were seven or eight years old). It can be anything at all—good or bad, important or unimportant—but it should be something you can describe as a one-time incident (something that happened only once), and it should be something you can remember very clearly or picture in your mind, like a scene.
> Now tell me about an incident or something that happened to you. Make sure it is something you can picture, something specific, and something where you can remember a single time it happened.
> As the student begins to tell the memory, listen for the visual and specific part of the memory. Some background details may be appropriate. Do not, however, spend too much time setting the stage with facts leading up

to or surrounding the incident itself. Instead, concentrate on what actually happened.

Phrases such as "we were always . . . ," "would always . . . ," "used to . . . ," or "would happen" suggest incidents that occurred repeatedly. Ask the student to choose one specific time which stands out more clearly than the others and tell what happened that one time. If one particular incident does not stand out over others, eliminate this event and choose a different early memory which can be described as a single incident.

Before moving on to the next memory, ask the following questions and write down the student's response:

Do you remember how you felt at the time or what reaction you had to what was going on? (If so), please describe it. Why did you feel that way (or have that reaction)?

Which part of the memory stands out most clearly from the rest—like if you had a snapshot of the memory, it would be the very instant that is most vivid and clear in your mind? How did you feel (what was your reaction) at that instant?

Our experience indicates that, although we can begin to see a student's basic beliefs and motivations in the first memory, the accuracy of these interpretations increases when they are based on additional memories. The counselor's assessment thus should be based on at least three memories. Typically, from three to six memories are collected. (p. 24)

The counselor can make the directions less specific by stating "I want to record a particular incident that you recall in the first seven or eight years of your life. Tell me what happened, what moment is most vivid, and how you felt at that moment." If the counselee follows the directions, the counselor then takes down verbatim what the counselee says. If the counselee doesn't follow the directions, the counselor may have to resort to a variety of other tactics. If the counselee is resistant or says "I can't remember any specific incident," the counselor might ask the person to make one up—to invent one. Most people at that point suddenly remember an incident that actually occurred. When that happens, the counselor is likely to suspect that the client is someone who tends to do the opposite of what is expected of him. Some people, on the other hand, are much more creative. They may intermittently invent and recall incidents; they may embellish a partially recalled incident; and, at times, they may claim they are unable to invent an incident. Of course, an invented incident is just as useful diagnostically as something that actually happened. Other creative variations are the attempt to offer recollections from a later age period and the attempt to give reports.

When people are unwilling to cooperate with the early-recollections process, the counselor should discuss with them the fact that probably they are unconsciously unwilling to reveal much about themselves—which is, of course, their prerogative. This insight often prompts a client to bring in some early recollections at an ensuing session.

Sweeney (1975) provides some additional guidelines about how to utilize the early recollections.

Is the individual active or passive?

Is he/she an observer or participant?

Is he/she giving or taking?

Does he/she go forth or withdraw?

What is his/her physical posture or position in relation to what is around him?

Is he/she alone or with others?

Is his/her concern with people, things, or ideas?

What relationship does he/she place him/herself into with others? Inferior? Superior?

What emotion does he/she use?

What feeling tone is attached to the event or outcome?

Is detail and color mentioned?

Do stereotypes of authorities, subordinates, men, women, old, young, etc. reveal themselves?

Prepare a "headline" which captures the essence of the event; for example, in relation to the woman's recollection of the ice cream: Girl Gets Job Done!

Look for themes and an overall pattern.

Look for corroboration in the family constellation information. (p. 49)

Watkins summarizes the value of early recollections:

> Early recollections (ERs) can be a useful and effective assessment tool in the counseling process. They often provide the counselor with considerable insight into a client's dynamics. . . . It is important, however, to understand that the assumed usefulness of ERs as a projective technique is based largely on critical opinion. The clinical usefulness of ERs has not been validated statistically. (Watkins, 1985, p. 32)

Watkins's statement concerning the lack of statistical validity for the procedure and abundance of favorable clinical opinion reflects the current Adlerian emphasis on practical procedures.

Identification of the Basic Mistakes

The summary of the family constellation and the interpretation of early recollections enable the counselor to specify mistaken and self-defeating perceptions. These perceptions are often very different from the guidelines of Adlerian "social interest," which emphasize the give-and-take, cooperative, equalitarian, and responsible nature of human relationships. Early recollections and the investigation of the family constellation frequently indicate self-interest, concern with power, avoidance, and withdrawal—all of which are identified as mistaken perceptions.

Mosak and Dreikurs (1973) offer the following classification of the basic mistaken and self-defeating perceptions.

1. Overgeneralizations. "People are hostile." The "all" is often implicit. "Life is dangerous," with the "always" implicit.
2. False or impossible goals of "security." "One false step and you're dead," "I have to please everybody."
3. Misperceptions of life and life's demands. In the extreme, one can observe these in the delusions and hallucinations. Typical convictions might be "Life never gives me any breaks" and "Life is so hard."
4. Minimization or denial of one's worth (Adlerians accept the worthwhileness of every individual). "I'm stupid" and "I'm undeserving" or "I'm *just* a housewife."
5. Faulty values. "Be first even if you have to climb over others." (p. 57)

Integration and Summary

One of the counselor's major tasks is to integrate and summarize the information gathered from the investigation of the client's family constellation, from the interpretation of early recollections, and from the identification of the basic mistakes. The goal of this diagnostic task is to extract from the information

a brief description of the individual's role within his family (either alone or in comparison with the roles played by the other members of the family), his major areas of success and failure, the major influences which seem to have affected his decision to adopt the role that he did, and perhaps also an inferential statement about his apparent major goals and/or conceptions of himself, others, life in general, or of some particular aspect of life, such as sexuality, physical handicaps, religion, and so forth. (Gushurst, 1971b, p. 31)

This process of integration should result in a clear, concise summary that reveals the client's mistaken and self-defeating perceptions, as well as her assets, so that the individual can easily recognize her own dynamics. The summary is presented to the counselee for her consideration and can be refined by discussing specific points.

> In summary, the Adlerian diagnostician proceeds by extracting the major features that appear in an individual's answers to the family constellation questionnaire, thereby obtaining a brief picture of his nascent personality; the individual's current outlook on life is then obtained by interpreting his early recollections; and the mistaken elements in his approach to life are then specified by comparing his contemporary convictions with those which seem to be required by the "logic of social living." Most importantly, when these diagnostic procedures have been completed, the individual has before him some very specific problem areas on which to focus, should he decide to change his life. (Gushurst, 1971b, p. 34)

Sometimes it is useful to dictate your summary of the life style in the presence of the counselee. Then the counselee, at the next session, reads it aloud. This procedure offers the opportunity to stop and discuss areas that raise questions. The counselor can learn a lot from hearing the counselee read and by being alert to slips and to what emphasis the counselee gives the reading.

Although this procedure may appear deceptively simple, it requires a good grasp of Adlerian theory to be clinically useful. One can synthesize and integrate the life-style material only by understanding the basic concepts of Adlerian psychology. The diagnostician must be able to recognize and articulate patterns.

> That is, he must learn to note that certain traits, because of an inner logic or necessity, tend to cohere; that if two or more traits of a certain kind are present in a given personality, certain other traits are likely to appear; and if these other traits do not appear, some explanation must be found for their absence. (Gushurst, 1971b, p. 31)

For example, if a person is passive and requires service from others, one can anticipate that she may feel helpless and tend to give up or that she will get her way by displaying ineptness and by withdrawing. If she cooperates, one can expect that she will do it by proving her "stupidity." Thus, the counselor must not only discern discrete patterns in the life style but understand how certain behaviors reinforce certain beliefs.

Because of the basic unity and pattern of the personality, one can identify a number of common life styles. Mosak (1971) provides a set of guidelines that facilitate analysis of common syndromes. As he states,

"The life style forms a unifying principle, a gestalt to which behavior is bound in accordance with the individual 'law of movement' " (p. 77). Mosak illustrates some commonly observed life styles:

The "getters," who exploit and manipulate life and others.

The "drivers," overtly overambitious, overconscientious, and dedicated.

The "controllers," who keep spontaneity and feelings in check in order to control life and ensure that life will not control them.

The persons who need to be right and hence feel superior to those whom they perceive as being wrong.

The persons who need to feel superior. These individuals, when they cannot be the best, settle for being the worst.

The persons who want to please everyone and who are always dependent on the approval and evaluation of others for their own self-esteem and worth.

The persons who feel morally superior because of high standards that elevate them over others.

The "aginners," who oppose all expectations and demands of life and who rarely know what they are for but who always seem to know what they are against.

The "victims," who pursue disaster and elicit the sympathy and pity of others. Victims are very creative. They are willing to suffer for anything—not just for a cause, as martyrs do—and they reveal a great deal of flexibility and imagination.

The "martyrs," who suffer like the victims but die for a cause. Often referred to as the "injustice collectors," they either silently endure or make their suffering very visible.

The "babies," who find their place by exploiting others through their charm and cuteness.

The "inadequate" individuals, who behave as if they couldn't do anything correctly and, therefore, constantly needed the help of others.

The "rationalizers" and the "intellectualizers," who avoid feelings and spontaneity and who are comfortable only in situations in which intellectual talents are valued.

The "excitement seekers," who despise routine and repetitive activity and who create and stimulate excitement.

Additional research findings generated out of the Department of Counseling and Psychological Services at Georgia State University seem to indicate that there may be fewer categories than those proposed by Mosak (Davis, 1979; Kaiser, 1978; Wheeler, 1980; Mullis, 1984; Wheeler, Kern, & Curlette, 1986). One must keep in mind, however, that these and similar typologies merely represent examples of various kinds of psychological movement. They are useful in that they give a concise word picture of behaviors and beliefs, but each life style is unique and must be understood in terms of its unique pattern regardless of proposed "types."

The aforementioned patterns are, of course, not the only life styles we observe. The counselor, therefore, must develop the capacity to see relationships among the various data and formulate new patterns. After certain patterns are identified, they are compared for similarities and differences. Areas of difference between the client and the rest of the family may be areas of competition, while areas of similarity may reflect alliances among the siblings, role modeling, or acceptance of family values. If parents set a highly competitive atmosphere, they will stimulate differences in siblings' attributes.

The information from the life-style analysis is valuable not only because it helps the counselor understand the perceptions of the counselee but, more importantly, because it helps the individual feel understood. This type of understanding transcends establishment of rapport and of a good working relationship; it creates faith in the counselor and stimulates hope that things can change. The counselor's reflection of feelings and empathy are important, but the kind of understanding we are describing has the power to stimulate movement. There is a great difference between dealing with someone who simply recognizes that you are angry and receiving from someone the insight that your anger is dictated by the belief "I know what is best." This kind of understanding goes beyond empathy and confronts you with the fact that you are deciding to display a particular emotion (for example, anger) and, therefore, you can also choose to respond differently.

Analysis of the life style helps counselor and client develop a plan for the counseling relationship and for the nature and direction of the counseling process. The life style and the mistaken or self-defeating perceptions that are presented to the counselee point to a number of beliefs and mistaken ideas that will reoccur in the course of counseling. The life style, then, is not a static, one-time diagnostic formulation but a consistent theme that is continuously discussed in relation to the client's approach to the various challenges of living.

INSIGHT

As you know, Adlerians believe that behavior develops not from what we are but from what we believe we are; that is, behavior is not the result of our experiences but of how we interpret them. Our behavior is based on our expectations and on the resultant self-fulfilling prophecies. We approach people in a friendly or hostile manner, and they respond in kind.

The insight phase of counseling is concerned with helping clients become aware of why they choose to function as they do. Although the counselor does not lecture or give advice, counseling is an educational process in which counselees learn about themselves. Through constant emphasis on beliefs, goals, and intentions, the individual's private logic is explained and discussed.

All of us operate with varying degrees of common sense and private logic. People who exhibit dysfunctional behavior, however, don't see life in terms of common sense but only in terms of their private logic. They solve their problems in a self-centered way that shows a lack of normal social interest and willingness to cooperate with others.

Adlerians interpret the pattern of behavior holistically, in terms of its unity. Therefore, they don't accept a dualism of intellectual and emotional insight and don't believe that the counselee should defer dealing with a problem while seeking to develop insight. Besides, intellectual insight may be only a ploy to keep the person involved in counseling instead of becoming involved in problem resolution.

Those who clearly indicate that they understand, yet make no attempt to change their beliefs or try on new behaviors, must be confronted with the purpose of such behaviors. By staying in counseling, clients publicly declare their good intentions to the counselor and to those close to them. By refusing to become involved or to make a commitment to change, however, these people defeat others' attempts to help them, while protesting their good intentions and well-meaning efforts. This is the situation that Adler called the "yes, but" game—"I know I should stop, but . . ."—with all its concomitant excuses, which reveal the person's psychological movement.

Interpretation is concerned with creating awareness of (1) life style, (2) current psychological movement and its direction, (3) goals, purposes, and intentions, and (4) private logic and how it works. Insight is created through constant reference to the basic premises of one's life style and to how these mistaken, self-defeating premises keep the individual from leading a successful and satisfying life.

The information that represents the basis for interpretation is derived from the person's here-and-now behavior and position in the family constellation. It also comes from hunches about the client's ordinal position and from an understanding of the individual's psychological position in the family constellation. As we have said, early recollections are used to clarify and sharpen the interpretation. Finally, inquiry about the various challenges of living (work, social contacts, sexual relationships, self-image, and spiritual concerns) provide insight into the motives and purposes of behavior.

Adlerian interpretation can be clearly differentiated from classical psychoanalytic interpretation. Adlerian interpretation is done in relation to the life style, which is the central theme. The interpretation is not done statically—in terms of a client's present position—but is continuously related to one's movement. It refers to the direction and course of one's transactions with others. It also alludes to where one is going and to what one expects to get by his behavior—to be special, to be in control, or to obtain special service. Thus, interpretation enables the client to see the pattern of movement and its meaning.

Characteristically, interpretation deals with the purpose of behavior and its consequences. The focus is on here-and-now behavior and on expectations and anticipations that arise from one's intentions. Interpretation is always done holistically, in terms of the meaning and scope of the pattern of movement. No attempt is made to analyze elements as discrete from the pattern.

Method of Presentation

The method of presenting an interpretation is very important. Interpretation is generally made tentatively: "Could it be . . . ?" "Is it possible . . . ?" "I have an idea about you I'd like to share." The open-ended sharing of hunches and guesses is powerful, because it relieves the counselor of the burden of being always right; one doesn't have to be perfect to offer a hunch or guess. It also provides a mirror through which the counselor can look at the client's behavior. Because the interpretation is offered tentatively, the client is not forced to defend herself and is truly free to agree or disagree. And when the counselor is wrong, this method of presentation enables both parties to consider other alternatives. The guessing method is a perfectly acceptable scientific process and is functional within the counseling relationship. If the counselor guesses correctly, the counselee feels understood. If the counselor guesses incorrectly, he has an opportunity to demonstrate the courage to be imperfect and to contribute another valuable element to the relationship.

There are times, however, when interpretation is presented confrontationally. This happens when there is a discrepancy between what one says he intends and what he actually believes. Discussing the purpose of this behavior helps the individual recognize the basic beliefs and goals that motivate his transactions in life.

At times, counselees are encouraged to interpret for themselves. Some believe that, if clients are able to interpret for themselves, the interpretation will be retained better. As counselees become familiar with their own life styles, they can start to contemplate their alternatives. To elicit a counselee's own interpretation, the counselor may ask "From what you understand about your life style, how would you explain the current experience you have just been describing to me?"

Goals

Occasionally, the counselor may offer an interpretation that is deliberately exaggerated, so that the client can see the ridiculous elements in her behavior. This type of interpretation has the same purpose as the paradoxical intention; both can, by their very extremity, influence or even create movement.

Generally, interpretation should not take place before trust and rapport have been established; however, a meaningful interpretation may actually build and solidify the relationship.

Since interpretation is directed at the movement and purpose of behavior, it also helps counselees begin to "catch themselves." An example of what we mean is someone who muddies up conversation by introducing the phrase "you know." Each person has his own idiographic meaning for that phrase; for some, it means "You know, don't you?" For others, it means "You don't know" or "Could you possibly know?" or "No one has ever known." And for still others, it means "You ought to know." Most people are unaware of how frequently they interject the phrase "you know." If they are interested in making their communication clear, they will learn to catch themselves in the act of muddying what they are saying. Often we maintain a symptom by being constantly on guard against it. Instead of fighting the habit of using the phrase "you know," the counselee is advised to catch himself saying "you know" and laughingly say "There I am, up to my old mischief again."

This ability to intervene in one's self-defeating perceptions as they are about to occur or to become aware of the purpose of one's behavior as it is happening epitomizes the goal of insight. By catching oneself and interfering with the undesirable behavior, one is learning to stop self-defeating patterns. This opens up the opportunity to practice active-constructive behavior and to replace faulty goals with positive goals. Examples of new beliefs and new positive goals that may result are "I belong by contributing" (goal: involvement); "I can decide and be responsible for my behavior" (goals: autonomy and responsibility for one's own behavior); "I am interested in cooperating" (goals: justice and fairness); and "I can withdraw from conflict" (goal: acting maturely by avoiding power contests and by accepting and understanding others' openness).

How an individual reacts to the counselor's interpretation provides guidelines for the next steps in the counseling process. Remember that interpretations are always made tentatively ("Could it be . . . ?" "Is it possible . . . ?"), so there is no need for the counselor always to be right. Also, a tentative approach ensures that, if the counselor is wrong, the counselee will not be harmed; he will simply indicate that that's not how he perceives things. If the client's response indicates that the counselor is wrong and the counselor is not upset by her failure to guess correctly, the counselee may benefit from learning that counselors also make mistakes and survive them unharmed. The counselor is modeling the courage to be imperfect which often teaches as much as an insightful interpretation. The counselee begins to see that the world does not come apart just because someone makes a mistake.

Results

If the interpretation is accurate and helpful, several things may occur. At the time of the interpretation, the individual may give a recognition reflex—a grin or smile indicating that what the counselor said makes sense. In other words, the interpretation "rings a bell" and is personally applicable or the counselee may have a contemplative look, which generally indicates that she is seeing some of her behaviors and attitudes in a new light.

Interpretation from the Adlerian frame of reference is never nomothetic (dealing with generalities) but idiographic, designed to fit the unique life style of each individual. Interpretation involves communication about all kinds of interpersonal transactions, with emphasis on purpose rather than on cause and on movement rather than on description. In other words, Adlerian interpretation is dynamic rather than static.

By exposing the hidden intentions responsible for the counselee's self-defeating behavior and by clearly illustrating them, the counselor helps the counselee see these intentions as unpalatable. This is what Adler was talking about when he used the expression "spitting in the patient's soup," which means that, though one may still eat the soup, it will never taste quite the same. The person may still engage in a self-defeating behavior, but will not like it.

REORIENTATION

In the reorientation phase, counselor and counselee work together to consider alternative attitudes, beliefs, and actions. The approach is to reeducate and remotivate the counselee to become more effective in her approach to the challenges of living. But the counselor must go beyond developing mere awareness of alternatives. The courage to risk and make changes must also be developed. This is often accomplished by focusing on the immediate interpersonal situation rather than on past experiences. By seeing how she can change within the counseling relationship, the client develops the motivation to experiment in other relationships.

Establishing Realistic Goals

A beginning step in reorientation is to clarify with the counselee what he wants. The relationship phase focused on mutual goal alignment, but now, in reorientation, there must be a clear establishment of the counselee's goals. The counselor attempts to determine whether the client's complaints are about the environment or about himself. It is important to make it clear that, as people change themselves, they also change their environments. Changing a belief such as "I must win every conflict" to "I am willing to cooperate, listen to others, and give in when appropriate" can have a major effect on one's relationships. The change will stimulate totally different responses in others, and, as a consequence, one's feelings, goals, and actions will also change.

It is important to determine whether the counselee's goals for change are realistic. Unrealistic goals will only discourage; for example, someone who has not been able to relate to women may decide to become involved with a popular and attractive woman. If this relationship doesn't work, he can justify his lack of success by taking the self-defeating approach of "See? I tried, but I can't make any progress." Instead of letting this person "prove" his faulty assumption that he is not acceptable to women, the counselor encourages him to establish the intermediate goal of becoming better acquainted with women.

> To initiate behavior change after the client has recognized his basic life pattern, the therapist may suggest, "Is this the kind of person you want to be? Could you think of another better way to act? What do you suspect will eventually happen if you continue this pattern for a long time?" (Nikelly & Bostrom, 1971, p. 104)

A new orientation toward people and the life tasks, which is the goal of the reorientation phase, comes about as the client's beliefs, perceptions, feelings, and goals become more appropriate and more in line with common sense. This phase actually involves showing how one's behavior and relationships relate to one's intentions and beliefs. The counselor mirrors to the counselee how his goals and intentions are chosen by him and by him alone and how they influence all his actions, feelings, and approaches to the tasks of living.

> The therapist must understand that the client behaves according to his interpretation of what is meaningful and significant to him. The client learns or forgets whatever serves his purposes; however, such selectiveness may hamper his sense of social relatedness and inhibit self-realization. (Nikelly & Bostrom, 1971, p. 105)

At this point in the process, the counselee is made aware that insight has little value by and of itself. It is only a prelude to action. *Outsight—* moving ideas into action—is the real aim of the process.

Problem Solving and Decision Making

Problem solving and decision making are basic skills in the action phase of the counseling process. They are employed to help the counselee explore and understand the problem adequately, so that the goal can be defined precisely. The next step involves considering alternative courses of action and helping the counselee examine and order his values. Each course of action is considered in terms of how it helps one realize one's goals and values.

Carkhuff (1973) schematizes this phase in terms of the following steps:

1. Define problem: develop accurate grasp of situation
2. Define goal: clearly determine task to be achieved

3. Develop alternative courses of action: develop means to achieve goals
4. Develop counselee's value hierarchy: describe things that matter to counselee
5. Choose course of action: evaluate course in terms of value hierarchy
6. Implement course of action: develop a way to act on a course of action

In the Adlerian counseling process, counselor and counselee align their goals, consider possible alternatives and consequences, evaluate how these alternatives will help the counselee meet his goals, and then reorient by taking a course of action. The counselor helps the counselee consider how his mistaken, self-defeating perceptions keep him from making effective decisions.

> Gina: I'd like to go on to medical school, but I'm not sure if I could do as well as I should. So maybe I'll teach biology.
>
> Counselor: You are not sure of yourself. Your belief that you have to be first or you are nothing seems to keep you from deciding in favor of medicine.

Seeing New and More Functional Alternatives

The goal of Adlerian counseling is active-constructive behavior that enables the individual to become more effective and happier. Any failure to take forward steps should be interpreted in terms of its purpose. Counselees are helped to see the purpose and the payoff of persisting in the self-defeating behavior. To that effect, it may be useful to get the counselee to ask "What is the worst thing that could happen if I changed?" The client is then likely to recognize that the "worst thing" is not so bad after all and that, as a matter of fact, changing the behavior will probably result in positive situations—for example, relating better with others. Through this process, clients learn once again the effects of the choices they continually make about life. Even more importantly, they see the power they have to change their beliefs, perceptions, and goals, and hence their feelings and actions as well.

The Adlerian orientation is primarily a motivation-modification system, not a behavior-modification system; that is, the focus is on changing attitudes, beliefs, perceptions, and goals, so that behavior will also change. This does not prevent the Adlerian counselor from suggesting from time to time "Act as if . . . ," encouraging the counselee to assume a certain behavior so as to start experiencing the world differently.

It is important to show clients how they create and maintain their own ineffectual approaches to the challenges of life. By creating a goal that is unattainable or by adopting a belief that is dysfunctional, people set themselves up for failure.

Jack believes "I can do as I please; I make my own rules" and also "I'm not as much as others." His goal is to find excitement. When things don't go well for him in school, he drops out. Not having salable skills, he gets a menial job that is everything but exciting or rewarding. To find excitement, he becomes involved with hard drugs. His belief that "I can make my own rules and do as I please" leads him to believe that he will not be caught.

The counselor's task is to help Jack see how these self-defeating beliefs get him in deep trouble and that they provide a false base of security. Jack needs to be helped to see that there are active, constructive ways of finding excitement, which will be rewarding instead of destructive. By changing his beliefs about himself and life in general, Jack will be able to consider a new and more challenging type of work and to develop confidence in his capacity to relate successfully to people.

Maria believes "It is dangerous to express feelings," "People are no good and treat me unfairly," "I must please others no matter what," and "If I'm not on top, I'm nothing." Her goal is to stay ahead of others by being right and in control. Since she is very unwilling to express her feelings, she has difficulty in her social and family relationships. Her hiding behind a facade of inconsequential talk creates and maintains a wall between her and others. Her children don't respect her and keep alluding to how inadequately she provides for the family. Maria uses the children's attitude to fortify her belief that people treat her unfairly. Instead of expressing anger at her family's lack of appreciation, she dejectedly accepts their criticism.

If Maria is to lead a more functional and satisfying life, she must start to express her real feelings and stop pleasing others at her own expense. The counselor helps to point out ways in which she does this and encourages her to find specific new ways to express her feelings and to feel OK about herself even if she is not on top.

Dreikurs (1967) states:

To motivate reorientation, I employ a mirror technique confronting the patient with his goals and intentions. Moreno also employs a "mirror technique" for similar purposes in psychodrama. Interpretation of goals is singularly effective in stimulating change. When the patient begins to recognize his goals, his own conscience becomes a motivating factor. Adler called this process "spitting in the patient's soup." However, insight into goals and intentions is not merely restrictive; it makes the patient aware also of his ability to make decisions, of his freedom to choose his own direction. (p. 70)

The focus on change involves helping counselees clearly see their self-defeating mistaken beliefs, mistaken ideas about human relationships, mistaken ideas about life's demands, and mistaken purposes and goals. When they see the interrelationships among these factors, counselees are in a position to change and move in a positive direction.

Specific Strategies

Among the wide variety of strategies that can be incorporated in the Adlerian counseling process are:

Immediacy
Encouragement
Paradoxical intention
Spitting in the client's soup
Acting as if
Catching oneself
Creating movement
Avoiding the tar baby
Task setting and commitment
Terminating and summarizing the interview

Immediacy

Immediacy means expressing how you are experiencing the counselee in the here and now. Since the immediacy dimension has the potential to upset as well as to advance the relationship, it is usually approached tentatively. If the counselee has progressed in self-awareness and self-understanding, the communication of immediacy can be more direct.

Immediacy is used to help clients become aware of what they are communicating both verbally and nonverbally. Healthy and mature persons communicate congruently. They say what they intend to say. In the immediacy aspect of the relationship, you make explicit the relationship between you and the counselee.

> Peter: I want to do something to help me get started; but it's no use. They are all ahead of me.
>
> Counselor: You say you want to get started, but I get the impression from your tone of voice that you have given up and are still concerned with how you compare with others.

In this example, you share your impression that the counselee is defeating himself.

Encouragement

Encouragement focuses on helping counselees become aware of their worth. By encouraging them, you help your counselees recognize and own their strengths and assets, so they become aware of the power they have to make decisions and choices (Dinkmeyer, 1972).

One's identity is a product of interpersonal relationships, because the feedback one receives is internalized and creates identity. If someone feels discouraged and inadequate, the lack of self-esteem produces dysfunctional behavior and failure to become involved in the tasks of life. Encouragement is the most powerful procedure available for changing the counselee's beliefs.

Encouragement focuses on beliefs and self-perceptions. It searches intensely for assets and processes feedback so the client will become aware of her strengths. In a mistake-centered culture like ours, this approach violates norms by ignoring deficits and stressing assets. The counselor is concerned with changing the client's negative self-concept and anticipations.

Encouragement can take many forms, depending on the phase of the counseling process. At the beginning, you let your clients know you value them by really listening to their feelings and intentions, and stimulate their confidence by accepting them as full and equal participants in the process. In the assessment phase of counseling, which is designed to illuminate strengths, you recognize and encourage the counselees' growing awareness of their power to choose and their attempts to change. In the reorientation phase, you promote change by stimulating the individual's courage. Thus, encouragement is a vital element of every aspect of the counseling process.

> *Gina:* School grades have little meaning for me. I could do it; but my teachers demand too much and go too fast.
>
> *Counselor:* You feel you could do the work at a different pace.

You sense the discouragement and value the counselee's belief in her own ability. If she accepts her ability, then procedures for modifying the pace can be considered. You demonstrate that Gina has resources.

Paradoxical Intention

Adler called the paradoxical intention "prescribing the symptom," and Dreikurs called it "antisuggestion." It is a technique in which clients are encouraged to emphasize or develop their symptoms even more. For example, if the child doesn't do her arithmetic homework, you might suggest that this is a good way to resist authority and encourage her not to do any schoolwork. If an individual bites his fingernails, you encourage him to bite even more and deeper.

Usually it is best to make the paradoxical recommendations for a specific period of time and treat them as an experiment. That is, you encourage counselees to see what they learn from the experience.

The paradoxical intention makes people dramatically aware of the reality of their situation and that they must accept the consequences of their behavior. When you confront a client with your paradoxical refusal to fight his behavior, the behavior becomes less attractive in the client's eyes. This procedure implicitly indicates confidence that, when the individual sees the problem in a magnified perspective, he will choose to change his behavior. Also, this technique can make the symptoms appear so ridiculous that the counselee finally gives them up.

> *Terry:* Mr. Smith is very unfair. He bugs me all the time, and, when I talk back, he sends me to the principal.
>
> *Counselor:* You feel that Mr. Smith is unfair. But why do you cooperate with him?
>
> *Terry:* Cooperate? Ridiculous! I never do.
>
> *Counselor:* It seems to me that you play his game. You say he gets you in trouble; but you could really defeat him if you didn't go for the bait. Can you imagine how he'd look if you didn't respond?

You suggest doing exactly the opposite and "winning" by failing to cooperate with the teacher. Actually, both student and teacher win.

Adler and Dreikurs taught that to maintain a symptom, one must fight against it. The paradox is often effective because, when the counselee comes for help, the counselor tells him to go back and do what he was doing. By no longer fighting it, the counselee may be free to choose.

Spitting in the Client's Soup

Adler's technique—which he also referred to as "besmirching a clean conscience"—comes from the boarding-school practice of getting someone's food by spitting on it. It is one application of the Adlerian strategy of modifying behavior by changing its meaning to the person who produces it. The counselor must determine the purpose and payoff of the behavior and spoil the game by reducing the behavior's pleasure or usefulness in the counselee's eyes.

> *Alan:* You've said that I don't function unless I can be first or best. I suppose I should give that up.

> *Counselor:* You can continue.
>
> *Alan:* I'm confused.
>
> *Counselor:* All I'm saying is that you always have to be so careful about being first that you don't try a lot of things you'd enjoy. But you are entitled to miss them if you want to protect yourself.

You point out that the individual has a right to insist on being first, but you also clearly show how that approach restricts him. The choice is still with the counselee, but it is now less palatable.

Acting As If

This is an action-oriented procedure used with the counselee who pleads "If only I could . . ."; it consists of suggesting to the client that, for the next week, he should "act as if"—he should behave how he wishes he could behave but doesn't believe he can. The counselee will usually protest that it would only be an act and that, in essence, he would be the same person. This is how Mosak and Dreikurs (1973) suggest you deal with protestations: "We show him that all acting is not phony pretense, that he is being asked to try on a role as one might try on a suit. It doesn't change the person wearing the suit, but sometimes with a handsome suit of clothes, he may feel differently and perhaps behave differently, in which case he becomes a different person" (p. 60).

> *Drew:* I just can't get acquainted with girls. If only I could be like Tom and walk up to a group and talk about the game. . . .
>
> *Counselor:* It's difficult for you to talk with girls. For this week, I'd like you to act as if you were Tom and just begin by talking about the game.

You suggest a limited task, such as acting as if Drew had the courage to talk to girls. The expectation is that the plan will work. If it doesn't, you explore what kept it from being a good experience.

Catching Oneself

Through confrontation and interpretation, counselees become aware of their goals. Once they decide to change, the counselor suggests that they learn to "catch themselves" in any behavior they want to change. At first, they will catch themselves too late and recognize that they have again fallen into the trap of seeking attention, trying to prove their power, or whatever. With awareness and practice, clients learn to anticipate the situation—both their self-defeating perceptions and the behavior that ensues. As a result, they can learn to avoid the situation or to change their behavior when they are in a situation that tends to stimulate the behavior in question. This approach requires a sense of humor and the ability to laugh at one's ineffective behavior instead of becoming discouraged about it.

> *Robin:*   I know I shouldn't, but I seem to keep getting trapped into power struggles with Jack.
>
> *Counselor:*   You recognize that he stimulates you to prove you are right.
>
> *Robin:*   Yes, we get into lots of quarrels, mainly over who's right.
>
> *Counselor:*   I suggest that, as you sense a struggle coming, you catch yourself—become aware that you're about to get involved in being right and more powerful—and just withdraw by refusing to get involved in the argument.

Creating Movement

The counseling process reorients clients toward a new perspective by helping them understand the purpose of their behavior. Often this movement occurs by mutual consent and interaction. When it does not, you have alternatives by which you can create movement.

No tactic, strategy, or other counselor intervention can succeed unless the client wishes to succeed. Strategies and tactics that can effectively move the client depend on the quality of the counselor/client relationship. The counselor needs to enlist the cooperation of the client, whatever her resistance to the reorientation process may be. Clients may lose faith in the therapist if they perceive any of the counseling techniques as threatening (Dreikurs, 1967, pp. 25–26). Movement tactics, such as surprise, should be used judiciously. Indiscriminate use of movement tactics—that is, a use that fails to consider the appropriateness of the tactic to each setting—will result in failure.

When you surprise a client, the client is hearing and seeing unexpected counselor behaviors. The purpose of surprise is to create movement by drawing dramatic attention to a specific behavior of the counselee.

One form of surprise allows you to agree, for the moment, with the client's faulty belief.

> *Claudia:*   Whenever I go out with boys, they always criticize me. I'll never date again!
>
> *Counselor:*   Yes, I agree. Don't ever date critical men again. They can't possibly have anything valid to say.

You have adopted the client's point of view, advocating her despairing remark about dating. Since the client has dealt with the issue in absolute terms ("never"), you reflect her certainty ("Don't date critical men again"). By temporarily agreeing with the faulty belief, you have focused on the belief and diplomatically pointed to the problems inherent in that belief.

Avoiding the Tar Baby

Allen (1971a) says this procedure is based on the recognition that, no matter how self-defeating a person's perceptions and methods of operation may be, they still remain in that person's eyes his most effective method. Hence, he defends them. The counselee's faulty assumptions and mistaken goals may be ineffective, but they make sense in terms of the counselee's biased perception and may yield some kind of payoff.

Thus, the counselee may attempt to fit you and everybody else into his perception of life. It is important for you to elude the traps and avoid confirming the counselee's anticipations. For example, some counselees may try to provoke you so as to substantiate their assumption that they are unlovable. If you fall in their trap, they can point out that even those whose job it is to like all kinds of people dislike them. Other counselees may try to discourage you to show that nobody can help them. Still others may try to trap you into making a decision for them, carry out the decision poorly, and then blame you.

As a counselor, you will attend to and encourage only those behaviors that help the counselee to mature psychologically and develop greater social interest. You will avoid power struggles, feeling hurt, or expressing discouragement about your attempts to help the counselee. This technique essentially requires altering the meaning of the behavior to the counselee. To do this, you respond in ways contrary to her expectations and perceptions, thus forcing her to give them up (Allen, 1971a).

> *Terry:* I can never establish a friendship in a short time. They reject me. Even *you* are angry that I'm not making as much progress as I should.
>
> *Counselor:* You would like to have me feel discouraged, but I'm not. Tell me how things are going.

You refuse to be trapped into defending yourself and, instead, redirect the counselee to look at the positive.

Task Setting and Commitment

Task setting and commitment are the steps counselees take to do something specific about their problems. Thus, these steps take counselees beyond simply considering alternatives and lead them to actual implementation of change. To be effective, the task should be specific and chosen by the client. You can, however, assist the counselee by creating awareness of the various alternatives.

It is essential that the task be for a limited period of time. Counselees are more resistant if they think they are signing up for life. When the counselee is successful at a specific task and within a limited period of time, you have something concrete to encourage.

The step of setting tasks and developing specific commitments helps the counselee translate new beliefs and feelings into action, generates energy for the process, and provides feedback for evaluating progress. When the task is not accomplished, you help the counselee evaluate the effectiveness of the plan. If the plan is not effective or appropriate, you revise it.

Terry:	I'm still having trouble making friends. People are so different here. I just can't get started. The popular kids all ignore me.
Counselor:	You're having trouble getting to know the popular kids. Whom would you like to know better?
Terry:	Well, I guess Jack. But I know he's too popular and too busy.
Counselor:	You recognize that your goals may be too ambitious. Who is someone else you feel you'd have a better chance to become friends with?
Terry:	Bill is somebody I'd like to know better, and he's not impossible. He's even talked to me.
Counselor:	What could you do this week to get to know Bill better?
Terry:	I'm not sure. That's the problem.
Counselor:	What's something he likes to do that you could do with him?
Terry:	He likes to play ball, and we could do that at my house or at the park.
Counselor:	You've decided to try to play ball together. When do you plan to ask him? What day or days are you hoping to play ball with him?
Terry:	I'll see him sometime, and we'll figure it out.
Counselor:	I think you'll accomplish more if you are specific. I would like you to set a day, even a time, to talk with Bill. Have in mind some days when you could play ball together.
Terry:	I'm not too sure, but I'll see him Friday morning, and I'll ask him about playing ball Saturday morning or Sunday afternoon.

As we said earlier, task setting involves helping the client establish a specific task—in this case, choosing a playmate. The goals of the tasks should be realistic, attainable, and measurable, so that, at the next meeting, progress can be discussed in terms of specifics.

Terminating and Summarizing the Interview

Effectively closing an interview is often a problem for the inexperienced counselor. You should have some idea of the minimum and maximum time the interview should last. Generally, 30 minutes with children and 45 to 50 minutes with adolescents and adults are sufficient counseling periods. Counselees should know when the interview begins and when it will be over. It is important to establish these limits not only for practical purposes (such as being available for the next client) but also because counselees often postpone talking about their major concerns as long as possible. If they are aware of time limitations, counselees will tend to get to the important issues more readily.

Termination deals with what has been discussed, not with new material. If the counselee brings up a new topic, you can suggest "That might be a good place to begin next week." Asking the counselee to summarize the interview helps you have a clear picture of the counselee's perceptions and intentions.

Counselor: Our time is up. I'm wondering what you got out of our session. If you could summarize it, I believe it would help both of us.

Robin: I recognize I do some things that bug the teacher, and I think I'll ask Marcia to help me with the homework.

In this chapter we have considered the basic elements of the helping relationship and the perceptual organization of effective helpers. Goals of counseling, a theory of change, and a number of counseling techniques have been described. The techniques must become a part of the counselor, not merely a professional procedure. They require a sensitive, empathic listener who uses active methods because he cares and because they are more likely to produce movement and change on the part of the counselee.

REFERENCES

Adler, A. (1958). *The practice and theory of individual psychology.* Patterson, NJ: Littlefield, Adams.

Allen, T. W. (1971a). Adlerian interview strategies for behavior change. *The Counseling Psychologist, 3*(1), 40–48.

Allen, T. W. (1971b). The individual psychology of Alfred Adler: An item of history and a promise of a revolution. *The Counseling Psychologist, 3*(1), 3–24.

Carkhuff, R. R. (1972). *The art of helping.* Amherst, MA: Human Resource Development Press.

Carkhuff, R. R. (1973). *The art of problem solving.* Amherst, MA: Human Resource Development Press.

Davis, J. B., Jr. (1979). Reliability and validity issues of Adlerian life style analysis. (Doctoral dissertation, Georgia State University, 1978). Dissertation Abstracts International, 39, 5060B.

Dinkmeyer, D. (1972). Use of the encouragement process in Adlerian counseling. *Personnel and Guidance Journal, 51*(3), 177–181.

Dreikurs, R. (1967). A psychological interview in medicine. *Journal of Individual Psychology, 10,* 99–122.

Dreikurs, R. (1957). *Psychology in the classroom.* New York: Harper & Row.

Dreikurs, R. (1967). *Psychodynamics, psychotherapy, and counseling.* Dubuque, IA: Kendall/Hunt.

Eckstein, D., Baruth, L., & Mahrer, D. (1975). *Life style: What it is and how to do it.* Chicago: Alfred Adler Institute.

Ellis, A. (1962). *Reason and emotion in psychotherapy.* New York: Lyle Stuart.

Gushurst, R. S. (1970). *The interpretation of early recollections.* Unpublished doctoral proposal, University of Chicago.

Gushurst, R. S. (1971a). *The reliability and concurrent validity of an idiographic approach to the interpretation of early recollections.* Unpublished doctoral dissertation, University of Chicago.

Gushurst, R. S. (1971b). The technique, utility, and validity of life style analysis. *The Counseling Psychologist, 3*(1), 30–40.

Kaiser, L. L. (1978). A study of the Adlerian life style in relation to psychiatric diagnosis. (Doctoral dissertation, Georgia State University.)

Kefir, N., & Corsini, R. J. (1974). Dispositional sets: A contribution to typology. *Journal of Individual Psychology, 30,* 163–178.

Kefir, N. (1972). *Priorities.* Unpublished manuscript.

Kern, R. M. (1982). Lifestyle scale. Coral Springs, FL: CMTI Press.

Kopp, R., & Dinkmeyer, D. (1975). Early recollections in life style assessment and counseling. *The School Counselor, 23*(1), 22–27.

Langenfeld, S., & Main, F. (1983). Personality priorities: A factor analytic study. *Journal of Individual Psychology, 39,* 40–51.

Mosak, H. H. (1958). Early recollections as a projective technique. *Journal of Projective Techniques, 22,* 302–311.

Mosak, H. H. (1971). Life style. In A. G. Nikelly (Ed.), *Techniques for behavior change.* Springfield, IL: Charles C Thomas.

Mosak, H. H., & Dreikurs, R. (1973). Adlerian psychotherapy. In R. Corsini (Ed.), *Current psychotherapies*. Itasca, IL: Peacock.

Mosak. H. H., & Gushurst, R. S. (1977). What patients say and what they mean. In H. H. Mosak (Ed.), *On purpose*. Chicago: Alfred Adler Institute.

Mullis, F. (1984). (Doctoral dissertation, Georgia State University.)

New directions in training. *The Counseling Psychologist* (Part 1). *3*(3), whole issue.

Nikelly, A. G., & Bostrom, J. A. (1971). Psychotherapy as reorientation and readjustment. In A. G. Nikelly (Ed.), *Techniques for behavior change*. Springfield, IL: Charles C Thomas.

Nikelly, A. G., & Verger, D. (1971). Early recollections. In A. G. Nikelly (Ed.), *Techniques for behavior change*. Springfield, IL: Charles C Thomas.

Satir, V. (1972). *Peoplemaking*. Palo Alto, CA: Science & Behavior Books.

Shulman, B. H. (1962). The family constellation in personality diagnosis. *Journal of Individual Psychology, 18*, 35–47.

Shulman, B. H. Psychological disturbances which interfere with the patient's cooperation. *Psychosomatics, 5*, 213–220.

Shulman, B. H. (1973). Confrontation techniques in Adlerian psychotherapy. In B. H. Shulman (Ed.), *Contributions to Individual Psychology*. Chicago: Alfred Adler Institute.

Sweeney, T. J. (1975). *Adlerian counseling*. Boston: Houghton Mifflin.

Watkins, C. E., Jr. (1985). Early recollections as a projective technique in counseling: An Adlerian view. *American Mental Health Counselors Association Journal, 7*, 32–40.

Wheeler, M. S. (1980). Factor analysis of an instrument developed to measure Adlerian life styles (Doctoral dissertation, Georgia State University, 1979). Dissertation Abstracts International, 40, 5032B.

Wheeler, M. S., Kern, R., & Curlette, W. (1986). Factor analytic scales designed to measure Adlerian life style themes. *Journal of Individual Psychology, 42*, 1–16.

7 Counseling Children and Adolescents

T he approach to counseling children and the approach to counseling adolescents differ enough to warrant treating them separately. With young children, most of the counseling is with the parents, teachers, or parent surrogates. As children become more verbal, they can be counseled individually and in groups. Adolescents (13 years of age and older) present unique challenges to the counselor or therapist. These challenges involve decisions about emphasis in therapy—whether to strive toward stimulating more autonomy or whether to work at helping the young person function within the system (school or family). Naturally, it will never be an either/or decision. The purpose of adolescent counseling usually involves increasing self-esteem and social interest.

Formal use of the life-style assessment is another element that differentiates child and adolescent counseling. In most instances, the use of Dreikurs's four mistaken goals and the knowledge of the child's family constellation make formal life-style assessment unnecessary. "Maturing," however, involves increasing self-deception and sophistication in hiding one's goals and motivations from oneself and others. Mistaken behavior on the part of young children is for the most part directed toward adults, since young children seek belonging through their relationships with adults. Youths, however, become more and more concerned with pleasing and belonging with peers and less and less concerned with pleasing adults. Peer pressure, the desire for excitement and experimentation, and the profound physical and psychological changes that are taking place are some of the elements that make counseling adolescents qualitatively different from counseling children.

COUNSELING VERY YOUNG CHILDREN

Many Adlerians believe that even preverbal toddlers can understand rather sophisticated psychological interpretations. To substantiate this view, its proponents point to the fact that, when the recognition reflex is elicited in a demonstration setting, toddlers clearly show that they understand the counselor's recommendations to their parents. These children realize the behavior in question is no longer going to "work," and they change, often rather strikingly, their way of acting. The following case, not unusual in family-education centers,* clearly illustrates the situation.

---

*Family-education centers (discussed in detail in Chapter 12) are community resources in which children, adolescents, parents, teachers, and other interested adults can learn more cooperative ways of living together in harmony, whether in the home or in the classroom. Counseling is done in public, in front of an audience. Mental-health principles are taught to the audience by interviewing volunteer families who have in the past been themselves a part of the audience (International Encyclopedia of Psychiatry, Psychology, Psychoanalysis, and Neurology, 1977).

Cynthia, age 19 months, was described by her mother as a destructive terror. She was constantly into everything, emptying drawers, tearing things apart, and creating a ruckus. Her mother was at her wit's end. Having been one of the eldest of a family of 12 children, she had considered herself competent as a parent until she began to deal with Cynthia. The fact that she could elicit no cooperation from her daughter was particularly galling since her profession was that of a labor mediator. She was deeply hurt by Cynthia's behavior and stated that she vigorously disliked her daughter.

The counselor postulated that Cynthia's goal was revenge and asked the mother if she would be willing for one week to go immediately to the bathroom, without any comment, each time Cynthia began tearing the house apart. In her desperation, the mother agreed, but predicted that she would be forced to retire to the bathroom at least ten times a day before Cynthia would believe her mother meant business. But she agreed to keep a chart.

The mother was dismissed from the stage, and Cynthia entered. She was an attractive toddler who didn't say a word during the interview but listened attentively. She had a marked recognition reflex when the goal of revenge was presented. Apparently, she felt that in some way she had been mistreated, so her feelings were hurt and she wanted to get even. The counselor then told her that her mother would go to the bathroom each time she began destroying something and asked her if she thought this arrangement was fair. Cynthia shook her head negatively. Finally, when the counselor asked Cynthia if she believed that her mother would actually carry through such a recommendation, the child looked pensive.

One week later, Cynthia's mother returned to the family-education center and reported that the relationship between herself and her daughter had undergone a dramatic change and that she enjoyed her daughter and was having fun with her for the first time since Cynthia was born. She also reported that on the first day she had retired to the bathroom six times, on the second day twice, and, except for one flurry the night before, she hadn't found it necessary to use the "bathroom treatment" again.

Probably the mother would have been fairly successful even without Cynthia's involvement in the counseling process. It is our impression, however, that Cynthia's new awareness of the goal of her misbehavior, coupled with the knowledge that her mother was going to deal with her differently, contributed significantly to a change that appeared almost miraculous.

In our experience, interviewing very young children is useful primarily for diagnostic purposes. As children become more verbal, they can be drawn into the counseling process itself, their cooperation can be enlisted, and their involvement and participation can be promoted. Furthermore, since Adlerians believe that every misbehaving child is a discouraged child, specific encouragement of the child by the counselor and, in the case of the family-education centers, by members of the audience, is a significant part of the counseling process. In the centers, younger children are often interviewed separately from their parents. Many of them enjoy being in front of the audience, particularly when audience members are asked to give feedback on what they sincerely appreciate about the children who have been interviewed.

We often have to see with our own eyes just how actively very young children influence those around them and, consequently, what an important role they play in the counseling process of other family members.

> Tina, 8 months, was the youngest of five children. The older four had all gone through periods of minor behavioral disturbances, and now the parents returned complaining about Tina. When, at the family-education center, the entire family was interviewed together, it became clear that this 8-month-old was tyrannizing the rest of the family merely by sucking on her lower lip. Throughout the entire session, Tina would periodically suck on her lip, and one of the parents or children would get up, walk across the room, and pull her lip out.

As children get older and more verbal, individual therapy is often the best way to deal with their problems.

> John, age 4, was badly bitten by a neighbor's dog. At the time of his referral, he had become enuretic, asthmatic, plagued with nightmares, and extremely fearful. In other words, he was behaving like a typical adult neurotic. Since litigation was involved, the child was interviewed by his attorney, who asked him to describe the incident. John did so by drawing pictures and writing under them "Bowser bit John," followed by the date. In John's case, although the parents needed help in understanding how to deal with the child, the therapists at the center elected to work directly with John in talking therapy.* John was certainly an exception, since the youngest child with whom talking therapy had been used at the center was 8 years old.

This case demonstrates that when we talk about feelings, beliefs, and purposes, the very young child understands.

---

*Talking therapy means just that—sitting down with the child and talking with him for part of the session, establishing a warm and trusting relationship, and, from time to time, gently challenging the child's mistaken views about himself and the world.

However, some nursery-school, kindergarten, and primary-grade teachers report success in their regular classroom group discussions, in which children are encouraged to discuss classroom affairs as well as their personal feelings and concerns. One of the most exciting therapy groups conducted at a family-education center was a group of 9- to 12-year-olds. Anyone who has seen a movie like Truffaut's *Small Change* or has seriously observed small children at work and play will not find it hard to believe that young children think deeply and are very candid and perceptive in discussing their thoughts and feelings with other children. Unfortunately, most adults are so prejudiced about what young children can and cannot do that they overlook children's capability to participate in the counseling process.

A counselor who works with young children needs to be familiar with the normal developmental process and its many variations. At the same time, the counselor must not misuse "developmental stages" and the like as a means of labeling children and failing to see and respect them as unique individuals. Every infant is born a full-fledged human being, and all infants quickly become actors as well as reactors, learning precisely how to influence adults.

The primary goal of counseling with families is to help the parents become a match for their children. The primary goal of counseling with children is to win their cooperation and help them see that it is to their benefit to operate with, rather than against, their parents. If a child is seen separately from her parents, it is essential that the counselor inform the child as fully as possible of what is discussed with the parents.

Nystulian Play Therapy

Nystul has developed a play therapy that applies Adlerian Psychology (Nystul, 1980).

Nystulian Play Therapy is based on seven assumptions:

1. The counselor attempts to establish a feeling of mutual respect with the child.
2. The counselor believes there are no maladjusted children, only discouraged ones; encouragement is, therefore, the main tool of Nystulian Play Therapy.
3. The counselor allows the child to feel understood by identifying the hidden reasons for her behavior. Children's private logic helps them move toward significance as they perceive it. You need to understand and accept the child from the child's perspective.
4. The counselor modifies the child's motivation for change by redirecting her teleological movement. Children are helped to become aware of the

incongruity of their short-term goals. DUSO identifies how children can solve problems in an active-constructive manner and provides learning experiences to implement practical short-term goals (Dinkmeyer and Dinkmeyer, 1982a, 1982b).

5. A Nystulian Play Therapy session starts with 15 to 30 minutes of the DUSO program and ends with 15 to 30 minutes of Creative Arts Therapy (depending on how much time is available).

6. The counselor uses natural and logical consequences to establish the necessary limits for anchoring therapy to the world of reality. Establishing limits with the child also establishes logical consequences. The limits must be enforced for the child to learn order and responsibility.

7. The counselor recognizes that parents and educators are important adjuncts to Nystulian Play Therapy. The play therapy is always accompanied by consultation with and educational programs for teachers and parents (Dinkmeyer, McKay, Dinkmeyer, 1980; Dinkmeyer and McKay, 1976).

COUNSELING OLDER CHILDREN

What we have said about counseling young children also applies to older children, except that children who are 6 or 7 (or older) can be counseled individually, in peer groups, or in family groups. It is important that counselors treat children of all ages with the utmost respect and courtesy, just as they would treat adult counselees. It is not necessary to change vocabulary or tone of voice, nor is it necessary to "get down to the child's level." Immature people are delightful with their creativity, imagination, intelligence, and spontaneity. Unfortunately, these characteristics are drilled out of most children.

There are not many children who are mentally ill, as we would use the term with adolescents or adults. But children may not be skilled in communicating verbally; activating personality patterns through other media may help them communicate. Dance, music, psychodrama, movement, and art all represent nonverbal channels that many children find quite comfortable.

The DUSO Revised Programs I and II (Dinkmeyer and Dinkmeyer, 1982) are excellent resources for counseling with children. The stories, primarily on cassettes but with text in the manual for those who prefer to read stories, are keyed to specific behavioral goals. They help children learn to develop an understanding of self, of others, and of choices. They provide the stimulus for discussion of issues that challenge the child. The format for discussions of each story includes:

1. Review of the story
2. Discussion of the feelings and behavior of the people in the story
3. Discussion of how the child might feel or act in a similar situation

In the D–2 kit, 42 discussion pictures illustrate experiences typical for students at this level and provide another opportunity to initiate meaningful discussion and exploration of effective ways to solve problems.

The Communication Activities are a unique contribution with considerable potential for child therapists (Dinkmeyer and Dinkmeyer, 1982). Skill development in the Communication Activities focuses on three areas: communication, encouragement, and conflict management. These skills were chosen because they are the basis of social interaction and because they are areas in which people commonly experience difficulty. The activities are interdependent and carefully sequenced; early lessons build the communication skills needed for the more complex conflict management activities. As students proceed through the lessons, they learn to clarify their own feelings and to express these feelings to others.

The child has an opportunity to develop skill in attending, listening to feelings, expression of feelings, empathy, reflective listening, and sending I-messages. There are also sequences of skills in encouragement and conflict resolution. Instead of leaving development of skills to chance, they are presented in an interesting sequence so they can be learned. This approach can make therapy more systematic and effective.

Instant Rapport

Children don't have the experience necessary to be good interpreters; so, although they are astute observers, they often come up with poor and mistaken interpretations. But most children seem able to change their views easily and quickly. It is easy to establish rapport with children almost instantly, as the following example illustrates.

> I am asked to see a 4-year-old for psychiatric evaluation. I go to the waiting room and escort the child to my office. I close the door and sit down. The child remains standing, and I ask him "Are you used to having people tell you what to do?" He may respond either verbally or nonverbally in the affirmative. Using the "goal-disclosure" method described by Dreikurs, I say "Perhaps I can guess why you don't do what people ask you to do." The child will usually give me some encouragement. I then ask him "Could it be that you don't do what you're asked to do so you keep people busy, thus letting them know that you're around?" I seldom get a response to this.

However, I frequently get a response to the presentation of the second goal: "Could it be that you want to show people that you are big and strong and that they can't make you do what they want you to do?" The child may respond with what Dreikurs referred to as the "recognition reflex." Even though he shakes his head negatively, there is a twinkle in his eyes and a roguish smile on his face. He may blush, and he may even attempt to hide his face. When I obtain this type of response, I know I am on the right track. I then assure the child in a variety of ways that he is in fact stronger than me and that I have no intention whatsoever of attempting to overpower him or force him to do things that he doesn't want to do. The most common response at this point is for the child to very neatly sit down, and from that time on we are friends. (Pew, 1969, p. 67)

Sometimes, the children's relief in discovering that an adult understands them is so great that it finds rather touching expression, often after relatively short interviews. For example, the child may shyly offer the therapist a piece of candy, shake her hand, or even give her a hug.

Instant rapport is, of course, easier to obtain with small children. We repeat: rapport necessitates the adult's basic respect for the child. When interview techniques are demonstrated publicly at family-education centers, observers often remark that the counselors don't talk with children any differently than they talk with adults. The reason is simply that children respond quickly to any adult who treats them with respect and doesn't talk down to them. Also, small children respond well to an adult's fair, firm, and friendly attitude and to the early demonstration that their behavior makes sense.

Whenever adults don't know what to do with children, they call them names (lazy, fearful, or aggressive) or use more sophisticated terms such as *minimally brain damaged* or *dyslexic*. Adlerian counselors are not satisfied with dealing with the observed behavior alone; they try to understand the purpose of the child's fear or aggression or incapacity to read. Only if we can understand the goal of the child's mistaken behavior are we able to plan *with* the child what approaches will be helpful to him.

Ideally, the counselor who works with school-age children will try to bring about general agreement among parents, school personnel, and the child concerning the best course of action. Frequently, the parents blame the school, the school blames the parents, and the child goes off scot-free. The counselor must avoid this kind of situation. Since counselors are often misquoted, a meeting of all parties concerned, *including the child*, is most helpful to achieve common purposes and goals. The counselor must recognize that most teachers are well qualified to teach children who want to learn or children who want to behave, but frequently have no idea what to do with children who don't want to learn or don't want to behave. Therefore, the counselor must be willing and able to teach teachers, as well as parents, the basic principles of working and relating with children.

CONFRONTATION IN COUNSELING

Adlerian confrontation is designed to put the challenge or problem directly before the child for the purpose of helping him understand why he behaves as he does. James and Myer have developed these ideas as an extension of the work of Adler, Dreikurs, and Dinkmeyer (James and Myer, 1985).

Some counselors are cautious about using confrontation, believing that it lacks empathy and caring. We believe a counselor who really wants to motivate change must at times challenge a client to make movement. Actually, as James and Myer indicate, avoidance of challenging techniques may indicate a counselor's lack of therapeutic involvement with the client.

Confrontation is obviously not an opening technique, but is based on development of rapport and caring. The purpose of confrontation is to create insight and movement. It often stimulates emotions that might not come to the surface under other situations. After confrontation, other techniques can help the child understand his feelings; for example, "When I challenged you, you looked as if you felt very hurt. Tell me more about that." James and Myer (1985) say: "Our notion is that confrontation breaks an impasse and at most gets a train of thought, emotion, and behavior of the child moving again. At the least, it hopes to bring varied, crystallized, and encysted feelings out in the open so that they can be fully explored."

Areas of confrontation include:

Confronting subjective views. The child is confronted with the private logic or hidden reason that to her makes the behavior acceptable. This type of confrontation makes the child aware of what she is doing at the moment.

Confronting mistaken beliefs and attitudes. The child is confronted with mistaken beliefs and attitudes that work against positive, social development. The focus is on basic convictions about one's nature, the world in which one lives, and the nature of life and its meaning. These basic convictions fill the blanks developed by Shulman: I am _____, life is _____, therefore _____ (Shulman, 1973).

Confronting private goals. This confrontation may be used when the child attempts to deny feelings the counselor believes are hidden.

Confronting statements may actually produce the "recognition reflex," a nonverbal indicator such as a sudden shift in body position or of the eyes and facial muscles.

Confronting destructive behavior. The client may become self-destructive by avoiding an issue passively or aggressively or by acting out and becoming aggressive toward the counselor. In this situation the counselor confronts the child with her behavior at that moment in the therapeutic relationship. This type of confrontation brings the client to an awareness of the here and now and how her behavior affects others.

ADLERIAN TECHNIQUES THAT CAN BE ADAPTED TO CHILDREN

Paradoxical Intention

Paradoxical intention involves having the child become aware of and even actually attempt to increase his own self-defeating behavior. The child is asked to practice, emphasize, enlarge, and develop the symptoms to a ridiculous degree. As the child becomes aware of the unproductiveness of the symptom, he usually gives up or changes the behavior.

In using paradoxical intention with children, you must be certain you are not in a situation of power or personal revenge with them. If so, they will work against you. Instead, the paradoxical intention can be treated as an experiment. Whatever it is that they are doing, have them do it in the extreme; for example, if the child is biting her fingernails, ask her to bite all her fingernails even more thoroughly. If she is trying to prove that she is independent, ask her to work without cooperating with anyone.

Creating Images

To work with imagery, suggest that the child mentally picture a threatening social situation. A fearful child might imagine a protective wall around him, then he could learn to imagine the scene in a less threatening way.

Acting As If

"Acting as if" is used when the child believes a situation is controlling his actions. Generally the child uses the ploy, "if only I could" to relieve himself of responsibility for the situation. By trying out a different role, the child often finds that he cannot only act a part, but can become a different person in the process.

Confrontation is a powerful, motivational tool for the counselor, but it cannot be used effectively unless a degree of trust has been developed in the counseling relationship. After trust develops, the child can be confronted effectively about passive or destructive behavior.

COUNSELING ADOLESCENTS

Adolescence is a recent invention, a product of Western, consumer-oriented, industrialized society. Adolescence as we talk about it is not recognized in many cultures. In some families and some communities, adolescence is now so prolonged that the term can include people up to age 25 (the age when some males finally complete their growth). This creates a rather peculiar situation since many young people mature earlier, at least physically and physiologically—puberty occurs earlier and full adult size is achieved earlier. Furthermore, today's adolescents are generally taller and heavier than their counterparts of even ten years ago.

The phenomenon of earlier physical development does seem to be leveling off, but the counselor must be aware of it, nevertheless. If for girls puberty is defined as the onset of menstruation, some girls reach puberty as early as 10 years of age, when they are in fourth or fifth grade. On the other hand, it is normal for some girls to begin menstruating as late as age 15 or 16. Although the onset of puberty in boys cannot be as clearly defined, there is still a wide range of what is considered normal. For example, a young man recently reported to a counselor that he did not develop secondary sex characteristics until he was 18 years old. These normal variations in physical development make generalizations about young people at a particular chronological age virtually impossible, thus complicating the task of counseling.

Another factor that contributes to the difficulty of counseling adolescents is the variety of views everyone has of the young person, including parents, teachers, peers, and the community at large. With the exception of some rural towns, it is difficult for an adolescent to find useful ways to contribute to the community. Many adolescents react by neglecting some of the standard role expectations and by emphasizing the social aspects of their development, particularly as far as peers are concerned. This behavior leads many parents and teachers to see adolescents almost as members of a different culture. The tendency of young people to adopt fads in clothing, language, music, dance, and so forth contributes to the adolescents' isolation from the general community. It is interesting, however, that many adolescent fads are later taken up by young and not so young adults. In a social sense, adolescents are thus often cultural pioneers.

Overcoming loneliness and achieving intimacy are major concerns for most adolescents, as is the more general goal of achieving belonging in the human community. Since useful avenues are frequently blocked, there is a strong tendency for adolescents to find belonging in ways that many adults find objectionable. Today, adolescence is characterized by an ever-increasing disregard for adults' opinions and an ever-increasing concern for the recognition and acceptance of peers. Since many adolescents view themselves as outside the mainstream of social and cultural expectations, it is not surprising that they tend to band together with other similarly isolated youths, seemingly at war with adult authority as represented by parents and school.

It is often difficult, however, to decide which generation we are dealing with. For example, by age 16, some adolescents are buying into the values of the adult society and, within a year or so, clearly see themselves as members of a different generation with regard to those who are two or three years younger. Adolescence is a period of examination of values, and young people find much to be skeptical of in society's values. But despite their apparent isolation from the adult community, the vast majority of adolescents really want to know what adults think, particularly the adults close to them and especially parents. This tremendously important fact, established by several national studies, is often overlooked by the adults.

Counselors always face a difficult dilemma. Should they put their efforts into helping adolescents accept what is frequently a faulty system? Or should they concentrate, instead, on helping adolescents develop a constructively critical attitude that, if coupled with a sense of responsibility and leadership, can bring about much needed change in the system? Unfortunately, many imaginative adolescents are considered trouble-makers by both the school and society, with the result that we lose the contributions these young people could make.

All the psychopathological conditions described in Chapter 4 are found in adolescents; however, the adolescent's ability to change rapidly often astounds the therapist. Psychiatric disturbances that in adults often necessitate relatively long-term therapy can change in adolescents within three or four counseling sessions. On the other hand, although nowhere is an attitude of optimism more important, the counselor must be aware of the frequency and depth of depression in many adolescents and the serious potentiality for suicide. For the most troubled or troublesome adolescents, a trusting relationship with one adult can literally mean the difference between life and death.

Life Tasks

In working with adolescents, either individually or in groups, it is helpful to keep in mind the life-task areas of work, friendship, love, getting along with oneself, search for meaning, and leisure and recreation. As we indicated in Chapter 3, each of these areas may be an important source of information for the counselor. A simple self-rating process is useful in understanding how adolescents view themselves. The self-rating can be expanded to take into consideration how the adolescents predict their parents will rate them and then, if the parents are involved in the counseling process, to see how parents do in fact rate their son or daughter (Pew, 1974). If extensive therapy or counseling is anticipated, a personal life-style assessment is indicated.

After rapport and a mutually respectful relationship are established, many adolescents can be helped by a systematic interview guide, Motivating Yourself and Others (Dinkmeyer and Dinkmeyer, 1983). This interview is accompanied by a cassette tape from CMTI. The interview can take place with the counselor, or the client can work with the cassette and bring the completed form to the session. The form is shown in Figure 7-1.

The interview helps the adolescent identify goals and strengths. The focus is on identifying "How Purposeful is Your Life" through specific questions and a rating scale. A series of incomplete sentences also examines motivating factors in the adolescent's life. There is an opportunity to identify the priorities that direct behavior.

Symptom Bearers

Many of the adolescents we see in counseling have in some way been elected "symptom bearers" for their family. What we mean by "symptom bearers" is illustrated by this case:

> Eleanor, age 15, a very talented musician, superb athlete, and good student, kept running away from home. She told the counselor that she would even take heroin to get herself into a drug-treatment center, so that she wouldn't have to be at home with her family. Her parents, ostensibly solid citizens, turned out to have a very unfulfilling marriage. The father dealt with the marital conflict by getting drunk. But when his daughter saw him intoxicated, her mother denied the obvious by simply stating "Father doesn't drink." The father also seemed unusually interested in seeing his daughter nude or partially clothed, although he never made overt sexual overtures. The more Eleanor ran away, the more controlling her father became, insisting that she must stay within the family to "help get the family together."
>
> As the family dynamics became clear, the counselor realized that Eleanor was the best adjusted member of her family—the one who could see clearly what was going on—yet she didn't know what to do about it. Once an informal foster-home placement was arranged, Eleanor made great personal strides, while the rest of the family required extensive therapy.

Eleanor was one of the lucky ones. Many young people deal with this kind of situation by engaging in drug abuse, juvenile delinquency, sexual misbehavior, academic failure, or even by attempting suicide.

Drug Use

Adolescence is a time for experimentation, and many youths become involved, to a lesser or greater extent, with consciousness-altering drugs. In counseling, we see three groups of these young people: (1) those who are merely experimenting, looking for kicks and peer approval; (2) those who are looking for a new personality; and (3) those whose discouragement is so profound that they are seeking oblivion. The drug scene is constantly changing and may be decidedly different from one school district to another. In the same community, students in one high school may use primarily marijuana, alcohol, and tobacco. Only a few miles away, students at another high school may be experimenting with all kinds of legal and illegal chemicals.

Although there is evidence that marijuana in itself is hazardous, one must question why a young person—or an older person, for that matter—would choose to get "high" several times a week, just as one would question why a person would choose to get drunk several times a week. What is missing in that person's life? What is she trying to avoid? Also, we have noticed that, when young people who have reported smoking several marijuana cigarettes every day stop using the drug, their behavior shows profound changes. While using marijuana, these youths fail to function effectively in any of the life-task areas. When they stop using the drug, they often make great academic progress, become gainfully employed, and find a place in their family, with their friends, and in their community.

The use of chemicals is so widespread among adolescents that any counseling should include exploration of this area. Counseling with anyone who is under the influence of any addictive substance is not likely to be very effective. Some youngsters are so heavily into drugs of one kind or another that only a residential-treatment approach is effective. We are seeing alcoholism even in grade schoolers, and alcoholism has certainly become a significant problem among adolescents. The use of tobacco is a major health hazard, which doesn't seem to be influenced by adult efforts to control it, partly, of course, because many adults exhibit in their own behavior that they are either unaware of or do not accept the facts concerning the dangers of tobacco use.

The major hazard posed by street chemicals is that most young people don't know what they are buying. Drugs may contain toxic additives or dangerous impurities. Young people may also take drugs in dangerous

Motivating Yourself and Others

Worksheet

Don Dinkmeyer, Sr., Ph.D.
James S. Dinkmeyer, M.A.

Directions: This worksheet is used with the "Motivating Yourself and Others" audiocassette. Listen to the audiocassette while completing the activities on this worksheet.

TYPICAL WAKING HOURS SCHEDULE

Directions: Keep a log of your current schedule and explore possible additions, deletions, and modifications.

Current Schedule	Goal Possibilities
6:00-7:00 a.m.	
7:00-8:00 a.m.	
8:00-9:00 a.m.	
9:00-11:00 a.m.	
10:00-11:00 a.m.	
11:00-12:00 a.m.	
12:00-1:00 p.m.	
1:00-2:00 p.m.	
2:00-3:00 p.m.	
3:00-4:00 p.m.	
4:00-5:00 p.m.	
5:00-6:00 p.m.	
6:00-7:00 p.m.	
7:00-8:00 p.m.	
8:00-9:00 p.m.	
9:00-10:00 p.m.	
10:00-11:00 p.m.	
11:00 p.m.-12:00 a.m.	

NOTES:

LIST #1
LIFELONG GOALS, AMBITIONS, AND INTERESTS

LIST #2
STRONG POINTS OF PERSONALITY AND CIRCUMSTANCE

LIST #3
WEAK POINTS OF PERSONALITY, BAD LUCK, AND FAILURES

LIST #4
SPECIFIC PROBLEMS AT THE ROOT OF YOUR CONFLICT

LIST #5
FUTURE GOALS

LIST #6
FUTURE PLANS

Immediate   Long-Range

FIGURE 7-1
Form for Motivating Yourself and Others

HOW PURPOSEFUL IS YOUR LIFE?

Directions: Take a moment to evaluate yourself on the following statements. For each statement, circle the number which represents how you usually feel.

Rate yourself from 1 to 7, with 4 being a neutral or middle rating. Use the 4 ratings as little as possible. You can comment on each statement in the space beneath each sentence.

1. In life I have...

1	2	3	4	5	6	7
no goals						very clear goals

2. My life is...

1	2	3	4	5	6	7
meaningless						purposeful and meaningful

3. If I could choose I would...

1	2	3	4	5	6	7
prefer to have been born into a totally different situation						would live my life over exactly the same way

4. In reaching my goals...

1	2	3	4	5	6	7
I have made no progress						I have succeeded completely

5. In thinking about life...

1	2	3	4	5	6	7
I often wonder why I am alive						Always see a reason for my being here

6. Concerning my freedom to make choices, I am...

1	2	3	4	5	6	7
as free as possible						completely bound by what others make me do

7. My ability to find a meaning and purpose in life is...

1	2	3	4	5	6	7
very great						very weak

8. My life is...

1	2	3	4	5	6	7
in my hands I am in control						out of my control

INCOMPLETE SENTENCES

Directions: Complete the following sentences to give you some awareness about your motives.

1. I am happiest when...

2. When I am under pressure, I...

3. Nothing makes me more furious than...

4. The main driving force in my life is...

5. I get discouraged when...

6. If I had my way...

7. What I like most about myself...

8. The best measure of personal success is...

9. I will do anything to...

10. Strength for me is...

11. My strongest feature is...

12. My claim to fame is...

YOUR NUMBER ONE PRIORITY

Each number one priority has a price that one pays to achieve that priority.

Priority in Belonging	Comfort	Pleasing	Control	Superiority
Strives to Avoid	Stress	Rejection	Humiliation	Meaninglessness
Price One May Pay	Reduced Productivity	Reduced Growth	Reduced Creativity Spontaneity Social Distance	Over-Burdened Over-Responsible

Additional copies of this worksheet and the audiocassette "Understanding Yourself and Others" can be obtained from CMTI Press. For a current brochure or to place an order, please write or call: CMTI Press ● Box 8268 ● Coral Springs, FL 33075 ● (305) 752-0793

FIGURE 7–1
Continued

149

combinations; the combination of downers and alcohol, for example, can be fatal. There is no doubt that a massive educational effort is needed in this area, but the bankruptcy of our educational system offers little reason for optimism.

What is the prognosis for adolescents who are deeply involved with drugs? As clinicians, we have seen many young people come through rather extreme and bizarre uses of chemicals and end up as fully constructive and unaffected young adults. We have also seen others—for example, those who have injected amphetamines intraveneously—who have never returned to their prechemical state and have never really recovered. Their history has been one of repeated hospitalizations, institutionalization, and therapy of all sorts.

Delinquency

Delinquency is a major problem among adolescents. A large study several years ago predicted that one of every four adolescent males would appear in juvenile court sometime during the teenage years and that the incidence of delinquency would increase among girls. The problem is compounded by the considerable confusion in the criminal-justice system, which results in many so-called "status offenders" (persons in need of supervision) being introduced to criminality through institutionalization when their only legal offense is being below legal age. The same behavior by an adult would not be characterized as criminal or even delinquent. Fortunately, some communities have begun to develop treatment and counseling programs aimed at keeping the adolescent out of the criminal-justice system. Since much of the delinquency is group related, generally the most effective counseling work is that done in groups. The unfortunate aspect of this need for group counseling is that most of those who are hired to work with delinquent adolescents have no training and background in group leadership or group dynamics.

Sex

Sexual experimentation results in a number of social problems. It has been estimated that, in the immediate future, the vast majority of adolescents will have experienced intercourse by age 17 and that one out of five babies will be born to unwed teenage mothers. In this area, too, there is a profound difference between the values of many adolescents and those of adult society. Our educational system, with few exceptions, does a poor job of dealing with the whole area of human sexuality, particularly as it relates to interpersonal relationships. Since the counselor of an adolescent can be almost certain that the youth will pose some questions or express concerns about sexuality, it is most important that the counselor think through his own values in this area. Although the willingness on the part of many adolescents to talk openly about sexuality is a positive element for the counseling process, such frankness may represent a problem for the counselor who is not prepared to deal with it.

School-Related Problems

Many adolescents express their rebellion against adult society and values by failing to conform to academic expectations. Since this is a complex area, we are reluctant to make sweeping statements. But one thing we can say with confidence: adolescents, like children, are not—for the most part—full-fledged partners in the educational system. Therefore, many of them feel justified in excluding themselves from the process. They fail to see a meaningful relationship between what goes on in school and what they see going on in society at large. In one rural Midwestern community, a hulking farm boy signed up for a class in knitting to express his frustration at the school system's refusal to provide courses in animal husbandry, agriculture, and other areas relevant to him and other future farmers.

The frequent conflict between the demands of the school system and the requirements of the adolescent for healthy growth and development poses a serious problem for the counselor. Unfortunately many school workers have no idea how to deal with troubled or troublesome adolescents. Frequently, a telephone call by the counselor in the presence of the adolescent—and with the youth's permission—to the appropriate person in the school is all that is necessary to win the cooperation of school personnel. In other cases, by the time an adolescent enters counseling, her reputation in school is so damaged that transfer to another system may be necessary.

Harold and John were the oldest in their senior class. They were both star football players as well as successful students. In the middle of the football season, Harold abruptly left the team, vowing he would never play football again. He found himself under a lot of pressure both at home and at school, and, as a reaction, began using alcohol and engaging in violent behavior against fellow students, teachers, and others. He was soon in trouble with the law, but, despite his ever-deteriorating relationship with the school, he was kept on the roll and even urged to participate in graduation exercises. By that time, however, he was in such bad graces with both students and faculty that he recognized he was likely to get in further difficulty by showing up at commencement, so he refused to go. At the same time, John was elected outstanding young man of the year.

In our opinion, Harold never received proper treatment. His case was so complicated that no one at his school was qualified to deal with it. Yet, the school was unwilling to take a strong stand and insist that Harold get appropriate therapy.

Many public schools all too often find themselves in a situation similar to that of Harold's. Some enlightened private schools do exercise the option of refusing to accept a student who, in their opinion, is heading for serious trouble unless certain conditions are met. The school must be assured that proper treatment is available for the student (and his family, if indicated), then, that such treatment is underway, and, finally, that it continues appropriately.

The Adolescent's Parents

The adolescent's parents are often a great source of difficulty for the counselor. The more the adolescent displays autonomy, the more resentful some parents become. And their resentment is frequently directed at the counselor. Counselors must be willing to maintain the strictest confidence with regard to their counselees while, at the same time, walking a tightrope with the parents, who often demand to know what their child is thinking or doing or feeling. When this occurs, family therapy is indicated, unless the adolescent is old enough to decide to work toward personal emancipation from the family. In many communities, parents maintain some legal responsibility and hold onto their adolescent children until they are 18 years of age. Sometimes counseling is primarily a holding action until the adolescent can strike out on her own. At the other end of the spectrum are adolescents who are so close to their families that they reach adulthood without having made a successful separation from their families. In these cases, too, the most hopeful approach is family therapy. Here is an example of one such case:

> George, 17 years old and a high-school junior, had never had a date with a girl, preferring to spend his spare time at home tinkering with gadgets. His mother, a widow, greatly enjoyed George's company. They were good friends and shared many common interests. Mother didn't date or engage in other activities outside the home. Toward the end of his junior year, George began developing symptoms in the form of anxiety attacks with chest pains. Initially seen individually, he was then introduced to group therapy. In both individual and group therapy, he gained a lot of insight, but there was no change in his behavior or reduction in his symptoms.
>
> Only after a number of joint counseling sessions did George and his mother begin to see how important it was that they develop their own lives, independent of each other. In the next several years, although George

continued to live at home, he completed his schooling, became a pilot, and used his interest in gadgetry to make several inventions on the job. His mother, a school teacher, became active in local politics and in various activities in her church. The previously pathological symbiotic relationship between mother and son developed into a cooperative, interdependent relationship that allowed each party to move out and become a person in his or her own right.

We have found it helpful to supplement parent counseling with reading *The Parent's Guide* (Dinkmeyer and McKay, 1983), which is based on Adlerian ideas. Parents are given the book at their first session and told to read specific chapters. In ensuing sessions, there are opportunities to raise questions and apply the ideas to their adolescent.

COUNSELING COLLEGE STUDENTS

Many college students are still adolescents by most definitions. It is estimated that one out of five college students will seek some kind of psychiatric service during the college career. For the most part, college mental-health services are essentially adolescent counseling. To be effective, however, a counselor must know something about the system in which the college student must operate, how decisions are made, who wields the power on the campus, and so forth. High-achieving college students seem particularly susceptible to some sort of breakdown. If they were successful in high school but for the wrong reasons, perhaps to be better than others, on the college campus they often show a dramatic reversal. Students who were the best at being "good" become the best at being "bad," and the reversal may appear as academic failure, sexual misbehavior, crime and delinquency, drug abuse, and all the classical psychiatric syndromes such as psychoses and neuroses. For most college students, group therapy is undoubtedly the treatment of choice; however, individual sessions may be necessary to build trust and allay fears before involving the student in a therapy group.

> Diane was a junior in an excellent liberal-arts college, yet she had never learned to read properly. She had become skillful at gleaning information by talking with other people and was achieving good grades despite having never completely read through an assignment. She had difficulties in her relationships with boys as well as with her elderly parents (she was an only child). Diane came to the psychiatric clinic looking for help in these areas but was so embarrassed about her reading disability that she staunchly refused to consider group therapy. The life-style assessment was

completed, and she was seen approximately ten times individually. During this period, Diane developed a trusting relationship with her therapist, who was also the cotherapist of an ongoing open-ended group. The next quarter, she joined that group and had a positive experience.

Diane's case is unusual in that most young people don't need so many individual sessions before joining a therapy group.

SUMMARY

Adolescence is a period fraught with difficulties. The successful counselor is one who can accept each adolescent as he is at the moment, who is nonjudgmental and flexible, and who can approach counseling with adolescents as a learning experience, for adolescents have much to teach counselors. Since adolescents develop most of their difficulties in group interactions, working out their problems in groups is generally the most effective form of therapy. Many of the problems that adolescents face are related to the way they are treated by society and at home. Therefore, to be effective, the counselor must remain somewhat detached. If she becomes too involved as an advocate for the adolescent against the family, school, or community, the effectiveness of the counseling is likely to be significantly reduced.

REFERENCES

Dinkmeyer, D., McKay, G., & Dinkmeyer, D., Jr. (1980). Systematic training for effective teaching. Circle Pines, MN: American Guidance Service.

Dinkmeyer, D., & McKay, G. (1976). Systematic training for effective parenting. Circle Pines, MN: American Guidance Service.

Dinkmeyer, D., & Dinkmeyer, D., Jr. (1982). Developing understanding of self and others, DUSO-1 Revised, DUSO-2 Revised. Circle Pines, MN: American Guidance Service.

Dinkmeyer, D., & Dinkmeyer, D., Jr. (1982). DUSO 2, Teacher's guide. Circle Pines, MN: American Guidance Service.

Dinkmeyer, D., & McKay, G. (1983). The parent's guide. Circle Pines, MN: American Guidance Service.

Dinkmeyer, D., & Dinkmeyer, J. (1983). Motivating yourself and others. Coral Springs, FL: CMTI Press.

James, D., & Myer, R. (1985). Adlerian confrontational techniques. National Elementary & Middle School Guidance Conference.

Nystul, M. (1980). Play therapy: Applications of Adlerian psychology. *Elementary School Guidance and Counseling* (Oct.).

Pew, W. L. (1969). Instant rapport with children. *Elementary School Guidance and Counseling, 4* (1), 67–68.

Pew, W. L. (1974, April). Taking your own psychological temperature. *Single Parent,* 5–7.

Pew, W. L. (1977). Family Therapy: Adlerian. In *International Encyclopedia of Psychiatry, Psychology, Psychoanalysis, and Neurology.*

Shulman, B. (1973). *Contributions to individual psychology: Selected Papers.* Chicago: Alfred Adler Institute.

8 Counseling and Psychotherapy with the Elderly

$\boxed{N}$ ot much is done for old people in our culture . . . Many persons seem to be changed when they are older, and this is mainly due to the fact that they feel futile and useless. They try to prove their worth and value again in the same way as adolescents do. They interfere and want to show in many ways that they are not old and will not be overlooked, or else they become disappointed and depressed. (Adler, 1956, p.443)

Besides this statement, Adler wrote relatively little about the elderly. Contemporary Adlerians have also written little about aging compared to what has been published on issues of childhood, adolescence, and adulthood. But one should not conclude that Individual Psychology has little relevance to the problems of aging. On the contrary, in his review of nine representative theories of personality and psychotherapy, Brinks (1979, p. 79) concluded that the Adlerian approach was the most comprehensive theory in explaining the biopsychosocial issues of aging. The purpose of this chapter is to identify some of the challenges involved in treating the elderly and to offer several applications of the theory of Individual Psychology to treatment of the elderly.

THE CHALLENGE OF COUNSELING THE ELDERLY

Today, 11 percent of the total U.S. population, more than 20 million people, are over the age of 65. Projections are that this figure will rise to 13 percent in 1990 and to between 17 and 20 percent by 2030. Although it is estimated that 85 percent of these individuals have a chronic medical illness and 20 to 30 percent suffer from a psychiatric disorder, the elderly have a relatively low utilization of health services, particularly, mental health services. Only 1 percent are in private and public psychiatric hospitals, another 2 percent in long-term care facilities, and only 2 to 4 percent receive mental-health outpatient services. The majority of this care is for organic brain disorders like Alzheimer's disease. Reasons for underutilization of services involve both their underavailability and the "gerontophobia" of mental-health providers. It is not simply a financial issue (Larsen et al., 1983, pp. 344–45).

A major challenge for professionals who work with the elderly is their attitudes about the aged. Gerontophobia refers to the professional's pessimistic outlook about achieving therapeutic success with clients over the age of 65. Professionals who believe that only a YAVIS patient—one who is Young, Attractive, Verbal, Intelligent, and Successful—is treatable, will likely be disappointed with the elderly patient. The professional is also likely to expect less progress, assume responsibility for things the individual is indeed capable of, and approach the relationship with an attitude of sympathy rather than empathy. Besides a different, and more realistic, attitude toward the elderly, a somewhat different set of skills is needed to be a geriatric counselor or psychotherapist.

THERAPEUTIC ISSUES UNIQUE TO THE ELDERLY: THE LIFE TASKS

For Adler, the life tasks of work, love, and friendship embraced all human desires and activities. He believed that all human suffering originated from difficulties that complicated the tasks, whereas happiness and a balanced personality resulted from successfully meeting the tasks of life with an attitude of social interest. Meeting the tasks of life is different for the elderly individual than for the child or young adult. Whereas attending school or working at a job or at home are the usual ways of meeting the work task, how does the elderly person contribute to the welfare of others? How does one meet the task of love when one's spouse has died? What about the task of friendship when one is bedridden or wheelchair-bound? Physical decline, loss of sensory function that causes social isolation, chronic degenerative disease, economic deprivation, loss of friends and spouse, and retirement are some of the factors that lead to the widespread inferiority feelings among the elderly. Thus, old age is an especially difficult period of life because factors that engender feelings of inferiority and inadequacy are on the rise while the ability to compensate for these feelings is decreasing.

A basic challenge for the counselor or therapist is to undercut inferiority feelings by helping the elderly person find *different* ways to meet the tasks of life. This means cultivating independent behavior, facilitating mental, emotional, and physical development, and encouraging whatever else develops social interest rather than diminishes it. According to Keller and Hughston (1981), early reports of physical decline and decreased capacity in the elderly have been overstated; recent evidence increasingly suggests that many elderly have the ability to further develop their potential in many physical, mental, and emotional areas. This research indicates that even when declines are noted in certain body systems, accommodation mechanisms usually permit varying degrees of adaptation.

With advancing age the cardiovascular and respiratory systems do show lowered efficiency, but are capable of continued development and exercise endurance. Many of the declines in the auditory, visual, and endocrine systems can be accommodated. Physiological changes occur in the sexual system but in no way preclude sexual functioning. Finally, normal changes in cognitive functioning are decreases in speed and abstract reasoning, whereas memory loss and concentration difficulties are abnormal. Thus, even amidst physical decline, there is potential for development in the physical as well as the emotional realms. Continued development depends on a sense of belonging and self-respect, and on the desire and opportunities for the elderly individual to maintain a sense of independence.

COUNSELING AND CONSULTING WITH THE ELDERLY

The most common mental-health problems of the elderly involve problems of daily living; problems that involve only one life task that do not generalize to the other life tasks. In whatever capacity the professional directly encounters the elderly person—as caseworker, psychologist, nurse, physician, paraprofessional, or administrator—effective counseling intervention is possible. Counseling intervention may take place in a formal one-to-one setting or in a group, but most often it occurs informally, usually in the context of some ongoing daily activity that would not normally be associated with counseling. These counseling interventions usually involve encouragement, information, or goal disclosure. At other times, more specialized techniques may be needed or a specific consultation must be sought.

Throughout this book we have described the counseling process in three phases: relationship, assessment, and reorientation. Some guidelines for each phase will be helpful in counseling and consulting with the elderly.

Relationship

The counselor should attend to these guidelines to establish a good therapeutic relationship with an elderly client:

1. Attitude. The professional's attitude should always be one of respect. You show respect verbally by using the counselee's surname, unless your client invites you to do otherwise, and nonverbally, by your unhurried and interested manner and your empathy for feelings, beliefs, and attitudes.
2. Voice. You should speak slowly and distinctly, and louder if there is any indication of hearing loss.
3. Touch. Whether a handshake, hug, or pat on the shoulder, touch communicates caring and concern. In our culture the usual social distance or

"personal space" is about three feet between people; however, most elderly are comfortable and seem to prefer that others sit or stand much closer than that.

4. Time. Keep interviews short, especially if the client tires easily. Several short sessions are better than one long session.

5. Focus. Be supportive and issue-oriented, especially at the first encounter. Encourage the client to express herself about general issues such as grief, loneliness, helplessness, and guilt.

Assessment

Always assess the individual's behavior in terms of the four goals or levels of unproductive behavior and their styles of coping. When possible, and as time permits, perform a brief life-style assessment. Family constellation material is especially valuable in understanding the client's functioning in group settings.

The Four Goals of Misbehavior (Dreikurs, 1953) are as valuable for assessing and intervening with problems of the elderly as with children. As you recall, Dreikurs describes a method for understanding children's misbehavior in terms of the goals of attention-getting, power, revenge, and inadequacy or psychological disability. Keller and Hughston (1981) describe the four goals, which they term the "four levels of unproductive behavior," and specific intervention strategies tailored to the elderly. Let us apply those goals (described in Chapter 2) to two cases involving the elderly.

Florence J. is a 78-year-old widowed female who regularly stations herself in the vicinity of the reception desk at the senior day-care center. She eagerly engages seniors, visitors, and staff in conversation. Increasingly annoyed but fearing they will hurt her feelings, the clerical staff has refrained from telling her that her interruptions diminish their job performance. In frustration, they asked the center's psychological consultant for help. Concluding that the goal of Mrs. J.'s unproductive behavior is probably attention-getting, the consultant offered four suggestions: first, that everyone consistently ignore Mrs. J.'s distracting talk; second, that everyone vigorously reinforce her positive, socially useful behavior; third, that she should be involved in group activities that will help satisfy her need for belonging and involvement; and finally, that the clerical staff apprise other staff of the plan and the need for consistency in implementing it, particularly regarding the first two points. Over the course of the first week in which the plan was implemented, the staff noted several changes. Mrs. J. spent less time in the reception area and more time participating in the activity groups. At the same time the clerical staff experienced less stress, were more productive, and felt they were more effective in dealing with seniors like Mrs. J.

Arthur S. is a 69-year-old single male who has resided in an intermediate-care nursing home for the past 12 months. During this time he has gradually withdrawn from nearly all activities. In the past three weeks he has taken meals only if they were served in his private room. He has not ventured into the dayroom or hall in the past ten days. The only time he showed any positive reaction to patients or staff was when a female nursing assistant offered him some candy bars on Halloween. The staff has tried repeatedly to engage him in conversation or activity, without success. Neither coercion nor threats seem to work. Eventually, no one asked or expected anything of him, believing it was hopeless to try. No medical condition could account for his behavior. The program's consultant was called in to help the staff evaluate the situation and set up a treatment plan. Since the likely goal of his unproductive behavior was judged to be disability, the consultant did not expect that Mr. S. would readily respond to encouragement and democratically-oriented initiatives that would ordinarily be effective with the other goals. The nursing assistant to whom Mr. S. had been most responsive was trained in behavioral shaping methods and willing to work intensively with Mr. S. The goal was to progressively reinforce Mr. S.'s active and socially useful behaviors, beginning with minimal nonverbal responses to others and moving to verbal responses, to initiating small conversations, to eating one meal per day in the dining area, to all three meals, and then to involvement in other activity programs. After he began responding to the reinforcement program, democratically-oriented strategies were begun. Concurrently, encouragement and support from other staff members and residents were used to further increase his personal and social skills.

Assess the individual's major risk factors in terms of the Life Tasks, particularly loss of spouse, friends, job, status, physical health, and independence. Other risk factors are social isolation (the extent and availability of social support systems such as friends, relatives, church and civic contacts); poverty; sensory deprivation (such as failing hearing and vision that increase the likelihood of misperceiving situations and others' intentions); and fears (particularly about dying, inacessibility to medical care, bank accounts, etc.).

Be aware of the individual's physical condition, and the degree to which the individual is able to be responsible for normal activities of daily living (ADLs). Be familiar with the effects and side effects of medications the person may be taking. The side effects of many drugs prescribed for the elderly noticeably affect mood and cognitive functioning. A number of medications used with the elderly commonly produce depressivelike symptoms, decrease in immediate and short-term memory, and insomnia. Although medical and nursing personnel have primary responsibility for medical matters, all staff need to consider the effects of physical condition and drugs on someone's behavior and feelings.

Reorientation

Be available to the client and the family if you are functioning in the counseling role, or to the staff if you are in the consultant's role. Be reachable by phone. If the counseling or consultation is one-time and informal, make it known that you will be available for formal follow-up if desired.

Always encourage social interest. Help the individual identify the possible ways she might meet the life task in question. Emphasize strengths and the potential for developing them at this stage of life. Help the individual identify those things they can still do for themselves and for others, and encourage them to keep doing them. Challenge them to do things they haven't believed possible or did not want to do, but for which they are physically capable.

Encourage self-esteem. This can be facilitated in many ways, but the technique of reminiscence and life review are particularly valuable with the elderly. The individual is helped to review the events of his life and see it as complete. This review reminds clients that life is a series of crises and struggles as well as accomplishments, and that they have persevered and triumphed. Helping the elderly individual frame his past in this way can motivate him to try or to persevere in coping with the demands of the present.

Encouragement is unquestionably the most important technique with the elderly. Encouragement is the primary antidote to inferiority feelings. Sharing courage and the belief that one is important and worthwhile empowers the elderly individual in the quest to reconsider and relinquish feelings of inferiority in favor of feelings and behaviors more consistent with social interest.

Involve the family as fully as possible. It is usually necessary to teach family members appropriate skills for dealing with their elderly relative as well as for their own coping. With few exceptions, the family needs help adjusting its expectations for the elderly member's functioning. Family expectations are often unrealistically low, so that their efforts to help actually result in decreasing adaptation and relinquishing responsibility and thus independence in the elderly relative. Standard counseling techniques help the family deal with the anger, frustration, and resentment that are related to caring for the elderly.

Develop a good working knowledge of available community resources and policies, especially legal and financial, involving the elderly.

Specific Techniques

Reminiscence Exercises

The reminiscence technique involves calling to mind experiences or facts from the past to reconstruct and add meaning to the past and thus to the present. This exercise can be done individually, but is particularly valuable as a structured group activity. The technique usually involves minimal written responses to stimulus items, such as "How old were you when you first saw a TV? When you first had a radio? What is the name of the first person you dated?" followed by group discussion. These exercises have been shown to stimulate cognitive processes, reduce depressive moods, stimulate common bonds, experiences, and beliefs among group members, and stimulate interest in activities. Keller and Hughston (1981) provide excellent materials for reminiscence exercises.

Contracting

Behavioral contracts are particularly suitable for dealing with the goals of power and revenge in the elderly. Contracts can promote desirable behavior while extinguishing undesirable patterns. The consequences for the desirable behavior are defined, clearly specified, and agreed upon by both counselor and the elderly client. It is extremely important to specify the particular undesirable behavior as well as the expected desirable behavior. It is too vague to say, "She is uncooperative; she should work at cooperating with others." Rather, "refuses to carry out morning household duties," "is discourteous to other nursing home residents," and "makes critical remarks to group members" are specific examples of undesirable behavior. Subsequent desirable behaviors might be: "will remove all dirty dishes from the breakfast table seven days a week," or "will make at least three encouraging remarks a day to other residents for the next five days."

Group Assembly

This group method is a variation of Dreikurs's Family Council concept for use in nursing homes and other long-term care facilities for the elderly. The assembly involves residents on a particular unit or wing of a facility who meet regularly to foster personal independence and social interest within a democratic environment. The assembly makes a number of assumptions: all residents must be treated equally and must practice mutual respect; nursing home policy directly relating to patient care is the business of all residents; and problems in the unit can best be worked out when all residents work on them. If at all possible, the assembly is chaired by a resident who keeps order and allows everyone an opportunity to speak. The staff may need to organize the first meetings, but experience shows that residents are able to take responsibility for the assembly to the extent that staff members refrain from active involvement. According to Keller and Hughston (1981), the group assembly can revitalize the depressing atmosphere of most dependence-oriented nursing homes.

Couples Conference

Like the group assembly, the couples conference can structure self-respect and dignity for spouses who live in their own homes. Keller and Hughston (1981) find that the conference provides a support structure that ensures that each elderly spouse has equal access to the marriage rule-making and goal-setting processes. The counselor helps both spouses develop skills such as active listening, "I" messages, and conflict resolution so that the couple can meet weekly, and on their own, discuss mutual concerns in their relationship. (*Time for a Better Marriage* [Dinkmeyer and Carlson, 1984] further describes the couples conference.)

GERIATRIC PSYCHOTHERAPY

If counseling primarily addresses problems in living that involve only one life task, psychotherapy addresses more global dysfunction. Research indicates that the most prevalent mental health problems of the elderly are related to organic brain syndromes (OBS), particularly dementias such as Alzheimer's Disease, alcoholism, major depression, anxiety states, hypochondriasis, and paranoid disorders (Larsen et al., 1983, p. 351). Many of these dysfunctions involve organic factors. It should not be surprising that many traditionally trained psychotherapists feel uncomfortable or unprepared for treating the elderly. Until recently, if any form of psychotherapy was available to the elderly, it was primarily individual therapy, and it was seldom available to the individual with chronic, progressive OBS. Many still believe that chronic OBS is an absolute contraindication for psychotherapy. Adlerian-oriented therapists like Brinks (1979, p. 148), however, have found that a combination of individual and group psychotherapy can actually slow the progression of chronic OBS.

Dr. Lillian J. Martin, a pioneer in geriatric psychotherapy, developed the "Martin Method" in the 1930s. Her approach was rather brief (about five sessions), problem-focused, and centered around a comprehensive assessment of the individual's life pattern. The therapist's role was to emphasize the individual's strengths and encourage and inspire them. Positive affirmations were used as a form of thought stopping and self-control, and homework assignments involving daily activities and future goals were expected (Karpf, 1982). Martin's approach appears to have been very Adlerian; needless to say, it was largely ignored by doctors and psychologists in favor of psychoanalytically-oriented approaches.

In the past decade, group, family, and behavioral approaches have appeared as stepchildren of individual approaches. A strong case can be made for therapeutic approaches that are problem-centered rather than primarily insight- or feeling-centered. Brinks (1979, pp. 149–50) believes the mechanism for therapeutic efficacy lies in training the patient to think and act nonpathologically. He has found that the primary reason for the success of geriatric psychotherapy is that a long life constitutes valuable experience in effective coping, and that brief, problem-centered therapy provides the additional training one needs to cope with the problems of aging.

Brief, problem-focused psychotherapy can be provided in individual, group, family, and milieu contexts.

Individual and Group Therapy

The guidelines for individual counseling apply for psychotherapy, except that a formal but brief life-style assessment and life review are usually done. Most geriatric psychotherapy occurs in an outpatient setting rather than in long-term care, inpatient settings. The reorientation phase may extend for five or more sessions and often involves concurrent family and/or group sessions. The focus is usually problem-oriented, with insight as a secondary goal. This case illustrates features of both individual and group therapy:

> Jeanine G. is a 69-year-old who was recently widowed after 48 years of marriage. She has been living alone and for the past 4 months has become progressively depressed. She noted feelings of depression and rejection and avoidance of her regular friends. Spontaneous crying, weight and appetite loss, and early morning awakening began around the first anniversary of

her husband's death. Her family physician believed she was suffering from a delayed grief reaction and placed her on a low-dose antidepressant, which soon resolved all symptoms except the feelings of rejection, isolation, and dysphoric mood.

Jeanine was referred to a geropsychologist who began a brief course of Adlerian psychotherapy. The therapist's assessment was that Mrs. G. was ineffectively functioning in all three life tasks and that her life style and coping strategies were of a person who needs to be liked and feels required to please others at all times. In individual sessions Mrs. G. learned that her rejection feelings—anger and hurt that her husband died and left her alone—were similar to those she had experienced at other times in her life. This included the time her father and grandfather died in the same car accident when she was a child, and resulted in her need to be overly concerned with others' opinion of her and her need to please them. She was encouraged to meet with a friend daily outside her home and plan an activity that she really wanted to do rather than simply acquiesce to her friends' plans. She agreed to this but found it difficult initially.

Concurrent with her weekly individual sessions, she was integrated into an ongoing therapy group of seven other elderly widows. She found that others experienced similar feelings of rejection and depression when their spouses died, and was encouraged and challenged by them to socialize with her friends and to assert herself with them. Three months after beginning psychotherapy, Mrs. G. noted several positive changes in her life.

Milieu and Family Therapy

Milieu approaches for the elderly have recently been implemented in long-term care (LTC) facilities such as extended care, intermediate care, and skilled nursing facilities. Often a sizable number of the residents of such facilities have Alzheimer's or other OBS conditions. In the past, these residents received only custodial care. Brinks (1979) describes in detail how an Adlerian-oriented milieu approach has been successfully implemented in several facilities. Research shows that custodial care tends to reinforce a pampered patient role, which often results in exaggerated disability, and that many patients who enter LTCs for purely physical reasons develop mental problems (Brinks, 1979, pp. 273, 287). On the other hand, an effective milieu program trains patients to care for themselves and others, instead of how to be cared for by others. These kinds of Adlerian-oriented milieu programs emphasize patient activities: exercise programs, work therapy projects, arts and crafts, and reminiscence groups; behavior modification in many areas, including incontinence (a problem for one-third of all patients in LTCs) and patient governance, including democratically-based councils or assemblies. Family therapy is often a feature of day-care programs for the elderly. It is particularly useful in connection with milieu programs, especially in dealing with the guilt, anger, and frustration that family members have about their elderly relatives. This case illustrates some of the features of milieu and family therapy:

> Joseph Z. is a 70-year-old married male who recently entered a nursing home with a well regarded milieu program. Following his retirement three years ago as service manager for a local car dealership, Mr. Z.'s family noted progressive memory loss, which was subsequently diagnosed as Alzheimer's Disease. He had been known as a strong-willed family man who demanded respect from friends and coworkers. Lately he would become lost while taking walks in the neighborhood he had lived in for the past 35 years. This, along with stubbornness, urinary incontinence, and combativeness, led to his admission into the nursing facility.
>
> Within a few weeks Mr. Z. was able to be integrated into many ongoing social, exercise, and work group activities in the milieu program. Encouragement, contracting, and behavior modification techniques counteracted his incontinence, stubbornness, and combativeness with more socially useful and independent behaviors. Despite the progression of his memory loss, Mr. Z. was able to participate in some of the reminiscence and group assembly sessions. Five family sessions were convened by the program's counselor for the express purpose of dealing with Mrs. Z.'s and the eldest son's guilt about "dumping" Mr. Z. in the nursing facility because they felt powerless to care for him at home. The family's underlying anger and resentment about his dictatorial manner throughout the years, the more recent combativeness, and other losses of control such as his incontinence, were therapeutically addressed.

SUMMARY

Adler's words that opened this chapter were penned over 50 years ago, yet are remarkably cogent today. Although more is being done for the elderly than in the past, much more is needed. Research confirms Adler's observation that inferiority feelings are widespread among the elderly, primarily because they can no longer meet the tasks of life as they were previously able. But to the extent that concerned and knowledgeable professionals and others can encourage and enable the elderly to find different ways of meeting the tasks of life, they can remain productive rather than resorting to such unproductive behaviors as attention-getting, power, revenge, or the various kinds of disablement that remain all too common in our society.

These annotated resources have been helpful to people who work with the elderly. Keller and Hughston (1981) and Brinks (1979) take an Adlerian approach to treating the elderly.

Brinks, T.L., ed. *Clinical Gerontology.* A quarterly journal, one of the few professional journals focusing on psychotherapeutic issues dealing with the elderly. Consistently theoretically sound and practically significant articles for counselors and therapists working with the elderly in all settings.

Brinks, T.L. (1979). *Geriatric Psychotherapy.* New York: Human Sciences Press. This author acknowledges the Adlerian approach as the most viable psychological system for treating the elderly. He emphasizes psychotherapeutic interventions with the more seriously dysfunctional elderly, including those with OBS and various psychotic processes. Chapters on treating the elderly in LTCs reflect the author's years of experience as a master therapist.

Busse, E., and **D. Blazer** (eds.). (1980). *The Handbook of Geriatric Psychiatry.* New York: Van Nostrand Reinhold. Probably the authoritative handbook in the field to date. This exhaustive reference for professionals covers every conceivable mental health concern of the elderly.

Keller, J., and **G. Hughston.** (1981). *Counseling the Elderly: A Systems Approach.* New York: Harper & Row. This book, with its acknowledged Adlerian orientation, focuses on the problems of daily living in the elderly, and specifically excludes issues of psychosis or OBS. Much of the therapeutic orientation focuses on the four goals or levels of unproductive behavior. An appendix provides excellent materials for conducting reminiscence exercises.

Mace, N., and **R. Rabins.** (1981). *The 36 Hour Day.* Baltimore: Johns Hopkins University Press. A comforting, encouraging, and useful resource for family members who wish to learn more about Alzheimer's Disease and related disorders. This well written book has become required reading for many professional courses and seminars on treating demented individuals.

REFERENCES

Adler, A. (1956). *The individual psychology of Alfred Adler.* In H.H. Ansbacher & R.R. Ansbacher (Eds.). New York: Harper & Row.

Brinks, T. (1979). *Geriatric Psychotherapy.* New York: Human Sciences Press.

Dinkmeyer, D., & Carlson, J. (1984). *Time for a better marriage.* Circle Pines, MN: American Guidance Service.

Dreikurs, R. (1953). *Fundamentals of Adlerian psychology.* Chicago: Alfred Adler Institute.

Keller, J., & Hughston, G. (1981). *Counseling the elderly: A systems approach.* New York: Harper & Row.

Karpf, R. (1982). Individual psychotherapy with the elderly. In A. Horton (Ed.), *Mental health interventions for the aging.* New York: Praeger.

Larsen, D., Whanger, A., & Busse, E. (1983). Geriatrics. In B. Wolman (Ed.), *The therapist's handbook,* 2nd ed. New York: Van Nostrand Reinhold.

9 Health Care Counseling

T here have been a number of changes in the delivery of health care services in the past few years, and there will probably be many more. The changes involve both services and service providers. Research shows that health care counseling can increase a patient's understanding of and compliance with a treatment plan, as well as satisfaction with the service and the provider, so it appears that counseling is part of the solution to the present health care crisis (Strecher, 1982).

Until recently, members of health care teams had little interest or training in the area of counseling. Now psychologists and other mental health professionals trained in counseling and behavior change skills are being actively recruited into health care. In 1979 about 39 percent of doctoral-level applied psychologists were employed in health care settings, and it is predicted that the figure will reach some 60 percent by 1990. Not surprisingly, one of the fastest growing divisions of the American Psychological Association is the Division of Health Psychology. It has been suggested that changes in the marketplace and in reimbursement patterns will alter the traditional image of the mental health professional as a psychotherapist. DeLeon et al. (1985) suggest that psychologists at the nation's largest health maintenance organizations (HMO) view and project themselves as behavioral medicine specialists first and psychotherapists second.

The need for professionals trained in health care counseling skills will continue to increase. With some additional training, professionals already trained in personal counseling and psychotherapy can be prepared to practice health care counseling. This chapter will look at the skills and knowledge needed for health care counseling from an Adlerian perspective. We will also address some of the major theoretical and professional issues unique to this field.

ISSUES IN HEALTH CARE COUNSELING

There are two kinds of health care counseling: health restoration and health maintenance/health promotion counseling. In health restoration counseling, the counselor intervenes to restore some measure of functional capacity in either an acute or chronic situation. Here is an example of an acute-care intervention:

> An elderly female, brought into the emergency room in the late afternoon, had dislocated her shoulder in a doorway. Several attempts to reduce the dislocation by manipulating the joint were unsuccessful and it appeared that surgery would be necessary to relocate the shoulder. The liaison psy-

chologist was called and noted that the woman was deeply apprehensive and tense despite the pain medication and muscle relaxant given her. He proceeded to calm and relax her with some guided imagery and the conscious suggestion that she was now so relaxed that her shoulder would gently slide into place. The orthopedic surgeon was subsequently able to easily reduce the dislocation.

With a chronic ailment, health restoration counseling might resemble the kind of intervention a rehabilitation counselor would use with a brain-injured youth recovering from a motorcycle accident.

Health maintenance and health promotion counseling, on the other hand, focus on maintaining or actually improving the current level of functioning. This usually takes the form of risk reduction for heart disease, stroke, or cancer. For example, health care counseling might be indicated for a middle-level female manager who has been passed over for promotion because of obesity and has been unsuccessful with several attempts at weight reduction and management. It could be indicated when previous attempts to manage stress, stop smoking, or to stay on an exercise program have been unsuccessful. It could also be indicated in situations where a hypertensive individual has difficulty remembering to take blood pressure medication, thus compounding other risks he has for a stroke.

For our purposes, we will limit our discussion to this second type of health care counseling, variously called "health promotion counseling," "lifestyle change counseling," or "behavioral medicine counseling." To avoid confusion, the designation "life style" retains its traditional Adlerian denotation as the individual's unique life plan or personality structure, while "life-style" will refer to an individual's personal health habits such as diet, exercise, use of drugs and other substances, strategies for managing stress, and so on. The health counseling literature prefers the use of "patient" rather than "client," and we will follow that convention in this chapter.

Health counseling and personal counseling or psychotherapy represent different ways of working with patients or clients. Compared to psychotherapy, health counseling involves a more action-oriented and participative relationship between a patient with a need to reduce health risks or change life-style patterns and a skilled clinician who can facilitate acquisition and maintenance of these health changes. The duration of treatment is usually brief, often no more than six to ten 30-minute sessions after a 60- to 90-minute initial evaluation session, and is oriented toward prevention. Treatment is based on changing health beliefs and behaviors primarily through information and instruction, as well as behavior modification, skill training, and cognitive restructuring. Insight is a secondary consideration.

There are five key factors in health counseling: negotiation, tailoring, compliance, relapse prevention, and multimodal intervention strategies. The reason for failure in most efforts at health maintenance/promotion is lack of recognition of these key factors. No matter how excellent the lifestyle change program, it is likely to fail if the patient perceives it as primarily the counselor's program. Extended discussion is usually needed to *negotiate* an agreement between the patient's and the counselor's expectations and involvement in a change program, and the specific ways the program is *tailored* to the individual's needs and the demands of his environment. Once planned and implemented, considerable effort must be accorded the patient's *compliance* or adherence to the program. Close supervision, training in self-management skills, and appropriate feedback is needed for the patient to continue new patterns of behavior. The counselor must prepare the patient for occasional slips, like the first cigarette for one on a smoking-cessation program. The patient learns to apply "brakes" so the slip does not escalate into a full-blown relapse. And so *relapse prevention* must be an intentional part of the change program. Finally, unlike most other kinds of counseling, an underlying assumption of health counseling is that *multimodal intervention strategies* are usually necessary to reverse deeply ingrained cognitive and behavioral patterns. Thus, cognitive, behavioral, and environmental change efforts must combine to effect habit patterns as well as physiological and biochemical changes. This multimodal approach usually implies the need for collaboration with other members of the health care team.

AN ADLERIAN APPROACH TO HEALTH COUNSELING

The counselor of health maintenance/promotion will find a great deal of theoretical and practical wisdom in the Adlerian approach to counseling and psychotherapy. Conceptually, Adlerians had been writing about holistic medicine for fifty years before the term became fashionable. Unlike the reductionism of modern medicine and health care, Adler spoke of the indivisibility of the person and the need to treat the whole person. He explained that bodily functions "speak a language which is usually more expressive and discloses the individual's opinion more clearly than words are able to do. . . . The emotions and their physical expression tell us how the mind is acting and reacting in a situation which it interprets as favorable or unfavorable" (Adler, 1956). Rudolf Dreikurs (1977) further developed Adlerian thinking on holistic medicine and psychotherapy.

Adlerians view somatic symptoms holistically as manifestations of life style convictions that are inwardly experienced and simultaneously outwardly expressed. Symptoms or conditions like smoking, obesity, hypertension, or chronic stress find their outward or organic expression through one or more of the following: a constitutional predisposition (organ inferiority) that makes it "available" to the person; "social modeling" by a family member ("everyone in my family smokes"); symbolic value to the patient (obesity as compensation for the loss of a love); or the organic expression may be chosen because it is fashionable. Bulimia, for example, is very common today, whereas hysterical paralysis is passé (Griffith, 1984).

Practically, the Adlerian notions of cooperation, life style assessment, and treating the whole person complement the health counseling factors of negotiation, tailoring, compliance, relapse prevention, and multimodal interventions. Adlerians constantly stress a participative therapeutic relationship based on cooperation and social equality; the notion of negotiation invariably fosters compliance or adherence to the treatment plan. Searching for the uniqueness of the individual's life style convictions is a key to tailoring a treatment plan. Another distinguishing feature of Adlerian therapy is the wide range of techniques, often used in a multimodal fashion, to effect change. On the other hand, relapse prevention is a concept that seems less well developed in Adlerian practice.

In an Adlerian approach to health counseling, health beliefs are a central feature. Health beliefs are the convictions that inform and affect a person's health and illness behaviors. As such, health beliefs are intimately related to one's life style conviction. Just as there is a self-view or image component to the Adlerian life style, there is a body image component. An individual's body image reveals much about susceptibility or immunity to stress and disease processes, as well as one's likelihood to minimize or be oversensitive to a stressor. Health beliefs are also reflected in one's world view. They suggest the value of an illness or a health condition, especially with regard to convictions about entitlement, superiority/martyrdom, and control/manipulation. The individual's life goal and strategies also reflect these health beliefs.

We will apply the three phases of the counseling and psychotherapy process to health care counseling: the means of developing the relationship and engaging the patient, conducting the assessment, and reorienting and consolidating the life-style change process.

Relationship

The relationship between counselor and patient develops much like that in personal counseling or psychotherapy. There are, however, some important differences in timing and intentionality. In psychotherapy the task of developing the relationship can be accomplished leisurely over the first three or four sessions, but because of the brief and focused nature of health counseling, achieving cooperation and a negotiated treatment agreement is the primary task of the first session. The first session is scheduled for 60 to 90 minutes and is the most important session. During this time the counselor must come to understand the patient's reasons and degree of motivation for wanting the particular life-style change. If the change is sought primarily to appease a spouse or family physician, this needs to be dealt with at the outset; if little or no intrinsic motivation can be elicited, the probabilities of limited success need to be confronted and openly discussed. A consideration of continuing or stopping treatment should be made.

Next, the counselor asks the patient the "three questions." The first involves a functional assessment: "How does your (obesity/stress/high blood pressure/etc.) interfere with your daily life?" or "How would your life be different if you did not have _____?" This general question is followed up by asking specifically about the life tasks of work, love, and friendship. The extent of distress accompanying impaired functioning is often related to the patient's receptivity to change. The counselor must be alert to the payoff or gain the dysfunction may provide the patient and its interference with change efforts. The second question involves the patient's personal explanation for the symptom or condition: "What do you believe is the reason for your (obesity/stress/etc.)?" The answer to this and follow-up questions begins to suggest the life style—health beliefs as well as how accurately the person perceives his condition and prognosis. The patient's accuracy will be one determinant of the amount of information and education the counselor will need to provide later. The third set of questions helps elicit the person's expectations for treatment in terms of both his and your time and effort and the expected outcome and satisfaction: "What specifically were you hoping to accomplish? In what time? What sort of involvement do you expect of yourself? And of me?" Next, the counselor should evaluate the patient's previous efforts to make life-style changes by eliciting specific information about number of attempts, length of time, extent of success, outside help, and reasons for quitting or noncompliance. These are important factors in the patient's current expectations for success or failure.

Based on this background information, particularly the patient's expectation for treatment and outcome, the counselor then proposes what he considers realistic expectations for a change program with broad timelines, level of involvement, and expected outcomes and discusses them in relation to the patient's. The discussion that follows constitutes the negotiation process from which a mutually agreed upon contract for change emerges. Often this agreement takes written form and is couched in performance-based language. Let's give an example of this first phase:

> Jean S. is a 28-year-old single middle manager at the national headquarters of a large insurance company. She was referred by her physician to a psychologist for help with a weight reduction program. The physician was concerned not only with her obesity but also a family history of early death from heart disease. In the first session the psychologist elicited the following information: Ms. S. came not only because of her doctor's referral but also because she was passed over for promotion twice in the previous nine months, presumably because of her weight, and because she has recently felt herself losing all control over her cravings for certain foods. She lives with her mother and stepfather amid considerable family discord. Her father, who was morbidly obese, died at the age of 40 of a massive heart attack, and her life has not been the same since his death.
>
> Jean S.'s responses to the three questions are noteworthy. First, she is able to function adequately at home and on the job, but says she has less energy for hobbies and social activities in the past two months. She attributes this to "stress" but does admit she is a little depressed about being passed over for promotion when she believes she was clearly the first choice were it not for her appearance. She indicates that she is 75 pounds over her ideal weight. Thus, her life task functioning is somewhat impaired but not grossly. Second, she believes her overweight is due to "family gland problems," noting that all her older siblings and her parents were also overweight. She is fearful that she too will die of a heart attack or stroke at an early age, saying "it's just a matter of time." Third, she believes that the best treatment for her is a liquid protein diet, which can result in rapid weight loss but which her doctor has refused to prescribe because of the cardiac risks. He has instead placed her on a 1200-calorie protein-sparing diet and an aerobic exercise program. She has heard that hypnosis has worked for some of her friends and was hoping the psychologist would try it with her. She has never exercised much, but is willing to try. It was learned that Jean had been on several "miracle" weight loss diets; she had lost up to 20 pounds in two weeks but gained it all back in a few days. She admitted that she was "addicted" to chocolate and whenever she was overstressed, particularly with family matters, she would go to her room and binge on chocolate.

The psychologist empathically reflected Jean's concerns about losing control and her fear of death, then proposed what he considered an appropriate treatment plan: rapid weight reduction of 40 pounds could be expected over 15 weeks on the doctor's diet plan and some kind of aerobics program with low demands at first, probably short walks, increasing in intensity every week, along with a behavioral approach to modify eating patterns and some cognitive restructuring to modify life style-health belief convictions associated with loss of control and body image. He further suggested a family session to clarify issues at home and help establish a support system for her weight loss program. After considerable discussion Jean agreed that exercise was really needed but was not willing to walk or jog because of joint problems. Both agreed that a group exercise program would be appropriate. She admitted that her reason for wanting hypnosis was "because it seemed like a quick fix" but that it probably would not be too helpful for that very reason. She was somewhat reluctant to have her family involved in her treatment, not thinking they had any effect on her, but she was willing to invite her family to one of the next six biweekly sessions and possibly to one of the four monthly follow-up sessions after she had lost the target weight. She had no reservations about the behavioral or cognitive restructuring approaches. By the end of their first session, a mutually negotiated treatment plan emerged that was put into writing and signed by both Jean and the psychologist.

Assessment

The assessment phase in Adlerian health counseling tends to be more focused and briefer than in personal psychotherapy. It attempts to understand the patient's present health beliefs and behaviors in terms of personal and contextual factors. The basic feature of the *personal factors assessment* involves an abbreviated examination of the life style if time does not permit a complete life style assessment. An abbreviated assessment would cover only those early recollections directly related to matters of health and illness. Other personal factors to be assessed are health beliefs and behaviors, past and current gains or payoffs for the current health condition or symptoms, and the extent and accuracy of the individual's knowledge about his condition. The earliest recollection should be sought; then it is helpful to elucidate health beliefs through special recollections, asking the patient to recall singular experiences when he or other family members or relatives were ill. Often responses provide valuable insights into the person's body image and life style convictions, particularly about entitlement, superiority/martyrdom, and control.

In terms of *contextual factors*, it is helpful to do a brief family constellation with a focus on family values related to health and illness behaviors, and to know about the health and illness behaviors of other family members or relatives that may have served as social models for the patient. It is essential that the counselor assess the patient's cultural health status, which, according to Allen (1981), consists of the "silent" attitudes and norms of one's family, social and ethnic groups, and community that influence and reinforce certain health behaviors and not others. Allen says we are all influenced by cultural norm indicators for exercise, smoking, stress, weight control, nutrition, alcohol and alcohol abuse, safety, and mental health, and has developed several paper-and-pencil inventories to elucidate these cultural norms. Let's return to our case example:

> Jean's first health-related early recollection was from her sixth birthday party, involving an argument between her parents about the amount of cake and snacks Jean devoured at the party. Her father was embarrassed; her mother defended Jean's overweight "as normal for a girl her age." Jean began to cry, complaining of a stomachache, and her mother called the family doctor, asking him to make an emergency house call. After the doctor assured the family that everything would be all right, Mother kissed Jean and whispered that she could eat the rest of the birthday cake and snacks whenever she wanted. Jean remembers feeling fearful and helpless while her parents were quarreling. A second recollection at age nine involved a shopping trip with her mother. Jean had picked out two dresses to try on, only to find that she couldn't get into them because they were three sizes too small. Her mother laughed at this and said: "Don't feel bad. I'll take you to lunch." Jean remembers looking at herself in the fitting-room mirror wearing the small dresses and saying sadly: "I thought it would fit" while Mother laughed. Based on her early recollections and other indicators of health beliefs, family values and beliefs about health and illness, illness models, and cultural norms, the psychologist developed this formulation: Jean views her inner self as small and inadequate, within a big, powerful body that commands attention. She sees the world as demanding and dangerous, especially for the assertive, but less so for those who are ill or obese. Therefore, her goal is to appear big and strong but to avoid conflict at all cost. Overeating provides an illusion of safety for her and focuses attention away from family problems, especially parental disputes. Since she failed to develop many proactive life skills, she is likely to feel out of control with job and family demands, and overeating thus symbolizes the control issue. Her payoffs for being ill and obese as a child were special parental attention that diverted attention from the bitter fights between her parents, and being allowed to stay home from school because of "illness" when tests came up and occasionally on gym-class days. Not surprisingly, early life health behavior history showed that she modeled the illness-obesity behavior of her natural father. Presently, her mother appears to be a good source of support for a weight management program since,

as in past weight-loss efforts, she was willing to prepare the special foods the diet required. Jean has a girl friend in the office who would probably be willing to serve a support function during lunch and break times. Finally, Jean's responses to a paper-and-pencil inventory showed that she subscribes to a number of cultural norms that appear to reinforce her life style convictions: "Being a few pounds overweight is perfectly natural"; "It's expected that if you lose weight through dieting you will gain it right back"; "Everybody loves a fat person"; "It's natural to eat when one is lonely or has hurt feelings", "Sweets are a special reward for good behavior and therefore are more 'rewarding' than most nutritious foods"; and "It's natural to be overweight if you belong to certain ethnic groups" (Allen, 1981, p. 113).

Reorientation

There are two main levels of intervention: the individual and the family levels. At the individual level, encouragement is the basic nonspecific intervention. Specific interventions include information and instruction-giving, cognitive restructuring, and behavior modification, including setting behavioral goals, monitoring and pattern identification, stimulus control, reinforcement, and relapse prevention training. (Some of these techniques are described in detail in Chapter 6.) Since relapse prevention is a relatively new approach, we will provide a brief overview and refer the interested reader to Marlatt and Gordon (1984), the definitive source on relapse prevention, for a detailed discussion.

Relapse prevention consists of teaching the patient both behavioral skills and cognitive strategies so she can avoid high risk situations and overly high expectations that could result in relapse, or to apply the "brakes" so that once a "slip" occurs it does not escalate into a full-blown relapse. The counselor also helps the individual increase her ability to cope with cravings as well as anxiety and other determinants of relapse. "Relapse drills," in which the patient is able to practice these learned skills, are an important aspect of relapse prevention.

Intervention at the family level has the express purpose of increasing compliance and minimizing relapse. Drop-out rates from life-style change programs are as high as 80 percent when no health counseling is provided. Enlisting the aid of social support systems like the family, co-workers, or friends is a critical task for both patient and counselor.

Not surprisingly, the more uninvolved and the more dysfunctional the family or the marital partner, the more the health counselor can anticipate problems in implementing any change program. To the extent that family members can be incorporated into the change program, the more likely the program will be successful. For example, Brownell (1984) reports that when the obese patient's spouse attended weight-loss sessions in which spouses were encouraged to modify their own eating habits along with the patients, weight loss and maintenance were greater than for the control group studies. Brownell also found that an unwilling spouse can and often does sabotage the patient's treatment program. Dishman et al. (1985) reviewed the research on compliance with exercise programs and concluded that spouses' attitudes toward the change program are probably more important than the patients'. If family members can be directly involved in individual or group sessions, they should be encouraged or even required to participate. If this is not possible, the family's indirect support should be enlisted. Doherty and Baird (1983) describe "family compliance counseling" as one way to enlist this support.

Family compliance counseling works like this: after the change program has been negotiated, the patient is asked to come to the next session with his family. The counselor begins the session by providing information about the health condition to all family members, and answers whatever content questions they have. This is done to set the stage for a family commitment to the change program. The counselor then asks for the family's reaction to the patient's health problem and about the proposed change program. Next, the counselor helps the family make a contract for compliance to the change program. He begins by asking the patient if he would like help from the family. Assuming the response is affirmative, the counselor asks the patient what kind of help he would like, and so on, until a family contract emerges. At this point the counselor can provide specific health promotion literature to family members to help clarify and increase their involvement in the program. Finally, a follow-up session is scheduled to evaluate the patient's progress and the family's support contract. Let's return to our case example:

> Already a contract for change has been negotiated and the assessment has suggested specific change strategies. A multimodal and collaborative intervention plan evolved. At the behavioral level, Jean was instructed in behavior modification methods for changing her eating behavior. Skill training in assertiveness was begun. At the cognitive level, the psychologist worked with Jean to challenge and restructure some of her life style convictions-health beliefs in a more socially useful direction. He reframed Jean's occasional relapses as slips rather than as failures. At the social support level, a family session resulted in Jean's mother's agreeing to prepare meals consistent with the prescribed 1200-calorie diet and to adopt the diet herself for at least the first 15 weeks. Jean enlisted the support of her girl friend at work, and also joined a support group run by the

psychologist for other business people who were involved in similar change programs. She joined a beginner's aerobic dance class at a local YWCA, since she did not feel she could motivate herself to exercise alone. At the physiological level, Jean continued to be monitored medically by her physician, and the psychologist and the physician conferred with each other over the course of the eight months Jean was formally involved with health counseling. After the seven biweekly sessions, four follow-up monthly sessions were planned, as well as a 12-month follow-up. At the end of the eighth month, Jean had succeeded in reducing and maintaining her weight within five pounds of her ideal.

Health Counseling in a Public Setting

Jean's case illustrates health counseling in a private practice setting. As an example of health counseling in a public clinic, we will look at the case of Jim:

Jim N. was a 42-year-old married salesman who had undergone a triple cardiac bypass operation nine weeks before being referred to the hospital's Cardiac Rehabilitation Program counselor. Jim was begun on a standard postsurgical exercise program in the hospital and had done well enough to be discharged to the outpatient program in three weeks. But after good compliance with the outpatient program for one week, Jim's attendance started to decline and he began to doubt that he would ever return to his job. Before the surgery, Jim described himself as a hard-working, hard-drinking, charter member of the salespersons' million dollar club. He had been under considerable pressure to close his company's largest account at the time he experienced the crushing chest pain that lead to his emergency surgery. Now he was unsure of his ability even to drive his car to the regional sales office, much less perform as a top salesman.

In response to the three questions, he mentioned his fear of having another heart attack and dying while jogging or riding his exercycle. With some embarrassment, he said he was unwilling to resume sexual relations with his wife for the same reason, nor did he wish to continue any exercise that could not be telemonitored as in the hospital program.

As the oldest child, Jim had assumed much of the responsibility for supporting his family. His alcoholic father had been injured in World War I and could provide only a meager disability check each month. Jim worked at a series of part-time jobs all the time he was in school to help meet the expenses of a family of seven. He was seldom ill, and when he was, his mother doted on him. He expects that he may never fully recover and has been considering the possibility of early retirement. But he does not think he is that bad off yet.

Jim's earliest health-related recollection was at age nine, when he developed a mild case of pneumonia. That rainy spring he had been working at an outdoor shoeshine stand for six to seven hours a day after school and about twelve hours a day on weekends for three weeks before succumbing to pneumonia. He recalls lying in bed feeling very weak and pained every time he breathed, while his mother told him how courageous and hard-working he was and his inebriated father shouted from another room that Jim was a quitter and would never amount to anything. Jim felt that he had failed and vowed he would never fail or become sick again. This and two other recollections showed that Jim viewed himself as having little self-worth and the world as a testing place that expected tremendous accomplishments from him. His goal was to prove himself through his job and even through sexual relations. His body-image was that of a finely-tuned sprinter who could successfully compete in short events but not endure the longer ones.

Both his wife and his boss were willing and able to provide all the social support he needed to comply with the treatment program. Jim and the counselor were able to negotiate a contract aimed at returning Jim to at least his previous level of physical functioning, with the possibility of his returning to work. With the collaboration of his physician and the program's exercise physiologist, the counselor worked with Jim on some behavioral and environmental restructuring and on challenging and restructuring some of his health beliefs. He met with Jim and his wife to discuss his health and his concerns about the risks associated with lovemaking and returning to work. The more Jim came to understand the basis of his fears of disability or death from a second heart attack, the more willing he was to comply with the carefully laid out exercise and nutrition prescription worked out with his physician and the exercise physiologist. Within six weeks Jim was able to return to work with a more realistic understanding of his needs and abilities. A phone check with him twelve months later found him promoted to regional sales manager and reporting a more satis-fying marriage.

Both of these cases, Jean's and Jim's, suggest some of the ways health counselors function. In the first instance, the psychologist provided a full range of services in a private practice setting over a period of several months. In the second instance, the rehabilitation counselor functioned in a more limited and focused role and for a shorter period of time.

THE PRACTICE OF HEALTH PROMOTION COUNSELING

The effective practice of health counseling requires that the counselor or psychotherapist be conversant with medical and health care terminology as well as with the biopsychosocial view of health and illness. The terms "behavioral medicine" and "health psychology" refer to the study of health and illness behavior from a behavioral science perspective. Handbooks by Stone, Cohen, and Adler (1979), Davidson and Davidson (1980), and Millon, Green, and Meagher (1982) offer a readable introduction and overview of this newly emerging field. Graduate level courses and postgraduate CEU programs are now commonplace, as are pre- and postdoctoral internships and fellowships in health psychology and behavioral medicine.

Counselors and psychotherapists who are unfamiliar with the referral process and working relationships with other health care personnel, particularly physicians, may be in for some surprises. For better or worse, there is a certain protocol and pecking order in the health care team. The counselor or psychotherapist who is flexible yet assertive can expect to be accepted and esteemed by other health care team members after a brief "proving" period. There are various ways to practice health counseling. The kind of health counseling described in this chapter is being done by counselors or psychologists who are paid by a behavioral medicine or wellness program in a hospital, clinic, or HMO. Jim's case typifies this application. A small but growing number of psychologists are involved in private health counseling, as in the case of Jean's counselor. A special issue of the *Family Therapy Networker* (January, 1984) presents some first-person accounts of health counselor-physician collaborative relationships in different practice arrangements.

Certain medico-legal issues emerge in the practice of health counseling. These are beyond the scope of this chapter, but we will mention one of the most important, which deals with the matter of diagnosis and treatment. Many states restrict the terms "diagnosis" and "treatment" of health conditions in verbal and written language to use by those licensed to practice medicine, dentistry, and podiatry, while other states extend this usage to licensed psychologists. By and large, other members of the health care team are intimately involved in the diagnostic and treatment process, but they must exercise care in the specific use of these terms in verbal and written communication with the patient, medical records, and so forth. Prudent judgment in this area shields the counselor from the increasing number of malpractice suits and claims of practicing medicine without a license.

REFERENCES

Adler, A. (1956). *The Individual Psychology of Alfred Adler.* H.L. and R.R. Ansbacher (Eds.). New York: Harper & Row.

Allen, R. (1981). *Lifegain*. New York: Appleton-Century-Crofts.

Brownell, K. (1984). The psychology and physiology of obesity: Implications for screening and treatment. *Journal of American Dietetics Association, 84*(4), 406–414.

Davidson, P., & Davidson, S. (1979). *Behavioral medicine: Changing health life styles*. New York: Brunner/Mazel.

DeLeon, P., Uyeda, M., & Welch, B. (1985). Psychology and HMOs: New partnership or new adversary? *American Psychologist, 40* (10), 1122–1124.

Dishman, R., Sallis, J., & Orenstein, D. (1985). Relationship between exercise and other health behaviors. *Public Health Reports, 100* (2), 158–171.

Doherty, W., & Baird, M. (1983). *Family therapy and family medicine*. New York: Guilford Press.

Dreikurs, R. (1977). Holistic medicine and the function of neurosis. *Journal of Individual Psychology, 13*(2), 171–192.

Griffith, J. (1984). Adler's organ jargon. *Individual Psychology, 40*(4), 437–444.

Marlatt, G., & Gordon, J. (Eds.). (1984). *Relapse prevention*. New York: Guilford Press.

Millon, T., Green, C., & Meagher, R. (Eds.). (1982). *Handbook of clinical health psychology*. New York: Plenun.

Strecher, V. (1982). Improving physician-patient interactions: A review. *Patient Counseling and Health Education, 4*(3), 129–136.

Stone, G., Cohen, F., & Adler, N. (Eds.). (1980). *Health psychology: A handbook*. San Francisco: Jossey-Bass.

10 Group Counseling and Group Psychotherapy

H uman behavior can best be understood in its social context, because it is the social context that explains the purpose of the behavior. For example, a child's behavior on the playground might be considered totally out of order if it occurred in a structured classroom. Children's temper tantrums may be effective with the children's parents but not with their teachers. Children learn this and have temper tantrums only in "appropriate" social settings.

The counselor or therapist who believes in the holistic, social, purposive, and decision-making nature of human behavior recognizes that groups are a most effective resource for influencing attitudes and behavior. Group counseling and group psychotherapy are an interpersonal process led by a professional trained in group procedures. *Group counseling* usually focuses on exploring typical developmental problems—for example, getting along with peers, being acceptable to members of the opposite sex, or becoming involved with school tasks. *Group therapy* is more concerned with the correction of mistaken assumptions about life or faulty approaches to the basic tasks of life. In this discussion, we will use the terms *group* and *therapeutic group* to refer to both group counseling and group therapy.

HISTORY

Group therapy has an interesting history. Although Dreikurs (1952) indicated that the origins of formal group therapy can be traced back to Franz Anton Mesmer's hypnotic sessions in Paris two centuries ago, group psychotherapy as we know it is basically a product of the 20th century. J.H. Pratt, a Boston internist, is credited with having been the first to apply group psychotherapy. In the early 1900s, he used an educational group approach to treat tuberculosis patients.

> The early period of group psychotherapy may be dated from 1900 to 1930. During this time the major steps toward a systematic use of the group method, called at that time "collective counseling," were made in Europe. Dreikurs (1952) reports the early efforts of collective therapy by Wetterstrand with hypnosis, Schubert with stammerers, Hirschfeld with sexual disturbances, Stransky with neurotic patients, and Metzl (1937) with alcoholics. In Russia, Rosenstein, Guilarowsky, and Ozertovsky (Ozertovsky, 1927) used the group method. In Denmark, Joergeson used action methods with psychotics (Harms, 1945). (Dreikurs & Corsini, 1960, p. 22)

There is some question concerning the relationship between "collective counseling" and our current forms of group therapy. It is clear that the early efforts never reached a degree of organization comparable to group therapy as we know it today, and that the psychiatrists who used the group method worked independently of one another. With the advent of totalitarianism in both Germany and Russia, these psychiatrists were forced to abandon group methods.

In 1928, Dreikurs published "The Development of Mental Hygiene in Vienna." In this historically important paper, he described in detail, possibly for the first time anywhere, the dynamic differences between individual and group therapy, which he called "collective therapy."

> Alfred Adler (1931), in his child guidance clinics, was probably the first psychiatrist to use the group method systematically and formally. Moreno (1953) started group therapy around 1910, using techniques completely unrelated to the concepts and practices of individual therapy. He later developed a theoretical framework, sociometry, for the group approach. (Dreikurs & Corsini, 1960, p. 22)

In 1931, Moreno coined the term *group psychotherapy,* which became the formal name of the new method.

The literature of group psychotherapy and group counseling developed slowly. From 1900 to 1929, only 31 papers on group psychotherapy were published in this country. The literature has expanded greatly in recent times. Articles can be found in *Small Group Behavior* (Beverly Hills, Calif.: Sage Publications), *International Journal of Group Psychotherapy* (New York: International Universities Press), *Group Organization Studies* (La Jolla, Calif.: University Associates), and *Together* (Washington, D.C.: Association for Specialists in Group Work, American Association for Counseling and Development).

THE NATURE OF THE GROUP PROCESS

The group process focuses on the beliefs, attitudes, values, feelings, purposes, and behavior of the members of the group. The interpersonal relationships that develop within the group make it possible for the members to become aware of their mistaken and self-defeating beliefs and actions and to feel encouraged to change them.

Requirements for membership are unique. People don't belong because of their status; they belong because they have problems and are ready to acknowledge and work on them. The focus is on helping members establish personal goals and, by challenging their perceptions, enabling them to cope more effectively with the tasks of life.

Group Interaction

Humans are involved in continuous social interaction and inevitably face the dilemma between serving their own interests and those of the groups to which they belong. It is within the group interaction that one can observe how an individual decides to belong to the group. Some believe "I belong only if I can please," while others believe "I belong only if they give me my way." It is the Adlerian bias that one's social interest and, eventually, self-interest can often be best served through involvement in the give and take of cooperative endeavor with the group. This type of involvement creates a communal feeling and enhances one's feeling of belonging. We are social beings who live in and are influenced by the social system and behave in such a way as to attain the approval of others. Our basic striving is to belong and to be accepted and valued. The methods we use to search for significance and recognition indicate how we decide to belong.

Psychological problems result from disturbed interpersonal relationships, reduced courage, and insufficient social interest. Yalom (1970) studied 20 successful group-therapy patients to determine the critical incident, or most helpful single event, for the members of the group. He found that, almost invariably, the incident involved some other group member and rarely the therapist. Yalom lists the components of the corrective emotional experience in group therapy:

1. A strong expression of emotion which is interpersonally directed and which represents a risk taking on the part of the patient;
2. A group supportive enough to permit this risk taking;
3. Reality testing, which allows the patient to examine the incident with the aid of consensual validation from others;
4. A recognition of the inappropriateness of certain interpersonal feelings and behavior or of the inappropriateness of certain avoided interpersonal behaviors;
5. The ultimate facilitation of the individual's ability to interact with others more deeply and honestly. (Yalom, 1970, p. 23)

The therapeutic group will invariably move toward becoming a social microcosm of the members' experiences. All participants begin to interact in the group as they do in their real-life interpersonal relationships. Sometimes the members may seek the same position they held in their childhood family. Members also display in the group their faulty beliefs and ineffective approaches to the tasks of life. The participants don't need to describe their problems; their behavior reveals their life style and assumptions about human relationships. The therapist, instead of hearing about how the members behave, observes and experiences the participants and their behavior, since each member's style of life eventually emerges in the various transactions among the members.

Interpersonal Learning

Interpersonal learning becomes impetus for change through the following process:

1. The group becomes a social microcosm, representing each member's social world.

2. Group members, through feedback and self-awareness, become aware of the purpose and consequences of their interpersonal behavior. Through feedback, which is congruent and caring, one's strengths and limitations are discussed. Unlike the typical social situation, in which one may not be able to communicate honestly, the group values openness and congruence—saying what one feels and means. Feedback permits one to learn from the transaction, because the message is not perceived as threatening and can therefore be accepted and internalized. This phenomenon occurs because feedback does not demand change, but rather the sharing of what one is experiencing and perceiving. The receiver of feedback is free to decide her own course of action.

3. For communication in the group to be effective, the transaction must be real and genuine. The participants must communicate their involvement and feelings about what they are experiencing, as well as the feelings others' communication provokes.

4. Change occurs as a result of (a) awareness; (b) involvement and commitment to make specific changes; (c) the amount of belonging to the group the member feels and the resultant importance of being accepted and valued by the other members; and (d) encouragement by members and by the group leader.

5. Through the process of trying on new behaviors and beliefs and learning that it is safe to change, the group member gains the courage to continue making positive movement.

6. The whole process can be described as setting a cycle in motion in which (a) perceptions and beliefs change; (b) courage and belonging enable one to try on new behaviors; (c) involvement and risk taking are rewarded by acceptance and belonging; (d) fear of making a mistake is replaced by the courage to be imperfect, which reduces anxiety and insecurity; and (e) as self-esteem and self-worth develop, one is able to try additional change.

RATIONALE

The Adlerian view that humans are indivisible, social, and decision-making beings whose actions have a social purpose adds value and meaning to groups. Verbal and nonverbal transactions acquire new significance when the members are understood as social beings. In the group, the individual's private logic, priorities, and the way he seeks to be known are revealed.

The group has some unique diagnostic and therapeutic qualities. In terms of assessment, the therapist or counselor doesn't have to conduct extensive interviews, because observing and understanding the social meaning of the group members' behavior makes the therapist aware of each member's assumptions about life and human relationships. The group can also provide the therapeutic advantages that come from belonging. The corrective influences and encouragement of peers—the members of the group—is often more potent than that of any other individual. It has been demonstrated that peers may have a strong influence on behavior. Most problems are interpersonal, and, for most individuals, alternatives or solutions are best developed in a social setting. Discouragement often begins in group interaction and can best be dealt with in a group situation.

The measuring stick for progress is one's increased capacity to meet the tasks of life, to give and take, and to cooperate—what Adlerians call social interest. An individual's capacity to interact effectively with other members of the group is a measure of social growth, which is one of the goals of the group experience.

An effective group offers these opportunities:

To belong and be accepted

To receive and give love and to have a therapeutic effect on others

To see that one's problems are not unique but are often experienced universally

To develop one's identity and to try on new approaches to the various social tasks of life

THE SOCIAL CLIMATE OF THERAPEUTIC GROUPS

The therapeutic group provides a unique social climate and an atmosphere in which the individual's psychological movement can be observed and, at the same time, corrected. The group setting also offers members the opportunity to develop new perceptions of their approach to the basic tasks of life.

Therapeutic groups are agents that promote values. A group accepts certain values and influences members of the group in terms of those values. The group therapy setting requires these conditions:

1. Members have their place regardless of deficits or assets. They are not judged in terms of any position or status they hold outside the group. They establish their own position inside the group and are accepted on that basis. The full worth of each member is taken for granted simply because he is a part of the group.

2. The members' capacity to reveal themselves honestly and openly is valued. Failing to reveal one's feelings, putting up a front, disguising hidden agendas, and covering up one's intentions—all accepted and even valued in certain other social situations—are challenged in the group. The group values congruence, the capacity to honestly reveal and share what one is experiencing.

3. Members learn not merely by verbal understanding. They are expected to put their insights into action as they transact with the other group members. Insight is not valued unless it produces "outsights"—that is, some action or reality testing.

4. The leader models attentive listening, caring, congruence, confrontation, and interpretation to help participants acquire these interpersonal skills. Members learn what behavior is expected and are encouraged when they produce the desired behaviors.

5. Members can express their true feelings without fear of permanently disrupting relationships. Interpersonal conflict between members is discussed and worked through, so members learn that conflict, when dealt with honestly, can produce improved relationships. The norms of the therapeutic group prescribe that participants continue to communicate despite intensive negative feelings they may develop toward one another.

CONCEPTUAL FOUNDATIONS OF THERAPEUTIC GROUPS

The Adlerian approach to therapeutic groups recognizes certain conceptual foundations of the nature of behavior:

1. All behavior has social meaning. Each transaction between and among members of the group has social direction and social intention. Members are encouraged to understand the meaning of the transaction in terms of that direction and intention.

2. Behavior can best be understood in terms of holistic patterns. Early in the transactions with one another, group participants are encouraged to become aware of the consistent pattern an individual reveals by her behavior within the group. Thus, the life style, which includes the characteristic pattern of responding and behaving, is exposed, understood, and dealt with in the group setting. The group is organized so as to reveal the life style of each member. Participants learn to understand one another in terms of each person's unique style of living. They facilitate

one another's development in various ways: by becoming aware of the faulty or mistaken assumptions that keep one from developing effective approaches to the tasks of life, and through willingness to process feedback about what one is experiencing.

3. Like all behavior, behavior in the group is goal directed and purposive. Members become aware of their own purposes and intentions and seek to understand the other members' behavior in terms of its purpose. Participants learn to confront one another not only with the expressed beliefs, attitudes, and values, but with the purpose of overall psychological movement. They soon learn that, while words can deceive, the psychological movement always clearly reveals directions and intentions. Someone may say he intends to change, but members of the group give more credence to what one does.

4. Members are encouraged to become aware of their own motives and methods for finding a place in this and other group situations. Group transactions help reveal how members seek to find their place.

5. The group has specific hopes for each member's positive psychological development. More importantly, there is also a criterion for determining development: the individual's capacity to belong to the group, to make a commitment, to engage in the give and take of life, and to extend his social interest.

6. Members are understood in terms of how they see themselves and their situation—in terms of their phenomenological field. They are actively encouraged to help one another understand how their perceptions influence their feelings and behavior.

These basic concepts about human behavior provide guidelines and structure for the social climate of the group, a climate in which members look at the transactions in terms of their patterns, social meaning, and purpose. The hypothesis is that, as members increase their social interest, feel belonging, and make a commitment to others, their emerging social interest becomes a major factor in their psychological growth.

THERAPEUTIC FORCES OF THE GROUP SETTING

The therapeutic forces that develop in a group setting are responsible for stimulating changes in the members' behavior. Thus, if a leader is to effectively influence development, she must be aware of the potential mechanisms that operate in the group and of their effect on the participants. Also, the leader must be aware of how she can facilitate the potential therapeutic effect of such mechanisms. The leader must accept responsibility for stimulating a climate that will promote growth, self-understanding, and commitment to change. Group mechanisms are the dynamic processes that occur in any therapeutic group, which, however, do not occur automatically as a concomitant of the group meeting. The leader consciously creates situations in which the mechanisms are likely to operate. When these processes do occur spontaneously, they must be recognized and encouraged. The mechanisms are catalysts for individual as well as group development.

Acceptance

Acceptance refers to the respect and empathy each one in the group receives simply because he is a member. When acceptance has developed, group members come to identify with one another and to have a strong communal feeling, expressed in the belief that "this is where I belong, and I can trust the members of the group to be concerned, caring and honest." Feelings of acceptance and belonging are an essential undergirding of the growth process. Acceptance is fostered as the leader not only models empathy but, when necessary, intervenes to help participants learn how to be more empathic with one another. Each member of the group has a need to belong, and the therapeutic group provides the unique opportunity to find one's place and be accepted without having to undergo instant change.

Altruism

There is a positive desire in people, no matter how discouraged by our current climate of competitiveness, to be of direct service and assistance to others. The group provides a situation that values altruism. To stimulate altruism in the group, the leader models and demonstrates it and encourages any attempt of the members to express altruistic feelings. The group is organized so as to include opportunities to exert and utilize altruism.

Transference

Transference refers to the strong emotional attachment that members of the group develop as a result of their intensive experience with one another. Transference may originally be directed to the leader but eventually is manifested toward members of the group and even toward the group as a whole. Transference can involve both positive and negative feelings. The group provides the opportunity to give as well as receive love. Transference and the identification the members feel for one another form the glue that holds the group together. Transference is experienced as a continuous flow of emotional support. Unless this kind of transference develops, the group doesn't have enough strong feelings, positive and negative, to make the group a therapeutic experience.

Spectator Therapy

Spectator therapy permits group members to achieve some understanding of their own concerns by hearing the concerns of others. If a member of the group has a problem and another member brings up a similar problem, the first person has an opportunity to recognize that her situation is not unique. She can also develop solutions by considering the suggestions that are being made in the group. The behavior of the other member can act as a mirror in which one learns about herself. It is important for the group leader to recognize that members can and do benefit from ongoing interaction even when they don't participate verbally. Through spectator therapy, one observes others, learns more effective interpersonal skills, and benefits from the transactions that occur in the group.

Universalization

Universalization is the recognition that one's problems are not unique. The more one recognizes universalization, the more one becomes aware that others share the same problems and the less one feels lonely and alienated from the rest of humanity. Recognizing the commonality of problems makes it easier to communicate one's own problems. The leader intentionally stimulates universalization by creating a conducive climate and by asking "Have any of you experienced that or felt that way?" An effective leader underlines similarities in thoughts, feelings, and actions by pointing them out clearly as they occur.

Feedback

Feedback refers to the learning process the group members undergo by sharing their reactions to one another. Psychological feedback is the reception of information concerning how others experience us. The purpose of feedback is to enable us to develop insight about our interpersonal relationships. Feedback enables us to explore our feelings, values, and attitudes, and reevaluate our faulty assumptions or mistaken perceptions. Authentic feedback requires the group members to be truly concerned and to care about one another. It also requires that participants recognize the feedback as an honest sharing of impressions that does not necessitate a change of behavior. Feedback, then, becomes a strong source for creating psychological movement. If members truly feel part of the group and if they are concerned about peer evaluation, feedback can be a strong motivational force for change.

Ventilation

The group setting provides an opportunity for its members to express a number of emotions they may have inhibited or repressed. This emotional release often reduces internal pressures. Through ventilation, participants learn to expose and explore their inner feelings, both positive and negative, and to recognize that the concerns they have about how they will be received are often just fantasies. By verbalizing strong feelings, members develop new insights that enable them to make therapeutic changes.

Reality Testing

In the group setting, participants can not only test certain concepts, but can work through actual relationships. This gives them the opportunity to see their behavior more accurately as it is experienced by others. For example, if a woman has problems relating to men, she can experiment in the group with new methods of relating to men. Thus, she doesn't have to wait until she is outside the group to get some real-life experience in dealing with her new insights. The group provides an opportunity to practice a new life style and new perceptions in a social setting that is accepting and nonthreatening and that, at the same time, provides open and honest feedback.

Interaction

The interactions that take place within the group make visible the goals and purposes of each member. We say "make visible" because leader and peers don't have to depend on what the individual says, but instead can observe the actual behavior. Words may deceive, but behavior seldom lies in its direction and intent. An individual may protest that he intends to help or cooperate, but unless he does it, his words are just words. Group interaction moves the participants beyond words into action.

GROUP COHESIVENESS

In the previous chapters, we have stressed the importance of the relationship in individual therapy. Yalom believes cohesiveness in group therapy is the analogue of the "relationship" in individual therapy (Yalom, 1970). *Cohesiveness* refers to the positive pull or attraction members of the group feel for one another. It refers to the forces that enable members to experience a feeling of belonging, solidarity, and a common bond. This cohesiveness creates conditions whereby the individual feels not only understood, accepted, and valued, but also free both to reveal herself and to accept feedback from group members. A cohesive group is one in which members have a high level of mutual understanding and acceptance. Cohesiveness helps supply the feeling of belonging that is essential to all the other therapeutic forces.

Dickoff and Lakin (1963) found that members who perceive their group as cohesive attend more sessions, experience more social contact with other participants, and judge the group as offering a therapeutic experience. Yalom (1970) says: "We have cited evidence that patients in group therapy consider group cohesiveness to be a prime mode of help in their therapy experience. There is tentative evidence that self-perceived positive therapy outcome is related to individual attraction to the group and to total group cohesiveness. Individuals with positive outcome have had more mutually satisfying intermember relationships" (p. 43). Cohesiveness is a crucial factor because, as we said earlier, understanding and acceptance by peers often have greater power and meaning for the individual than acceptance by the leader.

The significance of cohesiveness is best understood when we recognize that most persons who come to a group for assistance have problems in establishing and maintaining meaningful interpersonal relationships, in developing and maintaining a sense of personal worth and self-esteem, and in experiencing what it means to be an equal member of an equalitarian group. The group, because of its unique social climate, develops cohesiveness and provides an excellent corrective experience for these specific problems.

THE ROLE OF THE GROUP LEADER

The leader is responsible for forming, establishing, and keeping the group going. In the early stages, the leader is the only person with whom all the members in the group are familiar. Members expect the leader to assume responsibility for the group's growth.

The group leader must be sensitive to the forces that make the group a therapeutic experience. He is a facilitator who both creates and encourages situations in which participants provide emotional support, universalization, feedback, and opportunities to try on new behavior. These processes promote learning, personal growth, and cohesiveness.

The leader must participate actively in the development of norms that facilitate growth and interpersonal learning. He intentionally establishes a structure for the group and indicates guidelines for behavior, such as congruence, open interaction, involvement, nonjudgmental acceptance, confrontation, and commitment. Much of our social behavior is characterized by facades, surface interactions, inhibited expression of feelings, and other modes that are destructive to the development of a productive group. It is crucial to understand that the norms that govern the group don't come about automatically as a result of forming a group. Their development requires intensive effort on the part of the leader.

The therapist or counselor must recognize that, as leader, she must provide a model as well as technical expertise, so the group can move. In the formative stages of the group, the leader may need to use exercises that create productive interaction. She may explicitly point out interactions that don't implement therapeutic goals and reinforce and encourage any attempts of members to effectively utilize the group's therapeutic forces. Some leaders like to believe that productive groups emerge without their guidance and even consider the kind of intervention we have discussed as manipulation. Yalom (1970) deals with the issue directly: "The manipulation in therapy is often covert, implicit, and unplanned; however, it may be overt, explicit, and planned without sacrificing therapeutic effectiveness" (p. 88).

Spontaneity is an important factor in effective group work. it enables the leader to pick up on what is happening and turn the interaction into a growth-promoting experience. Leaders must use all their creativity and spontaneity, since both accelerate the progress of the group and provide a valuable model for the participants.

Group-Leadership Competencies

The group leader must be able to function in a continuously flowing process with all members, no matter how different their beliefs, feelings, and intentions. He must be able to create an atmosphere in which members can achieve their goals and learn to help one another grow.

The leader pays attention not only to the content of members' messages but to the method, setting, and timing of messages. How are the feelings conveyed—with considerable involvement or apathetically? Does the message indicate the person is trying to focus the interaction on himself or that he wants to stay with the here-and-now transaction? The leader is always aware of the purpose of the communication, and, when it is appropriate, confronts participants with their beliefs, feelings, and intentions.

Thus, while leadership requires someone who is open, honest, accepting, spontaneous, understanding, and congruent, these personality traits alone are not enough. The leader must be trained and skilled in all these techniques:

Structuring the group and communicating its purpose

Using interaction exercises and programs effectively

Universalizing

Dealing with the here-and-now interaction

Linking

Blocking

Encouraging and focusing on assets and positive feedback

Facilitating participation by confronting nonverbal clues

Facilitating I-messages

Paraphrasing and clarifying to stimulate reality testing

Offering feedback

Formulating tentative hypotheses

Setting tasks and getting commitment

Capping and summarizing

To make the meaning of these competencies and skills clearer, we will describe each of them and explain the rationale for using it in the group setting.

Structuring the Group and Communicating Its Purpose

Definition. Structuring the group and communicating its purpose are essential for effective therapeutic groups. Defining goals and setting limits give the group a purpose and direct its activity. For example, the leader may indicate that each person in the group is there to work on a specific concern, that they will all be sharing the concern, and that they will help one another. More specifically, the leader may structure by indicating that members are to speak directly to the other members about their feelings and use I-messages, which express what one is experiencing but do not mandate change in others. Structuring may also encourage members to focus on the here and now—that is, on the dialogue within the group, in contrast to a discussion of events that happened outside the group.

Rationale. By structuring the group, the leader helps members focus their discussions on matters that are meaningful and purposeful. Structuring enables the leader and the group to set limits and to focus on tasks.

Structuring is a demanding job, because the leader must be continually aware of what is happening and determine whether it is within the structure, goals, and purposes of the group. Once members are ready to stay within the structure, more productive group work is accomplished.

The following dialogues contrast ineffective and effective use of structuring.

Ineffective use

David: I can never be on time. This makes my girlfriend really mad.

Joan: David, tell us about your girlfriend.

Frank: What kind of girls do you consider attractive, David?

Leader: We are concerned about how you get along with girls.

If the group agreed and structured itself not to discuss personal problems unless the counselee volunteered such information, this dialogue is beyond the structure. Furthermore, David's personal goal is solving the problem he has in being punctual. Therefore, the above comments violate group structure. The leader should have interrupted the interaction to indicate a violation of contract.

Effective use

Lynn: Well, why are we here?

Ramon: Yes, silence makes me nervous (looking at the leader).

Leader: You have all met with me individually, but let's review our goals. Our purpose is to share our concerns and to help one another by relating honestly and by providing feedback.

Utilizing Interaction Exercises and Programs Effectively

Definition. To program a group, the leader chooses to initiate specific group behaviors at a specific point so as to create an experience for the members. Programming is in contrast with permitting the interaction to be spontaneous and following whatever course of interaction happens to occur. Programs are usually aimed at specific goals. They are structured experiences that can be used to get people acquainted, build cohesiveness, help members understand certain phenomena by experiencing them, increase feedback, and create awareness of various group dynamics and processes.

Programs or exercises that are generally productive include:

Get-acquainted activity, in which people learn one another's names and some information about various members' interests

Depth unfoldment experience (DUE), in which members share their most important experiences—those they feel made them who they are

Strength recognition, in which members are asked to recognize, acknowledge, and state their own strengths

Multiple-strength perception, in which a member, after listing his own strengths, has the group present their perceptions of his strengths

Paraphrasing, in which a member can talk only after he has paraphrased what the person who preceded him in the conversation has said

Learning to link, in which members are asked to show how previous statements by different persons are similar or different

Having members present their position in the family constellation and indicate how they are most like or different from their siblings

Having members indicate their number-one priority and have the group give feedback on the priorities they have observed

Rationale. Although some leaders are philosophically opposed to exercises and uncomfortable using programs, it is important to understand the rationale and timing of programs. Programs are usually most effective early in group life, since they tend to improve communication, increase cohesiveness, and reduce anxiety when new members and inexperienced leaders are uncertain about what is expected. Although some object that programs are anxiety provoking, one must recognize that the novel, unstructured situation of open-ended group life can itself generate considerable anxiety. The leader who understands the use of programs, is familiar with a variety of structured experiences, and knows how to use them appropriately can facilitate group movement. The purpose of programs and exercises is to promote members' growth and communication within the group. The following dialogue shows an ineffective use of this competency.

Anne:	Well, what should we do?
Laura:	I don't know what is expected of us.
Anne:	It seems so pointless without a topic.
Leader:	Now I'm going to show you how to become more involved with one another. Here is an experience . . .

The leader waited until the group was in a state of confusion and now, instead of working through it, proposes a solution. The leader should sense when there is a lack of understanding of purpose and a lack of skills and provide them in a more timely manner.

Universalizing

Definition. Universalization is the process by which a group leader makes group members aware that others share their concerns. The leader elicits responses that make it clear that there are elements of similarity in members' thoughts, feelings, or actions. The leader asks questions such as "Has anyone ever had that problem or felt that way?" In other instances, the leader shows how certain ideas and feelings are related. This requires listening for common themes and making members aware of those themes so they see that they have similar problems. By easing or, at times, even removing the feeling of isolation, universalization permits participants to realize they all share similar human concerns.

Rationale. Universalization is basic to group cohesion. For cohesion to take place, group members must have positive feelings about one another and see one another as equals. By helping members see similarities in one another, the leader increases the group's cohesion. The leader encourages the sharing of concerns, because sharing creates a bond among group members and promotes growth. Awareness of the commonality of problems also provides reassurance and gives participants the courage to learn ways of becoming more effective.

The following dialogues contrast ineffective and effective use of this competency.

Ineffective use

George: I take after my father—the bad side of him. When he asks for juice and someone brings him water, he gets real mad. I'm like that. If I don't get my way, I feel like hitting.

David: Yeah, when my sister gets to hog the TV every Friday night, I get angry and pick a fight with her. She always gets what she wants.

Leader: Why do you think she gets what she wants?

The leader could have pointed out the similarity of George's and David's problems. By asking the reason for someone else's behavior, the leader is taking the group out of the here and now and is missing an opportunity to show George and David that their feelings are similar.

Effective use

Marianne: I really like science books, and I want to read them. But I always have to ask somebody to explain what some words mean. They're too hard.

Leader: Is anyone else experiencing a problem like this?

Dealing with the Here-and-Now Interaction

Definition. This competency refers to the ability to deal with what is happening now, as it is experienced by the entire group as well as by the individual members. It means moving away from memories of the past and from plans for the future to awareness of the present moment. What is important now is *now.* To be concrete, specific, and in touch with one's sensitivities now; to refer only to those past events that are affecting one in the present moment; to be conscious of what is happening in this session rather than in the last—all this is part of the here-and-now focus in group work.

Rationale. Here-and-now interaction, as opposed to there-and-then interaction, is essential to the spontaneity, growth, and effectiveness of the group process. Dealing at length with distant concerns is like cutting off the group's oxygen supply; it is present worries and concerns, not past ones, that members are trying to reduce or satisfy. Lingering excessively on past feelings, without reference to the now, is a distraction that affects the growth of the group. Behavior is not caused by something that occurred in the past; behavior has a current purpose. If the group fails to deal with the here and now, it forfeits the opportunity to work through problems and eventually resolve them. Members may attempt to avoid the here and now by trying to talk about the past or about events outside the group. By talking about the there and then, participants may give the impression that they are confronting themselves honestly and thoroughly. If the counselor is aware of this tendency, she will try to lead group members to discuss here-and-now behavior.

The following dialogues contrast ineffective and effective use of the competency.

Ineffective use

Tom: I've never been very confident of myself. When I was a little kid, I used to hide behind the furniture when my mother had company.

Leader: Has this pattern continued?

Tom: Well, when I was in high school, I took as many babysitting jobs as I could on weekends so I could avoid going to dances and parties.

Leader: Avoiding people made you feel secure.

Laura: Gee, I used to feel the same way . . .

The group leader has failed to recognize what was happening. By not shifting the conversation to Tom's feelings now, rather than then, he has set a tone for the group to ineffectively wallow in what has happened.

Effective use

Tom: I'm not very sure of myself, and I don't know how to talk about myself.

Leader: You are not sure what is expected of you here.

Linking

Definition. Linking requires the leader to point out to group members the similarities and differences he detects in what members are saying, from the point of view of both content and feelings. Linking necessitates awareness of meanings. A comment may have hidden meanings, and the leader makes it clear to the group how a member's statement relates to the comments of another member. The leader can also link an individual's verbal and nonverbal messages.

Rationale. Linking allows the leader to show group members that their problems, although stated in different terms, are basically similar. This applies to feelings too; members are made aware of the relationship between their feelings and those of others, even if verbalized differently. The assumption is that linking promotes interaction. At the beginning, group interaction is often minimal and superficial. The interaction produced through linking promotes cohesion. The member's perception of these linkages and realization that her problems and feelings are shared promotes greater understanding of human behavior and willingness to contribute to the group. Members are more willing and free to interact because they perceive that the others are interested in understanding one another.

The following dialogues contrast ineffective and effective use of the competency.

Ineffective use

Ramon: Mom and Dad always call my friends' homes when I'm a minute late getting home. All of the guys rib me about it the next day and call me "Mama's little boy."

Tony: When I get home from school and just begin to relax, both my parents come at me and demand to see what I have for homework. If I don't have any—wow! The war starts! Sometimes they even call the teacher to check my story.

Leader: Have you ever thought of having your teacher sign a no-homework slip for you?

The leader has offered a possible alternative to Tony and left Ramon hanging alone. This procedure limits interaction in the group. Ramon probably feels that he was not heard and must wonder what this group has to offer. He will probably be less willing and able to contribute the next time. The leader should have tried to link the feelings of anger at not being trusted that both Ramon and Tony expressed. This would have made them both aware of the likeness of their situations and feelings and enabled them to contribute more appropriately to the present situation.

Effective use

Sally: I like to go to the show on Sunday afternoon. Every time I suggest it to my friends, they want to do something else, so I just go along with them.

Marianne: When we break up into small groups in class to do a project, I get a good idea, but, before I have a chance to say it, someone else talks about his idea first. Most of the time, I just let mine go, and follow theirs.

Leader: I hear both of you saying that you get mad at yourselves when you let your ideas drop and just do what the group wants to do. How do you feel about that?

Here the leader links both people's feelings and problems, thus helping Sally and Marianne realize that they are not alone.

Confronting

Definition. By confronting sensitively and perceptively, the leader enables members to become aware of discrepancies between their behavior and their intentions. The disclosure focuses on the purpose of the behavior. Disclosure is managed through tentative hypotheses—"Could it be?" or "I have an idea that perhaps . . ."—and deals explicitly with the discrepancy between what one says and what one does, or between the behavior and its purpose.

Rationale. The goal of confrontation is not catharsis or challenge. Confrontation is aimed at making one aware of his effect on others. It helps group members to view their behavior more clearly and to be more congruent and sharing.

Confrontation should be offered with empathy. By caring and being congruent and authentic, the confronter offers a gift of great value. The Hill Interaction Matrix (Hill, 1965), which is a method of evaluating group interaction, assigns the highest level of productivity to some aspects of the confrontation process. Hill believes that it is at this level that individuals go beyond superficial human contacts and become productive.

If the leader operates with empathy and regard, confrontation facilitates individual and group movement to new levels. The leader who confronts takes a risk by sharing with the new members how others perceive them.

It can be helpful to make participants aware of how they may be subtly provoking other members of the group. This confrontation, as developed by Shulman (1962), is based on the hypothesis that each person's behavior in the group can be seen in light of psychological movement in relation to other group members and that this movement reveals the member's intentions (Shulman, 1962).

After the purpose of the behavior is ascertained, the group, with the member's consent, responds to the member's behavior by complying in an exaggerated way with the member's mistaken demands. For example, if one wants to be special, extensive time in the session is spent treating the person as *very* special. In other words, the group acts out the type of world the member wants. Thus, the member's purpose is exposed and, through the group's focus on the mistaken demands, the behavior tends to be inhibited. This procedure is similar to paradoxical intention, discussed in Chapter 6, since it exaggerates the behavior and thereby makes it less satisfying. Adler called this technique "prescribing the symptom."

The following dialogues contrast ineffective and effective use of confrontation.

Ineffective use

Wayne: I have had lots of problems in Mrs. Kasey's class. She picks on me.

Joan: Yeah, she really is on you. I try to cooperate, but I won't let her treat me that way.

Leader: Tell me what you do.

Effective use

Wayne: I have had lots of problems in Mrs. Kasey's class. She picks on me.

Joan: Yeah, she really is on you. I try to cooperate, but I won't let her treat me that way.

Leader: Could it be you want to show Mrs. Kasey that you can't be controlled?

The leader takes the dialogue to another level by focusing on the purpose of Joan's resistance, but does so tentatively to permit Joan to consider the purpose of her behavior.

Blocking

Definition. Blocking is intervening in communication that is destructive to the group as a whole or to individual members. Since the leader's goal is the progress of the group, she tries to check communication that hinders progress. For example, one of the participants may try to manipulate the leader into expressing her feelings toward other members, because the member fears a direct confrontation and wants the leader to do his work for him.

Rationale. Through the blocking technique, the leader encourages members to express inner feelings. Members are pressed to come out in the open with a clear statement of "where they are," manifesting openly their beliefs and feelings. The blocking technique must be handled gently so that it doesn't come across as rejection.

Blocking takes several forms. The leader can block questions and make members come out with a clear-cut comment on their feelings and beliefs. The leader can block gossip by intervening and directing a member to speak directly *to* whoever he is talking about instead of *about* her. Blocking can also help members focus on the here and now of group life instead of the there and then. This kind of blocking directs attention to current interpersonal experiences and feelings. The tendency to smooth something over with a soothing comment needs to be blocked when the intensity of a confrontation needs to be continued to its resolution. Continuing certain types of honest confrontation produces growth. Blocking can also be used to stop the invasion of someone's privacy by someone else who is trying to guess that person's thoughts.

Blocking is like a traffic signal. Handled improperly, it causes a traffic jam; handled correctly, it results in smooth-flowing traffic. The true test of whether the competency of blocking has been well mastered is to note whether or not the group can fulfill its purposes. Blocking prevents being sidetracked by insignificant and harmful tactics.

The following dialogues contrast ineffective and effective use of blocking.

Ineffective use

Lisa: I don't like the way John always sits with his arms folded.

Lynn: Yeah, that bugs me too!

Leader: He's just not a part of the group.

The leader has failed to have Lisa direct her remarks to John. Lisa wanted the leader to say something to John that she didn't dare say herself, because she feared the confrontation.

Effective use

Frank (to the leader): I wish you would say something to Carol. She doesn't contribute anything to the group.

Anne: We all feel that you should say something to her.

Leader:	You would like me to speak for you? But I feel it would be more helpful for Carol if you spoke directly to her.
Frank:	Carol, how do you feel about my difficulties with my mother?
Carol:	I was afraid to say something because I thought you would laugh at me. To me, it seems as though you . . .

The leader effectively blocks the group's attempted gossiping. The comments are redirected to the member concerned. Her feelings are brought into the open, and a constructive suggestion is made.

Encouraging and Focusing on Assets and Positive Feedback

Definition. The leader is aware of the powerful effect of making assets and positive feelings explicit. Positive feedback from peers has considerable influence on our attitudes and self-esteem. The leader finds opportunities to focus on assets and to supply positive feedback. This encourages group members to do the same by offering encouragement to one another.

Rationale. The individual is often concerned about her place in the group and is generally much more susceptible to suggestions and pressure from peers than from the leader. The group is a value-forming agent.

The leader can help the group encourage participants' development. As the group sees and accentuates the positive, social interest is stimulated and members grow by their opportunities to interact positively. As genuine encouragement is fostered and practiced, the group becomes more integrated and cohesive.

The following dialogues contrast ineffective and effective use of encouragement and positive feedback.

Ineffective use

Tom:	I don't seem to be able to get acquainted with girls easily.
Laurie:	Yes, you do seem very shy.
Tom:	I guess that's it; I'm just shy.
Leader:	Let's talk about your shyness.

Here the leader falls into the trap of discussing an assumed deficit.

Effective use

Tom:	I don't seem to be able to get acquainted with girls easily.
Laurie:	Yes, you do seem very shy.
Tom:	I guess that's it; I'm just shy.
Leader:	I've noticed that you seem relaxed when you talk with the boys in our group. Why are you at ease with boys?

The leader is attempting to use Tom's strengths and transfer them to the area in which he doesn't function as well.

Facilitating Participation by Confronting Nonverbal Clues

Definition. "The facilitator is one who is concerned about having contact with the whole person—his thoughts, feelings, purposes and actions" (Dinkmeyer & Muro, 1971). To understand the language of behavior, the leader begins by noting whether one's basic organic, emotional, and safety needs are being met. The group member's set of assumptions about self and others is constantly confirmed and occasionally rejected through reality testing in the group. The leader helps group members become aware of the language of nonverbal behavior and of which nonverbal behaviors open or close communication channels.

The leader should know when to look directly at a member and when to sweep the whole group with his gaze. The leader should also be able to detect blushing, tension, excitement, weeping, and laughter in their incipient states.

Rationale. By helping members become aware of nonverbal behaviors that open or close communication channels, the group leader adds another dimension to the group communication. Members become aware of their own messages and learn to read the others' messages. They also learn to point out and deal with incongruencies in themselves and others.

The following dialogues contrast ineffective and effective use of the competency.

Ineffective use

Gary   (at the first meeting of the group, seats himself all the way in the back, away from the group)

Leader: I often feel that, when people hang back there, they really don't want to be in the group. Gary, is there somebody here you don't like?

The leader's comment is a direct attack on Gary's position. It could have been made more general by saying "Let's all move in more closely."

Effective use

Lisa   (intellectualizes about herself and dominates the group with her reflections and recollections)

Wayne   (begins to twist and stretch in his chair)

Leader: You seem agitated, Wayne. What's going on with you?

The leader is commenting only on Wayne's actions. It is up to Wayne, if he wants to and if he can, to make a connection between his own and Lisa's actions.

Facilitating I-Messages

Definition. The I-message is a message clearly directed to someone concerning the sender's feelings and attitudes. The group leader's task is to facilitate the exchange of I-messages by modeling, by providing examples, and by intervening when indirect messages (you-messages) are being sent. The task also involves intervening when someone asks questions instead of making a statement about her own feelings. The leader asks the member to make a statement instead of asking the question—for example, instead of asking "Why are you doing that?" stating "I'm very bothered when you do that."

Rationale. The I-message, as opposed to the you-message, is much less apt to provoke resistance and rebellion. When people send I-messages, their awareness increases, because they become aware that they are responsible only for themselves and because they are forced to identify with, clarify, and become honest about the messages they send. Senders of honest I-messages risk revealing themselves to others as they really are. It takes courage and inner security for a person to do so. I-messages state only what one's feelings are and do not demand change in the other person because of the statement.

A direct I-message in the group process eliminates the need for a third member to interpret and send the message to the member it was intended for. The rationale is that, when members learn to deal directly with each other, more feedback and honest communication develop. When members are not communicating with each other or are using dysfunctional communication, the group becomes ineffective.

The following dialogues contrast ineffective and effective use of the competency.

Ineffective use

Jerry: Jack keeps saying he can't help laughing at me, and I'm tired of it.

Leader: You'd like to punch him in the nose.

The leader's comment is ineffective because it picks up Jerry's feeling instead of suggesting that Jerry address his anger directly to Jack.

Effective use

Jerry: Jack keeps saying he can't help laughing at me, and I'm tired of it.

Leader: Jerry, I'd like you to speak directly to Jack and tell him how you feel about it.

Encouraging members to face each other concerning their feelings is much more effective. It helps participants face up to their feelings and get them out into the open so they can deal with them. As a consequence, group members are able to explore insights directly and not feel as though they are dealing with someone who is not in the group.

Paraphrasing and Clarifying to Stimulate Reality Testing

Definition. In paraphrasing, the leader selectively focuses on content and feedback—on the essence of what has been said. The leader mirrors the thoughts to make sure she has heard them accurately, then encourages members to clarify their assumptions, values, attitudes, and behavior through interaction in the group. The group provides a unique setting for going beyond the verbal and trying on behavior to study its appropriateness and effect.

Rationale. Paraphrasing helps members find out whether they are being understood. Through reality testing, one tries on a certain behavior, learns from it, and evaluates its effects. The group can then help him "see himself in action."

The following dialogues contrast ineffective and effective use of the competency.

Ineffective use

Sally: I've been having lots of problems with my mother.

Anne: I'm getting tired of your always bringing up your mother in this group.

Leader: Each person has a right to discuss what he wants. Let's be patient.

The leader fails to hear Anne's message.

Effective use

Sally: I've been having lots of problems with my mother.

Anne: I'm getting tired of your always bringing up your mother in this group.

Leader: You are pretty angry that Sally always talks about her mother. Could you tell us what you are experiencing when that happens?

The leader helps Anne to be heard and to clarify what she believes and feels.

Offering Feedback

Definition. The term *feedback,* first applied to the behavioral sciences by Kurt Lewin, relates to the process whereby we learn how others perceive us, so we can modify our behavior accordingly. In everyday life, opportunities to obtain accurate feedback are quite limited. The group provides the psychological safety that makes it possible for people to give and receive true and valuable feedback.

Rationale. Feedback serves two functions: (1) providing information about the effects of one's behavior on others, and (2) providing positive or negative reinforcement.

The more clearly the feedback is related to specific responses, the better. Feedback about each response is better than information about overall progress, and precise information at the time of a response is better than general advice about a sequence of responses. Feedback in the group seems most effective when it stems from here-and-now observations and when it follows the generating event as closely as possible.

In the process of feedback, individuals rapidly acquire a great deal of data concerning how they appear to others. The overly friendly type finds that others in the group resent her exaggerated friendliness; the man who weighs his words carefully and speaks with heavy precision discovers for the first time that others regard him as stuffy; a woman who shows a somewhat excessive desire to help others is told in no uncertain terms that some group members don't want her for a mother. Genuine feedback can be extremely upsetting, but as long as information is offered in the context of caring that is characteristic of groups, it can be highly constructive.

The following dialogues contrast ineffective and effective use of the competency.

Ineffective use

Emily: I somehow feel that it's so easy for me to put myself inside another person, and I guess I feel that . . .

Leader: Why is it so easy for you?

Emily: Probably, I'm just sensitive.

Leader: You're really lucky to be like that. How about you, Al?

In this example, the leader doesn't give feedback about how Emily's comments strike him but simply accepts and reassures.

Effective use

Greg: What I meant by being careful is that, if I'm not careful about how I say something, it's twisted on me.

Leader: I have the impression we can tell when you're being careful.

Greg: I guess so, but it's my way. That's when I get into arguments.

Leader: I have the feeling that being honest is very hard for you.

Formulating Tentative Hypotheses

Definition. Tentative hypotheses are the hypotheses the group leader makes about the purpose of a member's behavior in the group. The hypotheses help the group consider the purpose of behavior and become aware of the here and now by investigating what is happening in the moment.

Rationale. The leader offers a tentative hypothesis of behavior (that is, makes a disclosure) in an attempt to help the individual develop insight into her behavior by understanding its purpose. Since the group is itself a social setting, it affords members a situation in which they can observe the purpose and consequences of their social behavior. Although tentative hypotheses are directed to one person, they are valuable for the entire group, because there is often considerable similarity in people's mistaken perceptions and self-defeating patterns. Feedback from peers in the group may make the hypothesis more valid and provide additional insights.

Tentative hypotheses are most effective when they are offered at the right time, when the member is ready for them, and in the right way. The leader's attitude when she makes a disclosure is crucial, as is how she makes the disclosure.

Disclosure is concerned not with the causes of the behavior but with its purpose. The leader avoids making assertions about the behavior, which may be discouraging, but makes the person aware of what the purpose of the behavior may be. These revelations may evoke an immediate recognition reflex. The disclosure is made in a friendly atmosphere of mutual respect; the leader asks the individual if he would like to know why he behaves in a certain way and offers the hypothesis tentatively, in terms of "I wonder," "Could it be," "I have the impression," and so forth.

The following dialogues contrast ineffective and effective use of tentative hypotheses.

Ineffective use

Wayne: If the subject we're discussing in the group doesn't interest me, I sometimes yawn out loud.

Leader: You're obviously trying to draw attention to yourself and keep us busy with you.

The leader has offered a hypothesis bluntly, *telling* Wayne what his goals are rather than *hypothesizing* about what his goals may be. Confronted with this attitude on the part of the leader, Wayne is likely to become defensive and deny the possibility that this is the true purpose of his behavior. He may also resent the leader for making such an "accusation." He will certainly feel trapped.

Effective use

Wayne: If the subject we're discussing in the group doesn't interest me, I sometimes yawn out loud.

Leader: Is it possible that, because you are bored with what is happening, you yawn to keep us busy with you?

Here the leader has offered the same hypothesis but in a much less assertive and abrasive manner. Wayne can consider the possibility that the leader's hypothesis reflects his real intention, without feeling trapped. And he can accept the leader's insight as a helpful suggestion rather than as an accusation.

Setting Tasks and Getting Commitment

Definition. The leader sets tasks by helping members verbalize the job or task they have set for themselves in the group. The members clearly state what they hope to accomplish through their interaction with the other members of the group in an individual session or (as is more often the case) in the entire series of sessions. The more specific the statement of the task, the easier it will be to accomplish it. The group leader promotes specificity by first hearing what an individual is attempting to say and then encouraging him to verbalize his ideas and commit himself to doing the job. Encouragement may come in the form of helping the individual see the value of accomplishing the task. The member makes a specific contract and is expected to report back on his progress at the next meeting.

Once the task has been specified, the leader should try to help the member say exactly how he feels he can best accomplish the task. Here, too, specificity is very important; however, the leader may allow the individual to change the method to which he has committed himself, if it is not effective. The essential factor is for the individual to make some kind of commitment to the task he has taken upon himself.

Rationale. Task setting and commitment are both important to the group process because without them, little would be accomplished. It is important that the leader help all members become aware of some area they need to work on in the group. It is equally important that all members make some kind of definite commitment to follow through with the job or task they have set for themselves. Task setting and commitments usually occur early in the group, but they may be redefined as new perceptions and situations arise.

The following dialogues contrast ineffective and effective use of the competency.

Ineffective use

Maureen: I'm not sure what the purpose of this group is. I know I'm not perfect, but I don't know what the group can do for me.

Leader: Well, there must be something! With that attitude, nothing will be accomplished.

Maureen: I already did say what I feel. I don't know what the group can do for me.

Leader: You can't really mean that.

The leader is trying too hard to get Maureen to react. This kind of strong-arm tactic doesn't work, because Maureen feels far away from where the leader is. Force will not get people to participate.

Effective use

Maureen: I'm not sure what the purpose of this group is. I know I'm not perfect, but I don't know what the group can do for me.

Leader: I think we all share some of these feelings. The purpose of the group is to help us understand ourselves and relate more effectively with others. Is there something in that area you'd like to discuss?

Maureen: Well, I feel uneasy in large groups of people. Perhaps we could talk about that.

Leader: Would you want to discuss with the group this uncomfortable feeling?

Maureen: Yes, I think I would.

Leader: Can you tell us how you feel in large groups and how you would like to change?

Maureen: Well, I just can't get my thoughts out, and I'd like to feel more free and relaxed.

Here the leader does not try to force anything. Instead, he tries to get Maureen to decide on a task for the group. The leader doesn't give Maureen a task but lets her find one. Then he guides Maureen to explore the situation.

Capping and Summarizing

Definition: Capping takes place near the end of a session, when the leader helps the group ease up on the emotional side of the interaction and focus instead on its cognitive aspects. Thus, the group leaves behind deep emotional explorations and prepares to function in the typical world of social reality. The leader does this consciously by responding to content rather than to feelings, by looking at ideas instead of picking up on feelings. When an emotional point is raised, the leader uses capping techniques to change the subject to something less intense. The subject can be changed back to a topic previously discussed or to a new and less loaded topic. In using capping techniques, the leader must make sure that no member is left in a state of crisis. Participants should not leave the session feeling they cannot cope with their feelings. At the end of the session, the leader may want to "go around" and give each member an opportunity to make a final comment.

Definition: Summarizing is a way of looking at the themes that are coming through in the session. This can be done by the leader, by the members of the group, or collectively. It may occur during the session when the leader wants to pull together what has been happening and look at the meaning of the interaction. It can be stimulated by questions such as "What's happening here now?" or "Where are we?" In other instances, the leader will choose to cap and summarize to the group what she has been experiencing and what she believes is the emotional level of the group. The leader may choose to identify where various members of the group seem to be on certain issues. This can also be accomplished by asking members to indicate what they have learned and how they feel about what they are experiencing.

Rationale. Probably the most basic reason for capping is that it allows time for all members to get themselves together and back in touch with reality. Summarizing closes the session on a note of positive planning, lends a cognitive element to the interaction, and enables the group to tie structure and purpose to what has really been happening. Summarizing also provides all members with access to one another's perceptions and can generate new data for the group. Finally, it provides the leader with an accurate reading of what members of the group are experiencing.

The following dialogues contrast ineffective and effective use of the competency.

Ineffective use

Jerry: I'm really uptight.

Leader: Well, it's about time to close, so let's leave that for next time.

Perhaps Jerry is in crisis, and he is abruptly put off.

Effective use

Jack: I'm not really sure whether we have solved our problem or not.

Leader: What do you think you've learned so far?

The leader caps the discussion and requests a response to what has been learned to this point. This provides an opportunity to assess what development has occurred for Jack so far.

REFERENCES

Adler, A. (1931). *Guiding the child.* New York: Greenberg.

Dickoff, H., & Lakin, M. (1963). Patient's views of group psychotherapy: Retrospection and interpretation. *International Journal of Group Psychotherapy, 13,* 61–73.

Dinkmeyer, D., & Muro, J.J. (1971). *Group counseling: Theory and practice.* Itasca, IL: Peacock.

Dreikurs, R. (1928). The development of mental hygiene in Vienna. *Allg. Zeitsch. Psychiat., 88,* 469–489.

Dreikurs, R. (1952). Group psychotherapy: General review. *Proceedings of the First International Congress of Psychiatry, Paris, 1950.* Paris: Hermann.

Dreikurs, R., & Corsini, R. (1960). Twenty years of group psychotherapy. In R. Dreikurs (Ed.), *Group psychotherapy and group approaches.* Chicago: Alfred Adler Institute.

Hill, W.F. (1965). *Him, Hill interaction matrix.* Los Angeles: University of Southern California, Youth Studies Center.

Metzl, J. (1937). Die Arbeitzmethoden der Trinkerfuersorgestelle Brigittenau. *Int. Zeits. gegen den Alcohol, 35.*

Moreno, J.L. (1953). *Who shall survive?* New York: Beacon House.

Ozertovsky, D.S. (1927). *Zhurn. Neuropath. i. Psichiat.* (20) 587.

Shulman, B.H. (1962). The use of dramatic confrontation in group psychotherapy. *Psychiatric Quarterly, 36,* 93–99.

Yalom, I.D. (1970). *The theory and practice of group psychotherapy.* New York: Basic Books.

11 Adlerian Group Methods

A dlerians place great emphasis on the social meaning of behavior. Recognizing that, basically, most problems are social and interpersonal, they believe in the necessity of understanding behavior in its social context. This approach, common to all Adlerian therapists and counselors, still allows some differences in group procedures.

LIFE-STYLE GROUPS

Adlerian groups often employ the life style to develop self-awareness and understanding. Usually, members of these groups present enough information about themselves to compile a mini-life style, which covers the individual's relationship with parents, rating and trait comparison with siblings, and some early recollections. The leader provides a brief summary of the individual's mistaken perceptions, assets, and goals. In some groups, members indicate how successful they are in the various tasks of life.

The members' life styles and the way each participant copes with the life tasks are all "grist for the mill," since they enable group members to understand the perceptions, beliefs, goals, and values of the other members. The equalitarian nature of the group relationship is emphasized as the members get to know one another, participate in the diagnosis, and learn to guess or formulate tentative hypotheses about the purpose of each person's psychological movement.

Robert Powers, an Adlerian affiliated with the Alfred Adler Institute of Chicago, uses an educational approach to group therapy. All participants actually keep some notes regarding the life styles in the group. The fact that leader and members of the group have access to the same information about life style and interaction makes it possible for members and leader to treat one another as equals sharing in a learning experience.

This is Frank Walton's excellent guide, based on Powers's format:

Part I: A Guide for Presenting Yourself to the Seminar
A. You have ten minutes, uninterrupted, in which to tell us who you are.
B. Stay, as much as possible, in the *present tense*. Later on you will have an opportunity to tell us about your childhood.
C. Life challenges each of us, and each person is now approaching its challenges in a way unique to himself. Tell us about your responses to these challenges:
   1. What kind of friends have you made? What kind of friend are you? How do you get along with strangers in chance meetings? How do people treat you generally? How do you feel about other people, most of the time?

2. What kind of work do you do? What kind of worker are you? Do you enjoy what you are doing? Do those with whom or for whom you work appreciate your contributions?

3. Whom do you love? What kinds of problems have you had over loving and being loved? Do sex, closeness, and intimacy have a comfortable place in your life or not? What does masculinity mean to you? What does femininity mean to you? How do you measure up to whatever you expect of yourself as a man or a woman?

Part II: A Guide for Sharing in Responses

A. Someone has just spent ten minutes presenting himself. How did you receive what he presented?

B. Did you *recognize* things in yourself that he mentioned about himself? Was it easy to understand him or difficult? Did he sound strange or familiar?

C. How do you *feel* toward him? Did your feelings toward him change as a result of his presenting himself as he did? How?

D. Do you feel invited to *act* any particular way toward him? Did you welcome that invitation or resent it? What would you like to do *for* this person? What would you like to do *with* this person? What would you like to do *to* this person?

Part III: A Guide for Drawing Your Family Constellation

A. In childhood each of us learned how to define the *place* he had amongst others. Help the members of the seminar to see the kind of place you had as a pre-adolescent child in your family.

B. How many children were there in your family, and where did you fit in amongst them? How were you different from the others, and how were you like them? Which of the others was most nearly like you, and which was most different? What were you "good at"? What was hard for you?

C. What was father like? Who was his favorite? What did he expect from you? How did you feel about his expectations?

D. What was mother like? Who was her favorite? What did she expect from you? How did you feel about her expectations?

E. How did your parents get along with each other? What were their differences/arguments/fights about? To which parent did you feel closer? Why?

F. Were grandparents or other relatives important to you? How?

G. Did anything change at adolescence? How? What did puberty, physical development, and dating mean to you?

1. For boys: What did "being a man" mean to you? Did you think you would have been happier, luckier, better off if you had been born a girl?

2. For girls: What did "being a woman" mean to you? Did you think you would have been happier, luckier, better off if you had been born a boy?

Part IV: A Guide for Discussing a Family Constellation

A. Can you share any feelings about yourself in your family with the person who just told you about his childhood?

B. Can you understand this person better? How?

C. Can you see something in the way he presented himself initially which didn't make sense to you at the time?

D. What more do you want to know about this person?

E. Can you see a relationship between the *role* he played as a child, in his family and among other children, and the way in which he has tried to find a place in this seminar?

F. Each of us has the *private goal* of playing a certain kind of *social role*.

Parts I and II are repeated for each member of the group before the group moves on to Parts III and IV, which are also repeated for each member of the group. A fifth and sixth part can be added at the option of the leader. Part V would consist of obtaining two or three early memories, while Part VI would be devoted to the interpretation of the memories by the leader and participants. These additional segments are limited to ten minutes each in the fashion of Parts I through IV.

A group may terminate at the conclusion of Part IV or Part VI, or it may continue to meet periodically in order to help group members work at relating the increased awareness of the purposes and patterns of their behavior to the challenges of social living.*

ACTION THERAPY

Action therapy is a group procedure developed by Walter O'Connell (1972, 1975). The format is similar to psychodrama, but the spontaneous release of emotions is not an end in itself but a move toward honesty with self and others. People are understood as decision-making beings who seek to enhance their self-esteem; their mistaken perceptions and faulty methods are highlighted in the group process. The hidden purposes of behavior are revealed, and the individual is encouraged to develop more socially responsible motivations and purposes.

Although the techniques of Jacob Moreno, the originator of psychodrama, helped generate action therapy, O'Connell indicates that his own system is Adlerian because of the following elements.

1. Man is not viewed as a mechanistic system powered by a closed source of energy. Feedback and resultant fluctuations in self-esteem better fit our world-view (Frankl, 1963; Mowrer, 1963) and seem capable of explaining

*From "Group Workshop with Adolescents," by F. Walton, *The Individual Psychologist,* 1975, *12* (1), 26–28. Reprinted by permission of *The Individual Psychologist.*

our behavior, a necessary segment of the total treatment field (Oliver & Landfield, 1962).

2. We have worked ourselves free of intrapsychic overemphasis with its accentuation of infantile and pathological determinism in favor of behavioral responses amenable to change in the here-and-now.

3. The preference is for a diagnosis which attends to self-esteem, compensatory fantasy and extent of humanistic identification abstracted from behavior over time and changing external conditions.

4. Treatment is a process for correction of mistakes and stupidities instead of eliminating impersonal disease processes, and is carried out in a group setting which highlights the creative hypothetico-deductive life style of the individual (e.g., experiences lead to cognitions which are self-reinforced and call forth strong expectations and demands toward others). (O'Connell, 1975, p. 63)

Basic Concepts and Tactics

This is O'Connell's description of the basic principles and tactics of action therapy:

1. *Guardian principle.* Every member of the group should have a "guardian," who shows understanding and acceptance and treats the person with dignity.

2. *Responsibility.* The goal is to educate each person to be responsible for his or her own behavior. Although feelings of anxiety and guilt are uncomfortable, the use of illness as an explanation for goal-directed behaviors is discouraged.

3. *Outsight.* If self-esteem is low, acceptance and belonging must be increased. This is accomplished by getting outsight into the motives and feelings of others.

4. *Awareness.* This is the concept of the Internalized Sentences and Negative Nonsense. Action Therapy avoids pointing to the past and, instead, highlights the individual's immediate, automatic reactions to internalized sentences.

5. *Self-disclosure.* The leader's stimulus value as a positive-identification model is emphasized. The members will more often do as the leader does than as the leader says. (O'Connell, 1975, pp. 64–66)

Techniques

"The number of techniques employable in action therapy seem infinite" (Moreno, 1959). Our five-year experience has taught us the recurrent utility of the mirror, double, role reversal, aside and dialogue techniques. The reluctant patient has always, in our experience, become involved in acting upon his problems when a staff member has temporarily enacted his kinetic and verbal reactions through the mirror play. The patient is generally quite astounded that someone seems to know him so well (without retaliating) and is willing to expend time and effort toward one who basically feels so unworthy. The double technique also provides for staff participation, with the protagonist standing behind the patient while verbalizing feelings and "automatic" reactions (e.g., "I feel that I'll be punished for whatever I think or say. I'll try to wriggle my way out by saying something strange. I don't dare try anything more . . ."). Role reversal has remained an excellent vehicle for introducing anyone to his unfruitful arbitrary demands on others then launching the discussion and practice of attending to the needs of others as a means of cementing friendship bonds. In the aside the real feelings and hidden manipulatory games (Watzlawick, 1964) are verbalized although the patient or staff protagonist might be behaving in a defensive self-defeating style. Rather than aim an interpretation toward an uneasy avoiding patient and thereby compounding his lack of self-disclosure, staff or patients may debate the particular patient's motives and goals among themselves. Such an interchange (dialogue) is usually tempered with such overt themes as "We know you've learned this in the past . . . but you can change, if you want to and think it's possible . . . If you think we're wrong, tell us." (O'Connell, 1975, p. 67)

As O'Connell indicates, "Action therapy is a form of group therapy which is focused on what the patient can do for others, rather than on the patient as such" (O'Connell, 1975, p. 36).

Action therapy includes "lecturettes" on Adlerian theory, which explain in common language the participants' mistaken concepts and self-defeating beliefs and how these errors in living can be overcome. The need for self-esteem (significance or worth) and social interest are emphasized. The liabilities of low self-esteem are illustrated through examples of members' misbehavior, such as oversensitiveness, feelings of worthlessness, and unwillingness to risk imperfection. The courage to be imperfect is discussed, as well as the consequence of a lack of self-esteem—restricted social interest, which creates distance and either overdependence or active or passive competitiveness and aggressiveness.

A part of the lecturette is concerned with topics which help the director to get the group going, avoiding abstractions and past histories. One such topic is the specific error of lowering self-esteem and narrowing social interest in this present encounter. "We all do this. Why? And how? Why are you doing it right now?" Another topic is anxiety, feeling "certain" that something catastrophic is going to happen to one, beyond one's control. "What do you fear will happen? Tell the group in a fit of openness and honesty. Is it a fear of loneliness, of humiliation, of others detecting imperfections?" Still another topic is knowing another, i.e., understanding how he lowers his self-esteem and social interest in terms of outer and inner (cognitive) movements; knowing his hidden anxieties; understanding the nature of his habitual relationships (hyperdependent, cooperative, or competitive); lastly, knowing how he wants to be confirmed, as "what," and by what types of reinforcements, e.g., as the best speaker, by constant nodding and smiling of others. Ideally, all members know this information about all other members and are willing to share themselves, and confirm others. This builds authentic "community," and each member is able to mirror or double for every other. (O'Connell, 1975, pp. 38–39)

In action therapy, the members of the group, one at a time, volunteer to be the protagonist and contribute their concerns and challenges of living to the group. The protagonist's low self-esteem and negative nonsense are explored.

While working with the protagonist the director inquires from other members for similarities and understanding. "Why don't you understand Joe?" "What information do you need? What movements does he have to make before you understand him?" "What do you tell yourself about Joe to keep distance from him?" "What have you said or done to Joe to help him tell himself that he is (or you are) inferior as a person?"

The director might ask if others have had similar problems. "Let's see the hands of those who have had sex problems" (two hands up, ten arms motionless). "I see we have two guys with guts and ten liars (laughter). I've had sex problems too. What do you think of that?"

The director can play upon competition itself to precipitate insight into the goals of competition on the useless side and develop group cohesion. One statement might be, "The group's task is to find the most depressed guys. Who is the sickest?"

The director can capitalize upon competitive power struggles to stimulate sharing and practice of openness. When Harry, a sullen, violently-passive alcoholic, steadfastly refused to play the son who infuriated Harry and led him to drinking behavior, a bet was made with Joe. Joe, also on the stage because the director called for the group to select people with the "best tempers," was told by the director, "I'll bet you two bits you can't get Harry to play his son." Almost immediately the director lost his quarter and the group had a hearty laugh over their power to "defeat" authority. But authority in this case was not defeated since it also laughed and was pleased at the creativity of the group in demonstrating power struggles and provoking movement.

Guessing at another's constricting cognitions highlights the other's "creativity" (albeit of an unexpected negative kind) and focuses on the possibility of his making alternative choices. Guessing in itself is stressed because it is encouraging to realize that no one of us has absolute certainty and guessing is what we are all doing. Guessing at another's creativity also helps to show him a developmental route to the sense of humor through experiencing the tragicomic paradox, e.g., knocking oneself down while crying for help. The humor of unloving the self while demanding pampering from others, the humor of being the best or most perfect self-devaluator, can also be brought out through mirroring and doubling in action therapy. (O'Connell, 1975, pp. 39–40)

Emphasis may be placed on the paradox of having participants strive harder to accomplish their "symptoms." The lesson is "either stop your negative nonsense, or immediately increase it and learn to enjoy your misery more fully" (O'Connell, 1975, p. 41).

The leader or director moves to develop peer support, acceptance, and especially encouragement, stressing that self-esteem comes from positive reinforcement of self and others, from courage, and from social interest.

THE ENCOURAGEMENT LABS

O'Connell is also the founder of the *encouragement labs,* which developed because his concept of humanistic identification "conceives of man as having both a relatively stable inner core (life style or existential-humanistic attitudes) and an innate potential for social intercourse (the need for power, seen as the ability to stimulate or resist interpersonal change)" (O'Connell, 1975, p. 52).

The goal of the encouragement labs is to teach participants, through lecturettes and experiences, that they are not passive victims of their environments. "The principal lab premise is that social interest does not emerge full-blown in the absence of psychological complaints (symptoms), but needs to be explicitly taught, especially in a competitive society like ours where there are no institutionalized efforts to teach the movements and responsibilities of love" (O'Connell, 1975, p. 53).

Encouragement includes in its progressive repertoire of social skills the art of courage: giving and asking for feedback about peoples' reactions to one's behaviors and guessing at the goals of misbehavior (self and others). Encouragement in its most advanced state includes recognizing the importance of being open and self-disclosing and not provoking and reinforcing inequality (e.g., feelings of insignificance *or* feelings of significance in narrow noncontributory social roles). Encouragement labs point toward knowledge and practice of the humorous attitude, for there is no more encouraging or growth-precipitating person than one with a humorous attitude. Contrary to popular practice, encouragement is definitely not pampering. Yet almost one hundred students, asked to write on how they would encourage authority figures in their lives, gave examples more appropriate to pampering. In these examples, students behaved as if they had no right to give feedback, or if they did it would be ignored or retaliated against: so they made themselves discouraged. Encouragement is not such destructive pampering as telling a person what he wants to hear about how wonderful he is, completely ignoring his motivated mistakes. Encouragement is a process of getting the message across, loudly and clearly, that one is responsible for constricting or expanding his feelings of self-esteem and belonging. (O'Connell, 1975, pp. 53–54)

The encouragement lab includes lecturettes and exercises aimed at developing encouragement skills. The members of the group are taught to produce natural highs by increasing their self-esteem and social interest. Techniques include presenting opportunities to encourage various kinds of constricted individuals and using success bombardment (finding something good). Participants learn even to congratulate creatively arranged rejection and other forms of negative nonsense and misbehavior. They learn to give encouraging feedback, instead of reinforcing negative nonsense and negative behaviors.

These are some of the essential elements for practicing the encouragement process in dyads:

1. Attend through eye contact and attentive listening.
2. Paraphrase your partner's message and feelings.
3. Identify similarities between yourself and your partner, since acceptance encourages belonging.
4. Share yourself through authentic self-disclosure of your feelings.
5. Give each other feedback, sharing the impressions that have been developed.
6. Find something good about everyone in the group—even how creatively someone arranges for reinforcement of her behavior.
7. Tell how your partner has encouraged you.
8. Make guesses as to how you have helped the group.

Becoming a Positive, Encouraging Person

This workshop was developed from *The Encouragement Book: Becoming a Positive Person* (Dinkmeyer & Losoncy, 1980). The workshop is designed to develop self-confidence, the ability to encourage oneself, and skills for encouraging others. The workshop combines minilectures, exercises and experiences, discussion groups, opportunities for feedback, and practice in various facets of the encouragement process. The workshop leader sets forth the psychological basis of encouragement, which exists in Adlerian psychology, with specific examples. Participants learn the process of self-affirmation and self-encouragement.

Encouragement is treated as part of the process of stress management. Participants learn about progressive relaxation, imagery, and combating their unhealthy beliefs. They learn the process of developing a positive relationship with themselves. They learn to recognize their accomplishments and to differentiate between self-esteem and ego-esteem. The focus is on developing courageous, congruent behavior.

The *natural high*, as originated by Dr. Walter O'Connell, is presented. Participants learn the three steps of (1) overcoming constrictions, (2) encouraging, and (3) transcending or spirituality.

A section on humor teaches participants how to see things in perspective. The humor process teaches that we can respond to anything positively and successfully.

Encouragement skills are taught specifically and didactically, including:

Communication that involves listening and empathy

Focus on strengths, assets, and resources

Perceptual alternatives

Focusing on efforts and contributions

Identifying and combating discouraging fictional beliefs

The power of expectation

The encouragement circle is taught as a method for solving problems in a variety of settings. The workshop also includes an opportunity to apply this encouragement process to parenting, marriage, social relationships, and profession or occupation as well as to oneself.

SOCIAL THERAPY

Toni and Theo Schoenaker originated *social therapy* at the Rudolf Dreikurs Institute for Social Equality in Zuntersbach, Germany. The process is called social therapy because all humans are understood as social beings and all problems as social problems.

People are accepted in the group with all of their strengths and weaknesses. The basic assumption is that all neurotic disturbances and personality problems are not illnesses but exaggerations of problems we all hold in common. Change comes by making progress toward courage, affirmation of self, and social interest.

Social therapy groups are composed of 20 participants who meet seven hours a day for five days. Members are encouraged to familiarize themselves with the principles of Adlerian psychology before joining a group.

Like all Adlerian groups, social therapy groups function in an atmosphere of equality. Efforts are made to foster feelings of belonging and acceptance on the part of group members, and there is emphasis on the positive use of constructive feedback to promote self-confidence and change. As the Schoenakers (1976) state, "In Social Therapy, one expands usual behavior in a positive direction and dares to act on suggestions for behavioral change. We hope that self-confidence will be strengthened, that social interest and courage will increase" (p. 16).

Belonging and acceptance are created by emphasizing participants' mutual respect and responsibility for self and others. Disparagement and attack, as well as useless feedback, are therefore avoided. The goal is to experience equality and humanness instead of competition and rivalry. A basic rule is that nobody talks about the group members outside the group sessions. Social therapy exercises are organized and guided so that each person is aware that he is not there to fulfill another's expectations and that others are not there to fulfill his own expectations.

Exercises include relaxation to become aware of the body and its functions, respiration and movement exercises to help members regulate their respiration rhythm so it matches the rhythm of the group, and sound exercises to learn how to express oneself.

Each participant creates her own emotions and seeks to belong according to her life style. Mistaken ideas of belonging, such as "getter," "driver," "controller," "pleaser," and "morally superior," are discussed. Behavior is seen and discussed as useful and useless and as active and passive.

The ultimate goal is to help members believe they are good as they are and reduce their drive for self-elevation. In a meditative atmosphere, a member comes to state "I am I, and I accept myself as I am," "You are you, and I accept you as you are," and "You are you, and you are not here to live up to my expectations."

Each participant comes to understand aspects of his life style. Because of the unity of the personality, the overall psychological movement in the group helps each member understand his own behavior. As Adler stated, "An individual's every slightest action, every behavior symptom is characteristic of the whole individual, and, like a stone from the mosaic, it indicates the style of the whole. From the way a person talks, moves, reacts to certain events, the traits and characteristics of his life style can be more or less easily recognized" (Schoenaker & Schoenaker, 1976, p. 46).

To promote understanding of the life style, the group leader may suggest that the group move around in the room without speaking, taking interest in one another. As the participants move about, the leader may ask questions, in the first person, such as:

Am I interested in the other person or am I occupied with the question "What does the other think of me?"

Do I seek contacts or do I just wait?

Do I go where the most contacts can be made, or do I move where I can only meet a few people?

Am I friendly for fear of not being accepted?

Am I afraid not to meet enough people and to leave one out?

Am I so active in contacting because I want to control the situation? (Schoenaker & Schoenaker, 1976, p. 40)

After the activity, discussion focuses on what one has learned from it.

With the help of other group members, each participant tries to determine her number-one priority, the methods she uses to maintain the priority, and the price she pays for it (Table 11–1). "Try on a behavior"—

TABLE 11–1
Number-one priorities

Number-one priority	How the other may feel	The price you pay for your priority	What you want to avoid with your priority
Comfort	irritated or annoyed	reduced productivity	stress
Pleasing	accepting	stunted growth	rejection
Control	challenged	social distance and/or reduced spontaneity	unexpected humiliation
Superiority	inadequate	overburdened	meaninglessness

From *Adlerian Social Therapy*, a monograph by T. Schoenaker and T. Schoenaker. Copyright 1976 by Green Bough Publications, St. Paul, Minnesota. Reprinted by permission.

criticize while looking someone directly in the face, ask a person of the opposite sex out to lunch, or experiment with any other thing one finds difficult to do. The focus is thus not merely on insight but on outsight and action as well. Role playing, psychodrama, self-observation, relaxation, movement, and expression exercises all help the individual understand his mistaken beliefs and faulty approaches to the challenges of living and to see alternative, more effective beliefs and approaches.

TELEOANALYSIS: UNDERSTANDING SELF, OTHERS, AND THE PURPOSES OF BEHAVIOR

The *teleoanalytic workshop*, developed by Don Dinkmeyer, is designed to help participants become aware of their beliefs, values, goals, and style of life and to move toward more effective relationships with others by shifting from self-awareness (insight) to activated social interest (outsight).

The workshop is based on these Adlerian premises:

1. People are social, decision-making beings, whose actions have a purpose. All behavior has social meaning.
2. The members' life styles are expressed in their transactions with the group.
3. People's behavior is best understood by a holistic approach, which recognizes that psychological movement reveals the life style and unitary striving toward a goal. To understand the person or a specific behavior, one should seek to understand the purpose.
4. Social interest and courage are criteria for mental health.
5. Individuals are understood in terms of their perceptions, or phenomenological field. The subjective factors of biased interpretations and perceptions influence people's decisions.

The workshop is didactic (it includes lecturettes to provide information) and experiential (it engages the participants in experiences that bring into play their feelings, beliefs, and values).

Topics might include:

Self-esteem, self-image, self-acceptance

Social interest

Purpose and finalistic causality, goal striving, fictional goals

Search for significance, power (active and passive)

Understanding life style: family atmosphere, family constellation and psychological position, methods of training, early recollections, creative capacity to decide and private logic

Priorities and the triangle

Life tasks and challenges

Discouragement, failure to function, courage to be imperfect

Encouragement and courage

Unity of personality, holism, pattern

Social equality: horizontal versus vertical communication

Understanding and deciding feelings

Commonly observed life styles: driver, controller, getter, self-elevator, righter, pleaser, morally superior, aginner, victim, martyr, inadequate, excitement seeker

Mistaken ideas about self: I am special, entitled, something only if first, must be perfect

Self-acceptance, self-encouragement, being a winner

Exercises and experiences are carried out so as to develop feelings of belonging in the participants, through improved communication first in dyads, then in groups of four, then eight, and so on. Through this process, all the members become more visible, more transparent, and more congruent to one another. The exercises involve presenting oneself to the group in terms of one's strengths, priorities, self-esteem, family atmosphere, family constellation, and assets. A variety of Adlerian techniques are used, including Corsini's Behind-the-Back Technique, Multiple-Strength Perception, Role Playing, Action Therapy, Relaxation and Centering, Fantasy, Psychodrama, and Analysis of Psychological Movement and Purpose.

PSYCHODRAMA-ORIENTED ACTION TECHNIQUES

Insight can be gained by showing group members the underlying purpose of their behavior and their biased perceptions. The method developed by Shulman and one of his cotherapists, A. Starr, focuses on moving from words to action (Shulman, 1973). Since members may refuse to accept the group's interpretation of their behavior, this method helps them attain insight by letting them experience the group's reactions to the underlying purpose of their behavior. The group is directed to react in an exaggerated manner to a member's neurotic goals, thus communicating the message in a dramatic and forceful way.

Instead of only using words, action was employed. This is close to the approach of Moreno. . . .

The plan was discussed during a group session. It was agreed that the group would try to discover the purpose of the irritating and provocative behavior and would then, in an exaggerated way, respond to the behavior, in line with the provocateur's neurotic demands. "If he wants to be a baby, let's treat him like a baby and see if he likes it." (Shulman, 1973, p. 181)

Here is an example of the procedure, which involves selecting one of a member's outstanding faulty goals and how he achieves it in the group, and dramatizing the goal and the behavior:

John, a 26-year-old male, an only child, continually apologized for his behavior, remarks and appearance. He insisted that he was the most poorly endowed in the group, was stupid, unattractive, unmanly and that he felt inferior to all the others. The group first tried to help him by denying his self-description and pointing out his assets, but had become discouraged and antagonistic toward him.

His early recollection was: "I was running alongside a low (unfenced) porch, screaming with fright. My parents, sitting on the porch, saw me run but didn't see anything chasing me. They got up to look and saw that I was being chased by a tiny gosling, so small they couldn't even see its head from where they were sitting."

The patient thus tells us through his memory that he is absolutely inadequate. He has to run from something so small that no one else would be afraid of it. How can anyone expect him to face adult tasks? He cannot take care of himself; others must protect him and care for him.

The group decided to respond to John as if he actually were inadequate and worthless. They began to ignore him or to deride his remarks. They told him that he couldn't possibly have anything worthwhile to offer but that they suffered his presence because they were too kind to throw him out of the group. A common response when John spoke was, "There you go making stupid remarks again. You are just inadequate, nothing you say is worthwhile," or "If you say it, it must be wrong."

The procedure was used in one session only. John became very angry but did not show it. At the ensuing session he spoke of his anger and was surprised at how the group accepted his anger. Once he began to apologize and caught himself, saying, "There I go again," the group offered warm feelings and John felt he didn't have to display his inadequacy any longer. Surprisingly, the provocative behavior returned only at long separated intervals, and a simple reminder from another group member was enough for him to catch himself. (Shulman, 1973, pp. 181–182)

In his article, Shulman gives three more examples of how to apply the psychodramatic procedure—a procedure that is closely related to the paradoxical intention. He points out that being confronted with one's mistaken goals and suddenly becoming aware of them often lead to an imme-diate release of tension and can result in spontaneity of behavior. "At the moment when the person catches himself, which is a process of insight and reevaluation, the goals can change, and the defensive distance-keeping operations are, for the moment, at least, suspended" (Shulman, 1973, p. 186). The group setting stimulates cooperation and insights, which, together with the stressful experience, tend to move the person emotionally closer to the group.

The psychodramatic technique is based on the hypotheses that (1) all behavior is goal directed, (2) each member's behavior in the group shows his psychic movement in relation to the other group members, and (3) this movement reveals one's secret intentions—one's private goals.

THE MIDAS TECHNIQUE

A variation of Shulman's procedure is the "auxiliary-world" technique of Z.T. Moreno (1959), which Shulman called the Midas Technique. In this type of dramatic confrontation, the group member and/or leader act out roles that create for the individual the kind of world and relationships she would like to have (Shulman, 1973).

> Confronting a patient with his mistaken goals not only leads to greater spon-taneity of behavior, insight, and re-evaluation, but also promotes insight and re-evaluation in certain specific ways:
> 1. The patient is shown what his secret goal is.
> 2. He is shown that others are aware of his secret.
> 3. He is shown that it is acceptable to others and that they are even willing to help him achieve it.
> 4. However, by doing so, they indicate that what the patient has so greatly prized is not at all prized by the others. A thing that no one else wants tends to lose some of its value (as described by Papanek, 1958).
> 5. The exposé spoils the "ploy." The group is "spitting in the patient's soup" by behaving in an unexpected way.
> 6. The ensuing acute awareness of the patient's behavior and the knowl-edge that the group is focused on it tend to inhibit such behavior.
> 7. The invitation to perform takes the steam out of the patient and further inhibits the behavior.
> 8. Unless the group can be seen as refusing the neurotic demand, it seems unimportant to work so hard for it. If it is so easily had, why worry about it? If the group is willing to give in, why fight for it? (Shulman, 1973, pp. 192–193)

The following general principles apply to the Midas technique:

a. The technique and its purpose must be freely discussed and understood by the group members.
b. The purpose must be to help a member, not to discipline or humiliate him.
c. The atmosphere must be friendly. The group is engaged in giving a member something he secretly and/or unconsciously wants. It is not denying him or prohibiting him.
d. Consequently, the patient must not be made to do something he doesn't want to do. (Shulman, 1973, p. 193)

REFERENCES

Dinkmeyer, D., & Losoncy, L. (1980). The encouragement book: Becoming a positive person. Englewood Cliffs, NJ: Prentice-Hall.

Frankl, J. (1963). *Man's search for meaning.* New York: Washington Square Press.

Moreno, Z. T. (1959). A survey of psychodramatic techniques. *Group Psychotherapy, 12,* 5–14.

Mowrer, O. (1963). *The new group therapy.* New York: Van Nostrand.

O'Connell, W. E. (1972). Adlerian action therapy techniques. *Journal of Individual Psychology, 28,* 184–191.

O'Connell, W. E. (1975). *Action therapy and Adlerian theory.* Chicago: Alfred Adler Institute.

Oliver, W., & Landfield, A. (1962). Reflexibility: An unfaced issue in psychology. *Journal of Individual Psychology, 18,* 114–124.

Papanek, H. (1958). Change of ethical values in group psychotherapy. *International Journal of Group Psychotherapy, 13,* 435–444.

Schoenaker, T., & Schoenaker, T. (1976). *Adlerian Social Therapy.* St. Paul, MN: Green Bough Publications (monograph).

Shulman, B. H. (1973). A psychodramatically oriented action technique in group psychotherapy. In B.H. Shulman (Ed.), *Contributions to individual psychology.* Chicago: Alfred Adler Institute.

Walton, F. (1975). Group workshop with adolescents. *The Individual Psychologist, 12*(1), 26–28.

Watzlawick, P. (1964). *An anthology of human communication.* Palo Alto, CA: Science & Behavior Books.

12 Family Therapy

F amily therapy, which deals with the total family unit as the client, is a product of therapy developments that have occurred during the past two decades.

Adlerians have worked with family dynamics ever since Adler's demonstrations in the child-guidance clinics of Vienna. The Adlerian theory of the role the family constellation plays in the development of personality is decidedly different from psychological approaches that emphasize the triangle of the two parents and the child and tend to ignore the relationships between siblings. Furthermore, since Adlerians see all problems as social problems, they assign greater importance to the relationships between people than to what is going on within the individual (interpersonal versus intrapersonal approach).

These psychological principles are particularly applicable to family therapy:

We are all socially embedded in an interacting social system. Any movement by the individual or the family creates movement in all other components of the system. Family therapy can teach practical procedures for relating in the family.

Movement and actions within the family reveal purposes and intentions.

All events are understood in relationship to the pattern and the goal.

NATURE AND AIMS

When one or more members of the family are having problems, the whole family unit is affected in one way or another.

A couple with two sons, ages 10 and 14, are experiencing severe marital problems. The mother has developed profound depression with marked suicidal tendencies necessitating hospitalization. Before she is ready for discharge, the father, too, requires hospitalization for his severe psychosomatic disorders. When the entire family is seen together, it becomes apparent that these disruptions have been and still are a major source of concern for the children. The 10-year-old boy is worried that his parents will get divorced. The 14-year-old boy is keeping his feelings to himself; he has become more and more socially withdrawn and shows a tendency toward obesity.

In its most traditional form, family therapy is based on the assumption that chronic family conflict involves, in one way or another, all the members of a family and is responsible for the problems of one or more individuals within the family group. Therefore, family therapy should include all members of a family. Because of the Adlerian holistic approach, the object of treatment is a particular group of people who are currently forming an indivisible unit, a unique whole called the family.

Although family therapy may result in changes in the personal life styles of various family members, such change is not the primary goal. Adlerian family therapy is aimed at teaching a group of people how to better deal with one another and how to live together as social equals. This aim is accomplished by sharing with the family group the principles of democratic conflict resolution, by reorienting the family members away from destructive modes of communication, and, most importantly, by teaching all members of the family to be agents of encouragement. A major goal of family therapy is to increase the self-esteem and feelings of worth of family members while stimulating their social interest (Dinkmeyer & Dinkmeyer, 1981).

THE FAMILY THERAPIST

Although family therapists can come from a variety of disciplines, the complexity of family therapy necessitates that therapists be fully qualified professionals in their field, with considerable additional training in working with the family as a unit. If the therapy involves more than one therapist, at least one of them must have these qualifications.

We decry the current tendency on the part of some counselors to present themselves as family therapists merely because they sit down with the entire family. Family therapy is perhaps the most demanding of all the therapies, requiring broad life experiences on the part of the therapist as well as specialized training. Although not essential, it is helpful, for example, if the family therapist has also had the experience of being a parent.

Family therapists must walk a very tight rope. Empathy and concern are essential elements of the therapeutic process, but so is the capacity to maintain enough psychological distance to be effective and avoid being pulled into a destructive family situation. A family in trouble tends to divide into factions. The therapist or therapists often feel pressure to identify or side with one or the other faction. When there are two therapists, one therapist can, for a short time, be more understanding of one family member or one subgroup within the family, *if* the other therapist is able to remain somewhat aloof. But this kind of balance cannot persist for any length of time. For example, if one therapist becomes too understanding of the plight of an adolescent seeking independence from the family, the parents may consciously or unconsciously torpedo the therapy in every possible way so as to maintain (or reestablish) the old balance and prevent the adolescent's move toward autonomy.

STRUCTURE

Adlerian family therapists emphasize trusting psychological movement and its meaning. When what a person is doing seems confusing, it is clear that what he does is in line with his goals, even though he might not be aware of it at the moment; for example, he might say one thing and do the opposite.

Once family therapy has been agreed upon as the treatment of choice, initial sessions should, if at all possible, include all members of the family. After the entire family has been seen together as a unit, in subsequent sessions a decision may be reached to exclude certain members— for example, the very young.

Families often ask whether sessions can be held in the family home. While certain kinds of information can be obtained only with a "house call," therapists are generally in a strategically better position working on their own turf, so to speak. If the father, for example, is sitting in *his* own chair, drinking sherry and smoking a cigar, while the therapists are situated in less comfortable positions (often from which it is difficult for them to see or hear all family members), the effectiveness of therapy is significantly reduced by both psychological and physical factors. The ideal location for family therapy is a room large enough to seat all members, preferably in equal-sized chairs, in a circle, without distractions of smoking, refreshments, and so forth. This can, of course, present some complicated logistic problems.

Family members often ask early in the course of therapy about prognosis, a question that usually also refers to the probable duration of therapy. We believe that giving a prognosis is mischief. If we give a good prognosis, some family members might feel constrained to prove us wrong. If we give a bad prognosis, the prognosis is often interpreted to mean we don't think we can help. And, if we don't think we can help, we probably can't. As to duration, we usually ask the family to agree to meet six times and then reevaluate the situation at the end of that period. Sometimes more definite agreements are useful.

> A woman was quite doubtful whether she wanted to stay married to her husband, because she felt she was always being manipulated by him. From time to time he showed some temporary improvement, but his wife

didn't feel she could trust his long-range commitment to their marriage. The husband acknowledged that she was right as far as the past was concerned. However, he seemed to realize that he was likely to lose his wife and children if he didn't change his ways and wanted to do something about it.

Family therapy was recommended, and the couple reached an agreement to put off a decision about their marriage until they had been in therapy for six months. This agreement provided an important sense of stability for the children, who might otherwise have felt a great deal of concern as to whether their parents were going to stay married. This concern might have prevented them from becoming as deeply involved in family therapy.

Since family therapy is a specialized form of group therapy, the information about optimal duration of group sessions is applicable to families as well. Sessions of less than one and a half hours are generally not as effective; sessions that last beyond two or two and a half hours invite disruption on the part of family members and fatigue on the part of therapists. Ideally, family therapy sessions should be held weekly to give family members time to process what has gone on during the session and to carry out the specific recommendations they have received from the therapists. At least in the early stages, meeting with the family less often than every other week is apt to disturb the continuity of therapy and make each session almost a separate experience.

The Initial Interview

The initial interview establishes the nature of the relationship and what family members can expect. The therapist deals with various members of the family to get some ideas about their priorities, attitudes, and beliefs. It is important from the start to make some kind of contact or connection with each member of the family. The therapist talks with each member directly, asking them to tell a little bit about their perception of the problem, and comes to understand their meanings, feelings, and beliefs. Even though young children may not understand the purpose for being there, it is important to respect them and to get some idea about how they see relationships. In this initial phase, the therapist seeks answers to certain questions, even though they are usually not presented formally:

What does each person want to happen in the family relationship? What does each family member see as the main challenge or issue the family faces?

Are family members aware that the purpose of the session is to focus on change, and not just to complain?

What does it feel like for each person to live in this family?

Identify the family atmosphere. Is it autocratic, democratic, or permissive?

At this point the therapist also identifies family constellation information. It is important to identify the position of the father and mother in their families of origin and how they perceive their positions. It is interesting to note whether family members often have conflict with children who are in the same position that they were in as children. For example, if the father was an oldest child, is he having problems with the oldest child in this family?

Through this process the therapist begins to identify the roles various members play in the family. Do the family members have restricted roles or do they function in a variety of tasks? Have boundaries been set up? How confined do they feel to their roles?

Adlerian family therapy observes and notes certain family faults and weaknesses. Even more important, however, is the diagnosis and identification of the family's assets. From the first contact, the therapist asks himself: What are the general assets of the family as a unit? What are the assets of each family member? How can these assets blend into the family system? (Sherman & Dinkmeyer, in press).

DIAGNOSIS IN FAMILY THERAPY

The therapist is interested in identifying family goals and the transactions that result from the goals and beliefs. The therapist must also investigate priorities and how they influence certain characteristic patterns. As we have said, Adlerians investigate the private logic and goals by a procedure called the tentative hypothesis. The therapist suggests his hunches to an individual or the family as a whole, framing them tentatively: "Could it be . . ?" or "Is it possible . . ?" and alluding to the goal and pattern of behavior.

In the diagnostic procedure it is important to understand who is seeking change. More important, are they willing to change? What type of change do they desire for the family or individuals in the family and in themselves? It is always important to analyze and identify who resists change and to clarify the purpose of the resistance. Determine what reward the person gets for the resistance.

Family constellation and the psychological position of each member are basic to understanding the family. The family therapist uses traditional positional psychology information to understand how family position influences transactions among members of the family.

Encouragement is considered the most important technique for promoting change. Most interpersonal problems are the result of discouragement. Encouragement is the process of building an individual's self-esteem, enabling him to cooperate with other members of the family. The encouraging family therapist plays a significant role during the diagnostic phase of therapy. Instead of focusing only on the pathology, liabilities, and weaknesses, the therapist is equally interested in strengths, assets, and resources. The therapist becomes a talent scout who identifies assets that will enable family members to deal more effectively with the challenges of living. Therapists learn to look for and affirm positive movement or involvement. They try to see the positive side in anything that first appears to be negative (Dinkmeyer & Dinkmeyer, 1983).

MULTIPLE THERAPY

Probably in no other form of therapy is the concept of multiple therapy (therapy conducted by more than one therapist) so important as in family therapy. If the family is any larger than the parents and one child, it is virtually impossible for a single therapist to be both an active participant and an acute observer of all the verbal and nonverbal communication that goes on.

Ideally, cotherapists should represent both sexes, but that is a point of limited importance. What is truly important is whether the cotherapists impress the family as people who communicate well and who show mutual respect. This does not mean it is inappropriate for cotherapists to disagree. Occasional disagreement provides opportunities to demonstrate to the family that people can disagree without disastrous consequences and can resolve their disagreements peacefully and cooperatively.

Pitfalls

Preconceptions

For the most part, it is desirable for cotherapists to discuss various issues of the therapeutic process in the presence of the family, allowing family members to take advantage of and learn from the therapists' discussions. As with any other form of group therapy, it is important for the therapists not to begin the session with any preconceptions of what should happen. It is impertinent for the therapists to try to decide in advance what is most important to the family and how it should be approached.

Scapegoating

Many families "elect" a member as the scapegoat, or symptom bearer, for the family's troubles. A child is often identified as "the problem," allowing the other family members to avoid looking at themselves and facing the part they play in their problems.

> Betty, 14 years old, had been a problem to her parents "from the day she was born." Now she was failing school, experimenting with drugs, and associating with unsuitable companions. She was indignant that her mother wouldn't permit her to go to another city and visit her 19-year-old boyfriend, who was in prison. Her younger sister, Sally, was sweetness and light and goodness in every way. Father and Mother insisted that theirs was the best marriage ever. During family therapy sessions, all members converged on Betty, repeatedly implying in one way or another that the family would be just fine if it weren't for Betty's bad behavior. Sally was seemingly genuinely concerned about her sister but, at the same time, judgmental. The therapists were unable to get the parents and sister "off Betty's case," since these people, totally unwilling to look at the role they played in the family problems, insisted on scapegoating Betty.
>
> After hospitalization and several more family sessions, Betty disappeared and no one heard from her again. If the therapists had known in advance the seriousness of Betty's situation and the unwillingness of the family to stop scapegoating her, they might have arranged for Betty to be placed in a foster or group home.

Avoidance of the Here and Now

Another reason for scapegoating (or any other kind of faultfinding or standing in judgment) is the common need to avoid the here and now. By recounting in detail the "facts" of the past, including all the injustices each has suffered, family members avoid dealing with themselves and one another in the present. Other families avoid the present by being future oriented. In still other families, some members have become highly skilled at minding the business of other members while neglecting their own problems. Here is an example:

> At the first family therapy session, Mother began by saying that Joan, 13, was not going to talk. Joan actually sat behind her vivacious little sister, Karen. When Joan was asked a question, Karen answered for her. When

Karen talked about herself and described how she felt, her father listened with obvious impatience, bouncing up and down in his chair, until he could give an edited version of what Karen had said, explaining how Karen really felt and why she felt that way. Then, when Father expressed his disapproval of Mother's behavior at the country club, she interrupted him half-way through. His wife insisted that she knew what had really happened and that he wasn't speaking for himself but, rather, was repeating his mother's comments about her daughter-in-law. At home, the story was the same—each person interfering constantly with the others and injecting herself into the others' business. There were constant criticism, bickering, and marked defensiveness on the part of all the family members.

When therapists are faced with a family like this one, they have to be firm, insisting that each person speak for himself. Another situation often encountered in family therapy is the attempt by one or more family members to lead the discussion away from those present and talk instead of family members who are not present. Also, as we mentioned earlier, family members are often adept at taking sides, and will try to involve the therapist in the family feud. Many children in troubled families have become highly skilled at the divide-and-conquer process with their own parents and will try this technique with therapists, too.

Pity

It is essential that the therapists recognize and avoid the pitfall of pity. Feeling sorry for someone is a discouraging and demeaning way to treat another human being.

Johnny, 5 years old and the smallest in his kindergarten class, had not had a particularly good year. His teacher recommended that he repeat kindergarten. In a family therapy session, it became apparent that Mother felt terribly sorry for Johnny, believing that his whole future would be blighted by his present failure in school. In pursuing this subject further, the therapist discovered that Mother, too, had been held back while in school, that she had found this a source of constant discouragement, and that she was now taking Johnny's "failure" as a personal failure. When she learned to stop feeling sorry for Johnny, she discovered that her son had thought the whole situation through and had come to the conclusion that he would be better off if he could spend another year in kindergarten.

GOALS OF THERAPY

Simply stated, the overall goal of family therapy is for the therapists to work themselves out of their job by teaching the family to communicate accurately, honestly, and openly, with each member speaking for himself about his own ideas and feelings. This overall goal is the outcome of several specific goals. One is to teach family members to resolve their own conflicts by relying on the principles of (1) manifesting mutual respect, (2) pinpointing the issue, (3) reaching a new agreement, and (4) participating responsibly in decision making.

As we said, it is important for parents to learn to recognize the mistaken goals of their children's misbehavior. The process of learning is not easy, however, and may be more efficiently carried out in a family-education center or in a parent study group. Another goal of family therapy is to help members learn to be responsible for their own behavior and to become cooperative and contributing parts of the family group. For a family to operate democratically, parents often have to make major adjustments in their roles. Sometimes the adjustments cannot be made in family sessions but require individual sessions, group therapy for one or both parents, or marital therapy. Family therapists should not assume that all problems can best be handled by dealing with the whole family as a group.

Family therapy is used when the degree of conflict or the duration of the problems is such that more intense work is necessary than could be done, for example, in the family education center. However, family therapy can be enhanced if the family attends, at the same time, a family-education center, or if the parents participate in a parent study group. Family therapy is also enhanced when the parents read material that can help them carry out their tasks more successfully. Possible materials are *The Practical Parent*, by Corsini and Painter (1975), *Raising a Responsible Child*, by Dinkmeyer and McKay (1973), *Systematic Training for Effective Parenting*, by Dinkmeyer and McKay (1976), *Systematic Training for Effective Parenting of Teens*, by Dinkmeyer and McKay (1983), *The Effective Parent*, by Dinkmeyer et al. (1987), and *Children: The Challenge*, by Dreikurs and Soltz (1964). Private family therapy is more often used in situations that involve delicate personal problems.

TECHNIQUES IN ADLERIAN FAMILY THERAPY

Adlerian family therapy focuses on understanding and influencing psychological movement. The therapist is concerned not only with what is said but specifically with what people do and with their nonverbal communication. Transactions among people help us understand their goals, priorities, and beliefs.

There is intensive work with the methods the family uses to communicate with each other. A therapist is likely to note that communication seems to be from superior to inferior positions. Families are encouraged to focus their communication on the positive. The therapist makes some simple communication rules:

1. Each person speaks for himself
2. Speak directly to each other, not through the therapist or another person in the family
3. Listen and be empathic to other members' feelings and beliefs
4. Do not look for someone to blame

The therapist must remember to focus on real issues, not symptoms. The therapist observes transactions and interactions to determine the purpose of what is being communicated and how these patterns and beliefs influence the family's behavior. The real issue may have to do with some of the priorities we discussed earlier, such as control, superiority, getting even, or displaying power.

The therapist must also make it a point to be encouraging. Family therapy is in itself encouraging insofar as it includes these characteristics:

Each person now feels he is listened to

Members of the family are intentionally empathic and understanding

The focus is on strengths, assets, and resources of a relationship

There is a development of perceptual alternatives, first by the therapist and then by members of the group. Members learn to recognize there are positive ways to look at any negative situation.

The therapists apply other techniques of Adlerian counseling to a family as to other therapeutic groups.

Confrontation of the Private Logic and Beliefs

The private logic includes goals, ideas, and attitudes. Confrontation is the procedure by which the therapist, sensitively and perceptively, makes family members aware of the discrepancies between their behavior and their intentions, their feelings and the feelings they reveal, and between their insights and their actions. Confrontation thus stimulates therapeutic movement by mirroring to the family their mistaken goals.

Paradoxical Intention

Paradoxical intention or antisuggestion persuades one to produce the symptom one appears to be complaining about. The symptom is actually prescribed and the family member is encouraged to become even more "symptomatic." The paradox helps to reframe the system, and helps change the entire meaning a family gives to a situation.

Role Reversal

Family members often do not understand how others perceive their behavior. In role reversal we ask each person to act as if he were the person he is in conflict with. We then ask him to express as clearly and honestly as possible how he believes the other person perceives the relationship between the two of them, and how he perceives the family and how people are working together. The second person then has an opportunity to react, indicating which parts of the role reversal were accurate and which were not in line with her thinking and beliefs.

Resistance and Goal Alignment

Resistance in family therapy usually presents itself as a lack of common goals between therapist and family. Aligning goals so that all are moving toward the same purpose is basic to bringing about change. Family therapy becomes complicated if Mother is concerned about the children's academic achievement, Father pushes athletics, and the son or daughter is mainly interested in social life. From these confused purposes the therapist helps the family find areas of compromise so that they can live together more cooperatively.

Setting Tasks and Getting Commitment

The therapist works with the family to establish certain tasks and commitments to specific changes that the family and individual members indicate they desire. Setting the task occurs in the first session, when each member is asked to state his goals and what he would like to see changed. The more specific the task, the more readily it can be accomplished. Family members make specific contracts and are expected to share their progress at the next meeting.

Summarizing

Summarizing is a way to get at family members' perceptions and look at the theme of the session. The therapist may decide to have family members summarize what they have learned at the end of each session; the therapist also summarizes and clarifies commitments and tasks.

Resistance

Resistance is a difference between the goals of the family and those set forth by the therapist or a difference between the goals of different members or groups within the family. Resistance must be dealt with immediately.

One of the most effective ways to overcome resistance and get things moving again is to add another ingredient to the therapeutic process. This ingredient can be an additional therapist or other family members who are not locked into the nuclear family system or into the new system that has developed in therapy (which includes the therapists).

If there is disagreement concerning goals and if the addition of new elements to the therapeutic process doesn't help, termination of therapy may be contemplated and discussed. Termination must always be an option so the therapist must avoid becoming so identified with the counseling process that termination becomes a personal issue.

The Role of Absent Members

With some complicated family systems—for example, blended families*— there are often absent members who, although never physically incorporated into the family therapy sessions, cannot be ignored as significant influences.

> A woman lost her husband through death and married a widower. With her children and his children under the same roof, a complicated family system developed. He studiously avoided talking about his first wife, while she, even after several years, felt herself a stranger in another woman's home. If this family had undergone therapy, the man's first wife would have had to have been discussed because of her continuing influence on the various members of the family.
>
> In another family, one child with extremely severe behavior problems required institutionalization. The father maintained close contact with his son. The mother, instead, feared the boy and was unwilling to discuss the possibility of his return into the family. The other children were pulled first in one direction and then in the other, thus showing how deeply this absent member was still affecting the everyday life of the family.

In family therapy, we usually think of two generations, parents and children; however, in some instances, three or even four generations have been successfully incorporated into family therapy.

---

*A blended family is a family in which both partners bring children from a previous marriage into the new marriage.

In one family, the paternal grandfather had been living with his son and daughter-in-law from the day of their marriage. The wife resented every moment of his presence, which she considered a heavy burden. According to her husband, she consistently lined up the children against their grandfather. Successful therapy for this family obviously would have required consideration of the role of the grandfather.

FAMILY-EDUCATION CENTERS

In family-education centers, counseling is conducted in public. Volunteer (demonstration) families are interviewed by the cocounselors in front of an audience, which participates in the counseling process. As in private therapy, specific behaviors are identified and precise recommendations are offered.

Goals and Organization

The purpose of a family-education center is threefold: (1) to disseminate basic mental health principles to a large audience (actually, this is a form of community education); (2) to provide a resource for troubled families; and (3) to train parents, teachers, and others to work more effectively with children. Family-education centers may be housed in hospitals, churches, schools, or other public buildings.

Funding sources vary, but in many centers much of the work is done by volunteers. The staff of a family-education center includes the director or codirectors, who are professionals in the mental-health field and who have had extensive additional training and experience with the Adlerian model. In some communities, however, lay people have been trained to direct family-education centers under professional supervision. Other staff usually includes a coordinator, an intake worker, a recorder, and the director and staff members of the activity center.

The family-education center includes (1) the counseling center, where the volunteer families are interviewed with the participation of an audience, and (2) the activity center, where children and adolescents can engage in a variety of educational activities if they choose not to be in the audience of the counseling center. Members of the activity center staff are specifically trained to observe children and to present their observations for the benefit of the parents and counselors in the counseling center.

In most family-education centers, admission is free. Although audience members are encouraged to participate in the counseling process by offering suggestions and encouragement, participants can be as involved or uninvolved as they choose. The volunteer families that are counseled function as coeducators. They actually help the cocounselors teach Adlerian principles to the larger group through the interview process. The volunteer families will have been in the audience for several weeks before becoming a demonstration family. Also, they (usually) have learned basic Adlerian principles of child rearing. The cocounselors vigorously ensure that, no matter how great the participation of the audience, the family is in no way put on the spot.

A counseling session with a family often ends with the audience participating in an encouragement session. The audience is invited to give its honest reaction to the family's strengths and assets. They feed back the positive things they see about the family relationship and about the individuals in the family. Volunteer families are usually asked to return for follow-up sessions during which they describe their successes and failures with the techniques and principles they have learned. The interview in the center is enhanced by reports from the activity center, from the children's school(s), from the family physician, and from any other professional who is working with the family.

Adolescents are invited to attend the education center to be interviewed, even if their parents are unwilling to participate. When parents are present, adolescents and parents are usually interviewed together. If young children are involved, the cocounselors generally talk with the parents first. Some tentative agreement is reached about one or two family problems that can reasonably be tackled through specific recommendations during the coming week. Then the children are interviewed separately and briefly and informed of their parents' concern. Counselors, after validating the impression of the children's goals, tell the children what recommendations have been given to their parents. The children are then dismissed to go back to the activity center while the activity-center staff member reports her observations.

As the counseling proceeds and parents become aware of the goals of their children's misbehavior, they learn how to deal with it—what to do and what *not* to do. In other words, they learn what responses will reinforce the children's mistaken beliefs and what they should do to avoid them. They learn methods that reduce conflict and promote cooperation and harmony. For instance, when power conflicts are obvious, parents learn to sidestep conflict by removing themselves physically. If a child has a temper tantrum, the parents may follow the recommendation to retire to the bathroom until the child's tantrum subsides. The counselors also teach the fallacies of reward and punishment and how to use, instead, the principles of natural and logical consequences.

After parents have learned to get out of the power struggles with their children, the use of natural and logical consequences is introduced.

As family conflict diminishes, regularly scheduled family council meetings are recommended as a laboratory for democratic decision making, problem solving, and conflict resolution. With family council meetings, parents learn to teach responsibility by sharing responsibility, and children learn more self-reliance and great self-esteem. An important result is that both parents and children learn to encourage one another.

REFERENCES

Corsini, R., & Painter, G. (1975). *The practical parent: The ABC's of child discipline.* New York: Harper & Row.

Dinkmeyer, D., & Dinkmeyer, D., Jr. (1981). Adlerian family therapy. *The American Journal of Family Therapy, 9*(1), 45–52.

Dinkmeyer, D., Sr., & Dinkmeyer, J. (1983). Adlerian family therapy. *Individual Psychology, 39*(2), 116–124.

Dinkmeyer, D., & McKay, G. (1973). *Raising a responsible child.* New York: Simon & Schuster.

Dinkmeyer, D. C., & McKay, G.D. (1976). *Systematic training for effective parenting.* Circle Pines, MN: American Guidance Service.

Dinkmeyer, D. C., & McKay, G.D. (1983). *Systematic training for effective parenting of teens.* Circle Pines, MN: American Guidance Service.

Dinkmeyer, D. C., McKay, G. D., Dinkmeyer, D. C., Jr., & McKay, J. L. (1987). *The Effective Parent.* Circle Pines, MN: American Guidance Service.

Dreikurs, R., & Soltz, V. (1964). *Children: The challenge.* New York: Hawthorn.

Sherman, R., & Dinkmeyer, D. (in press). *Systems of family therapy: An Adlerian integration.* New York: Brunner/Mazel.

13 Marriage Therapy

I n marriage therapy, the relationship is the client. It is thus essential that both parties in the relationship participate in the therapeutic process. Therapy with one marriage partner is not marriage therapy.

The marriage relationship must be worked at constantly and nurtured like a tender plant. Because of the changes that are occurring in the traditional patterns of sex-role behaviors in our society, this may be truer today than it was in the past. The changing roles of men and women and the concomitant reduction of sex-role expectations are the source of special kinds of problems that many couples face today.

The shift toward equality between marriage partners began in the United States during the Great Depression, when high unemployment among men often made it necessary for the woman to become the breadwinner in the family. The shift became even more pronounced during World War II, as thousands of women moved into the labor force and discovered that they no longer had to be second-class citizens controlled by their husbands.

Just as husbands lost control over their wives, parents lost control over their children. Authoritarianism gave way to increasingly equalitarian relationships between parents and children. The old ways of relating in a marriage and in a family were gone forever. Couples were forced to try to live together in a relationship of equality for which they had no background or training. In the 1960s, the changing nature of the marital relationship was influenced first by the civil rights movement and then by the women's movement.

These changes are still going on, and the problems they generate for the marriage partners, as well as for the relationship, are still unresolved. The element of change is a potential source of conflict in any intimate relationship. Partners change but rarely in tandem. Consequently, the problems of differential growth in intimate relationships are quite special. By rejecting their subservient role of the past, women have also rejected the concept that their own growth and development as persons—rather than just as wives—have no validity or, at best, are of secondary importance compared to the success of the marriage. Many men still don't know how to function in a relationship other than as the "superior male." These men are baffled at their wives' demands for an equalitarian relationship, self-actualization, and sexual satisfaction.

MARRIAGE AS A SYSTEM

People are indivisible, decision-making beings whose actions and movements have a purpose. The pattern of interaction between spouses evolves into a system. The marital system reflects personal goals, beliefs, and priorities as well as the goals, priorities, and beliefs you share as a couple. When the spouses' goals are aligned, the marriage system functions smoothly.

When goals and beliefs conflict and are not resolved, the system produces dysfunctional behavior. The marriage therapist must understand the individuals and the system.

The Initial Contact

Because both marriage partners must participate in the process, the therapist always tries to see both parties together. In the first interview, the focus is on establishing an effective counseling relationship and on developing a working contract.

Establishing the Counseling Relationship

Establishing an effective relationship requires varying amounts of time and effort. For people who have never had a trusting relationship with anyone, establishing such a relationship may take considerable time. In some cases, it is easier for one partner to become involved in the counseling relationship than for the other. But, in general, establishing a relationship is easiest when the therapist can demonstrate to both partners that she understands their problems. To do so, the Adlerian therapist uses a number of shortcuts that permit the partners to see that some aspects of their personalities or some characteristics of their relationship make sense to her.

One of the most reliable methods is to pinpoint each partner's number-one priority (as we will discuss in more detail later in the chapter). When a wife with a priority of pleasing becomes aware of that priority, she also realizes the price she pays for it—self-neglect, reduced personal growth, and a grossly exaggerated significance of rejection. She sees, often for the first time, that she takes her husband's rather innocuous behavior as personal rejection, and she understands why. If the husband's number-one priority is control, he may, for the first time, understand how he brings about distance from others. This new awareness and the concomitant feelings of being understood and accepted make an effective therapeutic relationship much more likely, as we see in these two cases:

> *Therapist:* I can't entirely explain it, but I find myself feeling somewhat annoyed with you, John.
>
> *John:* Is it something I'm doing?
>
> *Therapist:* No, not really *doing*. I think it has something to do with your number-one priority. I'd guess that your priority is comfort. If

that is so, the more you strive for comfort, the less productive you're likely to become. The price people pay for a number-one priority of comfort is reduced productivity. I suppose my feeling annoyed has to do with my puritan work ethic.

John: You're perfectly right. I set goals for myself, but I never seem to accomplish as much as I want to.

Therapist: (to wife): Do you find it difficult to pin John down—to get him to deal with issues?

Beverly: I certainly do. How can you tell?

Therapist: Many people with a number-one priority of comfort behave like artful dodgers. The worst thing for them is to feel trapped. I think John has become very competent at avoiding conflict with you, which is a way of avoiding stress for himself.

Beverly: Well, I certainly appreciate that someone else understands what a big problem that is for me.

Therapist: I think that your number-one priority is pleasing.

Julie: You're probably right. If I'm not pretty sure that what I'm about to do will be accepted, I'm likely to pull back.

Therapist: And, if Bob fails to give you approval, that's a personal rejection.

Developing a Working Contract

Establishing a working contract requires, first of all, a clear indication on the part of the therapist that there is hope for the marriage. It is the Adlerian position that, as long as people are alive, they have a potential for growth. It is also the Adlerian position that any couple can, if their relationship is one of mutual respect and cooperation, work out their difficulties, regardless of how complicated and profound their problems are.

After asking both partners to explain briefly why they are seeking counseling, we ask early in the interview whether they want to stay married. If the answer is affirmative, we propose personal life style formulations before we look at the problems in the relationship. If one or both partners are doubtful, we might still propose that they hold off any decision making until we have completed the life style formulation.

Even if both parties agree that they don't want to stay married, we still offer to formulate their life styles. If they agree, the partners may learn something from the dissolution of their marriage that will reduce the likelihood of their repeating the process with another partner. If one partner wants to stay married and the other does not, we again suggest life style formulations, asking the partner who doesn't want to remain married to hold off on any action until we have completed that aspect of the counseling process. Sometimes, of course, a couple comes in for counseling as a final gesture to show that they have done everything they can do, but in fact have already made up their minds not to remain married.

We prefer to establish a definite contract that has an end point as well as a clearly defined initial arrangement. The arrangement usually entails six hours of counseling—enough time to complete formulation of the life style for each partner. At the end of that period, it is appropriate to renegotiate the contract. Sometimes the partners feel that, for the moment, that's as far as they want to go. In other instances, the partners feel they would like to spend some time working on their relationship alone and then return for more therapy. Others, after completing the life style formulation, want to continue working with the counselor on the relationship. If at the end of the life style formulation, it becomes clear that one partner needs ongoing individual therapy, an agreement is reached to resume the marriage therapy later with both parties.

The Absent Spouse

Sometimes a person comes in alone, complaining about the marriage and protesting vigorously that his or her partner will not join in marriage therapy. Our strategy in such cases is to ask immediately for permission to get in touch with the reluctant spouse, often by telephone on the spot. In our experience, almost invariably the other spouse agrees to come in and frequently is very cooperative.

After hearing about the absent spouse, we are often amazed to see how different he turns out to be from the description. We know, of course, that we are hearing a biased account and that, if the partner we are interviewing is angry and intolerant, we will hear mostly about the spouse's bad points. This is often accompanied by blindness to one's own defects. It is most important, to win the cooperation of a reluctant spouse, to point out that only he can speak for himself and that we would truly like to hear what he has to say. Speaking to only one spouse about a marriage relationship is like seeing two actors on the stage but hearing only one of them deliver his lines.

A man was referred to us by his family physician. His complaint was premature ejaculation. He claimed that his problem was medical and that his wife had nothing to do with it. He also repeatedly refused to let us get in touch with his wife. A life style formulation was completed, and, as a trusting relationship was established, we were finally able, with his permission, to get in touch with his wife and invite her to join us.

When she came in (willingly), she told, to her husband's surprise, quite a different story. He had never mentioned, for example, that he had left home several times, threatening divorce. Also, it became obvious in the course of the session that he didn't know the depth of her affection and her commitment to their marriage. A personal life style of the wife was completed in her husband's presence. Marriage counseling was initiated. Special attention was paid to the symptom of premature ejaculation, which we saw as a problem that originated from the marital relationship and that, therefore, had to be solved through the spouses' joint efforts. After a relatively short period of counseling, the couple had resolved their differences enough to want to keep working at their marriage.

Individual and Family Therapy

Individual therapy is sometimes indicated as part of the marriage therapy process; however, individual problems that are essentially unrelated to the marital relationship must be kept separate from those that are related to it. Even though one partner may seem to need more intensive individual work, it is important to stay away from the view that he or she is "the problem" in the marriage. Problems that might better be dealt with individually rather than jointly include unresolved grief over the loss of a parent, difficulty in relating to persons of the same sex, problems in discovering and mobilizing one's own strengths (which may require vocational or academic counseling), psychosomatic complaints, and problems related to chronic medical conditions.

In family therapy, it often becomes apparent that the problems of the family are essentially problems between the spouses and that the entire family will not run smoothly until husband and wife have worked out their differences. At that point, the family therapist often recommends marriage therapy, which sometimes can be done concurrently with family therapy sessions. At other times, family counseling is temporarily discontinued until marriage therapy has been completed.

THE MARITAL INVENTORY

The *marital inventory* was developed to provide a systematic approach to marriage therapy (Dinkmeyer & Dinkmeyer, 1983). It is used in conjunction with the brief Lifestyle Scale (Kern, 1982).

One of the values of the marital inventory is that it communicates a serious purpose to the diagnostic phase and to the entire relationship. The inventory helps the therapist align goals with the couple and determine what it is they want to see happen. The inventory helps the therapist distinguish between complaint, symptoms, and real issues by identifying the purpose of the symptom and clarifying individual priorities.

The inventory emphasizes being positive, searching for assets and strengths, and being encouraging. The theme is "What is right about the marriage?" and "Where are the resources for improving the relationship?" We do not emphasize diagnosing pathology but believe that identifying strengths, assets, and resources is essential for improving the relationship system.

The inventory helps identify the patterns in the relationship, such as who strives to be in control, who wants to get even, who is the peacemaker and compromiser, and who is interested in growth and change. The inventory thus assesses the life style of the marriage or the system. We believe that marital happiness is achieved insofar as each partner has good self-esteem, a willingness to cooperate, to give and take, and a sense of humor.

USE OF THE LIFE STYLE IN MARRIAGE COUNSELING

Assessment

Life style assessments are conducted in the presence of both partners whenever possible. Recreation of a style of living (Adler, 1958) is based on a fairly specific method of data collection. (Appendix A shows life style forms.) The family constellation is diagrammed, including brief descriptions of each member of the family of origin, with particular attention to all the parental figures who were influential in the formative years, as well as deceased siblings and other children who, although perhaps unrelated, were extremely close to the person. When this inquiry is carried out in the presence of the partner, the spouse may learn for the first time some significant elements of the partner's childhood. The nonparticipating partner is asked to withhold comments at this stage, because we are trying to get into the subjective world of the person whose life style is being formulated and the partner cannot contribute to our understanding if he or she wasn't there. It is important that the therapist pay attention to the person whose life style is being formulated and not be unduly influenced by whatever the other partner says.

The formulation of the life style is meant to provide us with an understanding of the individual's subjectivity; therefore, there are no "right answers." We are merely looking for overall patterns and trying to get some idea of this individual's place in the family. Brief inquiries are made into physical, sexual, and social development, and educational and occupational experience. Here, too, the partner often learns significant new things about the spouse which had perhaps never been discussed before.

In the area of sexual development, for example, a spouse may learn "secrets" that can be very upsetting.

Bess:	I want you to know that we were up all night after our last session.
Harold:	Yes, it was a very difficult time, and I don't know whether we have everything worked out yet.
Counselor:	What came up that was so disturbing? The information about Harold's early sex life?
Bess:	That's it. I was so sure that I had married an inexperienced man—a man that was, well, pure. And, then, to find that he had had all that sexual experience in the service. . .
Harold:	It wasn't that much. Only a few one-night stands. I never saw any reason to mention it.

The next part of the data collection is not specifically related to formulation of the life style but is, instead, a way of learning each partner's attitude toward oneself and the spouse in the various life-task areas. For this purpose, Adler's three life tasks of love, friendship, and work have been broken down into subdivisions: worker, friend, lover, spouse, relating to the other sex, getting along with oneself, search for meaning, relating to members of the same sex, parent, and player. The person is presented with a scale of 1 to 5 (1 being the highest rating) and asked to rate herself, for example, as a worker. The question we ask is "How responsibly are you attending to the task of work at this point in your life?" After the person asks this question and predicts how the partner will rate him or her, the partner is asked to give his or her rating using the same procedure. This is a way to bring the spouse back into the process, after he or she has been involved only passively for some time. "Taking the temperature of the marriage" often pinpoints trouble areas or areas that need to be more fully explored. The counselor gets some idea of how well the partners know themselves and each other and has a base reading to refer to later to evaluate the success of the therapy.

Next, early-childhood recollections and dreams are recorded verbatim. Both reveal subjective themes and melodies in a person's self-view and show how one finds one's place in life. Both partners are also asked to recall a song, a fairy tale, a nursery rhyme, a poem, a character from the Bible, a biblical story, a television show, a radio show, and a movie that made a special impression on them when they were children and to describe what impressed them about each item.

The counselor summarizes the data and interprets the early-childhood recollections and dreams. After the counselor lists the primary themes that have emerged (the individual convictions and guidelines about who one is, what life is, one's expectations, and what ethical considerations one operates with), both partners and the counselor cooperate in listing the strengths of the person whose life style is being formulated. Watkins (1982) developed a self-administered life style that is effective for obtaining certain types of information.

Summarizing the Data

When formulations are completed and typed, each partner receives a copy. At the session following the summary, the clients may be asked to read their summaries aloud. The counselor pays particular attention to word slips and to what the reader emphasizes and omits; there is always an opportunity to stop and clarify (Dinkmeyer & Dinkmeyer, 1982).

Meshing the Life Styles

"Meshing the life styles" refers to the process of learning about the relationship as the life styles of both partners become known. "We fell in love" people often say when asked why they decided to get married. The acknowledgment that one chooses the direction of one's love in accordance with one's fundamental purposes makes it possible to accept that one also decides whether or not to fall in love. Similarly, "we are not in love" is often given as a reason for separation or divorce.

Married people can discover that love is a byproduct of a cooperative relationship. Mates are chosen on the basis of much more knowledge than we are aware of at the conscious level. We tend to choose someone who will treat us as we expect to be treated. We accept someone as an intimate not on the basis of common sense but on the basis of our private logic—as someone who offers us "an opportunity to realize our personal patterns, who responds to our outlook and conception of life, who permits us to continue or to revive plans which we have carried since childhood. We even play a very important part in evoking and stimulating in the other precisely the behavior which we expect and need" (Dreikurs, 1946, pp. 68–69).

Couples who have lived together for some time discover that the very attributes that attracted them in the first place may later create dissonance. A quiet man who was attracted to a gregarious woman may complain later that "she never wants to leave the party." A passive woman who was attracted to an aggressive man may later complain that he wants to make all the decisions.

As we look at the two life styles together, we always find some areas of agreement. For example, both husband and wife may have as part of their personality styles what Adler called the "masculine protest"—a tendency to think that this is a man's world and that men have a better deal, are more important, have more power, and perhaps are more dangerous than women. In the case of the husband, this attitude results in beliefs such as "I must be a real man"; with the wife, in beliefs such as "I'm only a woman." Another couple may agree that life must be exciting and dramatic. We may also find sharp differences in how the partners view life and in what expectations they have of other people. Naturally, if people were psychologically identical twins, they wouldn't get married in the first place. Ultimately, the goal of marriage therapy is for the couple to realize how much tolerance there is for individual differences within the relationship.

Often the process of comparing life styles and pointing out the differences clarifies for the first time why the partners see life so differently. The differences can add great richness to the relationship, or they can be a source of conflict.

> Ruth and Jim consulted a counselor primarily because of Ruth's paranoid psychosis. She was constantly plagued with delusions and hallucinations. For example, she got "special messages" on television and billboards, and she believed that her husband was plotting to kill her and their children. The therapist chose to relieve her symptoms with antipsychotic medication and to work with both spouses together. It became clear that Jim was a computer-type person who depended on "pure logic." Whenever he and Ruth got into a discussion and he had the upper hand because of his "logic," Ruth would flip into her psychotic mode, thus becoming totally unreachable. As the therapist and both partners came to understand this process, the therapist could actually point it out as it was happening during the counseling session. The therapist was also able to make the spouses understand that Ruth's sensitive, empathic, artistic, "right-hemisphere" approach to life was what had appealed to Jim in the first place and that Jim's logical, decision-making, and problem-solving attitude had been a great source of security for Ruth. But in time, his "left-hemisphere" approach to life had become a problem, especially as it was related to intimate conflicts. Successful counseling centered on helping each spouse appreciate the other, including the way the other experienced life, and to see how both approaches had value to the relationship.

Ongoing Use of Life Style Material

Ongoing use of life style material is part of marriage therapy. The couple chooses to continue to work together after formulation of the life style. Each recurrent question in the relationship is examined in light of the personal life style of each partner. The therapist needs to have a summary of each life style in front of her at all times so she can refer to that material as questions arise. From time to time the counselor can ask, "Now that you understand your own life style, how do you explain to yourself why you do what you do? And now that you understand your spouse's life style, how do you explain to yourself why he behaves as he does?"

Many of the partners' questions and observations are just different ways of asking "Why can't he (or she) be more like me?" Formulation of the life style helps to answer that question and shows rather precisely the ways the partner is not like the other and is not likely to become like the other. Furthermore, it helps back up the counselor's repeated admonishments that one cannot control another person—something that people often attempt, in one way or another, in marriage. The life style is neither good nor bad; it just is. Within a given life style, there is a wide range of possibilities, but a goal in marriage therapy is to help each partner accept oneself as one is at the moment and become just as accepting of the other.

Reorientation of the Life Style

Reorientation of the life style can be considered a necessity, a luxury, or anything in between. In most cases, it is not necessary for either spouse to make basic life style changes, since most life styles are broad enough to allow a wide variety of behavioral possibilities. For example, a person with a "very" life style tends to see things in extremes: something is either all black or all white; a job is either done perfectly or not well at all. People with such a personality tend to think in superlatives; hence the term *very*. She is not merely a good cook; she is a *very, very* good cook. If someone has a relatively broad life style, counseling may be limited to helping that person become aware of the choices that are available within, say, the "very" life style.

Certain aspects of the life style may be so limiting, however, that the counselor or the client concludes that counseling should be aimed at changing the life style. An example illustrates this point, but note that this is not, strictly speaking, an example of marriage therapy, but rather of premarital counseling, since the woman's goal is to find out whether she can adjust her attitude toward men enough to find a mate.

> Sylvia had an unfaltering hatred of men. She had grown up in a male-dominated family that numbered four boys and only one girl (Sylvia). When she grew up, she ended up working in an all-male office. The result was that Sylvia had devoted her life to outdoing men, both as a child and as an adult, and had never felt anything but prejudice and dislike toward men.

When she came for counseling, the first hurdle was to develop a trusting relationship with the male cocounselor. Since she was being interviewed in a marriage-education center, on many occasions men in the audience had a chance to show her that they empathized with her and that men can be sensitive, tender, and gentle. Therefore, she was forced to reconsider her basic premise that "all men are bastards."

Eventually, she had readjusted her bias enough to enter a relationship with a young man. But, consistently with her life style, she chose a man who was likely to fulfill her negative expectations—which he did. However, at this point she was able to resume therapy, reevaluate what had happened, and see rather clearly what had brought her to choose a man who would be most likely to let her down.

If one person elects to work at changing his or her life style, this goal may be pursued in individual, group, or marital therapy. It may also be dealt with in a marriage education center, although, as in family education centers, the basic goal there is not therapy or a change of the life style. As counselors, we must continually guard against the conviction that one partner must *help* the counselor change the other partner. It is much more important for both partners to learn to accept themselves and their spouse as they are at the moment. Whether or not to strive toward basic changes in the life style ultimately becomes a matter of choice for the individual. If each marriage partner learns to understand and accept the other with all the strengths and weaknesses, life style changes may not be so important.

The forms of intervention in marriage therapy can then focus on a variety of goals—change of behavior, change of feelings, change of environment, or change of attitudes, which is basically aimed at changing the life style. None of these is exclusive of or unrelated to the others. Some people can make rather marked changes in behavior without any particular change in insight. Some people can learn to deal with their emotions by understanding the purpose of the emotion—that is, by understanding the goal they are pursuing. If and when they decide to change their goal, the emotions take care of themselves. Naturally no one can consciously change feelings; it is much more important to get to the point where one can say "I'm a pretty good person, and, if I feel the way I feel, I must have some reason for it."

Mini-Life Styles

Mini-life styles are utilized particularly in marriage education centers or in other types of brief counseling. A mini-life style involves merely an overview of the family constellation and atmosphere and the interpretation of two or three early recollections. This elucidates a few of the basic themes but is in no way a complete life style formulation, which usually requires at the very least one hour and often two or three, depending on the complexity of the childhood family and how the individual produces data. Here is an example of the use of mini-life styles.

> Sarah and Mike, a young married couple, work in the same office. She is the only woman employee there. From her comments, it is pretty clear that she has a difficult relationship with her fellow employees because of her lack of acceptance of male behavior. She is critical, for example, of their constant discussions of professional athletics and of their swapping "dirty" jokes. Mike, as a fellow employee, is not spared her criticism. Since all her colleagues are men, Sarah wonders whether there might be something in her life style that would cast light on her current situation.
>
> A brief diagram of Sarah's family constellation shows that her *Gegenspieler** was her older brother and that she revered her father. From one of her early recollections it appears that she was stunned at the sudden revelation of a flaw in a man's character. Another early recollection clearly shows that she was very impressed with how good and important men must be. With the help of the counselor, Sarah comes to see how these conflicting views of men can present problems in her daily work. The mini-life style also helps Mike, who, until now, has not been able to understand his wife's problems on the job.

THE LIFESTYLE SCALE[†]

The Lifestyle Scale is a thirty-five item paper-and-pencil inventory developed by Kern (1982). It is continuously being refined via validity studies and item-reliability analysis. It can be employed with couples, individuals, students, management personnel, and educational groups. It was developed for the purpose of attaining life style information on priorities that might be helpful in understanding one's relationship with a spouse or others, career decisions, managerial and conflict management styles, and how one responds to stressful situations.

The scale assesses factors such as control, perfection, pleasing, victim, and martyr, which can be further organized into three factors of *control*, *conforming*, and *discouraged*. Completing the Lifestyle Scale usually generates immediate interest and conversation by the couple or client. In

---

*The *Gegenspieler* is the child, often closest in the constellation, against whom the person plays in the childhood drama.

[†]The authors wish to thank Dr. Roy Kern of Georgia State University for his contribution to this section on The Lifestyle Scale.

addition, it helps the individual to feel understood and more likely to take suggestions from the therapist/counselor.

Interpretation of the inventory, regardless of setting, takes the form of how each scale relates to the predominant life style theme or factor. Some simple rules of thumb on interpretation may help:

1. Look at all scale scores and determine both the predominant theme (the high score on the factor) and the other complementary factors in the scale that help the individual deal with particular life situations or spousal relationships. For example, if all scale scores are at the mean with no "high score," it may indicate the client controlled the scale just as he wishes to control the spouse or life situations in general.

2. If there are two high scale scores, one might investigate how they complement each other; for example, a high control score with a high perfectionistic score may indicate a person who controls situations, people, and life's problems by being cautious, intellectual, and fearing to make mistakes. On the other hand, if the perfectionistic scale and pleasing scale are high, the individual may be more interested in pleasing the spouse to avoid making mistakes.

3. If the two factors of "victim" and "martyr" are higher than the other scales, there is a high probability that the individual has low social interest, low self-esteem, and is a likely candidate for assistance from the counselor.

4. A high martyr scale, coupled with pleasing or controlling, may indicate an individual who is having a crisis in a particular life task area but is not necessarily extremely discouraged.

5. Finally, the scale is also helpful in gaining information on what types of characteristics a client dislikes in others as well as situations that may be most distressing to her. For example, a low quantitative score on control may indicate an individual who resents or dislikes being involved with individuals or a spouse who exhibits controlling characteristics.

Factor Profiles

Conforming Scale

The conforming factor may be active or passive. It may have the ingredients of perfectionism and at other times pleasing. If it is active conforming, the individual's goal will be to seek approval from others, and to serve as a peacemaker or diplomat in interpersonal situations. The individual will be sensitive to others' needs and avoid confrontation and conflict situations. He will generally demonstrate caring characteristics and most likely appear to possess high levels of social interest.

The passive conformer "goes with the flow." He follows directions, is quiet, and on the surface appears somewhat shy. Passive conformers are usually excellent listeners who have difficulty getting their needs met because it is difficult for them to use "I statements" such as "I want . . . , I need . . . , I prefer. . . ."

The active or passive conforming factor represented by this scale suggests someone who is sensitive, a good listener, shy, apologetic, and who may experience difficulties in the areas of confrontation, conflict resolution, and getting his own needs met.

Control Scale

The active controlling scale indicates an individual who attempts to deal with life's problems by being logical, rational, controlling his emotions, and actively leading others. Others may perceive the individual as bossy, opinionated, unwilling to listen, and more prone to confrontation than cooperation. Relationships with others may be a contest of winning and losing. Assets of this theme are the individual's ability to confront and solve problems rationally and to meet conflict situations head on. Other assets include the ability to lead, organize, and follow through with assigned tasks.

The passive dimension of this scale may be characterized by the individual who appears cool and calm and gives the appearance of having most situations under control. He is quiet, shows few emotions, either positively or negatively, and seems to be difficult to "get to know."

Perfectionistic Scale

This factor seems to indicate individuals who wish to control others or conform with others' demands. One who scores high on this factor may portray characteristics of conscientiousness, thoughtfulness, sensitivity, and caution, or the perfectionism may be a strategy for gaining control of situations or others. Scoring high on this factor may indicate an individual who likes to complete tasks by himself, is conscientious, extremely sensitive to making mistakes, and somewhat obsessive and conservative in responses to life tasks.

Victim Scale

The individual who scores high on this factor and the martyr factor may show feelings of low self-esteem, discouragement, and low energy level. Symptoms take the form of being unable to control life situations related to career, relationships, or peers. Other behaviors include oversensitivity to others' feelings, difficulties in problem solving, and interest in avoiding problems or stressful situations. This individual usually exhibits passive behaviors until stress or conflict surfaces, then exhibits unpredictable behavior.

Martyr Scale

If not coupled with a high score on the victim scale, this factor may indicate an individual whose expectations of self and others are so high that she continually sets up problem situations at work, with others, or with loved ones that are characterized by criticism, frustration, and feelings of unfairness and falling short of personal expectations. Other behavioral characteristics may include criticism of self and others, overbearing expectations, and high levels of frustration in one or more of the life tasks of career, social relationships, or intimacy. The term "overachiever" or the Adlerian sense of striving toward superiority may best characterize this individual.

Use With Couples

The Lifestyle Scale is useful as a quick screening instrument in couples or marriage therapy. Identifying the varied life style factors or themes can immediately provide insight into potential problems in the relationship. In the early stages, couples may be confused as to what makes a complementary relationship. Therefore, if the therapist can, for example, identify one spouse as a controller and the other as a pleaser early in the therapy process, she can immediately begin to investigate how this combination enhances the couple's relationship as well as how it can create problems. If one spouse appears to be a controller and the other a pleaser on the surface, this would seem to be a complementary relationship; however, further investigation may uncover that this individual's controlling theme has a strong need to control by being perfect. If this is true, it may be hopeless to try to please this individual. Thus the mate in this dyad who is bent on pleasing may end up extremely discouraged.

If the therapist can help the couple to identify how these characteristics initially attracted them, the couple may be able to redirect their efforts toward recognizing that these life style themes can also inhibit problem solving and complementary interactions. The controller may not need to change as much as to redirect controlling tendencies in a more complementary way toward the spouse. The pleaser may also come to realize that seeking constant approval may need to be reevaluated and redirected in some other way.

At this point, the therapist has many choices. During one session she might assign an exercise in role reversal or communication techniques.

Whatever the suggestion or intervention, understanding the couple's life style via the Lifestyle Scale provides opportunities to improve problem solving.

Other Brief Techniques

Other techniques include "two points on a line" and the "hidden reason." In the first of these techniques, one finds an imaginary line that connects someone's two apparently contradictory attributes. This makes it possible to locate innumerable other characteristics along the same line.

> A woman described herself as the most pleasing of her siblings but also the one with the worst temper. The counselor found that the connecting line between these two characteristics was the woman's need to be the best. The other characteristics the counselor located along this line were that she operated with high-flown ambition and that, as long as she received from others the approbation she thought she deserved, she could be delightful; when things didn't go her way, she could be a bitch. She was like the little girl with the curl in the middle of her forehead: when she was good, she was very, very good, and when she was bad, she was horrid. When these lines were quoted to the woman, she was amazed to remember that her father had said the same thing about her when she was little. Here was a woman who wanted to be the best and if she couldn't be the best at being good, she would try to be the best at being bad.

The "hidden reason" is a technique for uncovering the rationalization process we go through when we decide whether to do something. We begin this thinking process fairly consciously, but then the process sinks below the level of consciousness, and we are no longer aware of it. And when we are asked why we behaved a certain way, our answer will be either a new rationalization or an honest "I don't know."

Searching for the hidden reason is best done in a group setting. Group members are asked to put themselves in the client's shoes and imagine what she might say to herself; for example, "I'm always late because. . . ." After a number of guesses have been made, the client is asked "Who came close?" and whether someone has hit on the client's private logic. At that point, the client will understand and recognize her hidden reason, just as the child recognizes his short-term goal when presented with the four goals. Sometimes the involuntary "recognition reflex" is so strong that it cannot be disguised. In marriage therapy, use of the hidden reason technique often allows both partners to understand their behavior and the behavior of their spouse.

CONFLICT RESOLUTION

Since Individual Psychology is an interpersonal psychology, all conflicts are seen as interpersonal. Adlerian therapists see problems that develop in a marriage as problems in the relationship. As we have said, many marital difficulties result from the spouses' attempts to experience an equalitarian relationship, without having the necessary background to enable them to treat each other (and others) as equals. Most human relationships are characterized by some degree of superiority/inferiority. Adler, as early as 1931, saw the fallacy of this approach and pointed out that equality is the only standard for a successful marriage. Whenever one partner tries to elevate himself or herself above the other, the relationship becomes shaky and temporary, because the partner in the inferior position will always attempt to reverse the situation.

Intramarital fighting not only does not solve the problem, but lays the groundwork for the next conflict. Only with courage and self-confidence can people face the challenge of cooperation. Dreikurs (1946) said that two misconceptions exist with regard to human cooperation: "One is the belief that resentment can lead to improvement. . . . The husband will gladly adjust himself to his wife's desires if he feels fully accepted by her. But he may drive in the opposite direction if he senses her resentment and rejection" (pp. 103–104). Another misconception about cooperation is expressed in the statement that "when interests clash, nothing can be done except to fight or yield."

Dreikurs's Four Principles

The Adlerian marriage therapist deals with all marital problems using Dreikurs's four principles of conflict resolution: (1) showing mutual respect, (2) pinpointing the issue, (3) reaching a new agreement, and (4) participating in decision making. Every marriage conflict involves violation of one or more of these principles.

Showing mutual respect is neither fighting nor giving in; it is neither overpowering nor capitulating. It is, instead, acknowledging that the resolution of conflict rests with understanding and respecting each other's point of view, not with winning or losing.

Pinpointing the issue takes into consideration the fact that behind most marital complaints there is a social issue. For example, a couple may complain about sex, in-laws, work, money, or children. Behind the complaint will be some threat to personal status, prestige, or superiority and some concern with who is winning or who is going to decide or who is right. The partners are specifically taught the technique of pinpointing the issue so they can learn to resolve conflicts on their own, without requiring the help of professionals.

Resolution of conflict is based on the understanding that partners fight because they have reached an "agreement" to fight. Therefore, to resolve conflict, a new agreement must be reached. Reaching a new agreement ultimately comes down to each party's stating "This I'm willing to do, with no strings attached." It is best to make the new agreement for a limited time; at the end of that time, the partners should reevaluate to determine whether the new agreement works.

Husband and wife must participate in decisions that affect them both. Participation is not limited to the decision-making process, but includes assuming responsibility for the decision. Violation of this principle (which unfortunately occurs quite frequently) reflects lack of respect for one's partner and is bound to be deeply resented.

> A husband came home and announced to his wife, rather emphatically and enthusiastically, that he had made arrangements for them to spend a weekend at a resort motel and had also made reservations for dinner at a fine restaurant. He was quite surprised and disappointed when his wife didn't show the enthusiasm he had expected. What he didn't realize was that, by acting without consulting her, he had shown little respect for his wife and violated the principle of participation in decision making.

Detailed information on conflict resolution, a simple self-help conflict resolution card, and extensive material applying this to typical conflicts can be found in *Time for a Better Marriage* by Don Dinkmeyer and Jon Carlson (1984b).

THE NUMBER-ONE PRIORITY

Someone's number-one priority often becomes particularly clear at a time of great stress or conflict. A couple who seeks counseling for their marital problems may be revealing their number-one priorities so clearly that the counselor has no problem identifying them and sharing his insight with the partners. In our experience, this is one of the most effective ways of demonstrating to the couple that they are understood, thus laying the foundations of a strong working relationship.

> *Loraine:* Al tries to control me constantly through criticism.
>
> *Therapist:* Could it also be that, with your number-one priority of superi-

	ority and your emphasis on justice and fairness, you compound the problem by criticizing him for his criticalness?
Loraine:	I think I see your point.
Therapist:	Would both of you agree to refrain from criticizing each other for one week and try, instead, to say something encouraging to each other every day?
Al:	I'm willing to do that. But how do I know that what I say is encouraging?
Therapist:	There are no guarantees, but encouragement means giving honest recognition for whatever you appreciate about your wife. Naturally, if she doesn't believe that about herself, she may not find it encouraging. How about trying it right now? What do you appreciate about Loraine?
Al:	She is very bright and has a good sense of humor.
Therapist:	And what do you appreciate about Al, Loraine?
Loraine:	He is honest and reliable.

The Number-One Priority: Choice of Partner

"The number-one priority: choice of partner" is a relatively new addition to Adlerian theory and practice. It appears that people may choose marriage partners on the basis of their own number-one priority; that is, people choose partners with whom they can be themselves and pursue their number-one priority. For example, a man whose number-one priority is control is likely to choose a wife who, he believes, will permit him to exert his leadership and organizational ability. If his wife's number-one priority is superiority, she may have chosen him because, at some level of awareness, she felt that she could be better than her husband.

Problems in marriage relationships develop when the individual moves toward the "only if" absurdity (an extreme form of the number-one priority), such as "Only if I am comfortable, do I really belong." The more an individual moves toward the "only if" absurdity, the higher the price. As marriage partners learn about their own and their partner's number-one priorities, they become aware of some of their partner's vulnerabilities. One of the tasks of the counselor is to teach each partner to be an effective agent of encouragement instead of attacking vulnerabilities.

Married couples seldom have the same number-one priority. The most common pairings are control/superiority and comfort/pleasing. If the counselor is skilled at pinpointing the number-one priority early in the initial interview, he has reached a valuable insight into the life style of the partners, which will help the clients feel understood and facilitate a good counseling rapport.

CHILDREN

When children are involved in the marital conflict, the whole situation becomes much more complex. It is crucial that the therapist convince the spouses of the devastating effects of using the children to get at each other.

> A couple who had been in a conflict situation for many years also disagreed on how to deal with their very troublesome "hyperactive" child. The youngster was eventually removed from the home and put in residential treatment. In her deep discouragement, the mother reached the conclusion that she couldn't tolerate the child in the household again. The father never accepted the separation from his son but never tried to work out the conflict.
>
> By the time the couple sought marriage therapy, the child's treatment was seriously handicapped by the fact that, since he couldn't return to his home, long-range planning was almost impossible. After the husband announced that his son was ready to come home and the wife refused to accept the child back, the husband decided that he would move out and take care of his son. This led to a most serious marital crisis, which culminated in divorce.

Children, of course, know when there is disagreement between their parents, and there is no point in trying to hide it from them. The children can be told very simply that their parents are having some difficulties and that they are working on them. Beyond that, it is usually not advisable to draw the children into the marriage therapy process. Occasionally, with adolescent or adult children, we have found it helpful to include the young persons in some of the sessions, if the children are deeply enmeshed in their parents' relationship. If a couple is planning divorce, we remind them that they will continue to be the parents of their children. We also try to help them see that there is an advantage to dissolving the marriage peacefully and cooperatively, thus maintaining some type of friendly relationship, if for no other reason than to make it easier for the children to deal with the disruption of the family.

Often, when a couple begins to think about the children and the effects of marital conflict on their growth and development, they can be led to more cooperation and less battling. In other words, as the partners begin to realize how selfish they are and to what extreme they are concentrating on what each is getting out of the relationship to the exclusion of anyone else's interest and well-being, they can be led back toward a state of higher social interest and more courage. On the other hand, we never recommend that couples stay together "for the good of the children." If a relationship is built on phony premises, the children will always sense it and suffer from it. A destructive marital relationship is hardly a decent model for children if they are expected to know later in life what a good marital relationship is like.

OTHER PARTIES

In our experience, it is unusual for a marriage relationship to survive the prolonged existence of another party in the life of one or both spouses. People today try in so many different ways to overcome loneliness and achieve intimacy that long-lasting monogamous marriage has almost become one item in the large list of alternate life styles. We believe that, ultimately, monogamy will again be seen as the most viable form of a lasting relationship between a man and a woman. We also think that people will choose a monogamous relationship not because of pressure from church, family, or state, but because of the advantages of the relationship for both parties.

Individuals must choose their own definition of monogamy and agree on that definition with their partners. A monogamous relationship might mean, for example, a long-term deep commitment on the part of both parties, yet still allow significant relationships with members of the opposite sex, from time to time, for both partners. Our marriage therapy experience, however, has taught us that a relationship with another man or woman is often merely a symptom, not a cause, of the degeneration of the marriage relationship. Frequently, an affair is revealed to the partner in an effort to get him or her off dead center. We say "revealed," but there are seldom any secrets in a marriage; the other partner usually "knows" at some level of awareness about the extramarital affair. And quite often the other man or woman is not nearly as important as either spouse believes.

GOALS AND RESISTANCE

In marriage therapy, we must always face the issue of limited versus ideal goals, which is another way of saying that counselor and clients must try to answer the question "How much therapy is enough?" For one individual, a relatively minor change in attitude about one aspect of life may be sufficient; for one couple, a recommitment to working at the marriage and greater tolerance of each other may be all that is needed. The therapist can often see that, ideally, a couple would benefit from extensive therapy, including basic reorientation of the life styles, but ultimately the couple must decide for themselves what their therapy goals will be.

Resistance develops when there is a lack of alignment between the goals of the couple and those of the therapist or between the goals of the two partners. Whenever resistance is detected, it is important to stop the counseling process immediately and attempt to negotiate a new set of goals that is acceptable to all parties. Sometimes negotiation leads to the agreement that goal alignment is not possible and that termination is indicated. No matter what the outcome, the process is essentially to work toward consensus. By "consensus" we mean not that everybody agrees 100 percent, but that everybody feels able to live with a particular decision, preferably for a limited period of time. Thus, a married couple may decide to suspend any major decisions and work on their relationship for two months, with the intent of reevaluating and renegotiating the agreement at the end of that time. If the counselor feels comfortable working within such parameters, a consensus is reached, even though the counselor might like to see the couple commit themselves for a longer period of time.

MULTIPLE THERAPY

As we indicated in Chapter 12, multiple therapy is therapy conducted by more than one therapist. The advantage of this approach is more evident in marriage and family counseling than in any other area. One counselor can work effectively with a couple, but two counselors add many additional dimensions to the therapy process, particularly if they represent both sexes. The ideal situation probably exists when the counselors themselves are married to each other and the two couples can sit together in "four-track therapy." When the therapist is a male, the wife may feel besieged by two males and is often tremendously relieved to have a female therapist introduced into the process.

Ted:	I think that Mary and I should meet each week and have an evaluation—particularly of how we are using our time.
Mary (in tears):	That's not what I'm talking about at all.
Male cotherapist:	I think Ted's idea has merit. It might be incorporated in a family-council meeting.
Female cotherapist:	What Mary is looking for is some appreciation. I suspect that the term *evaluation* sounds like she's going to be graded.
Mary:	That's just it. And, if I don't pass, Ted will have one more way to control me.

However, wives do not always identify with female therapists and husbands with male therapists. Frequently, the male therapist finds that, for some reason or other, he can understand the woman's point of view better, and vice versa. If the therapists are married to each other, their credibility with the couple is considerably higher, particularly if they are able to be open about the rough spots they have handled in their own relationship.

Female cotherapist:	I get so mad at Larry I could bite him. But when I have a chance to be heard for a whole half hour in a marriage conference, I often find that I calm down considerably.
Male cotherapist (to female cotherapist):	But you still always want some kind of resolution.
Female cotherapist (to male cotherapist):	Yes, that's true, and you seem to be able to function much better when things are left hanging.
Clients together:	That's just the way it is with us.

Whenever marriage therapy is faltering, the addition of another therapist to the ongoing counseling process or simply for consultation is extremely helpful. Cotherapy and multiple therapy can be excellent methods for training counselors and therapists, and it is quite possible to have three or more therapists working with a couple at one time.

Most couples are pleased to have more than one therapist. They often feel they are getting their money's worth, so to speak, and that the more therapists present, the more points of view are introduced into the therapy process. When a new therapist joins the process, the "temperature of the marriage" is often taken again to give the new counselor some idea of the quality of the relationship and of the present trouble spots, compared to those that existed at the beginning of counseling. Sometimes this reevaluation opens up new directions in the therapy process.

A couple had initially rated themselves 3 as lovers, and there was no discrepancy between the partners' ratings. When the process was repeated a few months later, both partners had gained considerably in their self-esteem and were much more assertive about what they wanted in their relationship. At this time, they still rated themselves 3 as lovers, but since they were rating themselves so much better in other areas, they were now able to bring up and deal with the problems they were experiencing in the area of sexuality. Therefore, the counseling focused for several sessions on the issue of sexuality. The spouses were asked to read McCary's *Human Sexuality* (1978) independently and to underline, with pencils of different colors, the things that impressed them. By doing so, both partners discovered there were areas of sexuality they didn't know much about. They were also advised to attend a weekend sexual-awareness reassessment session at the University of Minnesota. During this session, they were bombarded with multimedia presentations on all levels and participated in numerous group discussions. Finally, they were recommended various techniques of the Masters and Johnson type and asked to pay special attention to those that emphasized the importance of giving pleasure to the other partner.

With their increased sophistication, it became clear that the issue behind their conflict in the area of sexuality was often one of control. The partners were asked to conduct an experiment. During the first week, the wife was to make all the decisions concerning expressions of affection, tenderness, and sexuality. The following week, the husband was to be in charge. The partners agreed to the experiment and also to cooperate with each other to the best of their ability. She learned to be assertive and that it was OK to be the initiator. He learned that he didn't require immediate gratification every time he felt sexually aroused. Both partners learned to greatly enhance their own and the other's pleasure. As a result, they learned to deal more effectively not only with sexuality but also with parenthood, and their relationship with their teenage children improved considerably.

MARRIAGE EDUCATION CENTERS

Marriage education centers are patterned after family education centers. They are inspired by the same models and operate in the same manner, so you will find much of this discussion familiar.

The three purposes of marriage education centers are (1) to communicate to a large audience basic mental-health principles that lead to more joyful and cooperative living; (2) to provide a resource for troubled couples; and (3) to train other counselors to work more effectively with couples. Volunteer couples are interviewed in a public group setting and function as coeducators with the cocounselors. As the partners are interviewed, the cocounselors have the opportunity to teach the larger group what democratic principles are being violated in that particular relationship and methods of conflict resolution. The situation provides a unique setting for teaching principles of harmonious living as well as a unique source of encouragement to couples in the audience. By participating in the interview process, members of the audience realize they are not alone and that other couples have similar problems.

The cocounselors then give the clients specific recommendations and ask them to return to the center in a week or two to report on their successes and failures. Each interview with a couple ends with an encouragement session. The members of the audience are urged to give honest, sincere feedback about the strengths they see in the relationship and about everything else they appreciate in the couple.

Marriage education centers may be housed in hospitals, churches, schools, or other public buildings. Funding sources vary, but in many centers much of the work is done by volunteers. The staff of a marriage education center includes a director and a codirector, who are professionals in the mental-health field and who have had extensive additional training and experience with the Adlerian model. In some communities, however, lay people have been trained to direct marriage education centers under professional supervision. Other staff usually include the coordinator, an intake worker, a recorder, and the staff of the activity center for children and adolescents. Admission is free in most centers. Participants can simply observe, or ask questions, or volunteer to be the demonstration couple.

Although we speak of a marriage-education center, the volunteer couples are not necessarily married. They may be contemplating marriage or living together in a variety of alternate life styles, including homosexual relationships. In other words, they are two adults attempting to overcome loneliness and achieve intimacy.

The cocounselors try to see to it that the volunteer couples are not analyzed, diagnosed, or in any way put on the spot. Since many people consider their marriages too private to talk about, we are constantly amazed at how freely people will attack virtually any subject, given the trust, support, and encouragement that are generated in the marriage-education center, not only by the counselors but by the other participants as well.

Like the family-education center, the marriage-education center is an example of primary preventive mental-health care. Counselors are able to reach many more people than they could by talking with individual couples. This preventive aspect and the aspect of community outreach and education have particularly interested a number of hospitals. Often, the marriage-education center becomes a referral agent to other community agencies. In the course of two or three weeks, for example, we referred one young man to a local hospital for treatment of his depression, a young woman to another hospital for treatment of her schizophrenia, and another woman for residential treatment of her alcoholism.

MARRIAGE ENRICHMENT

Marriage enrichment began in January, 1962, when a group of married couples met with Father Calvo for a weekend marriage enrichment retreat.

In October of 1962, David and Vera Mace began leading marriage enrichment sessions for married couples throughout the United States, leading to the founding of the Association of Couples for Marriage Enrichment (ACME) and the Council of Affiliated Marriage Enrichment Organizations (CAMEO).

Marriage enrichment is a process in which couples learn to be more honest, intimate, and respectful. As they learn to align their goals, communicate more effectively, and resolve conflicts, they open the relationship to deeper involvement and enhance its quality.

The Adlerian-based marriage enrichment program we will describe is Training in Marriage Enrichment (T.I.M.E.) (Dinkmeyer & Carlson, 1984a). This is a skill-based, 10-session program. Program topics include: A Good Marriage Begins With You, Encouragement in the Marital Relationship, Understanding Your Relationship, Honesty and Openness, Communication, Communication Skills, Choice in the Marital Relationship, Conflict, Conflict Resolutions, and Self-Help Procedures for Maintaining the Marriage.

The session format provides for both content input, skill development, and experimental activity. A typical sequence in a session would include:

1. A communication-building activity
2. Discussion of an activity assigned the preceding week, as an opportunity to put the program concepts into practice in the relationship
3. Discussion of reading in *Time For A Better Marriage*
4. Responding to skill-building situations on a cassette
5. Application of the skill from this session
6. Summary and sharing of what each person has learned

SPECIFIC TECHNIQUES

In marriage counseling, marriage therapy, and marriage education, we teach couples specific techniques that enhance communication and cooperation.

Listening

To learn the listening technique, one partner agrees to sit down and listen to the other partner until he or she has finished, without any interruption or nonverbal static. Then, the listening partner has the option to respond by sharing the feelings and beliefs he has heard, and the partner who spoke first becomes the listener. This process is particularly helpful when one partner is very upset and the other one is not, yet needs to understand what is bothering the other. The partners need to be taught to listen empathically to the feelings, beliefs, and concerns that are expressed.

Paraphrasing

In this process, one partner makes a statement; the other is to refrain from answering until he has paraphrased to his satisfaction whatever the other has said. This technique is difficult for partners who, while one talks, busily compose their own response instead of listening. Before they are ready to practice at home, they must receive a great deal of guidance from the counselors.

Feedback

If one partner comes home tired, angry, or discouraged, the other partner is often all too willing to give feedback. With this technique, we teach the two to ask the discouraged partner "Would you like some feedback?" or "Would you like to hear my suggestions?" and be willing to take "No" for an answer. Sometimes the discouraged partner will say "No, not now." Sometimes she will say "Yes, I would like to hear your ideas, but at a later time." Through this technique, couples learn that feedback is accepted much more gracefully when it is offered courteously and tentatively. Partners must understand that feedback is only sharing how one is experiencing the other or the situation, and is not a judgment.

Marriage Conferences

The marriage conference is one of the most satisfactory ways of dealing with intense conflict situations. This technique, first described by Corsini (1967), is taught to couples in marriage-education centers. Often members of the audience try the technique, too.

The partners are asked to make a series of appointments to meet with each other for an hour at a time, in a place where they are unlikely to be interrupted. The appointments should be at least two or three days apart. With couples who are experiencing significant conflict, we usually recommend at least three appointments. The marriage conference is a self-help process that couples can carry out in their own time and at their own convenience. It is quite normal for couples who are using the marriage conference for the first time to report disappointment with the experience, unless they follow the directions carefully. Innovating is not advised until the couple have had some experience with the technique.

At the time of the first appointment and as a result of a previous agreement, one partner has the floor for the first half hour while the other partner listens silently and refrains from interrupting, making faces, or in any other way interfering with what the other says. We generally recommend that partners avoid television, radio, note taking, smoking, eating, drinking, or any other distraction. During one's half hour, one is free to say whatever one chooses and also has the option to remain silent. It is one's half hour to use as one chooses. At the end of exactly half an hour, the process is reversed, and the first partner becomes the listener. At the end of the second half hour, the conference is over. As a result of a previous agreement, the partners do not discuss until the next marriage conference any controversial items that came up during the conference. Noncontroversial items or any other subject can, of course, be discussed between conferences. At the time of the second conference, the process is repeated, except that the partners reverse the order in which they speak and listen.

After experimenting with marriage conferences, a number of couples choose to continue having them as a regularly scheduled event in their lives. Other couples choose to conduct couple council meetings, which then grow into family council meetings as children become part of the relationship.

> Kathy and George are both extremely busy professionals with complicated schedules. Devoting 15 minutes a week to a couple council, which they refer to as a "board meeting," has probably saved them from divorce. They sit down every Sunday and work out the schedule for the week, transportation, who's going to do what work, financial matters, and so forth—in other words, all the regular business of living together and operating a household.

Listing Expectations

Another helpful technique is to ask couples to independently write out their expectations for themselves, for their partner, and for the relationship. When they bring their lists back, the counselor reads each list aloud, checking with the other partner to find out whether the items on the list are understandable and whether they are considered reasonable. Sometimes the partners are asked to live for a month according to these expectations. Often items from the list provide springboards for further discussion.

> Sue and Jerry had never seriously considered having children. As Sue approached the conclusion of her academic career, she started feeling more and more strongly about having a baby. The fact that she was over

30 and most of her friends had children contributed to her feelings. While Sue was in school, Jerry had settled into a comfortable life style, and the thought of disrupting it with a child's presence didn't particularly appeal to him. Sue and Jerry's difficulty was compounded by their respective families' subtle and not-so-subtle pressures on them. When they wrote out their lists of hopes and expectations, it was obvious that, while Sue and Jerry were far apart with regard to the issue of having children, they were in almost complete agreement about everything else. Since neither felt ready to make a final decision in one direction or the other, they decided to discontinue their day-to-day discussion of the issue and bring it up, instead, every three months. This decision was also motivated by the fact that they were expecting many changes in their lives, with Sue becoming a full-time professional and Jerry considering going back to school at least part time.

Homework

We regularly prescribe homework, and the partners agree to commit them-selves to doing the prescribed activity. The kinds of homework are limited only by the imagination of the counselors and of the audience (when the counseling takes place in a center). For a couple who hasn't been away from their children for many months and resents the situation, the assign-ment may be to hire a babysitter and spend a weekend at a resort motel. For a couple who complains about sex but whose underlying problem seems to be one of control, the homework may require each spouse to take full responsibility and make all decisions in the area of sex and affection for alternate weeks.

Paradoxical Intention

One of the most powerful techniques in marriage counseling is the para-doxical intention. The partners are asked to go home and do whatever they have been doing all along, but to do it on schedule. For example, a couple who has been fighting all the time may be urged to carry on a 10-minute fight each evening, using the very same procedures they have always followed—but they have to do it every night and for 10 minutes.

Many couples can't believe that such a recommendation will do them any good. They have come for help and are being told by the helper to go home and do exactly what they had been doing before. But if they are serious about improving their relationship, they usually make an effort to follow instructions. The paradoxical intention is always put in the form of an experiment: "See what you can learn." Whether the couple follows the recommendation, they learn that they can choose when to fight and when not to fight. Frequently, couples have a great deal of difficulty carrying out the recommendation without laughing, and the absurdity of their fight becomes apparent to them.

> A man found himself attracted to a younger woman who worked with his wife. This attraction was particularly devastating to his wife because at the time she was suffering from a serious illness. Although the couple wanted to remain married, the husband found himself fantasizing a great deal about the other woman. A "paradoxical recommendation" was made to the husband: he was supposed to sit for 20 minutes after dinner each evening and fantasize about the younger woman. This recommendation was made in the presence and with the agreement of his wife. One week later, the man announced that his fantasizing had clarified the situation for him. He now realized that he wasn't really in love with this other woman and that he had been looking to her as a source of encouragement during a period of deep concern over his wife's illness.

> A couple reported that they had problems because of the husband's premature ejaculation. We asked them to have intercourse twice a day and without foreplay. We emphasized that the husband was supposed to ejaculate as quickly as possible. The reason for our recommendation was that a symptom cannot be maintained unless one fights against it. Under the right circumstances, the symptom of premature ejaculation often disappears. In fact, it is not unusual for a couple to report the opposite experience—that is, the man has difficulty ejaculating or even reaching orgasm.

Separation

Many couples keep the threat of separation dangling between them. In that case, we occasionally recommend that they separate. We do so when we suspect that a separation will help the couple realize how much they love and miss each other. We also recommend separation when the fighting in between counseling sessions is so extreme that the partners don't seem to have time or energy for any kind of conflict resolution or problem solving. Generally, however, separation is not frequently recommended. When it occurs, it is much more likely to have been decided upon by the couple than to have been recommended by the therapists.

OTHER HELPFUL PROCESSES

Parent Education

Parent education often results in better relationships between spouses. The principles taught in family-education centers and parent study groups, although specifically designed to improve adult/child interactions, are also effective in promoting equalitarian marital relationships. Consequently, as a couple learns these principles for dealing with their children, they also learn to apply them to their own relationship. Couples who have been devoting a great deal of time to fighting with their children often find themselves with free time once they have learned to deal with their children more efficiently. Although sometimes this gives them more time to fight with each other, often the marriage relationship is enhanced as the spouses learn to put things in perspective and to consider their marriage relationship first and their apparent parental obligations second. Many couples report that their marriage has improved considerably after family counseling, even though nothing specific was recommended with regard to the marriage.

Marriage Study Groups

The marriage study group is an outgrowth of marriage-education centers and of the emphasis on the benefits of study groups. A group of couples meet weekly for eight to ten weeks to study a book, such as Dreikurs's *The Challenge of Marriage* (1946), Hawes's *Couples Growing Together* (1982), or Dinkmeyer and Carlson's *Time For a Better Marriage* (1984). Study groups are led by lay people and depend on the ability of the participating couples to learn the useful principles and put them into practice on their own. When couples find this difficult, marriage therapy or marriage counseling may be indicated.

Couple Group Therapy

As pioneers in group therapy, it is not surprising that Adlerians have adapted the group process to marriage therapy. A group of five or six married couples is seen for two hours a week, usually for a limited period of time, perhaps ten weeks. Couples benefit from the group by identifying with and getting ideas from peers. They discover that they are not alone and that their problems are not unique. Ideally, the couples will also have private sessions, including formulation of their life styles. Couple group therapy may take place in conjunction with attendance at a marriage-education center.

TECHNICAL QUESTIONS

Frequency and Length of Therapy

The frequency of therapy sessions is often dictated by factors that are extraneous to the therapy process itself, such as financial considerations and available time. The optimal frequency seems to be once a week. This gives the couple enough time to work on things between sessions yet maintains the intensity of the counseling experience. After 8 to 12 weekly sessions, most couples can be seen less frequently, often returning at monthly intervals for checkups.

The length of each session in marriage therapy can probably be the same as in individual counseling, commonly the 50-minute hour. In cases of four-track therapy, we have experimented with two-hour sessions with very good results. Since it is often difficult to get the therapists and the couple together, it helps to have a longer block of time, particularly if the couple travels far for sessions. With a two-hour block of time, we are able to get into the relationship more deeply and still have enough time to bring about resolution. We have also experimented with more intensive kinds of therapy—for example, meeting with couples six or eight hours a day for three consecutive days. Although some of these couples had profound and complex problems, the process could be brought to completion by the end of the third day.

As we have said, marriage therapy can be combined with individual and/or group therapy. Generally, if one partner is receiving individual therapy, the marital relationship should not be part of that therapy process, and the therapist should insist on dealing with relationship problems only when both partners are present. When one partner seems to need a group experience, certain hazards should be kept in mind, such as the likelihood of the partners' differential growth and the possibility that the other partner may feel left out and worry about what is going on in the group. When these kinds of problems are present, participation in a couple group may be a better solution.

Marital History

In our experience, a complete marital history is seldom necessary. We obtain sufficient information by discussing the current situation and by doing the personal life style assessments. When we are puzzled and do not understand the dynamics of the relationship, however, it may be important to go back and ask the couple to describe in considerable detail their courtship, the early days of their marriage, and the various phases of their marriage relationship.

We look for recurring patterns and often see that the very things that attracted the partners to each other in the first place are those that, in their current fights, are brought up most often and objected to most strongly.

Mark appreciated Clara's sociability and witty conversation, but now, when they fight, he claims that she talks too much. Clara appreciated Mark's strong, quiet, and logical manner, but now, when they fight, she complains that he wants to make all the decisions.

Sexual Problems

The sex act represents the ultimate test of a couple's willingness to cooperate and contribute to each other's welfare. Therefore, it is not surprising that most "sexual" problems turn out to be relationship problems. We seldom find it useful to accept the couple's diagnosis that they have a sexual problem, thus dealing only with the symptom. Many couples report that, as their relationship improves, their sexual life improves also. If a couple has ever had a good sexual relationship, chances are they can have it again; if a couple has never had a good sexual relationship, it is more likely that we are dealing with sexual problems per se.

It is amazing how many couples are sexually ignorant. We often recommend that they read *Human Sexuality* by McCary (1978) and that they underline, with pencils of different colors, the portions they consider important. The couple can thus learn together through reading. They can also learn through various desensitization procedures, such as the multimedia sexual-awareness weekend for couples, patterned after the Sexual Awareness Reassessment Program at the University of Minnesota. Similar but less sophisticated experience can be achieved by having the couple see some of the more artistic "pornographic" movies or use other sexually arousing materials of high quality.

A complete sexual history is sometimes indicated to help clarify a confusing situation. In this case, the partners are asked to describe their early experiences with sex, both before and after they met, and provide a fairly detailed history of their sex lives up to the present. An important process, but one that can be conducted only by counselors who are very comfortable about their own sexuality, is to have the couple describe their lovemaking in great detail, from the beginning to the end of the experience. This often makes if possible for the counselor to identify the trouble spots and for the couple to learn a great deal about themselves and each other. We strongly recommend that such histories be obtained with both partners present, although sometimes one partner is unwilling to discuss certain aspects or portions of past sexual history in the presence of the other. Naturally, we must be sensitive to such situations, and hear him or her out in private, although we tend to recommend that partners be as open with each other in this area as they can possibly be.

Another technique is to ask each partner, in the presence of the other, to close the eyes and fantasize aloud an ideal sexual experience with the partner. Sharing fantasies tells both people things about themselves and each other that they have often been unable to verbalize and opens the door for sharing fantasies further on their own.

Although it is rare for sexual problems to have a physical basis, we do sometimes recommend a complete physical checkup if a couple has not had examinations recently or if either partner suggests in any way that he or she believes their sexual problems might have a physical basis. Although physical examinations seldom add anything new to the picture, they often alleviate the partners' anxiety.

ADDITIONAL STRATEGIES IN MARRIAGE THERAPY

Psychodrama

Psychodrama refers to a group of techniques in which the client acts out various situations so as to gain insight into and better understanding of the situation. For example:

> Shirley, age 24 and married, thinks she is in love with another man. She reports great torment in trying to decide what she should do. We ask her to sit half on one chair and half on another. We talk with her about how it feels to be sitting on two chairs, and we ask her to predict how long she will be able to remain in that position. We also ask whether she has some idea about which "chair" she is leaning toward. Then we ask Shirley "Do you think the chances that in one year you'll still be living with Al are larger or smaller than 50 percent?" She says "It's still 50/50." Had she said that the chances were greater than 50 percent, we would have told her that, on the basis of her own admission (at least at this moment), she really had decided to stay with Al. We would also have pointed out that the main issue then was how big a production she was going to make out of her decision.

In another psychodramatic technique, the partners change chairs, playing each other's role and experiencing each other. We use auxiliary egos, doubling, mirroring, and any of the other standard psychodramatic techniques, as well as spontaneous variations that we create on the spot.

Absurdification

This technique consists in taking what the partners say and carrying it to its ridiculous extreme. It is particularly useful with people who are prone to thinking in terms of either/or and in superlatives. Once the person has become aware of the absurdity of an extreme stance, we use every opportunity to confront her with it. For example, "Is it possible that everything in your life is in terms of *always*? Do you know anybody else who *always* suffers as nobly as you do? You must be a saint in disguise."

Prescribing What the Partners Already Know

One of the first questions we ask partners is "Can you think of something you could do in the coming week that would make a difference in your relationship?" Almost all partners know things they can do and that, for whatever reason, choose not to do. Generally, the only recommendation we offer in the initial interview is that each partner do those few things that he or she has mentioned. Also, we tell them to do them for a limited time, preferably until the next appointment. We don't want them to have the feeling they are committing themselves for life.

I'm Stuck With

We often ask couples to hold hands, look in each other's eyes, and tell each other, step by step, what they find difficult to live with both in the partner and in the relationship. One partner does this until he or she is finished, then the other partner repeats the process.

Diagnosis and Prognosis

Sometimes couples ask for a diagnosis. We have developed a unitary diagnostic system that simplifies this process. The diagnosis is always the same: chronic human imperfection. When the question of prognosis comes up, we simply say we don't know; we are not prophets, we don't have a crystal ball, and we can't read minds.

Redefinition

An important technique is that of redefinition. If Ralph keeps referring to Janet as stubborn, we redefine the characteristic as persistence and identify in considerable detail all the advantages Janet brings to the marriage because of her persistence.

At all times, and not just when we employ this technique, we try to help partners communicate clearly, using the right words, being specific and direct, and avoiding all that can confuse the message.

Guessing the Purpose

This technique has two advantages. If we counselors guess correctly, the person or couple feels understood. If we make a mistake, we have the opportunity to demonstrate our courage to be imperfect, which is what we are trying to teach the couple. And the more we guess, the more we sharpen our psychological sensitivity.

Placing Responsibility

Another related feature of our approach to marriage counseling is the willingness to go into each session with no script. We put the responsibility directly on the couple by asking them right away "What would you like to work on today?" If they wish to report on our previous recommendation, we will ask them to tell us what we recommended, rather than rely on our own memory or notes. We continue with "What did you do?" and "What did you learn?"

GROUP TECHNIQUES

Because of the complexity of the group in a marriage-education center, many techniques are used, some of which develop directly from the group.

Feedback

Counselor: You have heard Helen and George describe the situation when they were on vacation. What kind of feedback would you like to give them?

Counselor: Esther said that sometimes she feels so discouraged she wonders whether life is worth living and that she has even thought of suicide. How many of you have thought of suicide from time to time?

Of course, feedback can be successful only if clear ground rules are laid down: we do not permit analysis, diagnosis, or direct confrontation, and all comments must come through the cocounselors.

Counselor: It appears that Betty knows very well how to get into a fight with Frank. What suggestions would you have for her if she chose to stay out of the fight?

Audience:	She could go to the bathroom.
	She could tell Frank that she loves him too much to fight with him.
	She could tell Frank she hasn't time for a fight today but she would be willing to work him into her schedule sometime tomorrow evening.
	She could tell Frank that, if he keeps on pestering her, she's going to kiss him.

Encouragement cannot be overemphasized. We have never had anybody get an overdose of encouragement, and we consistently do everything we can, and stimulate the audience to do everything they can, to help increase the self-esteem of those being counseled.

Empathy

Counselor: Helen has described a very sad and poignant situation and feels she's the only one who has ever experienced anything like it. Would all of you who have known through your own personal experience what it's like to be in her boots come up on the stage and stand around her?

Information

Counselor: It is clear from talking with Peter that his wife is an alcoholic. How many of you have wrestled with chemical dependency in the family? What are the various resources available in our community?

Clarification

Counselor: It seems, Sue, that you still don't understand what I've been saying. Let me ask the audience if there are members who would be willing to try to restate it in such a way that it would make sense to you.

Taking Pressure off the Couple

When the going gets heavy, a useful technique is for the cocounselors to stop and have a conversation or turn to the audience and deliver a short lecture or have a discussion with the audience while one or both partners have a chance to compose themselves. Tissues are always available, often supplied by somebody in the front row.

Desensitization

Norman has never been able to tell his wife of 26 years what he thinks and feels about sex and what would please him. In fact, he can't imagine talking about sex with anyone. A lively discussion about human sexuality is stimulated with the help of the audience. Norman listens to what is being said, and, as the discussion proceeds, he finds it increasingly easy to actually begin to use some of the terminology himself.

Support

A particularly touching experience often takes place in a marriage-education center when, after formal counseling ends, the people who have felt empathy for one or both partners gather around them, giving them support and encouragement.

REFERENCES

Adler, A. (1958). *What life should mean to you.* New York: Capricorn.

Corsini, R.J. (1967). Let's invent a first-aid kit for marriage problems. *Consultant, 40.*

Dinkmeyer, D., & Carlson, J. (1984a). *Training in marriage enrichment.* Circle Pines, MN: American Guidance Service.

Dinkmeyer, D., & Carlson, J. (1984b). *Time for a better marriage.* Circle Pines, MN: American Guidance Service.

Dinkmeyer, D., & Dinkmeyer, J. (1982). Adlerian marriage therapy. *Individual Psychology, 38*(2), 115–122.

Dinkmeyer, D., & Dinkmeyer, J. (1983). *Marital inventory.* Coral Springs, FL: CMTI Press.

Dreikurs, R. (1946). *The challenge of marriage.* New York: Hawthorn.

Hawes, E. C. (1982). Couples growing together: Couple enrichment programs. *Individual Psychology, 38*(4), 322–331.

Kern, R. (1982). *Lifestyle scale.* Coral Springs, FL: CMTI Press.

McCary, J. L. (1978). *Human sexuality* (3rd ed.). New York: Van Nostrand.

Watkins, C. E., Jr. (1982). The self-administered life-style analysis. *Individual Psychology, 38*(4), 343–352.

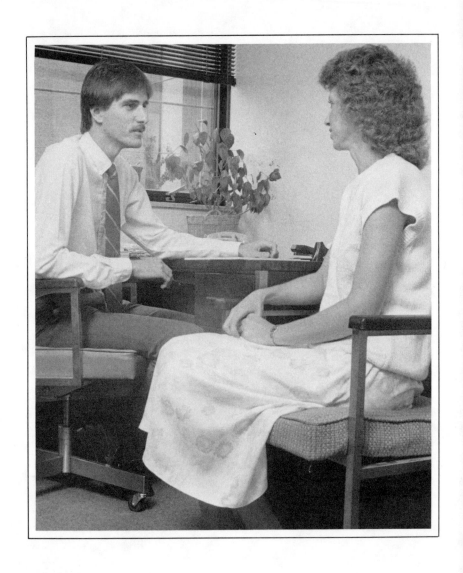

14

Individual and Group Consultation with Teachers

T he education process concerns not solely the students but the teachers, administrators, and parents as well. We have dealt with the counseling of students throughout this book. In this and the next chapter, we turn our attention to teachers and parents. Chapter 15 deals with the unique and highly successful strategy Adlerians use for parent education, whether in schools, agencies, or other settings. This chapter focuses on the counselor's relationship with the teacher.

The authors' extensive experience with American education includes successful efforts to establish the profession of elementary school counseling more than twenty years ago. Recently, financial pressures, the demand for a return to "basics," and other educational priorities have placed the counselor near the top of the list of "expendable" personnel in the school system. When counselors are often responsible for more than 500 students in a high school, or for perhaps all the students in an elementary or junior high school, the question "Since counselors cannot possibly be effective, why have them at all?" becomes less than rhetorical. The school counseling profession survives only if its services are highly visible and when people consider them essential to the entire school population.

Counselors have few chances of being effective, or even of surviving, if their job is narrowly defined as counselor/student interaction. There is much more to student counseling than working with students alone. For school counselors to be effective, they must be able to work with all facets of the education process. They may, for example, schedule classroom affective-education programs and activities. But if the teacher operates that classroom autocratically and demands that the children depend on her instructions, demands, and needs, the counselor's half-hour each week has no chance of counteracting the teacher's more pervasive influence.

School counselors must have skills that not only allow them to work with individual teachers on a request basis, but permit them to initiate group education and problem-solving experiences for teachers. The latter is preferable, since groups can be more productive and successful than individual consultation. Four advantages of the group model are:

Individual consultation with teachers places the counselor in the "expert" or "answer-man" role, where advice can be ignored or proven impractical

Teacher beliefs about human behavior are more likely to surface in a group setting, and the counselor can apply this internal frame of reference to how it shapes behavior

Peers are more able to identify faulty beliefs and have these perceptions accepted by an equal

Working with a group multiplies resources for each teacher's problem-solving needs (Dinkmeyer, McKay, & Dinkmeyer, 1980)

THEORETICAL FOUNDATIONS

Whether in groups or individually, consultation with teachers must be supported by a theoretical framework for understanding human behavior, and Adlerian psychology offers that framework. But first let us examine some of the principles teachers often use to understand behavior.

Common Mistaken Assumptions about Human Behavior

Behavior is a product of environmental factors

Jennifer is a problem child because she comes from a poor home—the other side of the tracks, so to speak. In other words, where you live determines how you behave. It seems almost unnecessary to answer the advocates of this theory by pointing to the countless cases of exceptional achievement and motivation among ghetto children and to the equally countless cases of apathy and failure among children who "benefit" from middle- and upper-class environments.

Behavior is a product of heredity

This view, expressed by the catchall phrase "The genes did it!" is more prevalent among parents than among teachers. The reason is simply that teachers have ample opportunity to make comparisons among their students and see clearly that heredity is only a small factor in a child's makeup. But some teachers may accept the heredity theory if they have had older brothers or sisters in their classes, or hear opinions from other teachers who have worked with siblings. They may hear statements such as "That family has no discipline" or "There's no father, so the oldest son does a lot of the disciplining."

Behavior is a product of age and stage of development

Those who hold this view see behavior as a function of chronological age—the terrible two's, the troubled teens, and so forth. Like the environmental view, the opinion ignores the wide variability among individuals—in this case, of individuals at the same age or "stage." It forgets the mature 12-year-old and the immature adult.

Behavior is a product of sex

Sex-role stereotyping is perhaps on its way out, but it accounts for differences in behavior by focusing on the sex of the child. Although not many people today say that girls are made of "sugar and spice" and "boys will be boys," these stereotypes still influence our children's choices. For example, boys still take more high-school math courses than girls do, at least in North America. In cultures in which sex stereotyping is absent or exists to a much smaller degree, differences in the boys' and girls' educational choices are unknown.

These four minitheories of human behavior explain away, rather than understand, behavior. What can a counselor do when a teacher subscribes to one or more of these "theories"? Short of having children change home, genes, age, or sex, these beliefs leave the teacher powerless to make an effective intervention.

Applicable Adlerian Principles

By introducing the teacher to the Adlerian theory of personality, the counselor can help the teacher understand students' behavior.

Behavior must be seen holistically

The individual is a whole, not a conglomeration of diverse and often conflicting parts. We cannot understand behavior if we focus on small fragments, or certain confusing behaviors, and ignore the overall pattern. Each bit of information is indeed correct, but it performs a limited, often useless, function in our effort to understand the whole person. If we focus exclusively on a student's extremely high IQ score, for example, we cannot explain that student's low grades. The two elements appear inconsistent until we recognize another factor—motivation. It is only through the broader picture of overall psychological movement that we can understand behavior.

All behavior has a purpose

When a child misbehaves, instead of asking "Why?" ask "What is the purpose of that behavior?" Our question aims at understanding the behavior, but we use a different framework for inquiry. When we start from the premise that all behavior has a goal (whether we like the goal or not), all behavior makes sense—children's behavior as well. As you may remember, Dreikurs saw children's misbehavior as the result of one of four goals: attention, power, revenge, or display of inadequacy. These goals are more easily recognized if the teacher first identifies the feelings the misbehavior provokes in her (as discussed in greater detail in Chapter 15).

All behavior has social meaning

All individuals, adults and children alike, seek to become part of the group. It is therefore especially important that the teacher understand the social environment and the interpersonal relationships a child chooses. When children don't succeed in their quest for belonging, they often resort to antisocial behavior if that behavior gives them the uniqueness they have been unable to achieve otherwise. The class clown, for example, feels that to be noticed by others is so important that he will risk being punished by the teacher if that is the price he must pay to achieve his goal.

Each individual must cope with the life tasks of work, friendship, and love

How each child approaches these tasks gives us an understanding of the child's life style and willingness to cooperate with others. In school, success at these tasks is revealed by the ability to function in schoolwork, by the capacity to get along with others, and by playing a sex role appropriate to the culture.

Each person operates on the basis of private logic

The overwhelming majority of students (and teachers) agree as to the logic of appropriate classroom behavior. Yet the private logic plays an important role in classroom behavior as in all behavior. Until we understand the child's private logic, we are unable to effectively change the child's undesirable behavior. The fact is that all behavior has a goal, whether we like the goal or not, and all behavior makes sense in light of its goal. Thus the class clown feels that it is logical to disrupt the class, no matter what the teacher's logic may be.

The bias of our private logic colors our interpretation of the world and results in the tremendous variety of our behaviors. These behaviors, whether political or religious preferences, styles of dress, or choices of words, are all "logical."

Behavior is always consistent with the individual's self-concept and life style

This principle enables us to distinguish one's patterns and themes—for example, "I count only when I'm being noticed; therefore, I must attract attention at all costs," "I must be in control; therefore, I won't hesitate to hurt or embarrass others," "I am incapable; therefore, I will not try." When we don't understand a certain behavior, we cannot invalidate it. Instead, we must seek to understand the private logic and self-concept that make the behavior meaningful and reasonable from the person's point of view.

All behavior reflects one's degree of encouragement or discouragement

When children tackle a new task, they have certain expectations about their probability of success. Encouraged or courageous children feel adequate and capable of coping with the task.

Discouraged children feel they cannot succeed; therefore, they will not try. Overambition, inadequacy, and high standards are all affected by the level of encouragement or discouragement the child experiences.

Adlerian psychology states that we choose our life style and determine our own behavior. We are both the products and the determinants of our behavior; each of us is at the same time the artist and the painting. The teacher and the counselor who share this view and wish to change a child's behavior have the advantage of knowing that an undesirable behavior can be changed because it is chosen. By offering the child the encouragement he needs, the counselor or teacher will have a profound influence on the child's behavior.

SOME COMMON ELEMENTS OF LEARNING THEORIES

Dinkmeyer and Carlson (1973, pp. 69–83) examined the learning theories of Piaget, Skinner, Gagné, and Montessori, as well as the phenomenological theory, the field theory (Bruner and Lewin), and the social-learning theory. They found common elements in these diverse learning theories that echo some of the Adlerian concepts we have discussed throughout this book:

Each individual has a uniqueness that is basic to the structure of one's personality

Consequences are part of learning, and reinforcement is one such consequence

Motivation results from a state of disequilibrium, which may be internally perceived, imposed by external elements, or a combination of these two conditions

It is important to understand the total situation, not just some components of it

One must try to identify with others, demonstrate empathy, and understand others' points of view

When dealing with children, one must take into account individual differences and begin where the child is ready to begin, which requires consciousness of the child's degree of readiness and willingness to cooperate with the child

When examining heredity and environment as components of behavior, environment should be given more weight than heredity

Learning occurs when behavior changes

Implications

Numerous implications can be drawn from these common elements of learning theories, but four points are especially relevant if one wants to challenge misconceptions about teachers. These four implications represent essential elements of the successful teacher/counselor relationship.

1. Teachers cannot be responsible for their students' behaviors. It is often assumed that the teacher must change the child; in fact, teachers must first change themselves. If the counselor allows teachers to realize this point themselves rather than offer it as a fact, the concept will meet with less resistance in the teacher's process of self-discovery.

2. Teachers must be more involved with encouraging the discouraged child than with praising the good or accomplished student. Because of this, we need to reexamine the use of grades in the classroom. As a form of external evaluation, grades often become an unnecessary reinforcer for the A student and a potent discourager for the D student. The counselor can facilitate teacher growth in this area by explaining the differences between praise and encouragement and by discussing with teachers some ways they can implement encouragement more frequently with their discouraged students.

3. Teachers cannot always protect their students from failure, whether in the classroom or on the playground. This point may seem to contradict our first point, but the underlying concept does not. Teachers are not responsible for their students' behaviors; therefore, they should not feel compelled to shield children from unpleasant experiences.

4. Teachers should attempt to provide greater balance between students' cognitive and affective needs. Our education system concentrates on the cognitive "three R's" and ignores another important set of R's; responsibility, resourcefulness, and respect. The counselor can concretely aid the teacher in this area by sharing value exercises, teaching reflective listen-

ing and other communication skills, and providing effective resources for the teacher to use in the classroom and share with the children.

There are two basic formats for implementing a successful teacher/counselor relationship: a one-to-one basis and small groups.

CONSULTING WITH THE INDIVIDUAL TEACHER

The counseling relationship with a teacher can take many different forms, depending on the teacher's expectations. Some teachers expect "expert" advice from the counselor, an attitude that reflects unhealthy dependence on the counselor.

> Mrs. Smith teaches a third-grade class. One of her students, Wanda, doesn't like to do arithmetic. Wanda spends most of math time daydreaming, doodling on the margins, and talking with other children. It is the talking with the others that really upsets Mrs. Smith. On one particularly talkative day, Wanda simply ignores the teacher's pleas for cooperation as well as her threats. Mrs. Smith, "at the end of her rope," decides to see the counselor.
>
> As Mrs. Smith approaches the counselor's office, she entertains several thoughts about the problem and its possible solutions. These thoughts, which are sure to get in the way of a successful resolution of the situation, are likely to be "I can't do anything anymore about this," "The problem is with Wanda," or "Our counselor will give me some good ideas on how to get Wanda to be quiet."

But the counselor must share more than ideas with the teacher; the counselor/teacher relationship is collaborative. If the counselor deals only with the crisis between Wanda and Mrs. Smith, she can give advice only on how to improve this specific situation. Predictably, this will ensure one of two things: if the crisis is solved, the counselor gets the reputation of being a "crisis fixer" and can count on a mounting number of crises that need fixing; if the counselor's advice fails, Mrs. Smith will be firmly convinced that the counselor has nothing useful to share.

The collaborative nature of the counselor/teacher relationship calls for the counselor to "give away her skills" so the teacher will be able to solve this crisis and the next crisis to come along, which will surely be different. This expertise is represented by the understanding of behavior (especially group behavior), by communication skills, and by problem-solving skills. Counselors must avoid becoming "answer men." They must examine their personal values and life style, to avoid falling into a trap; for example, a counselor who seeks excitement will not want to give up many crises. A counselor who needs to be in charge will not readily give up the opportunity to be an expert and perhaps try to place teachers in a dependent and inferior position.

The teacher seeking help is a critical resource in the consultation procedure. Does the teacher have certain beliefs or a life style that will impede collaboration? Just as the counselor as expert may cause problems, the teacher as advice seeker may interfere with the effort. This situation often occurs with teachers who don't see themselves as part of the problem they take to the counselor. The teacher is the client with whom the counselor must work; thus, the relationship between counselor and teacher is similar to the counseling relationship. There must be mutual trust and respect as well as mutual goal alignment.

But there are, of course, counselors who structure their job so that teachers will see them as experts who have all the answers. When counselors offer quick solutions off the top of their heads in the hall, teachers' lounge, or office, they create the image of the "medicine man." The result is that teachers, instead of focusing on their own behavior as contributing to the problem, go to the counselor to obtain a "prescription."

Teachers may tend to see counselors as special individuals who hold a privileged position in the school system; and often this perception is not entirely imagined. Counselors tend to have more freedom and unstructured time than teachers, and they frequently see students on an individual basis—a luxury that classroom teachers rarely have. Counselors must offset this view, which may well be true of traditional (and ineffective) counselor job descriptions.

Counselors must avoid crisis intervention, and must understand when a crisis is being used to manipulate their time. Crisis intervention is frequently unproductive; by making themselves available to teachers in noncrisis situations, counselors can transmit totally different ideas about their skills and avoid appearing as "medicine men." It is imperative that the counselor spend the first month of the school year getting to know the teachers on a friendly and unthreatening basis. The counselor must not come across as the "big person who stands up for the little people." Simply by spending time with the teachers in their own environment, whether the teachers' lounge or their classrooms after school, the counselor has immediate access to the teachers' points of view.

To increase the chances of teachers' self-referral, counselors must seek to achieve three conditions:

1. Through presentations at faculty meetings, newsletters, and personal contact, the school staff needs to be made aware of the full services the

counselor offers. The counselor creates the impression that he is available and valuable.

2. The counselor cannot hide in his office, seeing people only by appointment or being inflexible about requests for consultations.

3. The school administration must support consultation with teachers as a valid counselor activity and actively direct teachers to the counselor for this purpose. Many administrators, unfortunately, consider the counselor a crisis resolver, a bookkeeper, or an affective-education specialist.

The importance of goal alignment with the administration is often overlooked. The principal assumes the counselor will handle many details and paperwork that others don't have time for, and the counselor assumes others will handle these tasks. We recommend at least one meeting each year between counselor and principal to create mutual goals and understanding of expectations and expertise.

A counselor's concern with the school environment, with the image she projects, and with the services she provides is best summed up in a single question: "If the counselor is missing from the the building for one day, who notices and why?"

Systematic Procedure for Collecting Data

A systematic procedure for collecting information from a self-referred teacher helps to structure the initial meeting between counselor and teacher and provides an opportunity to listen to the teacher's problem (Dinkmeyer & Carlson, 1973, p. 179). Figure 14–1 shows one consultant referral form used to collect the necessary data.

Anecdotes

A vital technique in data collection is the anecdote. The anecdote is the recollection of an interaction between child and teacher that demonstrates the specific dynamics of the relationship. Returning to Mrs. Smith and Wanda, if Mrs. Smith were to respond to the counselor's request for an anecdote with "Today Wanda just didn't listen to me; she was so stubborn," her answer would be insufficient. The counselor helps the teacher reconstruct a situation to make specific behavioral evidence available; for example:

> For the past two weeks, I haven't been getting any cooperation from Wanda at math time. She doodles and daydreams, but what really bothers the class is that she talks with others all the time. I tell her to be quiet, and she will just for a while. But then she starts up again.

Exploring Beliefs

At this point, the counselor should ask Mrs. Smith for a tentative hypothesis as to the purpose of Wanda's psychological movement and ensuing behavior. This allows the teacher to share some of her beliefs about child behavior—her frame of reference. (From our example, we already have a clue that Mrs. Smith feels she must act "for the best interests of the class" rather than in response to her own needs.) Whether agreeing or disagreeing with the teacher's ideas (hypothesis), the counselor must at this point accept the teacher's knowledge and beliefs. Now counselor and teacher can begin to list the child's assets and strengths.

This tactic may seem strange to the teacher, who probably feels that it is irrelevant or useless to dwell on the good, when it is the bad that is the problem. But by becoming aware of how Mrs. Smith perceives Wanda as adequate, the counselor can help the teacher pursue an avenue that may lead to successful interaction with Wanda. What has worked in the past? What has been tried and hasn't worked? This procedure, included in the referral form in Figure 14-1 allows Mrs. Smith to become aware of her own effectiveness and permits teacher and counselor to move immediately from the specific problem into possible resources for solving the problem.

Tuning in to Feelings

After the counselor has established a cooperative relationship with the teacher and obtained specific behavioral incidents, the next step is to help the teacher ascertain her feelings about and reactions to the problem situation, so corrective actions can be formulated. The process must move into the teacher's affective domain, so that the goal of the child's misbehavior can be correctly identified. The consultation process lacks an invaluable asset if the counselor omits this step or allows the teacher to deny negative emotions.

Recognizing and identifying negative feelings may present the first major roadblock. A "good" teacher may feel it is important not to admit that a student can "get to me." Allowing the teacher to ventilate feelings that may becloud his point of view, especially in the crisis situation, is tremendously helpful. (It is assumed that the consultation meeting is conducted in a private environment.)

By indicating to the teacher that behavior is best understood in an *ABC* format (similar to that of Ellis's Rational Emotive Therapy), the counselor deals with the specific problem and shares skills the teacher can use in future problem situations.

This is how the *ABC* format works. *A* is the antecedent behavior that starts the problem. It may be a behavior of either the teacher or the child,

Child's name _____ Grade _____ Age _____
Teacher _____ Time available for consultation _____
Family constellation (by age) _____
Family atmosphere _____
Specific description of learning difficulty or behavioral difficulty:
Is the problem you are concerned with focused primarily on one of the following 5 areas? Please circle. These areas are listed only to suggest classifications at the moment. Obviously many problems will overlap.
1. Intellectual deficiency
2. Learning problems, educational adjustment, questions regarding placement
3. Emotional problem, personality maladjustment, social adjustment
4. Discipline
5. Delinquent tendencies
Please describe the problem briefly. Anecdotal observations would be particularly appropriate. The anecdotes should include the child's behavior, your response or reaction, and his response to corrective efforts (antecedent event, behavior, consequence).
Tentative ideas regarding reasons for the behavior: _____
Child's assets, strengths: _____
Corrective actions utilized to this point: _____
Procedures which work with this child: _____
Mutually acceptable recommendations: _____

FIGURE 14–1
Consultant Referral Form. (From *Counseling: Facilitating Human Potential and Change Processes*, by D. Dinkmeyer and J. Carlson. Copyright 1973 by Charles E. Merrill Publishing Company. Reprinted by permission.)

but, in either case, it produces a response from the other, *B. C* is the action the person who emitted behavior *A* takes in response to *B*.

The feelings that accompany each of these steps must be identified. The *ABC* method makes use of anecdotes, which are recorded economically. This is an example of the *ABC* method as Mrs. Smith used it:

A: Wanda was not doing her math.

B: I went over to her desk and said "Please stop talking. You haven't even finished the first page!"

C: Wanda stopped talking for a while, but I had to come over to her again. It seems that she will work only when I stand over her.
The feelings I had during all of this were, first, annoyance—"Nothing works short of personal attention"—and, later, frustration, even anger—"I have better things to do."

Finding Alternatives

Counselor and teacher may now make a tentative hypothesis about Wanda's misbehavior. The child may be seeking attention, since she stops misbehaving as soon as the teacher pays special attention to her. Another possibility is power, since Mrs. Smith expresses anger at her failure with Wanda.

The teacher must then examine the alternatives to her own behavior. She may, for example, decide to ignore Wanda and let her bear the consequences of her choice of behavior. Those consequences may entail having to do at home the work she didn't do in class, or being pressured by her schoolmates, who also object to her talking, but have so far not had an opportunity to express their annoyance, since Mrs. Smith was sure to step in. By seeking alternatives and recognizing their consequences, the teacher will find her own behavior becoming more functional and less conflictual. All the alternatives demand that the teacher change first.

RECOMMENDATIONS FOR CHANGES IN THE CLASSROOM

We cannot suggest specific changes for any particular setting. To do so would run counter to the Adlerian view that specific solutions come only from applying principles based on a solid theoretical framework, lest one slide into the expert/problem-solver role. These general recommendations suggest how to tailor-fit solutions to specific situations.

Encouragement is the significant element in the change process. When teachers want children to stop certain behaviors, they should ignore those behaviors and fill the void by encouraging and reinforcing other more acceptable behaviors. The relationship between child and teacher is a result of how the teacher chooses to influence the child, whether it is nagging, demanding, praising, encouraging, ignoring, or any one of the other alternatives open to teachers (Dinkmeyer & Dreikurs, 1963).

The logical consequences of the misbehavior are more effective than punishment. Consequences are a natural outcome of the misdeed, while punishment is often arbitrary and unrelated to the change the teacher hopes to induce. The child who chooses to come to class late will have to take on the responsibility of finding out what happened while he was not there, instead of being scolded or punished by the teacher. Punishment tends to obscure the punisher's intended message, whereas consequences allow the child to experience the results of his choice of behavior. It removes the teacher as a potential butt of anger and resentment and allows the child to learn from his own actions (Dreikurs & Grey, 1968).

The teacher should learn what behaviors will unintentionally reinforce, rather than diminish, misbehavior. A child who seeks attention and stops misbehaving when the teacher asks has in fact heard "I am paying attention to you" rather than "Please stop that." Also, power struggles occur when the teacher is determined to prove to the child that certain misbehaviors will not take place; often the teacher's feeling in this situation is "Who is in charge here, you or me?" (Dreikurs, 1957).

Counselors can provide teachers with an objective viewpoint of the teachers' relationship with their students. Effective teachers are both kind and firm; but many teachers are one or the other, and conflict results. "Toughness" promotes rebellion, resentment, and noncooperation; "softness" induces the children to run all over their teachers. Kindness conveys the teachers' respect for the children, while firmness conveys the teachers' respect for themselves, in turn encouraging the children's respect. This task is perhaps more easily accomplished in C-groups (discussed later in the chapter and in Chapter 15), where the teachers themselves can tell one another how they come across in the C-group or in the classroom. This averts the problem, common among teachers, of responding to counselors' suggestions with the attitude of "What do they know? They don't spend any time in a classroom."

Teachers need to learn to use the powerful forces of the group atmosphere already present in the classroom. One way to use these forces is to ask the class to make a tentative hypothesis about a certain misbehavior. When the teacher asks "Why do you think Bill is acting that way?" he may be surprised to discover that the students know the purpose of the misbehavior as well as the teacher.

Teachers can facilitate behavior change by approaching children from a holistic perspective rather than concentrating on the specific irritating behaviors. By understanding both the positive and the negative ways children seek significance in the group, teachers gain access to new strategies they can employ.

Responsibility can be a powerful tool for promoting change in the misbehaving child. Teachers often assign classroom chores or other responsibilities to children who have already proven themselves responsible. By not allowing the discouraged child to progressively accept new responsibilities, the teacher transmits the expectation "You can't do it anyway." The power of expectations cannot be ignored, since expectations enhance or discourage the child's self-image and development.

Teachers should be aware of the basic principles of human motivation—why a child will perform a certain task, for example. The American education system has twisted motivation from the need to belong to the need to please. This is why bad grades do not impress the child who is not concerned with pleasing or who has given up on belonging. Homework, too, is useless as punishment, because the child can interpret it not as punishment but as a logical extension of school.

Teachers should learn to anticipate children's actions and reactions. Strange as it seems, a good rule of thumb is for teachers to react exactly the opposite of their first impulse, for example, by ignoring the attention seekers instead of nagging them.

Teachers often talk more than necessary, perhaps on the assumption that talking will change the child. The counselor can help the teacher see that letting children bear the consequences of their actions is more effective than giving them lengthy admonitions. Act more and talk less!

A classroom council promotes cooperation among the children by making the entire class responsible for the atmosphere and tone of the classroom instead of the teacher. Dreikurs (1957) and Glasser (1969) made similar suggestions to increase the mutual responsibilities of teacher and child.

Often, the major contribution counselors can make to teachers and students has little to do with imparting specific knowledge. Stimulating professional growth in the willing teacher is the highest goal the counselor can seek. Teacher education often does not train teachers to deal effectively with behavior and motivation, even though these form the cornerstone of a child's growth and success. Encouragement and emotional support, as well as positive expectations, are preferable to a counselor's diagnoses, solutions, and evaluation.

WORKING WITH TEACHERS IN GROUPS

Rationale

The Adlerian holistic approach stresses the social significance and consequences of behavior. If the counselor does not provide an opportunity for teachers to interact in a socially significant climate—in groups, rather than in the limited one-to-one consultation—a potent, positive, problem-solving, and educational opportunity is lost. It is a unique inservice training opportunity.

Traditional inservice experiences neglect the therapeutic forces a group can provide. Working with teachers in groups can be the counselor's most important contribution to the school staff. Group work makes efficient use of time, allows education as well as problem solving to occur, and removes one of the biggest barriers to an effective teacher/counselor relationship. Counselors are no longer the experts who "don't know what the classroom is really like," but become members of a group of peers with whom they can share their feelings as well as their skills.*

The rationale for the group setting is that most problems for teachers originate in the group setting of the classroom. By working with teachers in a group, the counselor can see exactly how the teacher's life style functions in the group setting, whether dominating, accepting, passive, demanding, and so on. The group allows each teacher to function as an integral part of a group. This process gives participants insight into the group dynamics that operate in their classroom every day. The counselor's leadership skills shape the group experience so that each member benefits.

Teacher educational opportunities are seldom as valuable as this type of experience. The school schedule is not conducive to teacher group interactions. Indeed, by design, the teacher is a lone adult throughout the school day, except for faculty meetings and the respite of the teachers' lounge.

A number of unique therapeutic forces occur only in the group setting. The group can provide an unusual atmosphere of acceptance, so that each teacher receives constructive empathy from his peers. In sharing their experiences, teachers learn that their problems are not unique and that there is a universal quality to classroom situations. The group is a place where teachers can vent frustrations and express concerns and ideas. The group also provides the counselor and the individual teacher with a wealth of resources: the other teachers in the group. Each member of the group can become a supportive and therapeutic agent for the other members of the group.

Organization

The staff must be educated to the goals, purposes, and potential benefits of the teacher group, so the counselor's first contact should be with the administration. If the administration perceives the teacher group as limited and self-serving, the counselor must point out the benefits that will accrue for the students as well as for the teachers. Teacher groups also effectively provide inservice training. Compared to the results of a one-day, one-shot teacher workshop, the cumulative effects of the ongoing group can be far greater. The counselor must also explain the holistic basis on which the teacher group will function.

---

*The group setting described in this section is a C-group, so-called because, as discussed in Chapter 15, its main functions begin with the letter C.

Counselors must pay careful attention to the process and procedures they use to introduce the concept of group to the staff. Their goal should be to make the staff aware of the purpose and function of the group and they should be prepared to dispel some of the faulty beliefs teachers may have about groups. The group process is not psychotherapy; it is not intended as a remedial group for teachers who feel they have been designated as "inadequate" by the counselor or in some administrative evaluation.

It may be useful for the counselor to demonstrate during a faculty meeting what a teacher group will be like. This gives the staff an opportunity to vicariously experience a group and become aware of the value of the process. Counselors should make clear that the teacher group is not a sensitivity-training group, an encounter group, or any other group with which the teachers may associate it.

The group should meet once a week for at least an hour. Teachers make a commitment to stay with the group for at least six to eight sessions, at which time the group as a whole can evaluate the group's needs and possible reorganization. The group might meet during the lunch hour or immediately before or after school. Once the administration and staff see the effectiveness of the group, changes in scheduling, covering for classes, and other arrangements will take place. Counselors should not let imaginary barriers of time and space discourage their efforts to start a group.

The group should begin by establishing a few general rules about membership. No one should be allowed to join the group after it has started. New groups can be formed when interest arises. This allows the ongoing group to remain exactly that and avoid repeating groundwork and history. A physically comfortable and private area should be provided for the group, often the counselor's office. The group should sit in a circle so that each member can see all of the others and no member is "at the head of the table," especially the leader.

It is important that the group be heterogeneous. It should be composed of experienced as well as inexperienced teachers, so that teachers can share a diversity of classroom experiences and training. On the other hand, the group should be composed of teachers from approximately the same grade level. Great discrepancy in the age level of the students the group discusses can become a major handicap.

Group size must be limited so that each member has an opportunity to share in each session; about five teachers plus the counselor (leader) is ideal. Membership in a group is always voluntary and not by recommendation of other teachers or administrators. The counselor should have a brief interview with each volunteer before the first meeting. Teachers qualify for participation by two criteria: (1) having a concern they wish to share with the group and (2) wanting to help others with their concerns. The commitment to these two types of sharing qualifies the potential member.

Content

The first meeting of the group can be structured to allow all members to share something about themselves and listen to the others. The leader might take this opportunity to point out similarities in the concerns or ideas among the members. Therapeutic forces can be utilized immediately to generate cohesion and commitment. The leader must exercise control of the group and offer direction by providing the necessary psychological foundations as well as therapeutic forces. Introducing the Adlerian socio-teleological concepts of behavior promotes the group's problem-solving skills by providing a common basis for approach to problems.

Anecdote sharing is a technique for presenting situations to the group systematically. The format is the same as that in individual consultation. After teachers identify their feelings during the incident, tentative hypotheses can be formulated. While it is important for teachers to recognize the individual differences in their approaches to classroom management and communication, each group member must accept the common elements in their classrooms—purposive misbehavior, discouragement, and practical alternatives to ineffective methods.

Focus

Even though the leader will have clarified the purposes of the group and role expectations for members, the first few sessions are likely to produce a certain degree of confusion and anxiety. This is a new experience for most of the teachers, and there will be many attempts to clarify roles and test new behaviors.

The leader should be aware of several procedures that can make the group experience more effective. A primary challenge for the leader is to see that each member of the group has an opportunity to describe his unique situation so the others can offer feedback. For the typical C-group, this means that one teacher will hold center stage for no more than 15 minutes each session and that no fewer than three teachers will actively present their challenges or problems.

The counselor must use techniques that will both set the stage for and conclude a teacher's statements. When a particular problem appears especially complex, the leader might seek clarification of a specific aspect of the situation. For example,

> Leader: It seems that a lot of the kids are giving you different challenges. Is there any particular kid we could concentrate on, so that everyone here can respond to your situation?

The leader must not feel that she is the only one responsible for reacting to each teacher's contribution. For example, if a teacher shares a concern that is not relevant to the group, the leader can verbally or nonverbally solicit the attention and input of another teacher in the group. If participants feel a topic is relevant and the counselor does not, the counselor must then clarify the purpose and content of the group before continuing, lest the time be spent purposelessly.

The C-Group in Action

The following excerpt from the third session of a typical C-group composed of second- and third-grade teachers and the school counselor shows how the teacher group is structured.

> Leader: Okay, who'd like to begin this week? Do we have any feedback on how things went the past week and on some of the strategies we developed?
>
> Carla: That idea of ignoring Lisa's crazy behavior and trying instead to encourage some specific, good behaviors seems to be working! She doesn't make a big deal of going to the pencil sharpener anymore. However, she isn't too interested in doing "good" stuff.
>
> Craig: Was this the girl who didn't do anything unless she got some attention?
>
> Carla: Yes, we said it was attention-getting misbehavior and that I should ignore the problem behaviors and pay attention to good things she was doing. It's not easy to find some, though!
>
> Betty: Maybe you'll have to encourage some of the positive things Lisa does. I had an attention getter like this, and he wasn't too interested in cooperating until I came up with some ideas he liked.
>
> Leader: So, there were things he did over which you really had no control—in which he had all the power?
>
> Betty: Yeah, I got really angry about it one day.
>
> Michael: Then it seems that it was a power struggle rather than just attention-getting behavior.
>
> Betty: Ricky still likes to do certain things, as a matter of fact. Today we had a hard time figuring out where his lunch pail was.

Leader: It seems that Betty has something going on now, and your situation has improved, Carla. Can we move over to Betty for a few minutes?

Betty: I'm sure interested to see whether Ricky's goal is power or attention; I'm not too sure I see all the differences between the two.

Leader: Well, could you tell us about the lunch-pail incident?

Betty: As we were going to lunch today, Ricky complained loudly that he couldn't find his lunch pail. I had to hold up the entire class—I can't leave them by themselves—and look for Ricky's lunch pail.

Michael: It sounds like you were pretty annoyed by this.

Betty: Yes, he knew we had to wait for him. And then he remembered that he didn't bring his lunch, after all, and he didn't have the money to buy one. (Laughter)

Craig: He really had you cornered!

Betty: Yes, I was pretty angry, because I felt like it was a game, and I lost—not my temper, but the power struggle.

Leader: What would be the alternative to Betty's dealings with Ricky?

Carla: It would be to withdraw from the power struggle. But how do you avoid dealing with him and his lunch?

Betty: And this isn't the only time I get challenged by Ricky to see who's in control.

Leader: Okay, but let's return to the lunch situation. How would you withdraw from the situation?

Betty: Leave the classroom and let him deal with his problem?

Craig: Can you leave a kid alone? And what if he really didn't have money?

Michael: It's still his problem, and I think that probably he won't keep it up if there isn't any attention or prestige in holding up the class.

Betty: I can see the need to withdraw, but I'm not sure I can leave him alone. What would he do? (Pause)

Craig: I think it would be worth trying just to find out!

Betty: If this situation does come up again, I'll do exactly that and see what happens. I have a feeling that it will come up again, because Ricky was quite pleased with the results today.

Leader: He really got to you, didn't he?

Betty: Yes. Sometimes I do get into power struggles with the kids, but I feel pretty responsible about the classroom atmosphere, and disruptions really get to me.

Craig: The kids probably know it. They can tell if there are ways to control you.

This C-group has begun to understand the purposive nature of behavior and has presented a formula for identifying emotions that correspond to certain goals of misbehavior. Betty felt annoyed, even angry, at Ricky's disrupting the lunch line. By sharing the anecdote with the group, Betty has made it possible for the others to help her identify Ricky's probable goal, power. The alternative is to withdraw from any "power contest," and Betty has made a commitment to use an alternative response—to let Ricky be the owner of his own lunch problem. The final exchange between Craig and Betty demonstrates and acknowledges the purposiveness of behavior and the life styles that promote certain behaviors.

The counselor must monitor the group's progress during and after each session. As a session progresses, the leader must make certain that each member of the group becomes a "sharer" as well as a spectator. The leader must recognize and counteract inherent tendencies to be withdrawn and shy or verbal and dominating. Encouragement must be used to allow members to contribute and to recognize the value of their contributions. When a problem is presented, or an opinion or idea is needed, counselors can turn to a member, instead of responding themselves.

The leader must also terminate discussions that wander from the purpose of the group. The C-group is highly specific and focused. To change the focus of the group, the counselor must be willing to confront and redirect a topic. This often entails picking up a feeling of discomfort with the topic and finding the reasons behind the feeling. The leader often has to make the first few interventions, but can also encourage members, nonverbally and verbally, to contribute their feeling and ideas and express their concerns. The leader must exercise control of the group without becoming involved in a power struggle with members.

Evaluation

The leader may wish to refer to a list to identify, review, and evaluate the leadership skills employed during C-group sessions:

Structuring

Using introductory exercises as needed

Universalizing

Linking

Confronting

Blocking

Encouraging (recognizing assets and giving positive feedback)

Facilitating nonverbal clues

Facilitating I-messages

Paraphrasing

Providing feedback

Offering tentative hypotheses

Setting tasks and obtaining commitment from members

Capping and summarizing

Group leaders should be aware of how frequently they use each skill in the group and have specific examples of each skill. Leaders will also find that some of their interventions and activities in the group lie outside these skills. In those cases, the leader should identify the purpose of the interventions and activities.

Systematic Training for Effective Teaching

If counselors wish to expand the principles of Adlerian psychology into classroom settings, they must educate teachers. *Systematic Training for Effective Teaching* (STET) (Dinkmeyer, McKay, & Dinkmeyer, 1980) is a 14-session educational program for teachers that addresses this goal. It employs a three-step approach in each session:

1. New ideas (often alternatives to more common classroom practices, such as motivation techniques that use encouragement instead of praise) are presented.
2. The new idea is practiced in the STET group with audiocassette classroom-simulated incidents.
3. Each teacher applies the new skill in the classroom and reports the results at the following session.

The typical STET group is made up of 12 teachers who meet once a week for one or two hours. The program can be modified to reduce the number of sessions or number of hours in each session. We find that teachers often need additional skills as well as the remedial techniques outlined in this chapter.

REFERENCES

Dinkmeyer, D., & Carlson, J. (1973). *Counseling: Facilitating human potential and change processes.* Columbus, OH: Merrill.

Dinkmeyer, D., & Dreikurs, R. (1963). *Encouraging children to learn: The encouragement process.* Englewood Cliffs, NJ: Prentice-Hall.

Dinkmeyer, D., McKay, G. D., & Dinkmeyer, D., Jr. (1980). *Systematic training for effective teaching.* Circle Pines, MN: American Guidance Service.

Dreikurs, R. (1957). *Psychology in the classroom.* New York: Harper & Row.

Dreikurs, R., & Grey, L. (1968). *Logical consequences.* New York: Meredith.

Glasser, W. (1969). *Schools without failure.* New York: Harper & Row.

15 Parent Education

T he family exerts the most significant influence on the individual's development. Parents in particular are responsible for the atmosphere in which a child is raised. As pointed out earlier, the child's position in the family constellation also influences growth, and interaction with siblings develops certain beliefs about peers and others. When the family structure and atmosphere are troubled and unhealthy, a child's growth is necessarily affected.

> Parents exert a tremendous influence on the child. They are the earliest and often the only models a child has and it is from them that beliefs, attitudes, and techniques are chosen. It is the parents' behavior that generally establishes the atmosphere of the home, i.e., whether it is peaceful or warlike, cheerful or depressing, marked by warmth, closeness, and mutual involvement, or cold, distant, and detached. (Shulman, 1962, p. 34)

It has long been apparent to Adlerians that training is necessary if mothers, fathers, and others in child-rearing roles are to do a good job as parents. Our biological heredity does not guarantee the necessary skills. Past experiences are often the sole source of information from which we fashion our approach to rearing children. If parents and other parental figures are unsuccessful in their own experience, their children may be discouraged or, at least, without a good model for dealing with the multiple challenges of parenting.

In our society, the "average parent" and the "typical home" are becoming increasingly rare. The nuclear family has become only one of a growing number of life styles. An indication of the large number of children being raised in single-parent homes is the growth in recent years of the national organization Parents Without ·Partners. Grandparents and other relatives must often assume parenting roles for a child whose parents have jobs that allow little time at home. It is thus almost impossible to draw a meaningful picture of the "average" home and parent.

Because of the diversity, traditional parenting roles are often not successful. Many parents grew up in comparatively autocratic family situations that did not tolerate questioning parental authority. The basic shift toward equality in our society has not spared the family—on the contrary. If you have any doubts as to who is in charge today, just watch a parent try to subdue a rebellious 4-year-old who seems to have mistaken the supermarket for a racetrack.

Women and children, once submissive minorities, have achieved a status equal to that of the head of the household. The autocrat's approach of "Do as I say," which implies a superior/inferior relationship, is no longer appropriate or effective. Today's children are unwilling to be less than equal. When told to "jump," instead of asking "How high?" today's child asks "Why?" Aside from the contemporary scene, which makes the autocratic parent especially ineffective, there is an inherent flaw in the traditional autocratic methods. That flaw is the failure to produce responsible children.

Parents need to learn new techniques and approaches. They need to acquire new skills to create a more equalitarian and democratic relationship with their children. By "equalitarian" we mean a relationship based on cooperation and mutual respect. The movement toward equality can be beneficial for both parent and child only if the parent develops the necessary skills of listening, communicating, motivating, encouraging, and letting the child assume responsibility for his actions.

This shift toward a more equalitarian relationship has produced confusion and discouragement in many parents who lack real parenting skills. They have habits, catchall phrases, and often threats, but no substance or understanding that will work in the daily challenges and confrontations with their children. It is curious that we recognize and license the skills required to be a barber, a cabdriver, or any number of jobs, yet most of us would think it outrageous if we were to similarly limit parenting to those who are skilled. Not merely curious but tragic is that acquiring the essential skills of parenting is left to chance.

BRIEF HISTORY OF ADLERIAN PARENT EDUCATION

Croake (1983) summarizes the precursors to contemporary Adlerian parent education. Adler began this method in 1922 while establishing the first child guidance clinic in Vienna, Austria. Although the first public demonstrations of ongoing cases were with problem children, the public nature of this counseling allowed many "normal" parents and teachers to learn preventive methods.

By 1930, there were 32 clinics conducted by schools and parent-teacher associations. Adler's assumption, that educational approaches were the most effective treatments for emotional disturbances, spurred Rudolf Dreikurs to continue the development of educational demonstrations and written materials. As Croake (1983) states, "All of the current Adlerian parent education programs are based upon the teachings of Alfred Adler as interpreted by Rudolf Dreikurs."

RATIONALE

Parent education is badly needed. Its essential goal is to improve the relationship between parent and child by making more alternatives available and by promoting greater understanding and acceptance. Parent education brings an openness to new ideas and techniques that can be crucially important in resolving present problems and avoiding future ones.

The parent-education group represents not only a unique experience but also a unique approach that does not prescribe "cures" or therapy. Instead, it allows parents to utilize powerful and often ignored forces in traditional learning settings. It does not consist of lectures, programmed learning, or other individual forms of learning. Parent education is essentially interaction among group members, because its goal is to improve interaction between parent and child.

With such a pervasive need for parent education, the question is not whether parent education should be available but where and when it should be provided. It is often the counselor's responsibility, regardless of the setting. Traditional counselors may not be aware of the need until they recognize the conditions in a certain milieu or system that can be improved by parent education.

School counselors who deal with the child only in the school setting or on an individual basis neglect to consider the influence parents share with educators. Marriage counseling often centers on disagreements about child-rearing techniques. The very differences in the spouses' childhood experiences may ensure a divergence of opinions if parent education is not available to bridge the gap. The increasing number of single parents is symbolic of the different circumstances in which children are raised today. Parents cannot *directly* influence the quality of their child's school day or television viewing. As a matter of fact, they may run a poor third to these powerful elements in their children's lives (by age 17, the average child has had three hours of television for every two hours of school). Nonetheless, parents not only can influence but effectively determine the quality of their own relationship with their children.

Public and private agencies provide parent education for target groups or as an additional service for their clients. Community colleges allow parents to schedule their group sessions in the evening or at other convenient times. Adlerian family-education centers also offer parent education.

In parent education, the counselor's sphere of influence extends beyond the group, because the sessions also have an influence on the participants' spouses, children, and children's teachers. The number of people who are directly or indirectly influenced by a parent study group that meets for an hour or two each week can easily reach 50 or more.

BASIC ADLERIAN THEORY FOR PARENT EDUCATION

One of the goals of parent education is to teach, in simple and understandable terms, a theory of human behavior that can be practically applied in the home. In Adlerian parent education, this theory is in all respects similar to that used in consultation with teachers (see Chapter 14). A child's misbehavior is best understood by identifying its goal and the emotions behind it. Once they identify the purpose of the behavior, parents can develop alternative courses of action, which, in turn, will encourage alternative behaviors in the child.

It is important to discuss and understand this basic theory as soon as possible in the parent-education group. Often the first several sessions focus on the purpose of misbehavior. Topics in the next sessions include: emotions as a purposeful tool, I-messages, alternatives to punishment, and encouragement. The objective of ensuing meetings is to focus on specific techniques and skills.

Adlerians are not the only ones concerned with parent education. Behavior modification and transactional analysis, for example, have originated several books and study methods in this area. A casual review of talk shows, bookstores, and newspaper columns gives ample evidence of the wide variety of approaches and high levels of interest in parent education. Adlerians, however, have a special commitment to meet the need for parent education.

Most Adlerian parent-education groups use either a book or an educational program. Adlerian books that are especially helpful to parents include *Children: The Challenge* (Dreikurs & Soltz, 1964), *Raising a Responsible Child* (Dinkmeyer & McKay, 1973), and *The Practical Parent* (Corsini & Painter, 1975). The most widely used educational programs are *Systematic Training for Effective Parenting* (STEP) and *Systematic Training for Effective Parenting of Teens* (STEP/Teen), both by Dinkmeyer and McKay (1976, 1983).

THE FOUR GOALS OF MISBEHAVIOR

Adlerian parent education—an extension of the Adlerian theory of human development—teaches a pragmatic, systematic theory of child behavior.

The first step in parent education is to understand the four goals of children's misbehavior. Dreikurs (1957) classified all child misbehavior into four categories, each corresponding to the goal of the misbehavior: attention, power, revenge, and display of inadequacy.

The goal of the child's misbehavior is not apparent to most uneducated parents. They find their children's actions confusing and annoying and, in extreme cases, a cause of much frustration and bewilderment. When parents don't understand the purposive nature of behavior in general and of misbehavior in particular, they may resort to extremely damaging measures, such as physical or psychological abuse.

Although parents may at first react to the concept of the four goals with a certain degree of confusion or even skepticism, they eventually learn to identify the goals by using two techniques: their own response to the misbehavior and the child's response to the parent's chosen behavior. This approach allows parents to use themselves as accurate indicators of the child's behavior rather than to rely solely on the child. (See Table 15–1.)

Attention

Each of the four goals of misbehavior reflects a degree of discouragement in the child. The first goal, attention, has many positive aspects and is particularly appealing to children as they explore and discover the world around them. "Are you noticing me? Am I still here?" express the purpose of the child's attention-seeking behavior.

> Monica, a 3-year-old, adores her mother and follows her around the house whenever possible. At times she comes up to her mother and unties one of her shoelaces or tugs at her slacks. Although annoyed, the mother generally acknowledges Monica's behavior with a friendly "Hey!" or with a slightly less friendly "Stop it!" depending on how annoying the attention-getting behavior is. Monica is pleased that her mother recognizes her efforts to attract her attention, and she stops her efforts whenever she realizes that her mother doesn't enjoy what she is doing.

In this example, the mother is *annoyed* by the child's behavior and probably confused by her daughter's seemingly pointless efforts to annoy her. Monica's response to her mother's annoyance is to temporarily stop the behavior for the simple reason that she has achieved her goal—attention.

Once parents recognize their children's ability to make their own decisions based on their own subjective needs, misbehavior makes as

TABLE 15-1.

Identifying the goals of children's misbehavior.

Increased social interest ◄─────────────────► Diminished social interest

		USEFUL		USELESS			Child's Action and Attitude
		Active Constructive	*Passive Constructive*	*Active Destructive*	*Passive Destructive*		*The Message*

Minor discouragement ▲ | Deep discouragement ▼

Active Constructive	Passive Constructive	Active Destructive	Passive Destructive	Child's Action and Attitude / The Message
"Success" Cute remarks Seeks praise, recognition Performs for attention Stunts Overambition Impression of excellence (may seem "ideal" student, but goal is self-elevation, not learning)	"Charm" Excess pleasantness "Model" child Bright sayings, often not original Little initiative Exaggerated conscientiousness "Southern belle," (often "teacher's pets")	"Nuisance" Show-off Clown Restless Talks out of turn "The brat" Makes minor mischief "Walking question mark" (questions not for information but notoriety) Speech impediments Self-indulgence	"Laziness" Clumsiness, ineptness Lack of ability Lack of stamina Untidiness Fearfulness Bashfulness Anxiety Frivolity Performance and reading difficulties	"Nuisance" Show-off Clown Lazy Puts others in his service, keeps teacher busy. I only count when I am being noticed or served.
A criterion of Social-Emotional Maturing is "Social Interest" Respects the rights of others Is tolerant of others Is interested in others Co-operates with others Encourages others Is courageous Has a true sense of his own worth Has a feeling of belonging Has socially acceptable goals Puts forth genuine effort Meets the needs of the situation Is willing to share rather than "How much can I get?" Thinks of "we" rather than just "I"		"Rebel" Argues and contradicts Openly disobedient Refuses to do work Defies authority Continues forbidden acts Aggressive May be truant	"Stubborn" Extreme laziness Stubbornness Disobedience (passive) Forgetting	"Stubborn" Argues Temper tantrums Tells lies Disobedient Does opposite to instructions Does little or no work Says "If you don't let me do what I want you don't love me." I only count when I am dominating.
		"Vicious" Violent Brutal Steals (Leader of juvenile delinquent gangs)	"Violent passivity" Sullen Defiant	"Vicious" Steals Sullen Defiant Hurts animals, peers, adults Kicks, bites, scratches Sore loser Potential delinquent I can't be liked and I only count if I can hurt others.
			"Hopeless" Stupidity Indolence Ineptitude (Pseudo feeble-minded) (Inferiority complex)	"Feels hopeless" Stupid actions Inferiority complex Gives up Rarely participates Says "leave me alone, you can't do anything with me." I can't do anything right so I don't try. I am no good.

322

TABLE 15–1.

Continued

Corrections of Misbehavior

Teacher's or Parent's Reaction	The Child's Probable Goal and His "Faulty Logic"	Teacher's or Parent's Corrective Procedures	Teacher's or Parent's Interpretations of Child's Goal (to child) (Ask all questions in a friendly non judgmental way; and *not* at times of conflict.)
To be kept busy by child. To help, remind, scold, coax, and give child extra service. Is delighted by constructive AGM child. Is annoyed.	GOAL I. (AGM) ATTENTION-GETTING Child seeks proof of his acceptance and approval.	Give attention when child is not making a bid for it. Ignore the misbehaving child.	"Could it be that you want me to notice you?" "Could it be that you want me to do special things for you?"
"He occupies too much of my time." "I wish he would leave me alone."	He puts others in his service, seeks help. "Only when people pay attention to me do I feel I have a place."	Be firm. Realize that punishing, rewarding, coaxing, scolding, and giving service are attention.	". . . keep me busy with you?"
Feels leadership of the class is threatened. Feels defeated.	GOAL II. POWER Wants to be the boss.	Withdraw from the conflict. "Take your sail out of his wind."	"Could it be that you want to show me that you can do what you want and no one can stop you?"
"Who is running this class? He or I?"	"I only count if you do what I want."	Recognize and admit that the child has power.	"Could it be that you want to be the boss?"
"I won't let him get away with this."	"If you don't let me do what I want you don't love me."	Appeal for child's help, enlist his cooperation, give him responsibility.	". . . get me to do what you want?"
Dislikes the child. Feels deeply hurt. Is outraged by child. Wants to get even.	GOAL III. REVENGE Tries to hurt as he feels hurt by others.	Avoid punishment. Win the child. Try to convince him that he is liked. Do not become hurt. Enlist a "buddy" for him. Use group encouragement.	"Could it be that you want to hurt me and/or the children?" "Could it be that you want to get even?"
"How can he be so mean?"	"My only hope is to get even with them."		
Feels helpless. Doesn't know what to do.	GOAL IV. DISPLAY OF INADEQUACY	Avoid discouragement yourself. Don't give up. Show faith in child. Lots of encouragement. Use constructive approach.	"Could it be that you want to be left alone?"
"I can't do anything with him!"	Tries to be left alone. Feels helpless.		". . . you feel stupid and don't want people to know?"
"I give up!"	"I don't want anyone to know how stupid I am."		

From "The 'C' Group: Integrating Knowledge and Experience to Change Behavior—An Adlerian Approach to Consultation," by D. Dinkmeyer, *The Counseling Psychologist,* 1971, *3*(1), 63–72. Reprinted by permission.

much sense to parents as it does to their children. This is true even in the more "unacceptable" behaviors of power and revenge.

Power

The second goal, power, is sought by children who exaggerate their need to be in control. The power-seeking child is guided by the faulty belief "I can count in this world only if I am in control of everybody else."

Parental reaction to this type of misbehavior is often anger and a feeling of "Who is in charge here, you or me? (It's me, of course, but I wish you would accept that!)" The autocratic parent, a model many have had as children or employed in their own parenting, often becomes blinded by power-oriented misbehavior, since such behavior usurps the parent's autocratic rule and challenges authority.

Parents who choose to struggle with the child to determine who is really more powerful may win the battle but lose the war. The child who loses a power struggle over bedtime, playtime, and other parent/child issues may become even more convinced of the importance of power. Mother or Father show, by struggling for power, that it is indeed important to be more powerful than the child, so in the eyes of the child, power becomes even more valid and attractive.

Revenge

The goal of revenge is the result of a child's feeling hurt, betrayed, or otherwise unfairly treated. Children who seek revenge are trying to get even with the person responsible for the "injustice" they have suffered. Since it is unlikely that a child is able to retaliate directly—for example, by taking his mother over his knees and spanking her, just as she spanked him—he will try to get even in other ways.

A child is aware of what misbehaviors are particularly irritating to his parents and may choose to use one of them, such as abusive language, in revenge. The parent, unaware of the goal of the child's behavior, is likely to be confused by what appears as the child's senseless need to hurt and often returns the revenge in kind, thus perpetuating the cycle.

Display of Inadequacy

All four goals of misbehavior are expressions of a child's discouragement; the fourth goal manifests extreme discouragement.

Billy is the youngest of three brothers. On weekends, his father often takes the children to the basketball court, shooting and scrimmaging with the boys. Billy hasn't yet mastered the art of dribbling the ball. Whenever he gets the ball, he quickly passes it. Soon the weekend comes when Billy doesn't want to go to the court: "It's too hot out. Besides, I'm no good anyway." He has competed but, discouraged at his lack of progress, has decided to give up the pursuit altogether.

The child may use any of the four goals, depending on how she interprets the situation. Misbehavior does not necessarily progress through all four goals, beginning with attention and ending with display of inadequacy; however, they are increasingly discouraged behaviors.

The child's misbehavior will stop when the parent chooses to respond to the situation in a different way. Billy's father, for example, must recognize his son's goal and extreme discouragement with his basketball abilities. While Billy may not necessarily be aware of his goal, he is aware of its consequences. If he succeeds in convincing his family that he is inadequate, he will be excused from the embarrassment of being the "worst" basketball player, when in fact he is only the youngest. The father's corrective strategy for his son's behavior would include encouraging positive efforts, modifying the games so that Billy can compete on an equal level, and so forth.

BOOKS FOR PARENT GROUPS

A specific nine-session format has been developed for a book group that uses *Raising a Responsible Child*, by Dinkmeyer and McKay (1973). A typical format for a session includes five basic topics: discussion of the activity and homework from the previous session, discussion of the current reading assignment, a practice exercise, summary, and reading and other homework assignments for the following session. The leader may rely on prepared questions or allow discussion of the specific technique presented in that session—for example, natural and logical consequences. Often the leader's most difficult task is to focus the group's discussion.

Leadership also involves moving the group from discussion of theory into practical application of the theory to their own relationships. The practice exercise allows participants to work with a specific concept or skill, such as reflective listening. Some of the material presented in parent education relates to basic communication skills as they apply to parent/child communication.

Since the group implies a work commitment for each member, the leader must exercise discretion and skill to make sure each member has the opportunity to share new experiences. The leader may also develop a group expectation that reading and trying new skills are necessary activities and that involvement outside the group session is also part of the process. Obtaining commitment is often difficult in book-study groups.

Parent groups that use books have functioned successfully for many years. Their advantage lies in the availability of a single source for reading and referral; the drawback is that this type of group demands inherently motivated participants.

PARENT C-GROUPS AND STEP PROGRAMS

C-Groups

Parent C-groups are an adaptation of teacher C-groups and have similar goals—going beyond the study of principles into the sharing of experiences. Awareness of how we function and how our attitudes, beliefs, and feelings affect our relationship with our children is an essential element of the C-group. The *C* stands for the many forces that occur in the group:

Consultation, provided and received by all group members

Collaboration on the concerns of group members who work together as equals

Cooperation among members, so that they can offer and receive encouragement

Clarification of the concepts under discussion as well as of members' belief systems and feelings

Confrontation of the purposes, attitudes, beliefs, and feelings that interfere with successful modification of the parent/child relationship; if change is to occur, confrontation of old, useless beliefs must take place, and a norm of confrontation—not to prove who is right but to share discrepancies and observations—is established by the group leader at the beginning of the group

Confidentiality, which assures that members' concerns will be shared only by the group

Commitment to the tasks confronting each member, which go beyond reading the assignment and discussing it at the next meeting

Change, the purpose of involvement in the group, assessed by each member in specific terms, from the point of view of both rate and targets

STEP Programs

The STEP and STEP/Teen programs are perhaps the most widely used and researched Adlerian parent education materials. They have reached more than two million parents; STEP has been translated into Spanish, Japanese, German, and Greek. The publisher reports more than 41 research studies on the STEP program (American Guidance Service, 1986).

The group experience provided by STEP programs is based on sharing a parents' handbook that all members receive and study, on large group-discussion charts, and on taped exercises. Discussion-guide cards also structure the expectations of sharing, genuineness, and listening. A large leader's manual covers the format for each of the nine sessions that make up the program. The manual also contains additional information on necessary leader skills dealing with problem members and tape scripts. The leader has the option of sticking to a prepared format or linking together various activities he considers appropriate to a particular group.

The success of the STEP programs can be identified in three areas:

1. Parents learn from each other; the book is the "expert" and the leader functions as a facilitator.
2. The three-step process of discussing new ideas (which are often alternatives to commonplace parenting practices, such as natural and logical consequences instead of punishment), practicing the new ideas as a concrete skill within the group, and applying the skill in the home with the children allow the parent to understand, try, and apply the effective parenting methods.
3. The group leader is not integral to the success of the program. A follow-up study on 1,000 parents who participated in STEP groups indicated the leader was the most or least liked aspect of the group by less than five percent of respondents (Dinkmeyer, Jr., 1981).

STARTING GROUPS

Organizers of group programs for parents often face the problem of having more prospective participants than can be accommodated in a single group. When this happens, a waiting list is prepared, or the possibility of creating more than one group is investigated. Groups should not exceed 10 or 12 participants (excluding the leader), so that members can enjoy the advantages of the small group. It is important that participants have children of approximately the same age level, so that the basis of their experiences and challenges is somewhat similar.

STEP programs provide an introductory brochure and an eight-minute tape that outlines the focus of the program and some of the topics. When proposing a book group or a C-group, the leader will often wish to demonstrate one of the more enticing topics in the program, such as the differences between punishment and logical consequences or the purposes of misbehavior. Parents get a taste of the program and find that acknowledging their need for education is not a sign of weakness but rather a sign of intelligent commitment to growth.

This point is especially important and deserves the leader's full attention. In the absence of pat "explanations," parents must deal with the many possible reasons for becoming involved in an education program. Often a parent rationalizes that "It worked for my parents, so it'll work for me," yet realizes that a defensive posture does *not* work. In such cases, the leader must help the person appreciate the shift from autocracy to democracy that has left many parents without effective strategies for dealing with their children. It is not that parents lack ability, but that they lack skills and models. It is up to the leader to point out this essential difference and its implications to parents in need of help.

GROUP–LEADERSHIP SKILLS

Parent-group leaders must use certain skills to make group experiences truly constructive. These skills are similar to those required in other group settings, but the focus is on learning and on the universalizing quality of being a parent.

Structuring

Structuring allows the group to know exactly what will be expected of each member. Meeting times and places, length of sessions, and purposes and goals will all be used to structure the group. Structuring occurs during the group's first sessions. As the group progresses, the leader feels free to restructure it as needed. The leader must be constantly aware of what is going on in the group, so that she can determine whether the current situation is in the best interest of the group's stated goals and purposes.

Universalizing

Universalizing helps members become aware that their experiences are similar to others'. Parenting, one of the most universal experiences, provides many opportunities for members of a parent group to realize how much they have in common. It is up to the leader to tap this well of common experiences and bring the similarities to the surface for everybody's benefit. When a member shares a problem with the group, the leader can elicit reactions from the others by asking "Has anyone had a similar difficulty?" or some other open-ended question that invites participants to share experiences. Often a parent reacts spontaneously in agreement, verbally or nonverbally, and the leader can then encourage additional response from that member.

Linking

Linking is the process of identifying common elements in the group members' comments. A leader often finds that an idea keeps coming up time and time again—a "theme" of the members' experiences. With parent groups, this may be "Bedtime is usually pretty difficult" or "Sometimes, spanking is really the only way to get the message across." It is important for the leader to use these themes in positive ways to link members during the early stages of the group. Linking and universalizing promote cohesiveness, a feeling of togetherness, and a sense of purpose. Once a theme is expressed and detected, the leader can articulate the common element with comments such as "I sense that both Tom and Elaine feel concerned about their middle child." The leader can then briefly discuss the problems common to most middle children and possible new ways to dealing with them.

Feedback

Feedback allows members to hear how others perceive them. Effective feedback refutes the widespread notion that one cannot share honest feelings and ideas with others. As you know, feedback does not demand change; it simply tells someone how he or she comes across to others. The person must then decide whether to accept or reject the feedback. To make feedback a tool of growth, group members must be willing to accept the elements of risk, such as the possibility of rejection or attack, no matter how seldom the risk becomes reality.

Tentative Hypotheses

Members must also develop the skill to make tentative hypotheses. Questions like "What purpose did the misbehavior serve?" "What did the child do?" "Could it be that the goal was power?" "How did you feel when that happened?" promote understanding of behavior and the ability to apply the understanding and explore hunches about misbehavior. The tentative diagnosis also allows the parent to try alternative behaviors.

Focusing on the Positive

It may be difficult for parents to see the positive side of their children while they are immersed in a power struggle or other conflict. Yet the parents' ability to focus on the positive and to encourage their child's skills and assets often helps to change the child's behavior. The leader can model encouraging behavior by recognizing the changes and improvements the parents report. Parents often don't see improvement until others in the group help them realize that changes have taken place.

Commitment

Leaders must keep group members aware of their commitment to the group. They can accomplish this by reading a particular chapter in the book the group is using and by practicing a skill that has been discussed during the session, such as I-messages or logical consequences. It is important that the person make a commitment to perform, not just to try, the new behavior. Attempts based on low expectations actually inhibit growth. A leader can ask for specific commitments at the end of the session and, at the start of the next session, ask members to share their experiences with the new behaviors. Commitment may consist of simply agreeing to send one encouraging I-message every day or to spend five minutes with each child every night before bedtime.

Summarizing

The summary at the end of the session deals with feelings and ideas as they occurred at any time during the session. It may deal with the content of the meeting or with the commitment each member has made for the upcoming week. The leader can begin by asking each participant to complete the sentence "I learned. . . ." This procedure allows members to share what they have gained during the session and gives the leader an opportunity to correct or clarify confusions or doubts.

Encouragement

Encouragement is a skill that parents may find especially difficult and confusing. It is often mistaken for praise, a more widespread form of communication in our culture. The essential difference between the two is that praise generally focuses on externals, while encouragement recognizes inherent abilities and positive expectations.

GROUP STAGES

A parent group usually undergoes three stages, each of which requires certain skills on the part of the leader.

As the group begins, the leader may be seen as an expert, know-it-all, or problem solver. Participants may have high expectations about improved atmosphere and better relationships with their children, and may hold the leader accountable for the success or failure of their expectations. These expectations are often inappropriate and unrealistic, and must therefore be changed. "Fix the parent" is a more appropriate focus for the group than "fix the child." The leader must create exercises or experiences for members to get to know one another. An additional task the leader must perform in the initial stage is to align members' goals. Summarizing and the expectations the leader expresses for the group can make goals clearer and more attractive.

When parents realize that *they* must change before their children can change, the group enters a stage of lessened enthusiasm. Members question both the new ideas and the philosophy of the group's approach. Some of them stand firm in beliefs that the leader feels inhibit change. The leader cannot demand absolute compliance and complete acceptance of the model and ideas; yet, one member's discouragement cannot be allowed to spread to other members. Loss of enthusiasm, fear of failure, or embarrassment about current beliefs may all lead parents to question the value of change. By recognizing the tentative nature of the group's atmosphere, the leader can move on to situations that foster change and positive growth. If parents unintentionally use their high expectations to discourage progress, the leader must help them set realistic goals and recognize effort.

The final stage of group experience is characterized by improved relationships among family members, the parents' use of new skills, and new ideas about common situations. Change must be accompanied by willingness to assume responsibility for one's own behavior. All these characteristics of the final stage are strengthened by the member-to-member communication and encouragement that increase as the group progresses.

GROUP–LEADERSHIP PROBLEMS

Individual members of a parent group may interfere with the purpose and progress of the group, generally as a result of *resistance* to the group's direction. The member may or may not be aware of the intent of the interference, which often surfaces in the form of a "game." The common denominator of these games is manipulative behavior, expressed in any of the following beliefs and attitudes.

"Try and make me!" places the leader and the parent in opposite corners and challenges the leader to get the parent to comply with the leader's goals. It may take the form of active disapproval of the ideas presented in the group or of a direct challenge to the leader to prove her firmness. The group leader always tries to communicate respect for the parent's differing opinion but also stresses that the purpose of the group is to study the new ideas and not to make sure that each member accepts all the ideas.

"I'll try it" creates an expectation of failure and/or an inability to commit oneself to the idea. Firm and consistent plans are needed if expectations are to be realized. The leader can avoid this attitude by obtaining a commitment at the end of each session and by encouraging all progress reported at the next session.

"Talkers" may not realize that their stories, opinions, and generally overbearing verbal interventions disrupt the group's progress. In other words, they may not be aware of the game they are playing. Talkers focus only on themselves and fail to recognize the value of listening to others. Confrontation of the derailing behavior should be firm but friendly, such as "How does your comment tie into the topic of this week—the family meeting?"

"Intellectualizers" would rather discuss the merits of an idea than explore how the idea applies to their home. Their viewpoint often differs from the rest of the group. The leader recognizes the point of view but then moves on with the broader goals of the group.

"Yes, but" statements allow people to play both sides of the net. They seem to accept an idea but at the same time offer evidence as to why they are an exception to the rule. The leader might help these members understand the duality of their statements by commenting "I hear yes, but doesn't but mean no? I guess you'll have to make a choice!"

"Prove it" and other monopolizing behaviors demand full attention from leader and members. This game is played when a person believes "I count only when others notice me." A "prover" may ask for facts, research studies, or other evidence to "sell" him on the merits of an idea. The leader must not let the group get bogged down in these challenges, but direct attention to ideas that are more relevant to the group as a whole.

All games challenge the leader's ability to keep the group on target. Group education is a unique and often unfamiliar experience; leaders must set a tone and offer reasonable positive expectations of change and progress. Parents will express certain beliefs and emit certain behaviors that demonstrate their concept of parent groups. Whatever their concepts, the leader must keep in mind the paramount importance of the group's movement.

Games may appear because parent education asks parents to change so that their children will in turn change certain behaviors. Parenting skills develop as parents adopt new behaviors and attitudes. The degree of risk diminishes by setting realistic group goals and expectations and encouraging all efforts.

REFERENCES

Corsini, R., & Painter, G. (1975). *The practical parent: The ABC's of child discipline.* New York: Harper & Row.

Croake, J. W. (1983). *Adlerian parent education. The Counseling Psychologist, 11*(3), 65–71.

Dinkmeyer, D. C., Jr. (1981). *Parent Responses to STEP.* Unpublished doctoral dissertation, University of Florida, Gainesville.

Dinkmeyer, D., & McKay, G. (1973). *Raising a responsible child.* New York: Simon & Schuster.

Dinkmeyer, D., & McKay, G. (1976). *Systematic training for effective parenting (STEP).* Circle Pines, MN: American Guidance Service.

Dinkmeyer, D. C., & McKay, G. D. (1983). *Systematic training for effective parenting of teens (STEP/Teen).* Circle Pines, MN: American Guidance Service.

Dreikurs, R. (1957). *Psychology in the classroom.* New York: Harper.

Dreikurs, R., & Soltz, V. (1964). *Children: The challenge.* New York: Hawthorn.

Shulman, B. (1962). The family constellation in personality diagnosis. *Journal of Individual Psychology, 18,* 35–47.

Appendixes

APPENDIX A

Guide for Initial Interview Establishing the Life Style

Name _____ Date _____

1. Reason for coming:

2. History of this concern:

3. Current life tasks (how things are going in these areas); rate from 1 to 5 (a rating of 1 means that things are going very well; a rating of 5, that they are very dissatisfying):

   Occupation _____
   Friendship _____
   Opposite sex _____
   Self _____
   Meaning _____
   Leisure _____
   Parenting _____

4. Father's age _____ Occupation _____ Mother's age _____
   Occupation _____

Personality, type of person:	Personality, type of person:
Ambitions for children:	Ambitions for children:
Relationship to children:	Relationship to children:
Way you are similar/different from father:	Way you are similar/different from mother:

5. Nature of parents' relationship:

6. Other family information:

7. Additional parental figures:

8. Description of siblings; list siblings from oldest to youngest:
   Which is most different from you? _____ How?
   Which is most like you? _____ How?
   What kind of child were you?
   Were there unusual talents, achievements, or ambitions?
   Any sickness or accidents?
   Childhood fears?

9. Physical and sexual development:

10. Social development:

11. School and work experience:

12. Sibling ratings; list highest and lowest sibling for each attribute. If you are at neither extreme, indicate your position in relationship to siblings:

Intelligence	Critical of self
Grades and general standards of achievement	Charming; trying to please
	Sociable; friendships
Hardest worker; industrious	Withdrawn
Responsible	Sense of humor
Methodical; neat	Demanded and got own way
Athletic	Temper and stubbornness
Appearance	Sensitive; easily hurt
Mischievous	Idealistic
Rebellious: openly, covertly	Materialistic
Conforming	Most spoiled
Standards of right/wrong; morals	Most punished
Critical of others	

13. Early recollections. How far back can you remember? (Obtain recollections of *specific incidents,* as detailed as possible, including the client's reaction at the time.)

14.

Number-one priority	How the other may feel	The price you pay for your priority	What you want to avoid with your priority
Comfort	irritated or annoyed	reduced productivity	stress
Pleasing	accepting	stunted growth	rejection
Control	challenged	social distance and/or reduced spontaneity	unexpected humiliation
Superiority	inadequate	overburden or overresponsibility	meaninglessness

15. Summary:
Mistaken self-defeating perceptions:
Assets:

Life-Style Assessment*

Instructions:

You will be presented life-style information segment by segment. After each portion is presented to you, you are to react to the statements on the answer sheet according to the directions provided below.

This exercise will enable you to compare your evaluation of collected information regarding life style to experts in the field. As you accumulate more information, you may change your judgment regarding some of the statements you have made. That is expected to happen and is very common. *Base each judgment on all the information available up to that particular point.* Do not look ahead, but you are encouraged to look back to the previous information if it is helpful to you to do so.

How to mark the answer sheet:

I. First decide if the statement should be marked
   A. true
   B. false
   C. no basis for judging either way
II. Then decide how certain you are of your answer and select, by circling
   A. *1* for statements you are *very* sure of
   B. *2* for statements you are *reasonably* sure of
   C. *3* for statements you are *somewhat* sure of but which could easily be marked otherwise.

Examples:

	True	False	No Evidence
1. Alice is a power-oriented person	1 2 3	1 ② 3	1 2 3
2. Alice is a person who is a getter in life.	① 2 3	1 2 3	1 2 3

In #1 the respondent felt the statement was false and was moderately sure of his belief.

In #2 he felt the statement was true and was very sure of his answer.

Information from the Initial Interview

Appearance:

Jane is attractive and neat. She is a tall woman. Her clothing is expensive and stylish.

---

* Reprinted by permission of Dr. Thomas Edgar.

Occupation:

Assistant to the director of a national television series. Her salary is good according to her report.

Marital status:

Single. No steady or serious relationship with a man at the present time. She has never been married, although she has been engaged to marry three times in the past five years.

Present stated problem:

Jane expressed a feeling of general boredom with life. Specifically, Jane feels her work is not satisfying and that her work is not appreciated by her boss. Her social life is unsatisfactory. She would like a permanent, long-term relationship with a male, but none have appeared who even come close to being the person she is seeking for such a relationship. Jane cries easily as she discusses her unhappiness with life in general.

She does not feel accepted by her co-workers.

The Life-Style Inventory

Name _____ Jane X _____

Date _____

1. Bill   + 4½

> Very good to her.
> Took care of her.
> Bought her things.
> Got along well. Kind.
> Not scholarly. Athletic.
> Lots of boyfriends.
> Tall and skinny.

2. Jane   30

> Always had lots of girlfriends.
> Cute. Happy. Outgoing.
> Lessons—singing and dancing.
> Never shy.
> Good in school; teachers
>   liked her.
> Not good in sports.
> No boyfriends.

Sibling ratings

Most different from respondent:

How? He's much more interested and quiet. More conservative. Not as good a student as she is.

Most like respondent:

How? Same sense of humor. Same tastes, e.g., music (except for wife). Always very close.

Groupings (age, sex, etc.):

Which played together? Yes—he teased her a lot and drove her crazy.

Which fought each other? He'd hit her once in a while—a punching bag.

Sickness, surgery, or accident? No.

Unusual talents or achievements?

Respondent's childhood fears? The dark. Little people lived under her bed but wouldn't bother her.

Respondent's childhood ambitions? Theater—a star.

Most

Intelligence – equal

Grades – Jane

Industrious – Jane

Standards of achievement – Jane

Athletic – Bill

Daring – Bill

Looks – Bill

Feminine

Masculine

Obedient – Jane

Made mischief – Bill

Openly rebellious – Bill

Covertly rebellious – neither

Punished – never punished

Standards of right-wrong – Bill

Critical of others – Jane

Critical of self – Jane

Easy-going – both

Charm – Jane

Excitement seeker – neither

Most

Cheerful

Sociable – Jane

Sense of humor – equal

Considerate – equal

Bossy – Jane

Demanded way – Jane

Got way – Bill

Temper – equal

Fighter – both

Chip on shoulder – neither

Sulked – neither

Stubborn – neither

Shy – neither

Sensitive and easily hurt – Jane

Idealistic – Jane

Materialistic – neither

Methodical, neat – neither

Responsible – Bill

Withdrawn – neither

Spoiled – neither

Overprotected – Jane

Parental information

Father, Oliver, Age 54 Occupation: owns store

APPENDIX A

Never hit me. Always
even-tempered. Made me laugh.
Got along well with him. Loves to
sing and dance—interested in opera
and things she likes, too. Generous.
Anything he could do for family.
Never admits he's wrong.
Narrow-minded about certain things.
Somewhat protective of her. Worried.

Favorite? Nobody. Why?
Ambitions for children? Bill—loose
standards for him but college
expected; for me, none.
Relationship to children? very close.
Sibling most like father? Bill in
business.
In what ways? Jane: home
personality.

Mother, May, Age 49 Occupation:
housewife

Always got along well. Loved her
and felt close to her. Temper on her.
Wake up Sunday morning in rotten
mood and then apologize. She was
around and would let them have it.
Couldn't stand for being fresh or
pouting, but could have what they
wanted. Got a kick out of raising a
daughter. Very sensitive; not much
confidence in self. Nice person;
good-hearted. Got feelings hurt
easily.

Favorite? Nobody. Why? Wanted a
daughter, if anybody.
Ambitions for children? College.
Relationship to children? Do things
for me. Be giving.
Sibling most like mother? Both.
In what ways? Get feelings hurt
easily. Very sensitive.

Nature of parents' relationship

Very good marriage; but Mother feels inferior and Father feels confident. Similar
interests. Always together. A few fights over stupid little things. Father makes
major decisions. She raised kids. Father controls the money.

Physical development

13 at menses; school and Mother prepared her. Getting dressed to go out and
called Mother "God damn it; why now?" Took it lightly. Father went and got
Kotex from drugstore, and she went out. It was just a thing that happened. It
was time. It was a nuisance at the moment and always has been. No difficulties.
13 at first bra (didn't need it). Doesn't remember getting first time. Feels like she
could lose 5 lbs. now.

School information

B.A. in radio and T.V. from Iowa State. Always a good student except in math
and science. Partied and still got good grades. Good in writing and reading.

Social information

Always had lots of friends. With one friend, Beth, friends in grammar school through high school. Very close. Best of friends, but always competitive. Real cute and never trusted her with men/boys. Jane always felt Beth was doing things better than she did them. Very selfish, spoiled, and self-centered.

Sexual information

Dated one boyfriend in high school. Necking and petting (but not really into it). Intercourse first time at 21 years. Went with one boy in college who didn't turn her on (Peter), then did it at 21 (2 years later). Not good. Terrible. But John did turn her on, and she had a good time. Six or seven men since then, but Eric the most and the best.

Other family information

Additional parental figures

Early recollections

1. Age 2 yrs.   Crapping in my pants in the crib. Didn't say anything. Mother took care of "it." Father was annoyed when it happened. At night. I know it was wrong.

2. Age 3-4 yrs.   I was fat. On the beach. Had on just bottoms. Playing in the sand. I think Mother was there. I was in my own little world. Felt good.

3. Age 3-4 yrs.   During the day. Don't remember what I did. But Mother spanked me. It had something to do with Bill. I thought she was the meanest person in the world for hitting me like that. Mother said "Wait until Father gets home." I know he wouldn't do anything. Mad at Mother.

4. Age 6 yrs.   Bill tied me to a tree in the park. Another little boy was there. They thought it was funny. I was scared and thought they were going to leave me there the rest of my life. They left, and I screamed "Bill, Bill." They came back a few minutes later, untied me, and let me go. I didn't think it was funny and was mad at brother for making me look foolish in front of *my* peer, *my* boyfriend. Big brother acted like the "big shot." I was scared and then mad.

5. Age 5 yrs.   Fighting with two girls at recess. Just one at first, and then the other decided to help. One held my arms back, and I bit the stomach of the girl in front of me. She deserved it. Girl had mark on stomach for years. I felt bad afterwards.

342

6. Age 6 yrs. First grade. Teacher would send two people to thank another class for play given. Teacher asked for relatives to raise their hands. I raised mine and teacher said "Do you have a relative?" (She knew the family.) I said "Yes, a sister you couldn't know about. Her name is Emma." Teacher said "O.K." and let me go. I got nervous that I couldn't carry it off and realized it didn't make sense. Later, I was embarrassed and didn't feel right. I didn't feel guilty. Knew I wouldn't do it anymore. "That's what you get for lying. It doesn't make sense."

7. Age 7 yrs. Being on top of slide in playground. Afraid to go down and afraid to climb back down. 5th-grade patrol boys calling me down. Scared to death. Afraid to move either way. Finally slid down and felt relieved that I was off the slide and could go down. Embarrassed at all the attention.

8. Age 9-10 yrs. Girlfriend Jane and I crawled under barbed wire at Ravinia. Went on empty stage and sang and danced and had wonderful time. Scared we'd get caught. Feeling real good. Imagining orchestra and audience.

	True	False	No Evidence
1. Jane may provoke others to abuse her so she can feel morally superior.	1 2 3	1 2 3	1 2 3
2. She finds others to be unfair.	1 2 3	1 2 3	1 2 3
3. Jane, psychologically, is an only child.	1 2 3	1 2 3	1 2 3
4. Jane often feels victimized by life.	1 2 3	1 2 3	1 2 3
5. It is better for Jane to be on the edge of the action, not in the middle of it.	1 2 3	1 2 3	1 2 3
6. Jane, as a child, was actively engaged in competition with her brother.	1 2 3	1 2 3	1 2 3
7. She feels that, while she is not perfect, others are worse.	1 2 3	1 2 3	1 2 3
8. Jane expects others to exercise control over her.	1 2 3	1 2 3	1 2 3
9. Jane will tend to criticize other people a lot.	1 2 3	1 2 3	1 2 3
10. Jane is likely to become depressed often by the circumstances of life.	1 2 3	1 2 3	1 2 3

11. Jane questions her own femininity and would prefer being a male, given the choice. 1 2 3   1 2 3   1 2 3

12. One of Jane's mistaken ideas in life is: women are inferior to men. 1 2 3   1 2 3   1 2 3

13. Jane's family valued getting along with others. 1 2 3   1 2 3   1 2 3

14. Jane will tend to become frightened and/or furious when others try to control her. 1 2 3   1 2 3   1 2 3

15. Jane learned from her family that what she merely *wants* she needs. 1 2 3   1 2 3   1 2 3

16. Jane's parents modeled a sharing cooperative relationship. 1 2 3   1 2 3   1 2 3

17. People who try to prevent Jane from doing what she wants are liable to get hurt. 1 2 3   1 2 3   1 2 3

18. Jane was given responsibilities in her family. 1 2 3   1 2 3   1 2 3

19. Jane has a great deal of confidence in herself. 1 2 3   1 2 3   1 2 3

20. The family valued making the best of any bad situation. 1 2 3   1 2 3   1 2 3

21. Jane tries hard to find her way in life through conformity. 1 2 3   1 2 3   1 2 3

22. Jane's brother dominated her, much like her father. 1 2 3   1 2 3   1 2 3

23. Jane finds it difficult to work cooperatively with others. 1 2 3   1 2 3   1 2 3

24. Jane, when she finds herself in a difficult situation, will often be unable to act in *any* way. 1 2 3   1 2 3   1 2 3

25. Relationships are a matter of who is on top. 1 2 3   1 2 3   1 2 3

Nine Adlerian raters, all experienced in counseling and psychotherapy, were asked to complete the preceding Life-Style Assessment questionnaire. The responses are listed below. On the left are the responses based on information up to and including the family constellation. On the right are the responses based on all the information available in the Life-Style Assessment, including early recollections. The modal responses to each question are listed to give the readers using this questionnaire some standard to evaluate their own responses. (T = True; F = false; NE = No evaluation)

APPENDIX A

Question No.	Mode	Question No.	Mode
1	T2	1	T1
2	T2, T3	2	T1
3	F1	3	F1
4	T2	4	T1
5	F2	5	T2
6	T2	6	T1
7	T2	7	T1
8	T2	8	T2
9	T1	9	T1
10	T2	10	T2
11	T3	11	T3
12	T1, T2	12	T2
13	T1	13	T1
14	T2	14	T2
15	T3	15	T3
16	F2	16	F2
17	T3, F2, F3	17	T1
18	F2	18	F1
19	F1	19	F1
20	NE2, F1	20	F2
21	T2	21	T2
22	T2	22	T1, T2
23	T2	23	T1
24	T1	24	T1
25	T2	25	T2

The Life-Style Inventory

Harold H. Mosak, Ph.D.
Bernard H. Shulman, M.D.
Copyright © 1971, by H. H. Mosak
& B. H. Shulman

Name _____

Date _____ 198_____

1.   2.

3.   4.

5.   6.

Sibling ratings

Most different from respondent:	How?
Most like respondent:	How?
Groupings (age, sex, etc.)	Which fought each other?
Which played together?	Unusual talents or achievements?
Sickness, surgery or accident?	Respondent's childhood
Respondent's childhood fears?	ambitions?

Most to Least	Most to Least
Intelligence	Cheerful
Grades	Sociable
Industrious	Sense of humor
Standards of achievement	Considerate
Athletic	Bossy
Daring	Demanded way
Looks	Got way
Feminine	Temper
Masculine	Fighter
Obedient	Chip on shoulder
Made Mischief	Sulked
Openly rebellious	Stubborn
Covertly rebellious	Shy
Punished	Sensitive and easily hurt
Standards of right-wrong	Idealistic
Critical of others	Materialistic
Critical of self	Methodical – Neat
Easy going	Responsible
Charm	Withdrawn
Pleasing	Excitement seeker

APPENDIX A

Physical development

School information

Social information

Sexual information

Parental information

Father   Age   Occupation

Favorite?   Why?
Ambitions for children?
Relationship to children?
Sibling most like father?
In what ways?

Mother   Age   Occupation

Favorite?   Why?
Ambitions for children?
Relationship to children?
Sibling most like mother?
In what ways?

Nature of parents' relationship

Other family information

Additional parental figures

Early recollections

1. Age

2. Age

3. Age

4. Age

5. Age

6. Age

7. Age

8. Age

Summary of family constellation

Summary of early recollections

Mistaken or self-defeating apperceptions

Assets

Children's Life Style Guide (CLSG)

1. Family constellation

Name	Age	Education

Who is most different from you? Why?

Who is most like you? Why?

Tell about your life before you went to school:

2. Functioning at life tasks

If choice go to school/stay home, what would you do? Why?

What do you like about school? Why?

What do you dislike about school? Why?

What is your favorite subject? Why? Least favorite? Why?

What would you like to be when you grow up? Why?

Who is your best friend? At school?

Are you a leader or follower?

What do you usually do when you are with your friends?

When you play a game, are you usually picked first/last/middle?

3. Family atomosphere

What kind of person is father?

What kind of person is mother?

How do mother/father get along?

Which child acts most like father?

Which child acts most like mother?

When you misbehave, who disciplines you? Why?

What do you like to do best with mother or father? Why?

What do you like to do least with mother or father? Why?

What do your parents expect of you at home? In school? At play? In special activities?

What jobs do you have at home?

4. Rating
List highest & lowest sibling for each attribute (including yourself):

Intelligent	Responsible
Hardest worker	Sensitive, feelings easily hurt
Best grades school	Temper
Conforming, obedient	Bossiest
Rebellious	Materialistic

Helps around house	Friends (most)
Tries to please	Most spoiled
Wants their way	High standards of achievement; wants to be best
Most punished	
	Athletic
Critical	
	Strongest
Considerate	
	Prettiest
Shares	
	Cares about other's feelings
Selfish	

5. Early recollections

6. Three wishes

   If you were going to pretend to be an animal, which would you choose? Why?
   Which animal would you not want to be? Why?
   What is your favorite fairy tale or story? Why?

7. Summary:

   Mistaken self-defeating perceptions:

   Assets:

APPENDIX B

Adlerian Counseling and Psychotherapy Competencies

	Unsatis-factory	Good	Excep-tional ability
1. Can present the Adlerian theoretical foundations underlying the therapeutic process	____	____	____
2. Can explain the psychopathology of the neuroses and psychoses as set forth by Adlerian psychology—that is, purpose of symptoms, interrelationship of the neuroses, and so forth	____	____	____
3. Can describe and demonstrate the Adlerian counseling relationship	____	____	____
4. Can deal with the disturbances and defenses that interfere with the relationship, such as externalization, rebellion, inadequacy, and projection	____	____	____
5. Can explore the current situation and the way in which the person approaches the challenges of living and the life tasks	____	____	____
6. Can use the number-one priority as a clinical method to investigate one facet of the life style	____	____	____
7. Can identify and interpret the essential life-style information—that is, family constellation and family atmosphere	____	____	____
8. Can interpret and utilize early recollections in formulating the life style	____	____	____
9. Can identify here-and-now psychological movement and interpret it to the client	____	____	____
10. Can understand the commonly observed life styles, such as "getter," "driver," and "controller"	____	____	____
11. Is able to attend to the client's verbal and nonverbal behavior	____	____	____
12. Is able to align counselor/counselee goals	____	____	____
13. Can empathically understand and reflect feelings while understanding the purpose of the feelings being shared	____	____	____
14. Can paraphase and allude to a goal or purpose	____	____	____
15. Can confront clients with their subjective views, mistaken beliefs, private goals, or destructive behaviors	____	____	____

APPENDIX C

Adlerian Society and Publications

To obtain current information on the North American Society of Adlerian Psychology (NASAP), contact:

Neva Hefner
Executive Director
NASAP
159 N. Dearborn
Chicago, IL 60601
(312) 977-1944

NASAP publishes a Newsletter and maintains a list of current institutes, training programs, and workshops in Adlerian psychology.

The quarterly *Individual Psychology: The journal of Adlerian theory, research and practice* can be contacted at:

Guy J. Manaster and Jon Carlson, Editors
Individual Psychology
Department of Educational Psychology
University of Texas at Austin
Austin, TX 78712

NAME INDEX

SUBJECT INDEX

358